ED M... ty-three
years s... ...helicopter
flying hours, 645 of them in an Apache and was awarded the
Military Cross for his courage during the now legendary
...oom Fort rescue in January 2007. He wrote of that fateful
...ssion in the bestselling *Apache*. *Hellfire* is his second book.

This edition of *Hellfire* is interactive.

In the margins you'll find symbols – these indicate
that there are free extras available online.

Simply visit **www.harperplus.com/hellfire**
and enter the relevant page number. There you'll
be able to watch footage, see new images and listen to
audio commentary by the author.

We hope you enjoy this feature and would welcome your
comments at feedback@harperplus.com

By the same author

Apache

HELL FIRE

ED MACY

Harper
Press

First published in Great Britain by HarperPress in 2009

Copyright © Ed Macy 2009

Maps © HarperPress
Drawn by HL Studios

Ed Macy asserts the moral right to
be identified as the author of this work

A catalogue record for this book
is available from the British Library

ISBN 978-0-00-728820-5

Set in Minion by G&M Designs Limited, Raunds, Northamptonshire
Printed and bound in Great Britain by Clays Ltd, St Ives plc

Mixed Sources

Product group from well-managed
forests and other controlled sources
www.fsc.org   Cert no. SW-COC-001806
© 1996 Forest Stewardship Council

FSC is a non-profit international organisation established to promote the
responsible management of the world's forests. Products carrying the FSC
label are independently certified to assure consumers that they come
from forests that are managed to meet the social, economic and
ecological needs of present or future generations.

Find out more about HarperCollins and the environment at
www.harpercollins.co.uk/green

*In memory of
my grandparents
and their unconditional love*

CONTENTS

LIST OF ILLUSTRATIONS

Photographs not credited below have kindly been supplied by the author. While every effort has been made to trace the owners of copyright material reproduced herein, the publishers would like to apologise for any omissions and will be pleased to incorporate missing acknowledgements in any future editions.

First plate section

An Apache flies over Afghanistan's wide open expanse: Garry Stanton.

GPMGs being used from louch poles. *Unknown.*

A flypast on Task Force availability Day: © *Crown Copyright/MOD. Reproduced with the permission of the Controller of Her Majesty's Stationery Office/Army Air Corps.*

Firing CVR7 rockets in the dive. *Andy Wawn.*

The mighty Hellfire missile. *Reproduced with the kind permission of Lockheed Martin.*

The line-up of brand new Apaches. © *Crown Copyright/MOD. Reproduced with the permission of the Controller of Her Majesty's Stationery Office/Army Air Corps.*

Firing rockets outside Thumrait Airfield, Oman. *Mick Galston.*

Second plate section

The technicians work in the sweltering heat to rebuild the
  Apaches. *Capt PHL, 656 Sqn AAC.*

Kandahar Airfield looking east. *Capt PHL, 656 Sqn AAC.*

Flying west with the M230 cannon actioned. *Capt PHL, 656 Sqn
  AAC.*

The Red Desert. *Capt PHL, 656 Sqn AAC.*

Lashkar Gah. *Capt PHL, 656 Sqn AAC.*

The dust cloud of a Chinook landing at Task Force HQ. *Capt
  PHL, 656 Sqn AAC.*

Camp Bastion in the early days. *Capt PHL, 656 Sqn AAC.*

At the top of the drop. *Capt PHL, 656 Sqn AAC.*

Large maps in the JHF(A) Forward Ops tent. *Capt Jake, 656 Sqn
  AAC.*

The Green Zone. *Capt PHL, 656 Sqn AAC.*

Ed's flight ready to lift on Operation Mutay. *Unknown.*

A Chinook extracting 3 Para. *3 Para – unknown.*

Patrols Platoon vehicles. © *Lance Corporal Lee Hewitson.*

30 mm HEDP rounds. *Capt PHL, 656 Sqn AAC.*

Having gone back to Now Zad, 'Bitching Betty' screams MISSILE
  LAUNCH. *Mick Galston.*

Looking south over Now Zad town. *Capt PHL, 656 Sqn AAC.*

A Hellfire slips off the rail. *Andy Wawn.*

A Hellfire being fired in anger. *Andy Wawn.*

Damage from a Hellfire. *WIDOW TOC.*

The youngest air trooper officially opening up Camp Bastion's
  flight line. *Capt PHL, 656 Sqn AAC.*

Musa Qa'leh showing the route of the convoy. *Capt Jake, 656 Sqn
  AAC.*

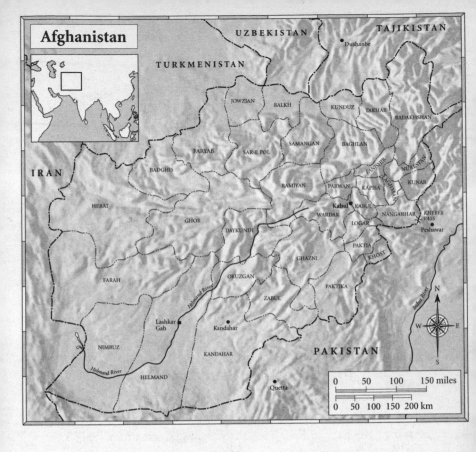

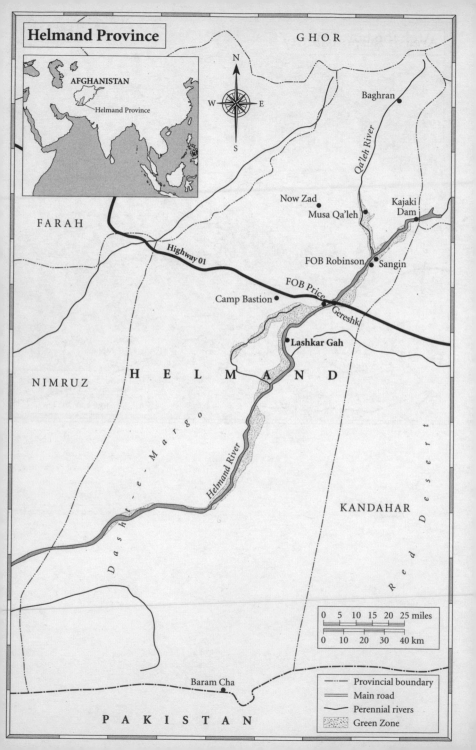

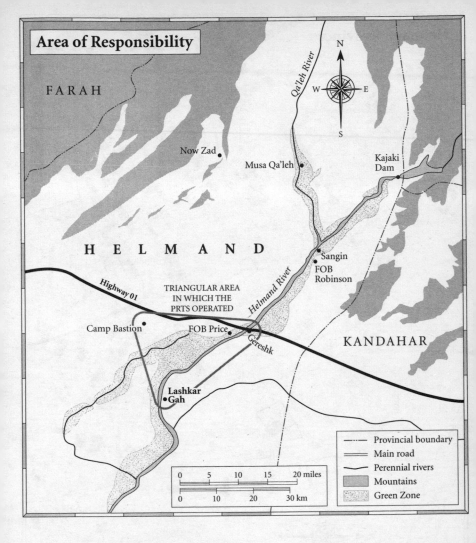

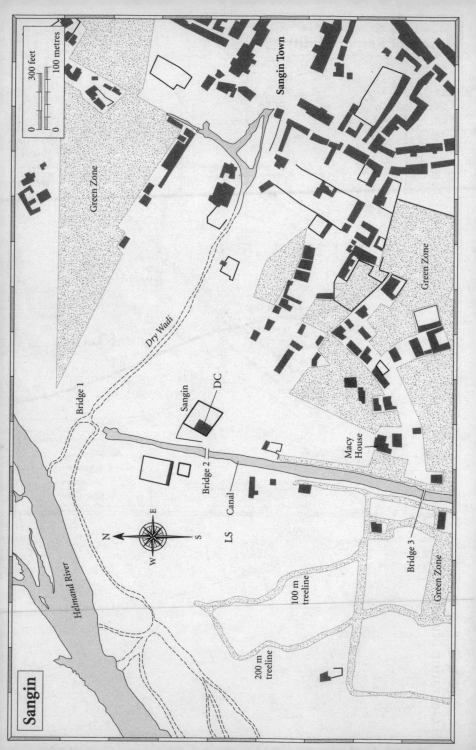

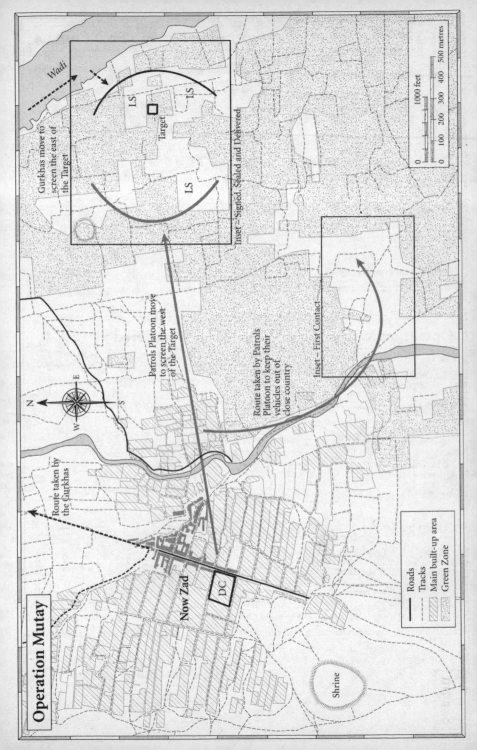

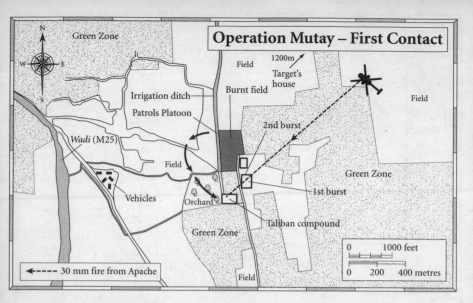

Operation Mutay – First Contact

Green Zone

1200m
Target's house

Field

Irrigation ditch
Patrols Platoon

Burnt field

2nd burst

Wadi (M25)

Field

Vehicles

Orchard

1st burst

Green Zone

Green Zone

Taliban compound

Field

0   1000 feet

0   200   400 metres

◄----- 30 mm fire from Apache

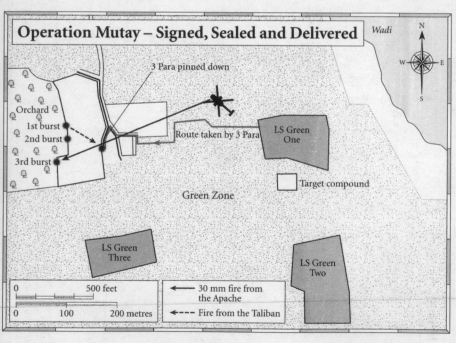

Operation Mutay – Signed, Sealed and Delivered

Wadi

3 Para pinned down

Orchard
1st burst
2nd burst

Route taken by 3 Para

LS Green
One

3rd burst

Target compound

Green Zone

LS Green
Three

0   500 feet

0   100   200 metres

◄── 30 mm fire from
the Apache
◄---- Fire from the Taliban

LS Green
Two

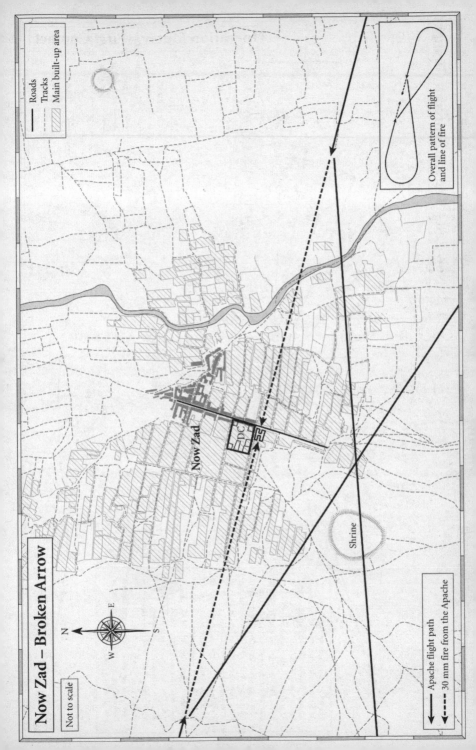

Now Zad – Broken Arrow

Not to scale

Roads
Tracks
Main built-up area

Now Zad

DC

Shrine

Overall pattern of flight and line of fire

Apache flight path
30 mm fire from the Apache

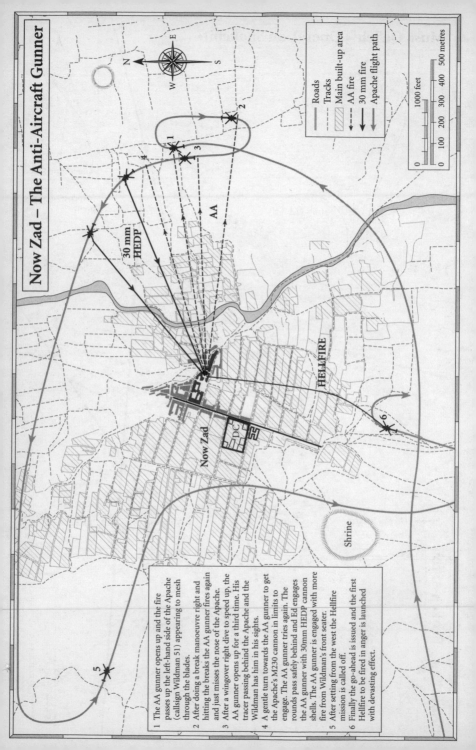

Now Zad – The Anti-Aircraft Gunner

Legend:
- Roads
- Tracks
- Main built-up area
- AA fire
- 30 mm fire
- Apache flight path

30 mm HEDP

AA

HELLFIRE

Now Zad

DC

Shrine

N
E
W
S

1000 feet
500 metres

1. The AA gunner opens up and the fire passes up the left-hand side of the Apache (callsign Wildman 51) appearing to mesh through the blades.

2. After doing a break manoeuvre right and hitting the breaks the AA gunner fires again and just misses the nose of the Apache.

3. After a wingover right dive to speed up, the AA gunner opens up for a third time. His tracer passing behind the Apache and the Wildman has him in his sights.

4. A gentle turn towards the AA gunner to get the Apache's M230 cannon in limits to engage. The AA gunner tries again. The rounds pass safely behind and Ed engages the AA gunner with 30mm HEDP cannon shells. The AA gunner is engaged with more fire from Wildman's front seater.

5. After setting from the west the Hellfire mission is called off.

6. Finally the go-ahead is issued and the first Hellfire to be fired in anger is launched with devastating effect.

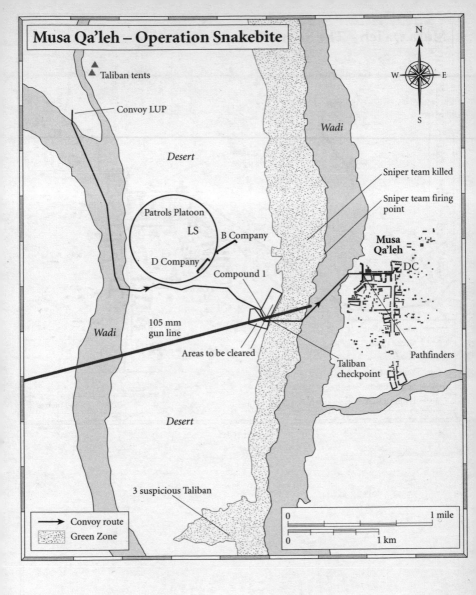

Musa Qa'leh – Operation Snakebite

Taliban tents

Convoy LUP

Desert

Wadi

Sniper team killed

Sniper team firing point

Patrols Platoon

LS

B Company

D Company

Compound 1

Musa Qa'leh

DC

Wadi

105 mm gun line

Areas to be cleared

Taliban checkpoint

Pathfinders

Desert

3 suspicious Taliban

→ Convoy route

Green Zone

N
W   E
S

0 ——————— 1 mile
0 ——————— 1 km

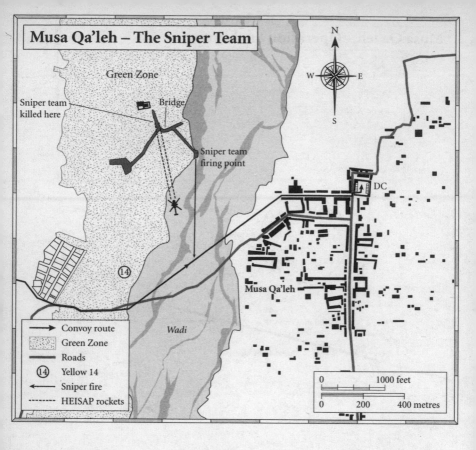

Musa Qa'leh – The Sniper Team

Green Zone

Sniper team
killed here

Bridge

Sniper team
firing point

N
W   E
S

(14)

Wadi

Musa Qa'leh

DC

→   Convoy route
     Green Zone
—   Roads
(14)   Yellow 14
←   Sniper fire
- - - -   HEISAP rockets

0   1000 feet

0   200   400 metres

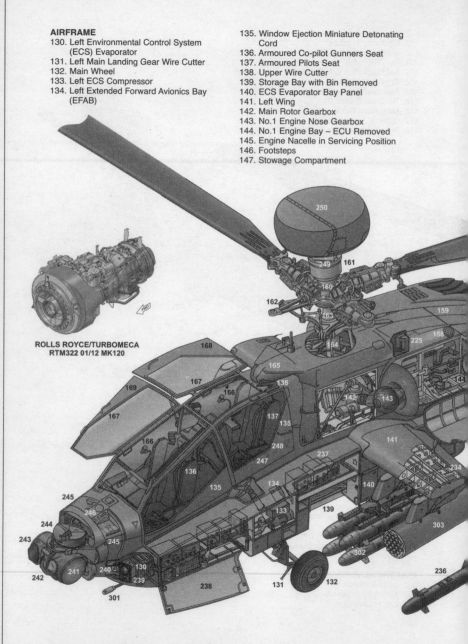

AIRFRAME

130. Left Environmental Control System (ECS) Evaporator
131. Left Main Landing Gear Wire Cutter
132. Main Wheel
133. Left ECS Compressor
134. Left Extended Forward Avionics Bay (EFAB)
135. Window Ejection Miniature Detonating Cord
136. Armoured Co-pilot Gunners Seat
137. Armoured Pilots Seat
138. Upper Wire Cutter
139. Storage Bay with Bin Removed
140. ECS Evaporator Bay Panel
141. Left Wing
142. Main Rotor Gearbox
143. No.1 Engine Nose Gearbox
144. No.1 Engine Bay – ECU Removed
145. Engine Nacelle in Servicing Position
146. Footsteps
147. Stowage Compartment

**ROLLS ROYCE/TURBOMECA
RTM322 01/12 MK120**

Apache AH MK1 Port view

148. Rear Fuselage Footsteps
149. Castoring Tailwheel
150. Moving Horizontal Stabilator
151. Tail Rotor Hub
152. Tail Rotor Hydraulic Servo
153. Tail Rotor Gearbox
154. Intermediate Gearbox and Cooling Fan
155. Tail Drive Shafts
156. Main Rotor Blade
157. Catwalk Access Panel
158. Pre-cooler By-pass Exhaust

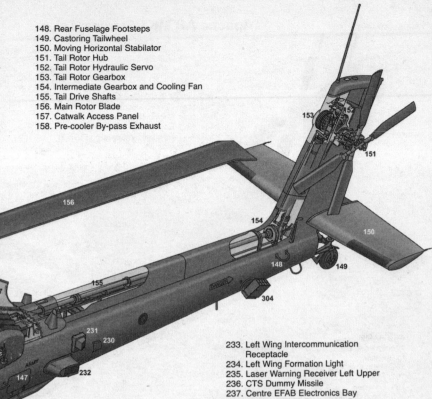

159. Catwalk Access Panels
160. Main Rotor Head
161. Integrated De-ice De-rotational Unit
162. MRB Strap Packs
163. Swash Plate Assembly and Scissor Links
164. Static Rotor Mast
165. Left Transmission Air Cooling Intake
166. Pilots and Co-Pilot Gunners Integrated Helmet and Display Sight System
167. Canopy Jettison – Miniature Detonating Cord
168. Pilots Crew Station Access
169. Co-pilot Gunner Crew Station Access Door

ELECTRICAL/AVIONIC
230. Left Aft Missile Warning Sensor
231. Rear Left Laser Warning Receiver
232. Left Flare Dispenser

233. Left Wing Intercommunication Receptacle
234. Left Wing Formation Light
235. Laser Warning Receiver Left Upper
236. CTS Dummy Missile
237. Centre EFAB Electronics Bay
238. Forward EFAB Electronics Bay
239. Left Forward RWR Quadrant Receiver
240. Left Forward MW Sensor
241. TADS Day Sensor Assembly
242. Target Acquisition & Designation Sight (TADS)
243. TADS Night Sensor
244. Pilot Night Vision Senor (PNVS)
245. Embedded GPS Bays (Left and Right)
246. CTS GPS Antenna
247. Outside Air Temperature Probe
248. Static Vent
249. Radar Frequency Interferometer
250. Fire Control Radar (FCR) Mast Mounted Assembly (MMA)

ARMAMENT
301. M230EI 30mm Chain Gun
302. Hellfire Missiles
303. 70mm Rocket Pod
304. Chaff Dispenser

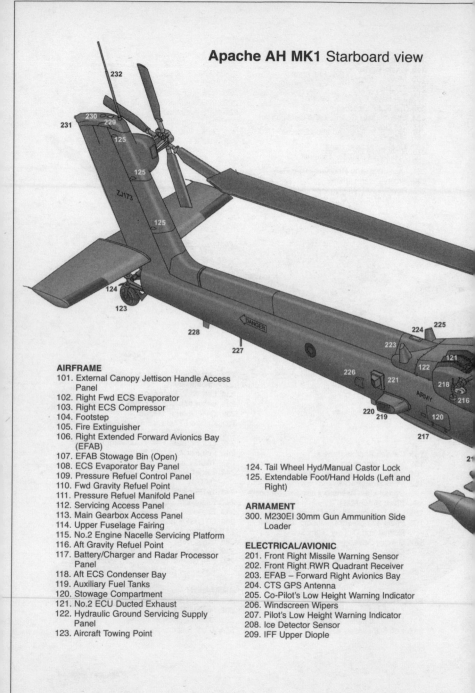

Apache AH MK1 Starboard view

AIRFRAME
101. External Canopy Jettison Handle Access Panel
102. Right Fwd ECS Evaporator
103. Right ECS Compressor
104. Footstep
105. Fire Extinguisher
106. Right Extended Forward Avionics Bay (EFAB)
107. EFAB Stowage Bin (Open)
108. ECS Evaporator Bay Panel
109. Pressure Refuel Control Panel
110. Fwd Gravity Refuel Point
111. Pressure Refuel Manifold Panel
112. Servicing Access Panel
113. Main Gearbox Access Panel
114. Upper Fuselage Fairing
115. No.2 Engine Nacelle Servicing Platform
116. Aft Gravity Refuel Point
117. Battery/Charger and Radar Processor Panel
118. Aft ECS Condenser Bay
119. Auxiliary Fuel Tanks
120. Stowage Compartment
121. No.2 ECU Ducted Exhaust
122. Hydraulic Ground Servicing Supply Panel
123. Aircraft Towing Point

124. Tail Wheel Hyd/Manual Castor Lock
125. Extendable Foot/Hand Holds (Left and Right)

ARMAMENT
300. M230EI 30mm Gun Ammunition Side Loader

ELECTRICAL/AVIONIC
201. Front Right Missile Warning Sensor
202. Front Right RWR Quadrant Receiver
203. EFAB – Forward Right Avionics Bay
204. CTS GPS Antenna
205. Co-Pilot's Low Height Warning Indicator
206. Windscreen Wipers
207. Pilot's Low Height Warning Indicator
208. Ice Detector Sensor
209. IFF Upper Diople

210. Right Pitot Tube
211. Right Wing Formation Light
212. VU1 & FM2 Full Band Antenna
213. Laser Warning Receiver Right Upper
214. Aft Right Avionics Bay with Cooling Grills
215. Nav. Light
216. Anti-Collision Strobe Light
217. Doppler Antenna
218. Right Side Airspeed and Direction Sensor
219. Right Flare Dispenser
220. VU2/UHF Blade Antenna
221. Laser Warming Receiver Right Rear
222. Safety Disarm Unit
223. Rear Right RWR Quadrant Receiver
224. Spine Formation Light
225. Rear Left RWR Quadrant Receiver
226. Right Aft MWS
227. IFF Lower Dipole Antenna
228. CTS UHF Antenna
229. Tail Formation Light
230. GPS Antenna
231. Tail Navigation Light and Bi Directional Radar Warning Receivers
232. VU2 & FM 1 Whip Aerial

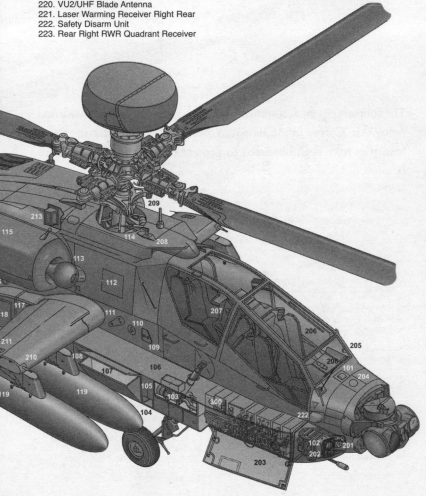

© AgustaWestland

The following is an account of operations involving 656 Squadron, Army Air Corps, in Afghanistan over several months in 2006. Identities have been obscured to protect the individuals and their families.

PROLOGUE

TUESDAY, 4 JULY 2006
Camp Bastion, Helmand province, southern Afghanistan

2255 hours local

The helicopter god was nearly out of miracles.

3 Para's A Company had never intended to stay in Sangin; they'd just dropped by to reassure the local elders that we were on their side. Then Intelligence reported that they'd walked right into the hornet's nest – the Taliban's only senior command and control location in southern Helmand – and the head shed ordered them to hold out at all costs.

Sangin had been under siege for weeks now; the Taliban had been hammering the place morning, noon and night. Their objective was simple: to injure a British soldier seriously enough to force a casevac helicopter insertion, and take out the 'cow' as it landed.

In the meantime they were amassing enough anti-coalition militia to rip the District Centre (DC) to shreds.

Thirty or so Paras were locked down in the platoon house, running perilously short of food and ammunition. Three of them had died a couple of days ago, and another was killed this morning while trying to secure the landing site for a casevac mission

1

launched to recover a badly injured survivor. The Taliban were a hair's breadth away from bringing down a Chinook with its crew, surgeon, anaesthetist, and the rest of the medical team on board.

We were called into Ops just before last light. More soldiers had been hit. One of them had spiralled from badly injured to critical. He'd last the night, but needed to be in the Bastion field hospital before lunchtime tomorrow. In any other theatre of conflict he'd have been Priority One and flown out immediately.

Lieutenant Colonel Stuart Tootal, Commanding Officer (CO) of 3 Para, only had a brief window in which to pull out his injured and Killed in action (KIA) and replenish the DC with men and supplies. The Taliban usually attacked ferociously at night, melted away before first light, then kicked back in with snipers after morning prayers. But now they knew that a casevac was imminent, we reckoned that rest and prayers would have to wait.

We'd been given permission to fire into known Taliban positions to prevent them from engaging the Chinooks. The enemy could only engage the landing site (LS) from two long, irrigated tree lines and a smashed-up building with four firing ports in its wall. I'd spotted a bunch of empty shells and an escape ladder there, so the ground troops had nicknamed it 'Macy House'.

Our plan was simple.

Jake and Jon in their Apache had the callsign Wildman Five Two and Simon and I in ours were Wildman Five Three. We would go in all guns blazing. We'd run in from the south with rockets then engage Macy House and the wooded hedge lines with 30 mm High Explosive Dual Purpose (HEDP) rounds as the Chinooks landed from and departed to the north. Bad light, the element of surprise and a curtain of dust from the Chinook rotors should do the rest.

It was blunt and effective, and we were good to go.

Until Whitehall intervened …

The Commanding Officer of the Joint Helicopter Force (Afghanistan) (JHF(A)) called the Officer Commanding 656 Squadron Army Air Corps (AAC) on a secure telephone to explain. He was put on speakerphone.

Major Will Pike, A Company's OC, had assured them that there were no civilians in that area of Sangin. They had also been made aware that a soldier had lost his life trying to secure the LS, and that a Chinook would soon follow. But the British government would not allow Apaches to use prophylactic firing into known Taliban positions. We could only fire in self-defence, or in defence of troops in contact.

In other words, we couldn't engage until we'd received incoming fire.

The CO apologised; he'd done everything he could. Whether we risked it was now down to us.

The OC, Major Black replaced the handset.

The surgeon confirmed that the soldier would die without his intervention, but it was down to Squadron Leader Woods. Woody was leading this casevac. He never asked his pilots to do something he wasn't prepared to do himself.

Eventually we agreed that the Apaches would go to Sangin early and cause a deception. We'd pretend we were out looking for the Taliban firing positions. Just before the Chinooks arrived we'd appear to find them at Macy House and in the woods and engage them; to satisfy the Rules of Engagement (ROE) we'd fire just in front of their positions.

With the plan set and Lieutenant Colonels Felton and Tootal satisfied we were doing all we could within the constraints of the ROE, we crashed out for another couple of hours. We'd be over Sangin at 0300 hours and the Chinooks would land forty-five minutes later – at first light.

* * *

We were up at 0115 hours and into Ops for 0130. Kenny, our watch-keeper, briefed us that Widow Seven Six – Sangin's Joint Terminal Attack Controller (JTAC) – would call the codeword Pegasus when the area around the DC was secure and we were cleared to engage.

During our couple of hours of broken sleep there had been another huge firefight. The Taliban had used mortars, Chinese rockets, recoilless rifles, Rocket propelled grenades (RPGs), a plethora of machine guns and small arms. We'd responded with B1 bombers, 105 mm light guns, Javelin anti-tank missiles, 81 mm mortars, .50 cal machine guns, machine guns and small arms.

'It's the fucking Alamo out there.' Kenny was a Lynx pilot and an ex-Para with over thirty years' experience, and he knew the score.

'Only bad news from me, I'm afraid,' Jerry said. Jerry was an RAF Flight Lieutenant, our Intelligence Officer. 'The threat remains very high and the risk to the CH47s is off the scale. They may not know there will be two, or have the exact time of your arrival, but Taliban intercepts have confirmed that they know we have injured men in Sangin, and they know a cow is coming.

'They've ordered all anti-coalition militia – every man with a weapon – to close in. The Apache is the only weapon that can really hurt them, and intercepts over the last twenty-four hours have been full of talk of bringing one down. More specifically, we have heard them say, "Bring in the Stingers and fire when they arrive. The mosquitoes are scared, so don't be afraid to shoot them down." Their morale is very high after the recent killings and they believe their plan to use up our ammo and force a resupply has worked. Any questions?'

The silence spoke volumes.

'Then all I can say is good luck …'

The chocolate bars were dished out on the short walk to the aircraft. Jake immediately paid for the privilege of eating into Jon's private stash.

'Do you actually know what time it is Dolly?'

Jake had got his nickname during our Apache training, when he shaved the odd hour off our fourteen-hour working days. As often as he could manage it, his family came first.

Jon restrained himself from singing the Parton theme tune to *9 to 5*, but he never failed to lift our spirits.

Sangin
0300 hours

'Widow Seven Six this is Wildman Five Two and Five Three. We are a pair of Apaches with four Hellfire missiles, thirty-eight rockets and 600 cannon rounds. Confirm you know of our deception plan?'

The JTAC would only speak to us on the secure frequency when we arrived in the overhead.

Jon and Simon set up a high orbit opposite each other around the DC, like two circling buzzards.

'Widow Seven Six affirmative. I don't care what you do as long as you get the injured out and reinforcements in. Confirm L Hour?' The JTAC wanted to know what time the Chinooks would hit the LS.

'Wildman. L Hour is set for Zero-Three-Forty-Five hours. H Hour is set for Zero-Three-Forty-Three hours. Confirm all men are east of the canal and no civilians have been seen west of the canal.'

'My position is at the building just west of Bridge Two over the canal. I have the injured with me. There are no troops further south or west than my position. Copy so far?'

We copied. The DC lay on the east side of the canal. To its south were trees and buildings that hid the Taliban. To its east the town sprawled for a couple of hundred metres to a now empty market-place and gave the attackers concealed avenues of approach. The dry wadi spread east beyond its northern entrance, splitting the town in two. The gap allowed heavy weapons and recoilless rifles uninterrupted fields of fire from the north and protection to melt away without fear of a follow-up. North-west by a hundred metres was the fast flowing Helmand River and the only safe avenue of approach for the load-carrying Chinooks. The canal stretched south as far as the eye could see, its tree-lined bank affording the Taliban a highway along which to move up to Macy House and the irrigation ditches surrounding the LS.

The JTAC, the protection party, the injured and the dead now occupied the only building west of Bridge Two. The LS was a 150-metre wide, 300-metre deep field south-west of them.

'And we haven't seen a civilian this side of the canal for weeks,' he continued. 'But be aware that the Taliban know you're here already. We've heard their commanders telling them to aim at the cow first – then the mosquitoes.'

We flicked onto the insecure Common Tactical Air Frequency (CTAF) so the Taliban could get the full benefit of everything we said. Jake began by telling us that he was looking to the south down the canal near Bridge Three 'where the Taliban killed our soldier'. Confirming he was dead may have raised their moral but we hoped it would also persuade them a Chinook wasn't inbound.

Neither of us was looking out for Taliban. We were too worried that we might miss the open ground when we did fire and hit their positions by accident. I'd spent the best part of four hours truing up the rocket launchers before we went to bed. It was strictly against the rules, but given the circumstances the CO had allowed me to do so.

I'd balanced an inclinometer on the live rockets and adjusted their launchers to the correct angles before tightening them. It broke every rule we could think of, and then some.

Jake had grabbed my shoulders with both hands and looked me straight in the eye before asking if I was 100 per cent sure. I told him that as long as he could shoot straight they'd work.

If we missed the target and hit the woods, or worse still our own troops, I'd be directly accountable for tampering with a live weapon system. They had to be bang-on, or I'd be banged up. Second chances were in short supply right now.

It was still dark. I could only make out the landscape from the thermal picture on the right-hand Multi-Purpose Display (MPD) screen just above my knee. The fields were dark and the river pitch-black, but the two tree lines positively glowed.

I aimed the Target Acquisition and Designation Sight (TADS) crosshair between them. Holding it steady I squeezed the laser trigger and pushed a switch.

T10 appeared at the bottom of my MPD screen, below the thermal image.

I now had the position stored, but the fear of an inquiry forced me to double-check it. I knew Jake would be doing the same a hundred metres further north.

We discussed looking for mortar base plates and heavy machine gun positions to give the Taliban something to talk about then lased and stored our firing positions in front of the 100 metre tree line on the LS.

T11 …

'Wildman Five Two this is Wildman Five Three,' I called. 'I have detected Taliban hiding in the buildings to the south of the DC.'

I hoped they'd assume I'd located whoever was waiting.

T12 – right in front of Macy House.

'Wildman Five Two,' Jake said 'I have Taliban in both tree lines to the south-west of the DC. Stand by.'

Neither of us had so much as begun to look for the Taliban.

We called the JTAC and he confirmed that the Taliban commanders were telling their men to stand their ground and fight.

It was now 0330 local.

The bluff and counterbluff had continued for the best part of twenty-five minutes – but they knew our ROE better than we did, so we just had to sit tight until the time was right.

Jake decided it was time to raise the stakes.

'Wildman Five Three this is Wildman Five Two. Fireplan: we will engage the Taliban in the trees to the south-west of the DC with Apache rockets. Copy?'

'Copied.'

'Then we will use the Apache guns. You shoot at the buildings to the south. I will shoot at the trees. Copy?'

I copied.

'We will fire from the south on my order. Kill all of the Taliban. Read back.'

I read it back as Simon banked us gently towards the south.

It was beginning to get light, but not light enough to bring colour to the silhouettes of trees, the canal that ran from Bridge Two or the rooflines of the town.

Four klicks to the south of the DC Simon and Jon turned back in a perfectly obvious and synchronised manoeuvre. We were nice and high so we stood out against the rapidly lightening sky.

We began to run in at forty knots.

Simon made the call we'd been waiting for on the secure inter-aircraft radio. 'I have two rotary icons on the FCR in the desert to the north-west. The Hardwood callsigns are inbound to Sangin and on time.'

'Widow Seven Six this is Wildman,' Jake called the JTAC on the secure frequency. 'Chinooks inbound; confirm we are clear to engage.'

I felt our nose dip and level again as Simon increased to ramming speed. A quick glance left with the naked eye confirmed Jon was 500 metres away and on level-pegging with us. We were in full view of the Taliban.

'This is Widow Seven Six. Pegasus. Clear hot. Clear hot.'

I pressed T10 and called 'Come Co-op' to Simon after I actioned the rockets.

'Co-op,' Simon replied.

The MPD confirmed everything I needed to know: co-op bottom right and T10 bottom left. My crosshair was smack in the middle of the field and I was hands off. The Apache would hold the TADS on the position without any help from me. More importantly I could see where Jake was supposed to be firing.

Please be dead on. Please hit the target …

'Running in to engage Taliban positions with rockets,' Jake said. That should encourage them to look south.

The range was counting down above T10.

3.5KMS … 3.4KMS …

'On Jake's executive word of command, Simon: match and shoot.'

'Match and shoot with Jake,' Simon replied.

The crosshair was static and Simon lined up the rocket steering cursor by adjusting our flight path. We were a hair trigger from firing.

'Engaging with rockets,' Jake called on the secure radio before switching back to the Taliban frequency.

3.0KMS … 2.9KMS …

'Wildmen engaging in five …' Jake paused to allow the JTAC a final opportunity to call off the firemission.

Nothing …

'Three … two … one …'

2.8KMS … Rockets peeled off both sides of our gunships with a whoosh.

I couldn't bring myself to look out of the cockpit window …

Their time of flight (TOF) crept down on the MPD.

TOF4 …

Four seconds to impact and they were far too high on my screen to judge if they'd hit.

'Hardwoods have about three klicks to run ...' The tension was getting to Simon too.

TOF3 ...

The rockets were still too high and fading fast to a pinpoint glow.

'Engaging,' Jon called, for the benefit of the boss back at Camp Bastion.

TOF2 ...

They began to drop down the screen, but far too slowly for my liking. Then they disappeared entirely.

What the fuck ...?

TOF1 ...

Two huge dust clouds blossomed right under my crosshair.

My focus shot up the screen; Jake's rockets had also landed bang on the button.

'Get in ...' I punched in T11.

Both sets of rockets had landed safely.

The TADS jumped right in front of the 100 metre tree line. I deslaved the lock because the rockets were so accurate. I moved the crosshair to a gnat's knacker away from the foliage and called to Simon to match and shoot again.

A gentle right bank followed by a roll out, then another set of rockets rippled off our gunship and landed with pinpoint accuracy. They too disappeared just before impact as their thermal signature matched the surroundings. A confirmatory glance told me Jake had matched us shot for shot. Simon and Jon were doing a storming job.

'Hardwoods have about a klick to run,' Simon said.

'Switch to guns,' Jake responded.

I had already slaved the TADS to T12.

I pushed up the weapon select button and the rocket symbology on my MPD was replaced by 300 rounds of cannon.

With the crosshair twenty metres in front of Macy House I let rip with a ranging burst. Ten white hot pins of light dropped down the screen. My heart started to pound as they passed through my aiming mark and headed towards the building. They ploughed into the ground with a metre to go, kicking up a column of earth and dust fifty metres high – enough to screen the LS from the sniper's positions.

'Fuck … that was close …' I changed the burst limit to twenty.

'Not close enough for my liking, but I'd still aim off a bit if I were you,' Simon replied before updating us on the secure radio. 'Hardwoods are about to cross the river and come into view of the Taliban.'

I deslaved the TADS from T12, adjusted the sight, lased and fired a twenty-round burst. I felt every one of them through my calf muscles as they poured off the gunship like steel rain.

I switched to the field south of the LS and ripped up the ground in front of the trees with a series of twenty-round bursts of HEDP bullets.

'They're over the river,' Simon called.

It was getting lighter by the second. I could now see that the south was well and truly blocked from view.

I switched my fire to the right, next to the canal bank.

Jake switched his left, further up the tree line.

We opened up in unison, providing a clear avenue for the Chinooks. Cannon rounds stitched their way along the edge of their approach path as they flared to land. The dust rolled south as the monstrous machines hit the ground. I fired fifty metres to their south-east and Jake did the same to their south-west – far closer than we had considered safe twenty-four hours ago.

No sooner were they down than they had lifted again.

We kept on ploughing up the LS until they were over the river and in the sanctuary of the open desert.

'Checkfire,' Jake ordered.

I stowed the M230 cannon.

The entire field was a dustbowl with a lone building in the north-east corner. A succession of Paras made their way over the bridge like ants in the pale dawn light. As the dust cloud drifted further south the last of them crossed into the DC.

'Wildman this is Widow. That's us all across safely and not a single shot fired.'

'End of firemission. You're clear back to Bastion. Thanks for the support – and stay on this freq for a Taliban update.'

We were only a mile from Sangin when he called back to explain what he'd meant. One of his interpreters with a radio scanner had heard a senior Taliban commander asking why they'd failed to shoot down the cows and the mosquitoes.

Their reply said it all: 'The mosquitoes were firing at us and we couldn't shoot …'

'Wildman copied,' I said. 'I don't think we'll get away with that twice …'

AIR ATTACK, AIR ATTACK

OCTOBER 1989
Aldershot, England

The echo of voices ...

The whisper of tyres on wet tarmac ...

A burst of blinding sunlight ...

The Royal Artillery (RA) instructor stood with his hands on his hips. A hint of a smile suggested he knew something we didn't. 'To be an effective anti-aircraft gunner, you have to be a very good judge of speed and distance.' He paced up and down in front of us like he was Captain Mainwaring. 'You cannot afford to waste shots. If you miss first time and adjust quickly, you may, if you're lucky, get a second chance, but only if the pilot's below par. If he's not, if he can fly half decently, like some of the Argies in the Falklands, he'll manoeuvre unpredictably and then it's spray-and-pray time. Spray, because that guy's jinking all over the sky and you'll never hit him in a month of fucking Sundays; pray, because by now he's seen your tracer and he knows where you and your little pop-gun are hiding.'

He tapped one of the four pintle-mounted general purpose machine guns (GPMGs). 'Now which of you sad, sorry bastards is first up?' He rubbed his hands and blew on them.

I pulled myself to my feet and squinted against the cloudless sky. Behind me, my 2 Para mates gave me some low grunts of encouragement. Behind them, I swore I could hear the sniggers of the RA captain's support team, but I didn't let that put me off. I expected nothing less. In the eyes of a young Para the British Army was divided between those wearing the coveted red beret and the rest – the crap-hats.

I'd been given a fifty-round belt of 7.62 and told to fire twenty-to twenty-five-round bursts at the bright red remote-controlled drone that would appear over the frost-bitten ridgeline any second now. Two posts set ten feet away at eleven and one o'clock determined my arc of fire. Outside them, my rounds would land in the nearby village. As a Para marksman, regimental honour weighed heavily on my shoulders, but how difficult could it be? The propeller-powered drone had a wingspan of a metre and a half; at this range it would be the size of a barn door.

The drone would be flying right to left, straight and level. Bang, bang; I'd collect my prize and we could all go home.

I heard a sound like a buzz-saw and pulled the butt of the GPMG hard into my shoulder. There. A bright red cross, its bulbous engine glinting in the sunlight, a hundred feet or so off the deck.

'Air Attack, Air Attack,' Mainwaring screamed at the top of his voice.

I placed the drone squarely in the centre of the sights.

Three, two, one … It passed the right-hand post and I gave it a sustained burst. The drone beetled on and disappeared over the ridgeline. I couldn't believe it. There was a chorus of wolf-whistles from the crap-hats as I breathed in the smell of burnt gun oil. I flushed with embarrassment.

Captain Mainwaring was in my face quick as a wink. 'Not so easy is it, son? Trouble is, you can't actually see where your rounds are going, can you? So this time, we're going to help you.'

A RA bombardier gave me a fresh belt of ammo.

'We're loading you up with 1BIT; now you'll be able to *see* where your rounds are going.'

(1BIT: one standard 7.62 mm ball round for every one tracer round (1Ball1Tracer = 1BIT).)

I'd be able to adjust my aim and walk the bullets onto the target.

The drone appeared again, nice and steady. With the belt of ammo draped over my left forearm I tracked it and pulled the trigger, spitting out red streaks the very moment it crossed the right-hand post.

Every single glowing round passed behind the stupid fucking thing by yards. I was so stunned I was unable to get in a second burst. The drone wobbled off and the catcalls intensified; some of them this time from my mates.

Mainwaring told me where I was going wrong. I needed to 'lead' the aircraft – at this distance, I had to aim a second in front of it and let it fly into the bullets. I should have known about this from the Saturday afternoon war movies I used to watch with my granddad; the ones where the Spitfire pilots talked about 'deflection shots' – firing at an angle ahead of a crossing enemy aircraft, taking its speed and distance into account.

Round three. This time, my lead was perfect, but for some reason all my bullets disappeared below the drone.

Next time, Mainwaring said, be aware of distance, then fire. Cheeky bastards had flown it further away than last time, catching me out. My lead had been good, but because of 'ballistic drop', the bullets had fallen well below the target. I'd show him this time!

Round four. My bullets passed behind it again. The drone-operator had increased its speed. Watch your range, Mainwaring told me, but don't forget the speed of your target.

Round five. It came screaming in from the left, jinking up and down as well as accelerating and decelerating. The dodgy bastards were taking the piss. I wasn't even close.

The laughter behind me grew to a cacophony.

'Am I right in thinking, Para-boy, that you're an SAS wannabe?'

I said nothing. I didn't like the way this was going.

'Didn't I warn you,' Mainwaring shrieked, 'that if you miss, the enemy aircraft will see your tracer and your position will be compromised? Stand by for incoming—'

I began to run.

I ran as fast as I could, legs pounding the rock-hard earth, arms swinging, as I made for the nearest cover, a concrete pillbox around 200 metres away. Over the whistles and catcalls behind me I heard the buzz-saw signature of the drone. The louder it got, the faster I ran. Cary Grant running for his life in *North by North-west* had nothing on me ...

The drone swept in behind me, drowning out the laughter.

I was still thirty metres from the pillbox when it slammed into the small of my back. I hit the ground and the lights went out. I thought I'd been split in two.

I tried to open my eyes, but couldn't. I heard people talking, but they made no sense. Where were Mainwaring and my mates? Where was I?

'You okay, mate?' a bloke said.

'I think he's dead ...' A woman's voice.

'He fell off his bike in front of that man's car. He was in the air, upside down, when the car hit him.'

I wanted to tell them that wasn't what had happened at all. I wanted to tell them I'd been on Salisbury Plain in a live firing exercise against a target drone when the bloody thing decided to go rogue and everything turned to ratshit.

Fuck! The pain ...

Someone was trying to move me. I felt like I was being pulled, pushed and prodded. Every time they touched me I wanted to open my mouth and scream, but I couldn't even whimper.

'I thought it had taken his head off. It hit him in the back and he was upside down, mate. His head went under the bumper and his feet went through the windscreen. His back must be broken.'

If my back's broken, why the fuck are you trying to move me? If my back's broken, how am I going to do SAS Selection?

They'll pay for this, I thought. *A drone goes rogue, hits me in the back and kills all my dreams. My God, I'll have them …*

'Get the boards. Quick.' Another woman. Stern, authoritarian.

'I tell you, he flew off the bonnet and then the guy drove over him …'

'Drove over his *head*,' the first woman said.

'No, it drove over his shoulder …'

Whatever, I thought. The pain that had threatened to overwhelm me was replaced by a feeling of immeasurable tiredness. I felt myself sliding and falling.

'Sir, wake up. Can you open your eyes for me?'

I opened my eyes and my confusion deepened as I slowly saw a black woman backlit by a bright orange halo. I thought for a moment that Diana Ross had come to take me away …

'Can you feel my hand?'

I couldn't, but all was not lost: I felt something on my face – the rain I could see sparkling in the glow of the street lamp.

'Can you feel me touching your fingers?'

I was aware of having hands and feet, but I couldn't feel her touching them.

'Can you grip my fingers?'

I couldn't. I couldn't move a muscle. I tried to shift my head, but it wouldn't respond. Nothing responded. I couldn't even speak. I was totally fucked.

The woman unzipped my Barbour jacket. 'Sweet Jesus, he's wearing a bin-bag under his coat.' At best she must be thinking I'm mad and at worst a weirdo pervert.

Leave me alone, I wanted to tell her, because all I want to do is sleep.

Suddenly and with no warning I felt like I was being hit on the back of the head with a road worker's mallet every time my heart beat.

'Yeah, he arrested,' a paramedic yelled. 'He's military. Suspected spinal and internal injuries …'

I couldn't open my eyes but at least the pain was telling me I wasn't dead.

I wanted to go to sleep again, but a voice in the back of my head told me I needed to stay awake.

And someone seemed to be shoving the end of a broom shank deep into me, just below my rib cage, next to my spine. Every time the ambulance hit the tiniest bump it felt like it was going to burst through my chest. I was John Hurt in my own nightmare version of *Alien*.

We hit a pothole and I suddenly found my voice. I screamed – full throat, full belly. It filled the ambulance and blotted out the sound of the siren.

'Fuck me!' the paramedic said.

I passed out again.

'Corporal Macy, can you hear me?'

Of course I can hear you; just give me some bloody morphine …

Then: *closed abdominal injury, mate*, the voice at the back of my head said. Fat chance of the love-drug.

The pain had got worse.

If I couldn't put up with this, how would I ever be able to pass Selection? Fuck Selection, I'm tired …

'Corporal Macy, *can you hear me*?'

I opened my eyes a crack and found myself blinking against bright, brilliant white. No wonder people said they saw angels in places like this. They were delusional; just like I was now.

A guy in a green smock leaned over and shone something into my eyes. 'You've been in an accident, mate.'

Now there's a surprise.

My head and back were on fire. I tried to move my feet and legs, but couldn't. With a supreme effort, I managed to raise my head and shoot a glance down my body.

I was on a bed wearing a green gown, in an operating theatre with a lamp suspended over me. It was pushed up and switched off. Maybe they'd already given up on me ...

A six-inch square rubber block was strapped tightly to my belly. The strap had some kind of winch attached to it. It was fucking killing me.

At least I now knew why I was paralysed. My wrists and ankles were cuffed to the bed with more straps.

'Can you tell me where the pain is?' the guy in green asked.

'Everywhere,' I said. 'Please, morphine ...'

Someone else approached the bed, a stethoscope around his neck. They looked at each other, then at me. 'Not yet,' he said. 'Can you tell us where it hurts most?'

He injected my right arm with a clear liquid from a big syringe. Whatever it was, it wasn't pain relief.

I screamed.

'My back is killing me.'

'Where specifically?'

'The small of my back. Please. You've got to give me something for the pain. I'm begging you—'

He cranked the handle several notches. The clicks were like machine-gun fire. I screamed again.

'I'm sorry, Corporal Macy, really I am.'

Like fuck, I thought, as another wave of pain crashed through me. The lights went out again.

* * *

My torso sprang upwards as soon as they took the tension off the strap. They lifted me onto another bed and finally relieved some of the pain.

They'd had to pump X-ray dye into my arm to identify the source of my internal bleeding. Then they'd squeezed the blood out of my kidneys. When they released the pressure, the blood had seeped back into them, the rupture clotted and my life had been saved.

'Think of your internal organs as being connected together by pipes.' The junior doctor's bloodshot blue eyes were set in a broad, unsmiling face. 'When you get hit as hard as you did, all your organs get thrown around and the pipes connecting them detach. Then you bleed internally and the bleeding can't be stemmed. You die from a loss of circulating body fluid. We think you were hit at about 50 mph, a lot faster than is considered survivable. Fortunately, your stomach muscles are so strong and your body so fit that the impact did not rearrange your internal organs as it would have for most people, so all your pipes remained miraculously connected. The force of the collision did, however, rupture your kidneys and damage a number of other organs. Your heart arrested as it fought to keep you alive. You arrested twice, in fact.'

He smiled. 'You're a very lucky man. The surgeon couldn't operate and didn't give you more than a 20 per cent chance of pulling through. Thank God you've been keeping yourself fit, Corporal Macy. By rights you should be dead.'

Funny what you dream about when you're on the point of checking out. Being pursued by a drone across a military firing range must have been on my mind because we'd recently done anti-aircraft drills at Larkhill.

'What hit me?'

'You don't remember?'

I'd have shaken my head if I wasn't in so much pain.

He told me that a number of witnesses had come forward. I'd been cycling along Queen's Avenue, close to the barracks. It was dark and it had been raining.

Slowly, it came back to me. I remembered the orange glow of the street lamps and their reflection in the puddles as I'd held my bike's front wheel between the yellow lines at the edge of the road. I'd followed the same routine for several weeks: two hours in low gear at full pelt with a bin-bag under my clothes to raise my temperature and make me sweat. After that, I'd get off the bike and go for a long run.

I'd been getting myself fit for SAS Selection.

Something had hit my right handlebar; I remembered the bang. I'd looked up and seen a Volvo. It had overtaken too close and clipped me with its wing mirror. I'd struggled for balance and my wheel had clipped the kerb and I'd careered into the oncoming lane.

I remembered headlights very bright in my face, the world turning upside down and then something colliding with me …

The rest was filled in by the policeman who came to take my RTA victim's statement.

When the front wheel of my bike locked at ninety degrees I'd gone over the handlebars and been hit by a car going too fast in the opposite direction. I was totally inverted when it ploughed into me, its radiator grille striking me in the small of the back. My head went under the bumper and my feet went through the windscreen. The driver had slammed on the brakes but not quickly enough to prevent him ploughing over my shoulder. No wonder I was a complete fucking mess.

I finally summoned the courage to ask the doctors the only question that mattered. SAS Selection. What were my chances?

A big fat zero, as it turned out. They told me I'd been lucky not to be invalided out of the Paras. The good news was that they were discharging me from hospital; I was heading home – if you could call army accommodation on the edge of Aldershot 'home'.

Over the next few months, my mates came in to bathe me because I was in too much pain to move. I had a livid purple bruise from the toes on my right foot – where it had gone through the windscreen – all the way up my leg, across my arse, my back and my shoulder, finally petering out somewhere under my hairline.

After several weeks, I started to walk again with the use of a putter and a pitching wedge. As far as 2 Para was concerned, this wasn't a military injury; in the old days it was a case of 'get on with it and let us know when you're capable of fighting again'.

I was in too much pain to even think about that.

Months later when I was sent back to hospital for another check-up, they spotted my other injuries; the ones they should have discovered before they discharged me.

I'd suffered multiple fractures all over my body and some had healed in the wrong positions.

Like the guy said, my fighting days were over.

ARRESTED AND TESTED

I'd joined the Paras in 1984 and thought I'd found my niche in life. Being accepted by this elite regiment had been my sliding-doors moment. The accident had slammed the doors firmly back in my face.

I was born and raised in the north-east, but, as a kid, constantly found myself in trouble. My parents split up when I was very young. Against my will I remained with my mother as did my younger brother. He was even more out of control than me and ended up in a secure institution; a boarding school for the 'socially challenged' they called it back then. One day he was with us, the next he was gone. He was the closest thing I had – the only real constant in my life – and I was angry that 'they', whoever they were, had taken him from me.

I didn't know at the time that my mother couldn't cope. Looking back, though, I wasn't surprised. We were like the Bash Street Kids on crack, my brother and I; trouble through and through.

When I wasn't skipping school, I was fighting the playground bullies and generally causing mayhem. It was only by a complete fluke that I managed to avoid a correctional institution. I had good reason to be grateful. However hard I thought I was, I'd seen the movie *Scum*, starring a young Ray Winstone, and didn't like the look of it one little bit. A Residential School for Boys, Special School, Borstal or whatever you want to call these places – it would have killed me. It's a miracle it didn't kill my brother.

As soon as I could leave school, I did, and without a qualification to my name.

Finally back in the company of my father, I took a job as an engineering apprentice at a small workshop ten miles from home. The high point of my apprenticeship was turning, milling and drilling the portholes for Britain's first iron-hulled warship. HMS *Warrior* was under restoration in Hartlepool dockyard and I had an important job to do. It was the early eighties, unemployment was going through the roof, and I thought I'd live and die in the north-east.

A thousand fox doorknockers and sixty-seven poorly paid portholes later, my work on *Warrior* was done – and so was I, until I met Stig down the pub one day. A local hard man, he was home on leave from the Paras. Two things impressed me about Stig. He had money – more money than I thought possible – and he could tell a story. Most of his stories concerned the Falklands, where the Paras had just been in the thick of it. If I could join the Parachute Regiment, I reasoned, I'd not only have money, but would end up seeing the world – even better, fighting in far-flung parts of it.

Stig laughed when I told him this, but when he saw I was serious he told me I'd have to train and train hard. So I pounded the beach every day before and after work; come rain, wind or snow, it didn't matter. Gradually, I built up my fitness. When it became easy, I tied a rope to a tractor tyre, fixed it round my waist and ran up and down the beach dragging the tyre behind me. People thought I was mad, but in August 1984 it got me where I wanted.

I was a fully fledged member of 2 Para by April of the following year, but as time passed, even that wasn't enough: I set my sights on joining the SAS. Being in the Paras was no guarantee of passing Selection. The SAS needed specialists, so I concentrated with every fibre of my being on becoming the battalion's best signaller, then on coming top of the combat medics' course. Nothing was going to stop me achieving my goal. Or so I thought.

On a cold, rainy October night in Aldershot, the Paras' garrison town in Hampshire, some twat in a Volvo clipped my bike and sent me over the handlebars. Flying through the air, upside down and facing backwards, I was hit by a car driving too fast in the opposite direction.

With their unorthodox methods, the surgeons saved me from death by internal bleeding. Too bad the hospital didn't also check if I'd broken any bones before it discharged me. By the time I'd got a second opinion, my right foot, both ankles and right hip had set in the wrong positions. They were completely fucked, as were my back, knees and right shoulder. Not only was I out of contention for the SAS, I was medically unfit for duty in any front line regiment.

To compound matters, the hospital had 'lost' my medical records. Closing ranks, they'd removed all the evidence. It was like my case never existed.

As far as the lads alongside me saw it it didn't make much difference: my soldiering was over. But I refused to accept a desk job and the quest was on to find a way back into combat without a Bergen.

A mate of mine suggested I should apply for the Army Air Corps (AAC). 'You want to be in the thick of it?' he said. 'You could end up flying for the SAS.'

He showed me a book. Inside was a photo of a pilot in an army helicopter, his eyes blacked out with censor-ink. Behind him were four fully tooled-up members of the Special Air Service. He was right. If I couldn't fight for the SAS, maybe I could fly for them. How cool would that be? I could get back to the front line without getting off my arse.

All I had to do now, I figured, was to con my way past the medicals that awaited anyone who wanted to become a pilot. Fate had already stepped in and given me a hand. Because I had no recent medical records, there was no paperwork to attest to the fact that little over a year ago I'd been mangled in a life-threatening accident.

Although 2 Para weren't keen on anyone leaving eventually my application was processed. I passed the aptitude tests and managed to bluff my way through the medicals.

Switching from the Paras to train as a pilot – provided I was accepted – meant I'd be stuck as a corporal for another four years, but I wasn't rank hungry. I was on a mission.

Within weeks I was told I'd been accepted for 'grading' at Middle Wallop, the AAC's main airfield a stone's throw from Salisbury Plain.

Grading was a process for assessing a potential pilot's ability to listen, absorb and replicate simple flying manoeuvres. It was a baseline test that included ground school and was designed to see if we had the ability to cope with the army pilots' course.

I was to start in July 1991.

I didn't know if I could fly or not, but by hook or by crook I would give it everything I had.

I was waiting outside the clothing store for my flying suit when a giant of a man nudged me out of the way with a dismissive, semi-hostile look and threw a pair of tatty old gloves onto the counter. The civvie behind the counter half-jumped to attention, threw the man-mountain a sickly smile and laid out a nice new pair of pristine white chamois-leather gloves in front of him.

'There you go, Mr Palmer. Your size if I'm not mistaken.' They must have skinned a whole mountain antelope to make just one pair for him.

Mr Palmer never said a word. He flicked a glance at my maroon beret, leaned into my personal space and stared into my eyes. I figured he either had something against the way I wore my silver-winged cap badge – 2 Para style – round by my left ear, or he just didn't like Paras, full stop.

He gave me a thin smile, tucked his gloves into his pocket and walked out.

I filed Mr Palmer's name away. I had other things to worry about right then. The trouble with grading was the fact that none of the instructors – crusty old pilots who had been in the RAF, but were now civvies, well beyond retirement age – gave you any feedback on your chances of success. I had no idea how I was doing.

Captain Tucker called us together in the Chipmunk hangar briefing room. A tall, softly spoken, well-to-do Royal Electrical and Mechanical Engineers officer, he was a candidate just like us, but because of his rank he was the grading course leader. We were told we needed an average score of fifty for each exercise. There would be twelve exercises altogether, with a final handling assessment tacked on the end.

When they debriefed us, the instructors wrote everything down in blue A4 ring binders that had our names on the spines.

I desperately wanted to know what was in my binder.

Standing outside the hangar with the smokers one day, I could see through the window into the room where the instructors kept them. The folders were in a neat row on the second shelf of a steel cabinet. As I glanced nonchalantly past the smokers, in came Chopper Jennings, one of the instructors, and locked the cabinet. Then he opened the top-right drawer of the desk, lifted out a big orange folder and flung in the key. Jennings took the key to the drawer away with him, but that didn't bother me. I could pick a drawer lock, no problem. Doors didn't present an obstacle either.

I asked one of the ground crew what time the hangar opened the following morning. I told him I wanted to practise my checks in peace. Six, he told me, and from that moment my mind was set.

I told my Para mate Chris my plan but he wasn't getting up early. He didn't want me to tell him if he was failing; only to let him know if he was passing.

Suit yourself, I told him.

The next morning, I hung around for the ground crew to open the hangar and push out the 'Chippies' – our De Havilland Chipmunk T10 training aircraft – into the crisp summer morning light. I crept past them, made my way to the corridor and reached the door to the office. Skills I'd learned from my mates at school for cracking locks and flipping Yales came in very handy. The key for the steel cabinet was where Chopper Jennings had put it. I opened the cabinet and selected the folder with 'MACY' on the spine.

I was scoring 54s and 55s. Each piece of airmanship was carefully marked. I studied the details closely. Mr Fulford, my sweet old instructor, had marked me down for not looking out enough. This, he said, could lead to a mid-air collision, and would need to be rectified if I was to become a pilot.

No sooner said than done, Mr Fulford.

I looked at my mate's folder and he was bombing big-style. Then I looked at some of the other guys to see how they were doing. Only a few were doing okay, the majority were borderline and some were totally losing it.

When I got back, Chris asked how he was getting on and I told him I hadn't been able to get into the office, but would try again. What else could I say?

The following day, bombing along in my Chippie with Mr Fulford behind me, I made sure that my head never stopped moving as I scanned the Hampshire skies for other aircraft.

When I broke into the office and sneaked a look at my file the following day, I was gratified to see that my situational awareness had improved greatly, but I needed to work on my navigational accuracy.

Your wish, Mr Fulford, is my command.

My eighth sortie was to perform a loop. I went for it, big-time. Approaching the top of the loop the blood drained from my thick skull and my vision became impaired by dark grey spots. By the time I had the red and white bird completely inverted, the spots had grown and merged and I was totally blind.

From the tone of his voice I could tell that it had caught nice Mr Fulford out too.

'Are … your … wings … level …?' he gasped.

I didn't have a clue; I was fighting a losing battle to stay conscious.

I grunted my reply.

I woke to hear the Gypsy Major engine screaming, quickly pulled out of the dive and levelled back off at the altitude I had started my first aerobatic manoeuvre. That's it, I thought. I must have failed now. But the following morning I'd somehow got away with it.

By the ninth sortie, I'd accumulated enough points to chill out a bit. I stopped sneaking into the office after my tenth flight, knowing I was almost home and dry.

Along the way, I had also learned why they'd given Jennings his nickname. He wasn't some helicopter ace after all; in fact, he'd never flown choppers. He just marked us so harshly that he chopped more people off the grading course than any other instructor. It was all I needed to justify my early morning sorties. You had to fight fire with fire.

On the day we were due to leave, two weeks and thirteen flying hours after the grading course started, we were lined up outside the Flying Wing Chief Instructor's office in rank order.

Decision time. I knew pretty much who had passed and who had failed, but there were still a few borderline cases I wasn't so sure about.

As a corporal I was way down the line, just behind my pal Chris.

A lieutenant was called into the office. I held my breath, knowing he was about to have the carpet pulled from under him. He emerged a moment or two later, punching the air. 'I've passed. I'm a training risk, but I've passed.'

I knew that from the files. How on earth did he scrape a pass?

A sergeant came out looking devastated. But from my peeks at his file I knew he was better than the lieutenant.

What the fuck was going on here? My heart sank; it seemed little better than a lottery.

I began to panic. What if I'd blown it in the last few sorties? Had I taken my eye off the ball? That was it, I convinced myself; the lieutenant must have greatly improved in the final few days and the sergeant had let down his guard.

Jesus. How had I done?

Chris slunk in and reappeared with the inevitable news. His grades were awful.

Then it was my turn, the moment of truth. The Flying Wing Chief Instructor, the Chippie Chief Instructor and a high-ranking, big cheese AAC officer were all ranged behind a table in front of me. I came to a halt and saluted. I could see my heart pounding through my shirt. This was it. This was my one shot.

'Corporal Macy, how do you think you have done?' the Big Cheese asked.

I wasn't prepared for a question. Don't be cocky, don't be an introvert either, I told myself. The result was jumbled nonsense. 'Er, I think I could have done better, because I put myself under a lot of pressure and, well, if I was to be given a chance, I—'

'Passed,' the Flying Wing Chief Instructor snapped. 'Congratulations.'

A big grin split my face. 'Really? You're sure?'

'You had the highest score. You're free to go.'

'Thank you, sir, sir and sir.'

I gave them a salute that nearly broke my wrist. I spun on my boots, slammed my left heel into the floor, deafening the old codgers, and marched out, quickly dropping my head as I emerged.

Outside, a marine corporal called Sammy was about to go in. I raised my head and said sombrely, 'Mate, I failed. Good luck ...'

His face fell.

Naughty, I knew, but Sammy was a Royal Marine Commando – the time-honoured arch enemy of the paratrooper. He was in on my spying game and had been tracking his performance through my daily updates. He knew he had eight fewer points than me at my last peek.

He'd find out he'd done all right soon enough.

When he reappeared a few moments later I was running around the corridor with my arms outstretched, humming the 'Dam Busters March'. He chased me out into the summer sunshine.

'Maroon machine *one*, cabbage head *nil*,' I shouted gleefully.

Later, I went to see Colonel Edgecombe. Colonel Greville Edgecombe was – and still is – an Army Air Corps legend. He explained the AAC's ethos, how it was all about tapping into the army's skills base, so that each flying squadron had a resident expert for each task. There were engineers, tankies, infantry, artillery, medics, signals operators, chefs and clerks. I wasn't sure what skills the clerks would be able to bring to the table – our pay was always getting cocked up – but I was happy to hear that we'd have a few chefs on board. Para food was great and I wanted it to stay that way.

The colonel told me that only four out of the fourteen candidates had passed with flying colours and had been formally accepted for training. My pilots' course was set for November, four months' time.

On my way out, I heard that Mr Palmer was in the building. I darted into the bogs until I knew he'd left.

By now, I knew that he wasn't plain old 'Mr' Palmer at all, but Darth Vader, the most feared instructor in the Army Air Corps. Knowing I'd be back in a few months' time, I couldn't afford another brush with him.

I had been given a reprieve. I was determined to become a pilot – and not just any pilot. I was going to fly for the SAS, and nobody, not even the Dark Lord of the Universe, was going to stop me.

SKYLINED WITH NO BACKUP

MAY 1992
Fremington Camp, Devon

Fremington Camp was a miserable blot on an otherwise beautiful landscape. Its huts had been built during World War Two and looked as if they'd been through the Blitz. The windows dripped with condensation, the frames were rotten and a number of the panes were cracked or broken. The wind whistled between the gaps, bringing the moist, salty tang of the sea into the improvised Ops room. If I'd been based here I'd have slit my wrists long ago. Thank God we were only passing through.

The Gazelle was the army's training helicopter. I loved flying the nimble little single-engine machine with its huge perspex bubble canopy. I'd been taught how to 'autorotate' so I could carry out an emergency landing if the engine failed, and how to do basic night-flying. I'd then gone on to more advanced techniques: flying low level, landing in confined areas, advanced navigation and instrument flying.

I was six months into the pilots' course. I'd done another thirty hours on Chipmunks, passing 'Basic Fixed Wing' and the ground-school exams that went with it, which allowed me to transition to 'Basic Rotary Wing': learning how to fly a helicopter.

From the very outset we operated under a 'three strikes' rule – three mistakes and we were out. From an initial twenty students on the course, we'd already lost four guys during the fixed wing phase, then three more during my fifty hours of instruction and solo practice during Basic Rotary Wing.

We were now on the 'Advanced Rotary Wing' or 'tactical' phase of our training: learning not only how to fly a helicopter, but how to fight in it.

Tim, a 2 Para mate on the course ahead of mine, had introduced me to the 'cheat-sheet' routine. Ground school involved exams on fourteen different subjects, from basic flight principles to meteorology and navigation. As there were only ever three different papers set for each subject, the drill was for students to acquire these papers – and the answers – from students on earlier courses. No one ever failed a ground-school exam; the challenge was not to get 100 per cent and give the game away.

Tim's pal Billy was the only bloke anyone knew of who didn't do this and since he looked like a dark-haired version of Dan Dare and I was impressed by the way he applied himself to flying, I decided to follow his example. In the Air Corps, I had glimpsed the life I wanted. I would have to touch every base if I was to become an SAS pilot.

Rejecting the cheat-sheets paid off when the instructors decided to set a new paper on every subject for our intake. Blind panic ensued and more guys fell by the wayside.

I listened cautiously, therefore, to those who recommended cheat-maps for the advanced tactical course: recce positions that had been highly marked during previous exercises. When we got to Fremington and were briefed on our 'mission' – to identify an 'enemy' vehicle convoy heading from the east on the B3042 towards the A377 – I took one look at the cheat-positions and decided to formulate my own plan.

I walked into the ad hoc planning room – little more than a broom cupboard – and studied the three faces gazing expectantly at me.

Herbert and Bateman, the two instructors, looked like they wanted to eat me for the breakfast none of us had had yet – and wouldn't get until we returned from the sortie. The other guy, a fellow student called Mick Baxter, was peering at me so intently I thought his eyes might explode.

'Right,' I began, trying to sound authoritative, 'for the purposes of this exercise, I am the patrol commander and I am going to lead us out. I am flying with Mr Herbert and you, Corporal Baxter, will be flying with Mr Bateman.'

Mick's Adam's apple bobbed in his throat. Warrant Officers Herbert and Bateman were already busy with their clipboards.

Today's exercise was about reconnaissance: finding and observing enemy convoys while maintaining tactical superiority; seeing and reporting without being seen.

After briefing the met, air traffic and timings I proceeded to the execution of the mission. 'When we leave here, we're going to follow this valley south-east.' I pointed to a black line on the map behind me. 'We will conduct an under-wires crossing here, where the pylon line crosses the River Taw.' It was the lowest point of the pylons just south-east of Chapelton.

'There are no roads and no villages nearby, so there's every chance we won't be seen. We'll continue to fly the marked route until we reach the confluence of the two rivers at Copy Lake, our Final Rendezvous point. Then we'll continue up to the OPs, catching the vehicles at the very end of their route, here …'

The two instructors scribbled away furiously. This was my big departure from the routine suggested by the cheat-maps. The instructors' preferred Observation Positions for viewing convoys moving through this area were a few miles to the east, on a wooded ridgeline with an unrestricted view of the B3042. In my book, they also allowed unrestricted views of our helicopters. We would be skylined while the enemy blended in with their surroundings – absolutely the opposite of what I felt we needed to achieve. The eye is drawn to movement and I knew that positioning our Gazelles on top of a ridgeline in combat would be suicide – an open invitation for an artillery barrage. And if the convoy stopped we would be heard; the wind would carry the noise of our aircraft directly towards it. They were shit positions.

I'd done a thorough map-study (something they called 'inter-visibility' in the Paras) and had found a spot at the bottom of a valley with an equally good field of view. We could see the convoy easily, and wouldn't miss them since they'd be at the end of their route. I could pop myself and Mick between the trees beside the river, and a huge hill behind us would provide a stealthy backdrop; our green recce helicopters would blend perfectly with our surroundings. In the unlikely event we were seen, we had a fantastic escape route that would allow us to melt away in a heartbeat. Bonzer.

'As soon as we're at the FRV, both our aircraft will point towards each other and we'll carry out our drills,' I continued. 'Anti-collision strobes, navigation lights and transponders will be switched off. We will not emit at all. A full 360-degree turn will signal that I'm ready to move. I will know you're happy, Mick, when you turn your nav lights off. I will then depart and you will follow me to our OPs.'

To get to our OPs we would manoeuvre through the trees until we ended up eyes-on the road. We would wait there, masked by the trees and our backdrop, until the convoy appeared. We'd count the vehicles, wait until we were sure we had the lot, then skedaddle back for the debrief.

'Any questions?'

Baxter still looked like he'd swallowed a yo-yo. The instructors said nothing. Like driving test examiners, Herbert and Bateman would sit silently beside us until we got back to camp. They'd only tell us how we'd done when we were back on the ground.

By way of chit-chat, I asked Herbert what he'd done before joining the Army Air Corps.

ACC, he said, in some place I'd never heard of.

Army Catering Corps. If we fucked this up, at least we could count on a Full English.

We took off just after the sun came up and headed out towards the exercise area. The wind dropped; Devon spread out before us in all its glory and the sea twinkled behind us. We slipped under the wires together fourteen klicks from the FRV, barely six feet off the ground, either side of the river, and began nap of the earth flying – at tree-top height, using the low ground for cover, to keep below the radar horizon. With a final klick to run I dropped down to fifteen feet and began to weave between the trees. I could see Mick a tactical bound behind, following me nicely.

We were as stealthy as any helicopter could be both from the ground and the air – small, camouflaged, and very hard to spot at this height unless we had to fly around someone out walking his dog.

The Gazelle wasn't always quiet. It was difficult to pick up rotor sound from a distance because it was light and had a fenestron tail rotor – thirteen blades housed in a Venturi – but its gears and bearings did emit a high frequency whine when it was in the hover.

The sun had crested the hills to the east of the FRV point. My goldfish bowl of a cockpit was beginning to warm by the time Mick's lights were finally extinguished, signalling he was ready. I led the way, a few feet off the ground, climbing for fences and gates.

As an ex-Para, I knew the value of terrain-masking ingress and egress within an area of operation – no matter whether you were on foot, in a tank or a helicopter.

I wound us through the belt of trees until we arrived in the OPs. I spotted the road in the distance, uphill through the gaps in the trees – sunlight glinted off a handful of cars threading their way along the dual carriageway towards the Cornish border. The OPs were awesome. The trees cast their shadows across us; even God wouldn't know we were here. We were nice and early and all we had to do now was sit and observe.

Mr Herbert took over the controls and I grabbed the pistol grip of the Gazelle Observation Aid, a sight like a periscope built into the canopy above the left pilot's seat. I peered through its rubber browpad and positioned its field of view on the road nearly a mile away. Eventually I spotted the headlights of the first of the four-ton lorries as it crested the hill to our south-east.

For the purposes of the exercise, the four-tonners represented main battle tanks; the Land Rovers that accompanied them were supposed to be armoured personnel carriers (APCs). We had been told roughly when to expect the convoy but not how many vehicles would be in it. After five minutes, I counted five four-tonners and six Land Rovers. Now I just had to wait and see if it was a split convoy or if there were any stragglers. Five minutes passed, then ten. Glancing through the trees to my left, I could almost feel Mick's frustration. No matter. I was doing this by the book. As a soldier, I knew that battlefields weren't neat and ordered – that you should always expect the unexpected. I didn't want to get back to Fremington to be told I was on Strike One because we'd missed a second convoy travelling a few miles behind the first.

Only when we were approaching our fuel 'bug-out' point did I decide that it was safe to return. I led Mick back to the FRV and he led us back to the camp. We landed with just enough fuel to have coped with a diversion should we have come face to face with unexpected enemy on our return.

After shutting down the Gazelles we were directed into the improvised briefing room while our instructors checked in with the convoy to see if we'd been spotted.

'How did you think it went?' Herbert asked as he closed the door.

I knew that my flying was okay, so the only thing he could fail me for was the mission itself. 'We achieved our mission, sir,' I replied. 'We got there in plenty of time and concealed ourselves before the enemy turned up. We counted the vehicles and I'm confident we didn't miss any. I'm pretty damn sure we remained undetected throughout, and on the egress. I don't think it could have gone much better, to be honest.'

Herbert arched an eyebrow. 'Really?'

Uh-oh …

'How do *you* think it went, Corporal Baxter?' Bateman said.

Mick took his face out of his hands and glanced at me before replying.

'We achieved our mission,' he said without blinking.

Herbert let rip. 'Your choice of OP was piss poor. You waited far too long and the information you brought back was untimely.'

Mick's face disappeared into his sweaty palms again and I could feel my blood begin to boil.

'What you should have done is find an OP further to the east so you could have picked the convoy up sooner,' he barked. His slightly ruddy face was turning a deeper shade of crimson.

He walked over to the map. 'If you'd chosen one of these two positions in this area here' – he indicated the points I'd been advised to use by my peers – 'you'd have detected the vehicles a lot quicker. Then you could have carried out the task and returned to camp a great deal sooner. But you waited till you were almost out of fuel. You not only endangered two helicopters, Corporal Macy, but you were late in providing valuable tactical information to your commander.'

I looked at him. Fuck, I thought, he's having a laugh ...

I took a deep breath.

'Well?' His face looked as though it was about to burst into flames.

I gave him my answer as slowly and calmly as I could manage. 'With all due respect, sir, I've been recceing positions for years. Sat on a bare-arsed, skylined hill like that, we might as well have been flying a banner behind us saying "over here".'

Mick's head began to move from side to side. I wasn't sure whether he was just questioning my approach or looking to escape through a crack in the floorboards.

I continued, undeterred. 'If the sun, glinting off our bubble cockpit, didn't give us away first the noise surely would have, because that position is directly upwind. And I didn't hang around the area for the hell of it. I waited because there was every chance that the first vehicles were just the vanguard of a bigger convoy. I needed to be sure that there weren't any others.'

They looked at me in disbelief and then at each other.

'Sir ... If I'd left too early and more vehicles had turned up, I'd have brought back the wrong enemy strengths and the commander tasked to destroy them could have found himself getting killed in his own ambush. That convoy was travelling at about twenty miles an hour, allowing us time to plan an ambush – making my information both 100 per cent accurate and very timely.'

Herbert was unimpressed. The marks he gave me said everything: I'd almost failed.

At breakfast with the rest of the students I completely lost it. 'In a real battle, skylined on that ridgeline like that, we'd have been shot clean out of the sky. Instructors – put 'em in combats or out in the field, expose them to real tactics and a little rain and they'd fucking melt! Herbert doesn't have a tactical bone in his fucking body!'

Everybody had stopped eating. My marine buddy Sammy, who I'd spoofed the day we received our grading results, eventually said what everyone was thinking. 'You're supposed to pass the course, you tit, not teach the instructors tactics and declare war on the system.'

'You were a gnat's cock-hair away from getting us both failed for not using their OPs,' Mick said. 'We only scraped a pass because your plan was bombproof. If we'd made one tiny error they'd have fucked us with it till our arses bled. You need to fucking wise up, Para-boy.'

After Fremington, I flew with three different instructors. Up until then, I'd had pretty good grades. The new instructors were assigned to find out what had gone wrong with Herbert and me. Fortunately, they put it down to an aberration.

Fremington taught me a lesson every bit as valuable as tactics and tactical awareness. It had taught me coursemanship – when to speak and when to keep my big stupid trap shut. No one liked a smart arse, and in my determination to get into the thick of it, I'd forgotten a crucial ingredient: humility.

CHOPPER PALMER'S WINGS

MAY 1992
Middle Wallop, Hampshire

No one at Middle Wallop wanted to find himself in the cockpit with a 'chopper', especially when it came to exams, and, as I'd already discovered, there was no instructor more feared than Darth Vader.

Mr Palmer and I had already crossed swords once and that was enough. I hadn't forgotten our first encounter: his huge frame filling the doorway as he'd strolled into stores for a new pair of gloves, glaring first at my beret, then at me. Ever since, like everyone else on the course, I'd gone out of my way to avoid him.

Late in the month my luck finally ran out.

After returning from Devon, I had several days more flying to do before my Final Handling Test – make or break day, when I would either earn my wings or get booted off the course. First there was a halt in proceedings beforehand because of the International Air Tattoo, a huge fly-in, normally organised by the RAF but staged this year at Middle Wallop.

IAT (or 'RIAT' as it is known today – they've added a 'Royal' to it) is the biggest air show in Europe. Hundreds of military aircraft take part, from vintage Hurricanes and Spitfires to modern fighter jets and combat helicopters. It's an organisational nightmare because tens of thousands of spotters descend on the event and traffic has to be diverted around the southern half of England. Marshalling this number of aircraft is a huge job and falls pretty much to the host base to organise; we students were told that we were the 'work party' – the guys on the ground responsible for ensuring the visiting pilots taxied and parked where they were supposed to. The man in charge was none other than Mr Chopper Palmer.

Everybody groaned.

I knew I hadn't helped matters by wandering around the place with the maroon machine on my head and sporting a set of Para wings on my arm like they were the only ones that mattered – before I'd realised that all that Para stuff wasn't necessarily the best way of becoming an AAC pilot.

On the day before the Tattoo I walked over to the air traffic control tower to get a bird's eye view of the proceedings, to orientate myself before the show started. As I wandered from window to window, getting my bearings, wondering how we'd fit all the aircraft in, I turned to see a petite, middle-aged woman engaged in a meaningful conversation with one of the controllers. I tuned in, because I'd overheard her mention that she had a couple of sons in the Paras.

I didn't think any more about it until, on her way out, she said her goodbyes and the controller beside me said: 'Bye, Mrs Palmer.'

'Mrs *Palmer*?' I asked when she had disappeared from view. 'Chopper's wife …?'

'The very same,' the controller said. 'Nice, isn't she?'

She was. Lovely, in fact. Something I found very difficult to square with her enormous husband and his fearsome reputation. But then it began to dawn on me. Maybe, on our first meeting, Palmer hadn't been psyching me out; maybe I'd misread that stare.

If the guy had a couple of sons in the Paras, perhaps it had signalled something else – an affinity, maybe? Jesus. Could it be that Chopper's reputation was not all it was cracked up to be? Could he be a regular bloke after all? How else could he have ended up with such a charming wife?

Armed with this heretical thought, I left the control tower and headed round the corner for my briefing. My fellow students were already waiting.

I fell into line just before Palmer appeared, looking like thunder. His eyes met mine and they seemed to bore right through me. He gave me that thin smile again and boomed: 'Right. I need a second in command. Who's going to be my two-eye-see?'

You could have cut the air with a knife. Nobody said a word. The only thing missing was *The Good, the Bad and the Ugly* theme music.

From nowhere, I felt myself stick up my hand. 'I will, sir,' I said.

Palmer growled something and stormed off in the direction of the hangars.

'What did he say?' I asked Sammy.

'He said, "Thanks, you knob. You've blown any chance you had passing the course. You can go back to being a meat-bomb right now."'

'Seriously. What did he really say?'

'He said, "Para, Para in the sky, living proof that shit can fly."'

As I made to pelt off after Chopper Palmer, Sammy held me back by my shirt. 'Are you fucking mad, Macy?'

'Probably,' I said, tugging myself free.

In fact, I was feeling happier than I'd felt in ages. My hunch – and it was based on some pretty solid first-hand evidence – said that, a pound to a pinch of shit, Palmer wasn't quite the chopper he was cracked up to be. And since in the game of roulette that determined which instructors would be assigned to us for our Final Handling

Test there was a fair chance I'd be getting Mr Palmer, I figured that – unlike Fremington – time spent in reconnaissance would not be wasted.

Part of me still couldn't quite believe what I was doing. I felt like a circus performer who was about to put his head in the lion's mouth.

When I caught up with him, Palmer started to brief me on the admin task. As he did so, he glanced at my beret and told me something I already knew – that one of his boys was in the Parachute Regiment.

'Is he in White Feathers One or Grungy Three, sir?' I asked. 2 Para had sent 1 Para white feathers for missing the Falklands and 3 Para, quite frankly, needed to wash.

He smiled. 'That would make you Bullshit Two, I guess.' He knew I was 2 Para from the blue lanyard I had wrapped around my shoulder.

I was about to reply when I saw a shadow racing across the ground between the hangars. I looked up. The first aircraft to arrive at the show was a helicopter. I couldn't tell what kind. I held up my hand and squinted against the sunlight.

As the machine banked on its final approach, I got my first proper look at it. It was the ugliest thing I'd ever seen – big, dark and angular, it resembled a menacing primeval insect. It came into a slow hover right in front of the tower and hung in the air. Then, nose down, nodding to a crowd of onlookers that had lined up to gawp at it, it crabbed towards a ground handler armed with two orange paddles before finally thumping down onto the ground.

Chopper Palmer swore under his breath. All I caught was something about Yanks.

'Sir?'

'Fly like that with me, Macy, and I'll mince you up through the fenestron of your Gazelle.'

'What is it, sir?' I wanted to get off the subject of going anywhere near a helicopter with him.

'That,' Chopper Palmer said, with a tinge of admiration in his voice, 'is a United States Army AH Sixty-Four Alpha. You ought to be able to tell by the unorthodox approach that it isn't from around here. It's known as the Apache.'

It was the first combat helicopter I'd seen up close. The Apache, I knew, was one of four helicopters competing for a UK MoD contract that would see the British Army equipped with a dedicated attack helicopter for the first time in its history.

As things stood, the Army Air Corps was equipped with two kinds of rotary wing aircraft: the Gazelle and the Lynx (not including the special Gazelles and A109s used by the SAS).

The Gazelle was generally employed for training, liaison and reconnaissance, but could be used for emergency casevac and move a couple of lightly kitted-out troops but that was about it – a valuable but limited asset.

The Lynx Mk7 was an anti-tank helicopter armed with missiles on each side. It was seriously underpowered and suffered badly when it came to moving even small amounts of troops. It was also hindered by the fact it needed a door gunner, reducing its load-carrying capacity and restricting the access from one door. The choice was missiles or troops – it couldn't handle both. And its Tube-launched Optically-tracked Wire-guided – TOW – missiles did not cut the mustard. It was supposed to be our first line of defence against enemy armour, but if it had ever taken on the massed ranks of Soviet T-72s on the West German plains, it would have been massacred. And the lessons of the recent Gulf conflict said that it wouldn't have fared a whole lot better against some of the lesser equipped armies still out there. Waiting for the TOW missile to be manually tracked all the way to the target, it was a sitting duck.

As a result, the impetus to equip the Army Air Corps with a dedicated attack helicopter, one that had been specifically designed for the role, had gained momentum, and the Apache was the main contender. It was battling for the contract, valued at upwards of £2 billion (and that was just for the airframe, not including the simulators or associated equipment), against three other machines: the German-Franco Eurocopter Tiger, an anglicised version of the US Bell Cobra called the Cobra Venom, and the Rooivalk, an ugly brute from South Africa. The Apache's presence at the show was a sign that the competition was hotting up.

I'd never seen anything like it. I was totally mesmerised.

Later, I asked Mr Palmer if I could take a look at it up close. He did better than that: he walked straight up and asked if I could sit in it.

The pilot, looking bored in a pair of mirrored Ray-Bans, was only too happy to oblige. Seconds later, I dumped my camera on the grass and was hauling myself into the rear cockpit – the pilot's position.

Glancing around the cockpit, I could see that it was a world away from the small, flimsy, plastic analogue world of my Gazelle. The Apache was huge, robust and instead of all of the normal instrumentation it had the bulk of its data displayed in the centre of the instrument console.

'Smile, son.' I looked out to see Chopper Palmer pointing a camera at me.

I wasn't sure what had made me happier – sitting in a machine I swore to myself I'd fly one day, or knowing that Chopper Palmer wasn't the Dark Lord after all.

The gunner's position in the front was dominated by a big metal block jutting above the MPDs that looked like a cross between an inverted periscope and something you'd find at a coin-operated peep-show. 'This,' my tobacco-chewing Texan friend told me, 'is something we call the ORT: the Optical Relay Tube. By lowering your eyes to the ORT it allows you to see the enemy using direct viewing optics.' He showed me a pink lens that covered the right eye, 'Look through that,' and then pointed to the MPDs, 'or at them, and you see what the Apache sees.' He spat out some tobacco. 'You can see the radar picture, the image projected by the gunner's thermal imaging system or his daylight camera, the pilot's thermal system … well shit, son … any one of 'em, at any given moment, all at the flick of a switch.'

'Fun's over, Corporal Macy,' Chopper said. 'We have some marshalling to do.' He walked off, forcing me to run after him again.

Three days after the show ended, we were back in the classroom again, preparing for our last few sorties before the dreaded Final Handling Test.

Before we knew it, it was late June. WO2 Bateman was putting the flying programme together. He was attempting to avoid pairing particular students with a particular Aviation Standards Officer if they had a good reason for not wanting to fly with him. The floor erupted. 'Not Chopper Palmer, sir, he hates me …' 'Don't give me Darth Vader, I'll pay you any money …'

I hadn't shared my belief that Palmer's bark was worse than his bite; I knew no one would have believed me. I stuck my hand up and announced that I wanted to fly with Chopper on my Final Handling Test.

The laughter was immediately replaced by a silence you'd only expect to find in libraries and monasteries.

'That's good, Corporal Macy,' Mr Bateman replied, 'because *Mister* Palmer has asked to fly with you.'

Catcalls, wolf-whistles and cries of 'teacher's pet' bounced off the four walls and Sammy called me a brown nose.

'I wouldn't be so quick, marine,' Bateman said. 'You must have been right up Mr Palmer's arse with your Para mate here, 'cause he's asked for you too.'

The lads had seen me getting on with Darth Vader, but Sammy hadn't been within thirty yards of him. Sammy called what he thought was Bateman's bluff.

Bateman replied, 'I think Mr Palmer said it was something to do with "Para Para in the sky" …'

I was off like a shot with Sammy hard on my heels, calling me every name in the matelot's dictionary of profanities.

I walked out to the aircraft nice and early on the day of the test. It was a beautiful summer's morning. An old Battle of Britain airfield, Middle Wallop had remained the largest grass airfield in the country and was as perfect a setting for an air base as you could imagine. The sun was just poking through the trees on Danebury Ring, the site of an ancient hill fort to the east.

I usually loved this time of day, but I felt troubled. It wasn't simply that this was the day I'd find out whether I had what it took to become an army helicopter pilot; I was seriously worried that I'd underestimated Palmer. Moments earlier, as I'd been briefing him on the flight, he seemed to have reverted to his old ways. As I'd scribbled away on the whiteboard in the briefing room, recounting what I'd be doing on the sortie, Darth Vader had just stared at me – the laser stare that everybody had been so alarmed by when we'd first arrived. Gone was the genial bloke who'd opened up the Apache for me and taken my picture. In his place was a big, taciturn bear that looked like he was eyeing me up for breakfast.

'Any questions, sir?' I'd asked when I'd finished the briefing.

'No.'

'I'll see you at the aircraft then, sir.'

'You will, Corporal Macy, you will.'

After walking around the aircraft, I clambered into the cockpit and tried to focus on my pre-flight checks. When I'd got all my maps ready, I set about programming my navigation aid. When I'd done that, I went over everything all over again.

Glancing back at the hangar, I spotted Palmer, larger than life, helmet on, visor down, striding across the grass towards me.

His gait, his whole demeanour seemed to be saying: don't screw with me; don't even talk to me.

My name's Chopper Palmer and I've got a reputation to protect.

A reputation he'd flexed only yesterday morning when he failed one of our course before they'd even taken off.

You arsehole, I said to myself, you requested this guy – and now he's going to fail you.

He walked round the aircraft, opened up the flimsy little door and began to position himself in the commander's left-hand seat. He was so big that he bounced me out of mine, but he didn't seem to notice. He squashed me against the perspex as he leaned over to put on his straps and he didn't notice that either. How was I supposed to fly this thing?

As I continued with my checks two things dawned on me.

The first was why he'd been nicknamed Darth Vader. He sat completely immobile, head forward, visor down, and had the scariest breathing I'd ever heard: a long, slow, deep, throaty breath in, a pause too long for a mere mortal to survive, and then a rush of air out.

The second was why he chopped more students than the rest. I was nervous, worried and my hands were visibly shaking. If we were having a fight I'd be in my element, but sitting here in this cramped cockpit knowing that he held the power to end my long quest was becoming unbearable. I was about to fail because I was struggling to hold it together. He was a chopper because students just dissolved in front of him.

I fired up the Gazelle's single engine – no problems there – but my first real test came when I needed to check behind me to ensure no one would be decapitated when I engaged the blades. Palmer was so big I couldn't see past him.

I spoke into my intercom. 'Can you check left please, sir?'

'No.' Palmer continued to look directly in front of him, his visor hiding any expression he may have had.

Parts of me were starting to die. What the fuck was this? 'Unless I check left, sir, I can't start the blades. I might chop someone's head off.'

He squashed me again as he grudgingly looked left. 'Clear.'

My sense of foreboding deepened. I thought of everything I'd been through – grading, a whole year spent learning how to fly – and it had come to this: cramped in a tiny cockpit with a gargantuan instructor who seemed hell-bent on failing me.

Somehow, as we made our way over the Hampshire countryside, I forced myself to concentrate. I simply had to do my best; I had to hold it together. For most of the rest of the flight I was somehow able to zen out Chopper Palmer's brooding presence, despite the fact that I remained squashed into my side of the cockpit by the man's enormous bulk.

Bit by bit we completed the test, until, right at the end, we came to the clincher: Practice Forced Landings. I carried out several PFLs that I thought were pretty good. Then, as we were approaching the airfield with the test minutes from completion, he suddenly said, 'I have control', chopped the engine and we plummeted earthwards.

As emergency landings and autorotations went, it was the best I'd ever seen; so expertly done, in fact, that he bled away the last reserves of energy in the Gazelle's freewheeling blades in a beautiful flared landing that ended in the helicopter's skids literally kissing the grass.

As we slid to a standstill I was so awestruck by this textbook display that I failed to take on board what he said next. It was only when my mind replayed the instruction that I realised he'd asked me to take off again and given me a grid reference.

I'd missed it.

He'd suckered me, the old bastard. I'd thought the test was over.

I was summoning up the courage to ask him for the grid reference again when he turned to me. 'Farrar-Hockley's fallen off a ladder in his greenhouse. He's got a pitch-fork up his arse. We've got to get him to hospital, pronto. I take it you know who I mean by Farrar-Hockley, Corporal Macy …'

'Farrar the Para,' I answered as I checked the grid I thought he'd said.

General Farrar-Hockley was a bigwig who'd retired a decade earlier and looking at the grid Chopper bloody Palmer had just given me was apparently living in Harewood Forest, a few minutes' flight-time away.

What I didn't know was whether this medical emergency was for real.

I pointed the nose in the direction of the general's house.

On the way, I checked the map and noticed that the general lived in an area that the instructors used for confined areas – a place that was extremely difficult, if not nearly impossible, for a helicopter to land in – though it wasn't on the cheat-maps.

I flew cautiously around the outside of a clearing that constituted the confined area. Every time I looked down, it looked smaller and smaller. I drew this to the big man's attention.

'So get me in there before we run out of fuel,' he demanded. 'Farrar's in a bad way.'

I stared at the tiny gap in the trees, hoping for inspiration. It was touch-and-go. I didn't know what to do.

'Are you going in or what?' Half-drowned by the crackling comms and the scream of the Gazelle, Palmer's voice still managed to sound like a megaphone.

Make-your-mind-up time, Macy. Palmer wasn't interested in debates or discussions. He wanted decisiveness and action.

What was the right answer? What was I supposed to do?

I took a deep breath. 'No sir. I'm not going to make it.'

There was a pause, then: 'Nor could I. Take me home.'

I breathed a sigh of relief. But Palmer hadn't finished with me yet. As we approached the airfield, he reached forward and chopped the engine on me.

Suckered again …

I applied my autorotation skills, dumping the collective lever I had in my left hand to store the energy in the blades so I could use it to cushion the landing. We dropped like a stone and the tone of the blades rose an octave as they freewheeled faster and faster.

At about fifty feet I pulled up the nose to slow the speed and as we dropped through twenty-five feet I gave the collective a sharp pull to arrest the rate of descent. The speed was now about thirty knots and we'd dropped to five feet as I levelled her off by pushing forward on the cyclic between my legs and pulling up slowly on the collective, using up the stored energy. I could hear the blades slowing and at the point we would have fallen out of the sky we touched down. We were running fast and bouncing around a bit but I'd got her on the ground before finally skidding to an untidy halt; scraping a slight zigzag in the grass in the process. Engine-off landings were not my strongest point.

With sticky palms, I sat there waiting for Palmer to issue me with fresh instructions. Instead, he pulled on the rotor brake, threw off his straps and opened the door. This time, he really was finished. Just before he unplugged his helmet he said, 'Do you have any points for me?'

Me? Points for him? I just wanted him to get out before he produced another hoop for me to leap through.

'I'll let you into a little secret, Corporal Macy. If you keep that up you might live long enough to fly the Apache. No debrief points. Well done.'

With that he bounced me off my door one last time before gently closing his and taking off across the grass. When he was several strides from the helicopter, it dawned on me that I'd passed.

BOOBY-TRAPPED
IN NORTHERN IRELAND

MAY 1997
1,500 feet over Crossmaglen, South Armagh, Northern Ireland

'Gazelle Five, this is One Zero Alpha. All callsigns are now firm, over.'

I pulled the transmit button on the cyclic. 'Gazelle Five, roger, wait out.'

I put the Gazelle into a shallow turn and turned to the guy on my right. 'Look down now, Scottie, and you can see where each brick in the multiple is. The most important element of working with foot soldiers is to identify where each and every man is. If the IRA kick off you need to know exactly where to look.'

Scottie peered down through the bug-eyed canopy. 'Hellooo,' he said, pretending to wave to the men on the ground. Not that they stood a hope in hell of seeing us; we were stooging around above them at 1,500 feet. A 'brick' was half a section – four men – the British Army's standard unit in Northern Ireland. A multiple is three or more bricks.

I was sitting in the left-hand seat, the commander of Gazelle 5, an aircraft with 665 Squadron, 5 Regiment Army Air Corps. 5 Regiment was the AAC's Northern Ireland Regiment to which I'd been posted for five months the year before.

Scottie, my pilot, was sitting in the right-hand seat. My job today was teaching him how to support foot multiples, a skill I'd acquired during my first posting to Northern Ireland four years earlier. As laid-back as Scottie appeared to be, he was also a damn good pilot. We were both sergeants and had known each other since I'd arrived in Dishforth after graduating from Middle Wallop. Scottie was a 'posh jock'. He had a soft accent and a high-pitched voice that got even higher whenever he got excited. He spent most of his money on cars, clothes and watches.

Scottie took over the flying so I could use the camera.

'One Zero Alpha has just entered Lismore,' I said, 'and taken up positions by the first house on the right. One Zero Bravo is behind them on the Dundalk Road covering the rear to the north.' I gestured for him to look out of the window again. 'One Zero Charlie has moved forward on the Dundalk Road to cover the south.'

One Zero Charlie was on both sides of the road, with an RUC policeman, looking along a straight stretch with good avenues of approach.

'One Zero Charlie is in the most vulnerable position,' I continued, 'because a vehicle can approach from the south, take a shot and scoot off. You need to keep an eye out along the Dundalk Road in both directions. If you see any vehicles, yell, because I'll need to warn the multiple commander. Large vehicles like covered tipper trucks and lorries could contain an IED. Keep a watch for them.'

'Okay, Ed.'

Before the multiple moved off again, I needed to scout ahead to find its vulnerable points – areas of particular threat in the vicinity.

'One Zero Alpha, this is Gazelle Five. I have identified all of your men. Can you send me your VPs for this area, over?'

A broad Ulster accent responded. 'One Zero Alpha, aye, we only have the one. Once we move forward up Lismore we'll cross a junction on our left leading south along Lismore Park. Can you see it, over?' The multiple commander was clearly a guy with local knowledge.

I could see the junction he meant. I told him it was clear.

'Gazelle Five, roger, over.'

'That's a bad crossing for us, mate,' the Ulsterman said. 'We've been shot at from that road before and the bastards have escaped onto the Dundalk Road and got away to the south, over.'

'Gazelle Five, roger, wait out.'

All of this was new to Scottie, although it shouldn't have been. Not that I blamed him. There had been a procedural breakdown in the way Gazelles had been supporting multiples in Northern Ireland and without remedial action I knew that more of our boys on the ground were going to die.

The threat level was high. Aside from IEDs and ambushes, it was the era of the South Armagh Sniper, a guy armed with a .50 calibre sniper rifle who'd taken out seven of our lads in the past five years. He was still out there. Our job was to provide top-cover, to scout ahead for anything that constituted a potential threat to the multiple on the ground. The Gazelle was an ideal platform for this role. Thanks to its powerful high-resolution, thermal-imaging camera system, we could stare down the throats of anyone down there, even from this altitude.

'Look along this road on my TV monitor, Scottie, and you'll see a lone vehicle at the dogleg bend facing south. That's a good shooting position, and the car is facing in the escape direction.'

'How do you know if it's a threat?'

'You don't yet. You need to see if the engine is warm on the thermal camera and to see if anyone is in the car or ready to jump into it.'

I pointed at the screen. The car was stone cold, with no occupants and nobody nearby. Had it been used recently, I would have detected the white heat glow of the engine block, even through its bonnet.

Scottie was quick to chip in. 'Do we give them the all clear?'

'No mate, this is what we do.' I got on the radio again. 'One Zero Alpha, this is Gazelle Five. I have a white Ford Capri at the dogleg halfway down the road on the left-hand side. It is cold, no occupants and no one hanging around, over.'

'One Zero Alpha, wait out.'

I turned to Scottie. 'We don't know the threat here, buddy. All we can do is let him know what's around the corner. He decides what to do about it.'

'How's that going to help him?'

'He'll be talking to base now; they'll pull a file on all Ford Capris and also check out the colour in case of a respray. If it's reported stolen, they won't go anywhere down that road, because it's likely to have an IED in it.'

'Gazelle Five, this is One Zero Alpha. That vehicle is registered to the house that it's parked outside, but thanks anyway. Are we cleared to move, over?'

'Gazelle Five, I've not quite finished looking around. Wait out.'

I looked at Scottie again. 'Okay, buddy, now that their VP appears clear I need to check the area they're about to move into.'

At the edge of the town there was a small close, shaped like a sickle, with an alleyway leading off it. The multiple would move past it in the next thirty metres or so.

'Look into every place a bomb could be left, or where trouble could come from, because you don't want the multiple split up, Scottie. If you look on the monitor now, you'll see a known trouble-spot called The Crescent.'

Scottie peered at the screen. 'There are three kids playing football down there.'

'What do you think we should do?'

'Tell the multiple commander. They need to know what's at the end of the alleyway.'

'Right. Paint the picture to the guys on the ground, so they're ready to respond.' He was picking it up fast.

After they set off, I explained to Scottie that he was responsible for the rear and the periphery of the multiple and should warn me of any vehicles – or anybody, for that matter – approaching from blind positions.

'Okay, what next?' he asked.

'I'm looking into Lismore. There's a little cul-de-sac down there where they're scheduled to do a house search.'

I scanned forward, letting the Gazelle's powerful thermal-imaging camera do its thing. Lismore was just forward of the area the multiple was patrolling. The ability of the camera to stare into people's living rooms, from this height and far higher, never ceased to amaze me. I let the camera rove through the streets and alleyways. It was a warm, late spring day. Wild flowers bloomed in the neighbouring fields. I could see it all. It was strange, then, that apart from the three kids playing football, no one was around.

A movement at the edge of the screen caught my eye, a curtain billowing in the breeze. The window on the first floor was wide open.

I scanned to the next house and noticed that its windows were open too. It was the same all along the street …

Fuck.

'One Zero Alpha, this is Gazelle Five. Go firm, go firm now! I have large combat indicators in Lismore, wait out.'

'What is it, Ed?'

I pointed at the screen. 'The bins are out in this cul-de-sac, but not in any of the others. They don't do bin collections in just one street. And take a look at the windows. What do you see?'

'It *is* almost summer, Ed.'

'Do *you* leave all your windows wide open when you go out to work? Look at the other houses in the area. Only a couple have theirs open.'

'I know a bin can have an IED in it, but what's the significance of the windows?'

'The IRA won't piss off the locals. They'll tell them there's a bomb in a bin. That's why the place is deserted. The windows are open so the pressure from the blast doesn't blow them in. I may be wrong, but this stinks of a set-up.

'It couldn't be a booby-trap bomb because our guys won't even touch a twenty-pound note on the floor in Crossmaglen and the IRA know that. The bomb would have to be set off by a command wire or remote control. I couldn't see any wires, but I didn't see a living soul down there either, except for the lads and their football. Stand by, Scottie, I'm about to transmit again.'

I told One Zero Alpha the form. There was a pause, then he came back to me; he didn't want to go near the place, but did want to question the three lads.

I told him how to corner them by moving a brick out onto the Dundalk Road first and another down the alleyway.

Scottie watched One Zero Charlie by the Dundalk Road and I surveyed the three lads as the men of One Zero Alpha moved towards them.

'One Zero Charlie, this is Gazelle Five. The lads are headed your way.' I could see them break into a run towards the Dundalk Road.

'This is One Zero Charlie cutting them off.' I could hear his breathing quicken as he ran.

I turned to Scottie. 'And that's why you need to know where everyone is and what their callsigns are.'

The lads ran back into the cul-de-sac and were promptly confronted by the men of One Zero Alpha.

Zero One Bravo was covering the alleyway and Zero One Charlie the entrance to the Dundalk Road. The three lads were cornered.

'It's making sense to me now,' he said.

'You don't need to gawk at our boys,' I told Scottie, 'because they're not going to shoot themselves. You need to be looking ahead of them and on their flanks. That's where trouble's going to come from if it's out there. Take a look, for instance, across the Dundalk Road and across that first field there. There's an inverted T-shaped tree line. Do you see it?'

'Got it,' Scottie said.

'Keep an eye on that place, buddy, because that's an awesome sniping position.'

'Why?'

'It's got a good clear shot, cover from above and a great escape route, making it hard for us to follow anyone who bugs out of there.'

'How do you know this shit, Ed?'

'Because I've been a foot soldier. I see things from up here. But I also see them from down there.'

The radio crackled. 'Gazelle Five, this is One Zero Alpha. The three lads are local teenagers and the way they're behaving makes our copper suspect there *is* an IED in the area. He knows these guys. They're usually pretty gobby, but today butter wouldn't fucking melt … Our job's done, Gazelle Five. We're heading back out onto the Dundalk Road and back to the station, over.'

'Wait out.' I explained to Scottie that we now had to go through the routine all over again, covering them on the journey back.

'One Zero Alpha, Bravo and Charlie, this is Gazelle Five. Your only threat is from a wood line to the east of One Zero Charlie. It's across the field on the other side of the Dundalk Road. We'll keep an eye out for any snipers, over.'

'Thanks, mate, over.'

'No worries, buddy, out.'

We turned and headed back the way we'd come.

It was my second tour of Northern Ireland. My first had been in 1993 – not counting the time I had deployed there on the ground as a Para in 1987 – and this time it was a very different ball of wax. In 1993, when I'd been in Belfast as part of City Flight, covering foot patrols in and around Belfast, I'd flown with ex-infanteers, AAC guys who like me had previously been soldiers. They'd all had a natural feel for the tactical picture on the ground and it showed in the way they flew. Somehow or other, this skill had been lost in the four years I'd been away.

My first unit after graduating from Middle Wallop, 664 Squadron, 9 Regiment Army Air Corps, was located at Dishforth in Yorkshire. With it, I'd been on exercises in Belize, Kenya and the United States.

In the five years I'd been an operational pilot I was having the best fun it was possible to have with my clothes on.

As a newly qualified AAC helicopter pilot, there were two platforms I could aspire to: the Gazelle or the Lynx. Most elected for the Lynx because it was armed and as aggressive a flying machine as the army possessed at the time, though that wasn't saying much. I went for the Gazelle because it formed the heart of the AAC's covert 'Special Forces Flight'.

I loved the Gazelle. It was the sports car of the skies while the Lynx was the family saloon. The Gazelle, being a two-seater, could sneak in almost anywhere, which is why the Special Forces liked it. And it had excellent performance; it could get up to 13,000 feet – quite a height for a helicopter – no problem.

Because it was small and made of 'plastic and Araldite' it was extremely hard to detect on radar when it was down in the weeds. It was also an extremely useful surveillance platform, because you

www.harperplus.com/hellfire

could hang things off it – Nightsun searchlights and thermal-imaging cameras for starters – and at stand-off ranges, because of its size, it was pretty difficult to detect from the ground.

I'd been doing everything I could to tick the boxes that would get me selected for the Special Forces Flight. I'd done my Aircraft Commander's Course, which allowed me to fly in the left-hand seat, and I'd racked up as many flying hours as I could. A couple of tours in Northern Ireland couldn't hurt either, I figured.

The second time I got out there, in December 1996, I'd found the place in a mess.

Someone who's new in-theatre, who doesn't know the callsigns or the flying regulations, is usually put through a routine known as 'supervised duties' until he or she is proficient with the set-up. Although I didn't need to sign up to supervised duties because I'd previously been in-theatre, I did so nonetheless, because the place we were flying out of, Bessbrook Mill, was extremely tight – it was the busiest base in the province – and had very strict flying procedures. I wanted to be sure I knew the ropes. I reckoned a stint of supervised duties couldn't hurt.

I flew out on my first sortie with a qualified commander. Tully sat in the left-hand seat; I sat in the right. We were called out to Crossmaglen to assist in a 'P-Check': a multiple on the ground had gone into a staunchly Republican area to haul in a suspect for questioning; we were to provide top-cover for them. We'd barely arrived over the suspect's house when the radio sparked and I heard the multiple commander's voice.

'One Zero Alpha, leaving Crossmaglen now.'

I glanced at Tully. No reaction. I picked up the 'patrol trace' – the map that indicated the route the multiple would take. There was nothing marked, no tasking; merely a callsign, the one we'd just heard. When I looked at the image on the TV screen in front of Tully's knees, I realised that he wasn't scouting ahead or to the sides of the multiple for possible threats; he'd got the camera trained on the multiple itself.

'What are you doing?' I asked.

'I'm filming the multiple. Why?'

'Filming their deaths more like,' I said under my breath. I got on the radio. 'One Zero Alpha, this is Gazelle Four. Go firm, go firm.'

I watched on the screen as fifteen men dropped to the ground.

Tully looked horrified. 'What are you doing?'

I told him and in no uncertain terms. Now we could see where our multiple was, we were at least able to identify who the good guys were.

As I circled above them, I asked One Zero Alpha to point out his VPs for me. He immediately said they were approaching Sniper Alley, a known hot-spot. I spent several good, long moments studying the street for things that shouldn't have been there: bins, skips, tipper trucks, command wires and suspicious-looking vehicles. I saw nothing that raised my hackles and signalled as much. Afterwards, he thanked me for what I'd done, saying it had been an 'awesome patrol'. In my book there was nothing awesome about it at all; it was supposed to be routine.

The problem was confirmed, when, over the next week or so, I flew with several other pilots who were every bit as lax as Tully had been in the way they covered multiples on the ground. It wasn't their fault; they didn't know any better. Realising I wasn't going to make myself popular by sticking my nose in, I decided to speak to the RQHI – the regiment's qualified helicopter instructor, the guy who defined the way we flew. James told me he was aware of the problem and said it was a knowledge-based deficiency; it's why we had supervised duties. I told him the best, perhaps the only, thing to do was to write a document that standardised air-ground-air procedure. James told me to 'crack on'.

So I wrote it all down: how a multiple functioned and what it might be called upon to do (P-checks, vehicle checkpoints, ambushes, searches, whatever). I then calibrated the threat it faced in any given situation and put the two together. The final ingredient was what we could supply in our Gazelles – how we could detect and alert them to IRA command wires, dustbin bombs, snipers, ambushes and so on. I then combined the ground and air pictures and came up with a set of procedures – kind of a 'how to provide multiple support by numbers' that anybody arriving in-theatre for the first time could pick up, read and follow.

When I'd finished, I ran it past some infanteer mates. They had no idea how much support our helicopters were able to provide them with.

Heartened by their reaction, I took my draft document to the squadron's 2i/c.

'Very good,' he said, flicking through it as I stood in front of his desk. 'But if you'll allow me to say so, Sergeant Macy, it needs a bit of a polish – i's dotted and t's crossed, that kind of thing. You don't mind, do you, if I ...?'

'Be my guest,' I said. I'd written it as a functional document, not a piece of Pulitzer Prize-winning literature. If someone wanted to tart it up for the brass, I was delighted.

A few weeks later, when I was due to go back to the UK, I'd asked the 2i/c if he'd finished tarting it up; he told me he still needed to do some work on it. He'd let me know when it was done.

That was the last I thought about it until we were practising multiple support procedures over Yorkshire a few months later and my co-pilot mentioned that there was an excellent document on the subject he'd read while deployed in Northern Ireland. 'It covers all this stuff, Ed. I'll give you a copy.'

As I flicked through it, I was delighted to see that 95 per cent of what I'd written had been left alone – it really had just had its i's dotted and t's crossed. Then I saw the 2i/c's name and signature at the bottom.

I gave a rueful smile. The important thing was that it was out there.

It would have a particular resonance almost ten years later in the dusty wastes of Afghanistan.

Then the UK MoD went and ordered the Apache.

It had won out against its rivals in a massive procurement deal – for a cool £4.13 billion, the Army Air Corps would acquire sixty-seven AgustaWestland-built machines, simulators and equipment to operate them. They'd look the same as their American counterparts, but would be very different on the inside. Instead of the standard General Electric turboshaft engines of the Boeing-built originals, the WAH-64D, as the British variant was known, would be equipped with RTM322s – built by Rolls-Royce – with almost 40 per cent more power. The Apache that Chopper Palmer had organised for me to sit in at the International Air Tattoo, which was impressive enough, had been revamped as a total thoroughbred.

What to do?

The Apache was due in AAC service in 2003, which technically gave me time to deploy with the SAS and still left time to apply for Apache selection. The latter, not surprisingly, had become the hottest ticket in the Air Corps. Every pilot with half an eye on the top rung of the ladder would put his name down for a place on the conversion course. To ensure I got there, I knew I'd need to be way ahead of the curve.

Fortunately, I had a plan.

BOMBING FREDDIE MERCURY

11 SEPTEMBER 2000
British Army Training Unit Suffield (BATUS), Alberta, Canada

My Gazelle was parked in the middle of the Canadian prairie. The sun was high and the sky was clear blue. Somewhere above me I could hear a lone bird calling. Lying on my back, I scanned the heavens, trying in vain to locate it. No matter. I popped another piece of straw between my teeth, closed my eyes and tried to doze, but I was out of luck there too.

Fuck me, I thought, didn't these Pathfinders ever put a sock in it?

Next to me was a Special Forces Land Rover filled with three lads from the Pathfinder Platoon – a small unit designed and trained to fight behind enemy lines; 16 Air Assault Brigade's equivalent of the SAS.

They were swapping stories about how they'd have solved the previous year's Kosovo conflict. It was full of harmless machismo – but it went on endlessly. Two of the guys favoured covertly parachuting behind the lines; the third was adamant that an 'infil' by land was better. Both ended with a bloody assault on Slobodan Milosevic's heavily armed Belgrade headquarters. The outcome, needless to say, was a foregone conclusion: Brits one, Serbs nil.

I was in 3 Regiment now, on a two-month exercise fighting a tank battalion, day in day out to get ourselves onto a war footing.

My flight commander, co-pilot and co-ABFAC, Dom, groaned beside me. 'Can't they just shut the fuck up for a moment? Some of us didn't get much sleep last night.'

'Paras,' I told him. 'A gobbier breed you couldn't hope to meet. I used to be one.'

'Don't I know it, Staff?' Dom said. 'And your gob is going to get us into trouble one of these days.' He rolled over and blocked his ears.

Dom was a captain and I was a staff sergeant, the 2i/c of our flight. Dom was public school, vertically challenged and took no shit from anyone, not even me. He was a soldiers' officer and always considered his men before himself. He wasn't the most gifted pilot, but he more than made up for that in the brains department.

We were having a break from kicking tanky arse and were concentrating instead on the fine art of Forward Air Controlling – FACing, as it was politely known in the trade. The Pathfinders were FACs – Forward Air Controllers. Dom and I were Airborne FACs or ABFACs. We did exactly what they did, but from the comfort of our Gazelles. The Pathfinders thought we were a couple of soft pussies, but I'd done the stripped-down Land Rover routine before my accident and knew where I'd rather be.

The radio sparked into life. 'Any callsign, any callsign, this is Starburst Two Four. How do you read?' The accent was Canadian. The 'how' came out sounding like 'hoe'.

The Pathfinders' game of Belgrade-or-bust ground to a halt before they could inflict further damage on any other rogue states.

'Okay, who's up first?' one of them yelled in our direction.

I offered it to them. In a six-month period, a FAC needed to control a certain number of jets and hit the target to remain qualified. In the past two months alone, I'd notched up more than twenty 'controls' – easily enough to remain in business. It was only polite to let them have a go.

Dom and I listened as they contacted Starburst Two Four and brought it in for a practice bombing run. Aiming for the only man-made edifice on a plain the size of Kent was hardly *Krypton Factor* material. The second Pathfinder directed a further T-33 at a tank hulk approximately 200 hundred metres from the building.

Dom started to snigger.

One of the Pathfinders, a little lad with a Freddie Mercury moustache, asked us what was so fucking amusing.

'Nothing, mate,' Dom said. 'Really. Excellent work. Bravo.' He gave him a slow handclap.

Freddie dropped over the side of the vehicle and looked like he wanted to do to Dom and me what he and his mates had talked about doing to Slobodan Milosevic. I jumped to my feet. Dom, the chicken, retreated behind me.

'Looks like you guys need to get some more "controls" under your belt,' I said, trying to sound helpful.

Well done, Macy; that came out beautifully.

'Funny guy,' Freddie said. 'Dodge, put this arsehole out of his misery will you?'

His mate picked up the handset. 'Your target,' he said to the inbound jet, 'is a helicopter ...'

'He'd have to be half blind to miss my little green sports car on the top of this hill,' I said.

The T-33 was built under licence by the Canadians and renamed the CT-133 Silver Star but the name never stuck. It looked like something from *Thunderbirds* as it flew in towards us. The big, cigar-shaped body and huge fuel tanks perched on the tips of two thin wings lined up on the hill. We heard a beep over the radio as it roared overhead – the sound that indicated he'd pickled off a simulated bomb.

The Pathfinder grinned as he spoke to the T-33 pilot. 'Roger. That's a Delta Hotel. The chopper is a goner. I'll be sure to tell its proud owner.'

'Delta Hotel' meant direct hit.

They all rolled around laughing and high-fiving.

'Playtime's over,' I said. 'You've got twenty minutes to hide. Then I'm coming for you.'

Silence returned to the prairie.

'Fuck off,' Freddie said. '*You* …?'

'I bet you tossers a night out in Medicine Hat that I can hit you and you won't even know where I am,' I told him. 'If you can find me and send an accurate grid reference to me before I bomb you, you win. Otherwise you buy the beers.'

'Game on, crap-hat.' This was intended as the ultimate insult; they knew I was an ex-Para.

They mounted up and prepared to set off. The next jet was due in twenty minutes. I put my hands over my eyes and started to count, hide-and-seek style: 'One, two, three …'

'Hey,' one of them shouted, 'we're not ready yet!'

'… seven, eight, nine …'

They roared off in a cloud of dust.

As promised, I gave them a twenty-minute start. Then I took off and headed south. It wasn't long before I spotted their dust trail. I followed them with my optics from a decent stand-off range of about eight kilometres, until I saw them stop on the edge of a depression. It was a good position, but I knew they would move the minute I sent their coordinates to the T-33; we were sharing the same frequency. As soon as I opened my mouth they'd be off like rats up an aqueduct, and it'd turn into a rolling goat-fuck trying to hit the bastards on the move.

It was time to get sneaky.

FACing is a finer art than most people think. A low level jet couldn't find its own targets. When you were a few hundred feet over enemy territory approaching Mach 1, it was nearly impossible to tell the location of the enemy and, even more importantly, of your own forces. That's when you needed a FAC, or, as they were sometimes also referred to in-theatre, a 'Jaytac' – a Joint Terminal Attack Controller (the same thing but theatre specific). FACs and JTACs did the same thing.

As fast jet pilots generally didn't have any time or inclination to loiter over hostile territory in the low level environment, the FAC's job was to identify the target, 'buy' the bomb and deliver it on-target as quickly as possible.

We popped up to their south and held the Gazelle in a hover so the Pathfinders could see us. Once I was sure they had us registered I dropped behind cover and got Dom to pop up every few minutes in a different position, always to the south of them to draw their eyes away from my intended OP. Our little game of cat and mouse was on …

'If they guess our next position, you're going halfers on the night out.'

The colour drained from Dom's face. The Pathfinders were known for putting it away.

A few minutes later, two fresh jets turned up and checked onto the FAC frequency.

'Any callsign, this is Starburst Two One and Two Two. How do you read?'

I was quick to get back to him. 'Starburst Two One, this is Spindle Eight Zero. If you work with me on this frequency and get Two Two to go onto the spare frequency, another callsign will control him later.'

'Starburst Two One, copied.'

'Starburst Two Two, copied and changing freq.'

I called Starburst Two One and he confirmed that they were Lockheed T-33 Shooting Stars too, jets older than my father, but good enough for my purposes. I told him that his target was an SF Land Rover, but that I was struggling to find it.

I told Dom to get behind cover then move round the range to the north-west as fast as he could so the Pathfinders wouldn't know where we were.

They would be looking for us in the south and after that call they'd assume I couldn't see them and hopefully sit still.

I switched to the spare frequency so the Pathfinders couldn't hear us and contacted Starburst Two Two.

Freddie fucking Mercury would be listening out on the other frequency for me to send his coordinates to Starburst Two One, not having a clue I was actually working both jets.

'Starburst Two Two, this is Spindle Eight Zero.' I gave him Freddie's coordinates first. North five-zero, three-five, zero-five, decimal six-six. West one-one-zero, four-eight, four-five, decimal niner-zero.' Then his height: 'Seven-six-zero metres.'

I told him the target was a Special Forces Land Rover.

I'd get the T-33 to attack from over the ridge behind them. If I did it right, they wouldn't even see it coming.

I continued into the microphone: 'Mandatory attack heading, two-one-zero degrees magnetic. Friendly helicopter, four point three kilometres north-west.' He now knew where I was and, after all, we didn't want a blue-on-blue, a friendly fire incident …

I couldn't use my laser on the target for fear of blinding them, so called 'Negative Lima', which signalled as much to the T-33 pilot.

'Readback,' I said. He read the attack back perfectly. I pictured him turning onto this attack run.

'Call when ready,' I said.

A moment later, he signalled he was.

I flipped frequency back to the one the Pathfinders were on for a few seconds to put them off the scent that I was working Starburst Two Two on another frequency. I called Starburst Two One, letting him know that I had found the Land Rover to my north, but needed a few more minutes to get the exact coordinates. Without the correct coordinates they'd be too cool to run just yet.

I flipped the frequency back.

All being well, the Pathfinders would still be looking south just as we were arriving in the north-west.

'Starburst Two Two, running in …'

Dom pulled us into our new OP. I could see the Land Rover to the east-south-east of us – 4.3 klicks away. Perfect.

A quick glance to the left and I saw the T-33 a couple of hundred feet off the deck. It could do 570 but had throttled back to about 400 knots – which still looked fast.

'Your target is an SF Land Rover,' I said. 'Twelve o'clock, four miles is a depression, a wadi, running right-left. Call when visual.'

A momentary pause, then: 'My target is a Land Rover. Visual with wadi, sir.'

I kept talking. 'Short of the wadi is a scar on the ground. Long of the wadi is a track running away from it.'

'I have a white scar short and can see an online track dropping into the wadi,' Starburst Two Two said. He was homing in nicely. The Pathfinders, meanwhile, would still be waiting for me to give their coordinates to Starburst Two One on the other frequency.

I continued the talk-on, drawing the pilot's eyes ever closer to the target. 'Twelve o'clock, two miles, track. Target Land Rover is on that track, blind to you. Your side of the wadi. Caution late acquisition.' I was warning him that he would acquire the Land Rover late because it would be blind to him on a reverse slope.

'Got the track dropping into the wadi, possible late acquisition,' he acknowledged.

'The target Land Rover has started moving south-west.'

The Pathfinders had cottoned on and were making a break for it. They must have heard the aircraft.

The T-33 began to climb.

I gave Starburst Two Two another steer. 'Twelve o'clock, one mile, dust trail.'

He replied almost instantly. 'Tally target, one vehicle heading south-west.'

He had the target and began to dive directly at it.

The final confirmation I needed was unique and swift: 'Target crossing the bridge now.'

I waited until I was 100 per cent sure he was pointing at the Pathfinders. 'Starburst Two Two, you are clear dry on that target.' 'Dry' was the command to practise a bomb-drop but not to release any actual munitions.

'Clear dry, sir.'

As he passed over the top we heard the distinctive beep of him simulating a bomb drop off the rails.

'Starburst Two Two, this is Spindle Eight Zero. That's a Delta Hotel. You are cleared back onto the original frequency.'

'Starburst Two Two, good control, changing freq …'

I took over the controls of the Gazelle, changed back onto the original frequency and flew directly at the Pathfinders. I keyed the microphone. 'See you guys in Medicine Hat. Looks like you're buying …'

They gave me the two-fingered salute as we passed overhead.

FACING TOMMO

I only had one place left to look. I told Andy that the tanks had to be hiding behind the small hillock in the dry wadi bed.

'Easier said than done …'

Andy wasn't wrong. We'd been up here training with Striker armoured fighting vehicles a couple of days before and the terrain was distinctly unfriendly: a network of narrow valleys cutting through steep-sided hills. The Strikers had fired their wire-guided anti-tank missiles from the ridgelines as we brought in fast jets. It was like a giant game of splat-the-rat. If we got pinged, we'd have to come to a hover, spot turn and fly back the way we'd come.

'If we get caught here, the tanks will kill us. Keep it low and slow and use the pedals to boot us round if you see anything.'

'Pedals? While we're still flying?'

I'd forgotten Andy Wawn was a brand spanking new pilot.

'I'll follow you through on the controls and take over if we get caught with our pants down. If I shout "I have control" I want you to cut away faster than lightning because we won't have time to hand over properly.'

I made a mental note to teach him how pedals could assist a turn. It was a tricky manoeuvre that wasn't officially in the manual – and with good reason. The nose drops and tail rotor authority teeters on out-of-control; get it wrong and the tail breaks away. You'd end up spinning out of control and smashing into terra firma.

Andy flew us up the valley, just below the skyline, fifty feet off the deck and high enough to spin us round and drop the nose without crashing. I held the controls lightly; the light wind from behind us made them slightly sloppy and unresponsive. We both looked anxiously at the bend 500 metres ahead.

We were both expecting the worst. The enemy tanks could be just behind the bend. We'd be so bloody sharp that the boss had refused to come in with us. He was waiting at the mouth of the valley to bring in artillery and fast jets should we get zapped. We'd know if we'd been shot down because the BATUS Asset Tracking System (BATS) box in the back would register a hit and we'd have to land.

With 400 metres to go I craned my neck to the right to see that extra foot around the bend.

I caught a splinter of light to my left, at the periphery of my vision. No sooner had I picked it up than it was gone again.

With 300 metres to go I heard a very light swishing sound. I glanced at Andy. He made more weird noises through his microphone than Darth Vader; it was one of his party tricks.

He glanced back. 'What?'

'Look where you're goi—'

Before I had time to finish the swishing sound turned into a high-pitched screech. By the time I'd turned to see what it was, it had become a blood-curdling banshee wail. I could hear it over the sound of the Gazelle's whining gearbox and engine, and my helmet's hearing protection. Whatever it was, it was less than a foot away from me. It was as if the devil himself was running his fingernails down the world's biggest blackboard …

'I HAVE CONTROL,' I yelled, and flicked my head forward again, fast enough to rattle my eyeballs.

I knew then that what was trying to kill us had us so firmly in its grasp that there really was no escape.

We were at thirty knots, with the valley walls pressing in on both sides. The ground was strewn with boulders fifty feet below.

Hundreds of white strands were suspended in the air in front of us, and more were joining them with every passing nanosecond. We were caught in a giant web. The homing aerials on the Gazelle's nose had been bent back until they were touching the windscreen.

'SWINGFIRE WIRE,' I bellowed.

The Armoured Fighting Vehicles (AFVs) on the ridge must have fired a wire-guided missile. As these things shoot down range they spew out a thin but incredibly strong metal wire; this one had been left draped across the valley in front of us. Our blades had picked it up and spun it around the Gazelle, winching us in towards the hill-side.

I flicked on the radio. 'Mayday … Mayday … Mayday …'

As I fought to cut back our speed the screeching intensified then was punctuated by a series of high-pitched pings as the tension in the wire increased. I prayed we wouldn't lose control of the main rotor.

I was barely keeping us airborne. First we'd been netted; now we were being reeled in. It was only a matter of time before the wires would tighten on the exposed tail rotor drive shaft as it spun at over 5,000 rpm; we were about to be garrotted.

I snatched a glance to our right. The hilltop was too far away; I pointed the nose towards the slope, using a rock as a marker, and shoved the cyclic forward.

Prairie grass ten feet in front of us filled the bubble cockpit. We were going in, head on.

Andy went into Pantomime Dame Mode: 'I'm too young to die …'

'Shut the fuck up,' I screamed back.

With an almighty yank back on the cyclic the nose came up forty-five degrees to match the rake of the slope. I kicked us left a little and dumped the collective lever halfway down. The skids hit the hillside hard and for a moment it looked like we'd stuck solid.

Then we began to slide backwards.

'Nooo …' Andy yodelled, but before he could draw breath we shuddered to a halt again.

The rock I'd been aiming to use as a chock was stuck behind the left skid and holding us fast.

My right hand shot up to the fuel cut off lever. The engine whine stopped instantly and the screeching began to fade. I pulled the collective up to slow the blades before pulling on the rotor brake.

Silence.

Andy gave me the biggest grin I'd ever seen.

'Do you have any fucking idea how hard I was working?' I said. 'And how close we just came to dying?'

He just kept smiling like a halfwit.

'Have you got anything to say?'

'As a matter of fact I have.' His expression became instantly serious. 'Can I have a fag in here? Cos my door's wired closed and I'm gasping …'

He wasn't wrong. We were trussed like a turkey.

Twenty minutes later our flight commander and the CO came sliding down the hill towards us. After the CO had taken pictures, a technician cut us free so we could assess the damage. The wires had all but severed the tail rotor drive shaft. Steve McQueen would have been proud of us. He'd used the same trick in *The Great Escape* to snag himself a motorbike.

'Should have been collected in after firing,' the CO said. 'For you two, the war is over.'

I pulled a copy of *Low Level Hell* from my jacket and waved it at him.

'The Bible says we need to pick up another bird and get right back out here, sir. The war's not over yet.'

'You'd pick a fight with your own shadow, Macy, given half a chance. Come on, I'll give you a lift.'

A week later our two Gazelles were sitting on a hill, awaiting the battle due to kick off in the small hours of the next morning. This was the big one, as real as it got at BATUS, and I wanted to show what our Gazelles were made of.

We were due to mix it with artillery fire, tank rounds, armed recce cars, mounted machine guns, mortars, Milan anti-tank missiles, jets dropping bombs and our own Lynx helicopters. It was what we had all trained for – as close to a real battle as it was possible to be – and I knew we were more than capable of acquitting ourselves well.

Lieutenant Colonel Iain Thomson was here to validate our regiment during the final BATUS exercise. Tommo was the revered CO of 9 Regiment Army Air Corps. He was a legendary leader and knew how to get the best out of his men, but he was a scary bastard too.

He held the power of life or death – he was there to assess whether we were ready for war fighting. I was determined not to let our side down.

We had a BATS box fitted into the rear of the Gazelle, in place of one of the seats. It would transmit our position at all times to Exercise Control. Excon was the hub of the mock battle, where the invigilators watched the conflict play out on a giant screen.

We had been on the prairie for six weeks and after a disastrous beginning had kicked tanky arse in every battle since. I wanted Tommo and the brass to know how good we were, how fast and low we could go, how quickly we could pick up the enemy and how we could shape the battle for the commanding officer. We were the

www.harperplus.com/hellfire

CO's scouts and wielded more power than our little helicopter looked capable of.

The bloody 'Red Tops' were our only problem – Gazelles painted a horrific shade of anti-collision Day-Glo red, flown by range officers whose job was to ensure that we flew within safety limits. They could hand us a yellow card if we flew into the wrong area or in front of somebody else's weapon system. Worse still, they'd give away our position by hovering over us at a couple of thousand feet. Because we went fast and low, the 'enemy' tanks relied on the Red Tops to track our stealthy battle positions.

Following my first protest the Red Tops were told to fly low and behind us, but the bastards still managed to give us away because they never flew low enough. They needed to see the big picture, to ensure safety procedures were being observed. As a result, the tankies brought more artillery down to shoot us out of the sky. I'd been told quite firmly by Excon to wind my neck in; there is no way I was going into this battle without the Red Top escort. End of story.

If there was one man this side of the pond that could get in their way it was Tommo. I couldn't ask him because he didn't know me and would probably tell me to wind my neck in as well, so I told Excon that Tommo didn't want us given away by Red Tops. I reckoned they wouldn't dare speak to him, so we'd get to fly alone.

Job done. Or so I thought.

Tommo strode over to the four of us like he was going to convert me between the posts.

I was alongside Andy Wawn. As an ex-tanky he'd taught me a whole lot of Standard Operating Procedures – how to find his old mates, interpret their intentions and lull them into inescapable ambushes. Andy was a cheeky fucker who loved a confrontation. He cupped his hand around my right ear. 'You know when I said "we" should bluff Excon?' he whispered. 'Well that was like a Royal "we". I'm just the chauffeur here. Better get your boxing gloves on, Macy.'

'You lot,' Tommo announced, hands on hips, '*will* be followed by Red Tops in the morning.'

I heard my flight commander stifle a groan. Dom didn't know I'd bluffed Excon; he thought we'd been given permission.

Man or mouse time, Macy. I took a step forward.

Out of the corner of my eye, I saw Dom wince as I fronted up to the CO. 'Sir, every battle we've ever been in those Red Tops have given our position away.'

Tommo bristled. 'And you are?'

'Staff Sergeant Macy, sir.'

'Well, Staff, I'll just get them to fly low level behind you. How about that?'

'Sir, we've tried that and they still give our position away. At dawn we'll be looking into the sun and won't be able to see very well, so we'll be constantly on the move. Having them there is like having the hand of God pointed at us.' I paused. 'The tankies spot them every time …'

Tommo looked at me much as he might an insect moments before he crushed it. 'I don't see where this conversation is going, Staff Macy, do you? This exercise is fucking dangerous enough.'

My mind was fizzing.

'I couldn't agree more, sir. The Red Tops will be blocking our routes out, and won't see us against the low sun. They're supposed to be there for safety reasons, but could cause a mid-air collision.'

'Staff Macy, if you think for one moment I'm allowing you out without a minder, you're very much fucking mistaken.'

'Sir, we have a transponder onboard that will track our position perfectly. It's displayed in Excon on the big map board. We've tested it and it works great. And we have our comms if necessary. There should be no need for Red Tops.'

He hesitated for a moment. 'If you disappear off that board for a second, you're for it.' Tommo had clearly had enough of the conversation. He fixed me with a last beady stare. 'Do I make myself blindingly bloody clear?'

'Yes, sir.'

He stormed off, and I turned to find Dom holding his head in his hands. Tommo wasn't a man to cross and the BATS boxes had been known to be temperamental.

'Let's just live with the Red Tops', Dom said. 'It's only an exercise.'

I couldn't blame him for worrying. He was on attachment from the Scots Dragoon Guards and praying that the AAC would take him on; he had a lot to lose.

'Don't worry, Boss. I'll check 'em before we take off.'

An hour before dawn, I leaned into the back of each Gazelle, switched on the BATS boxes, and wandered over to the Excon Portakabin where a sergeant confirmed that Hotel Two Zero Alpha and Hotel Two Zero Bravo had, indeed, registered on their computerised map.

I got back to the boss. 'We're on,' I said. 'Let's go.'

It had to be a hundred to one against both transponders failing. Tommo wouldn't be too pissed if one dropped off radar; he knew we worked as a pair. As long as we won he'd be doing too many back flips to care.

Staying nicely hidden and looking into the morning sun was proving unworkable. Whatever was sneaking through the wadis below the horizon was invisible to us.

'Hotel Two Zero Alpha this is Hotel Two Zero Bravo. We need to outflank them in their own backyard,' I called to Dom. 'I'm blind …'

'One Zero Alpha, my thought exactly. Your lead.'

'Head along that wadi there.' I pointed the way. 'We need to keep this low and fast. Get me eyes-on those tanks and don't even dare come into the hover; we'll be too sharp.'

'Awesome dude,' Andy said. 'But how the fuck are we going to see them if you won't let me hover?'

'I'll tell you when we get there.'

Andy was in his element. 'Yee-ha, low level hell. This is what I joined up for.'

The floor passed beneath us at an alarming speed and proximity.

'There'll be hell to pay if you clip a ridge or fly through wires again. Bring the speed back a touch.' Height and speed were both okay, but Andy was getting a fraction overexcited. I didn't want an action replay of our Swingfire stunt.

Dom called a halt to our advance when we were close enough to bump into the tanks' advanced recce. He scanned a stretch of ground that ran for about 500 metres up to a small bank directly in front of us. 'Move,' he called.

'Moving.'

I told Andy to get me behind the ridge.

His voice rose an octave. 'I'm ten feet off the shagging floor ...'

'Then you're ten feet too high.'

The skids barely touched the ground as we scooted across the crest of the hill.

'Run the aircraft onto the ground and don't come into the hover. You'll kick up too much dust.'

He skidded to a halt and turned to me. 'What the fuck now?'

'Sit tight.'

I unstrapped, climbed out and ran up the bank.

Peering through my binos I spotted the vanguard of the tanks.

Twenty minutes later we were behind them and slightly off to one flank. There was no way they'd expect that.

The CO was ecstatic and moved his Lynx into place. The artillery opened up the show and then we brought in wave after wave of fast jets, only breaking to drop more artillery on them. In what was now a well-rehearsed manoeuvre, a squadron of Lynx simultaneously unleashed their misery on the tanks before disappearing again.

The show wasn't over. A handful of tanks had been hiding behind a fold in the ground and were now running with nowhere to hide. I called in a pair of Lynx and we all moved to head them off. We provided cover on either side of the Lynx; we were well inside the tanks' sector now and had to be on our guard. The Lynx hammered the last of the tanks and we bugged out to the greatest news of all. One of the Lynx had dispatched the tank regiment's CO, a man that had never once been killed on the prairie.

When we landed back at Excon, Tommo was waiting for us, arms akimbo and feet as far apart as they could be. I was looking forward to hearing what he thought of us managing to get in behind the enemy and smack the CO too.

'Get your fucking flight commander,' he boomed at me. 'I want a word with the both of you.'

Shit. I'd flown right along the boundary, but I was sure we'd not crossed it. Dom would have alerted me. A moment or two later, we were both standing in front of Tommo.

'Where the fucking hell have you two been? You promised me I would be able to see you at all times, and yet you never appeared on the map once!'

My flight commander looked devastated. Tommo wielded a shed load of power in the Army Air Corps and was destined for the highest of appointments. He could kill careers with one swipe of his pen.

'I checked the system before we took off and we were on the map, sir ...'

'Another one of your promises, Macy? What do you expect me to believe? You're not on radar, no one knows where you are, and all of a sudden you two know the location of every fucking tank in

Canada. If you switched the transponders off you are both for the fucking high jump. Do you hear me?'

'Sir …' I pointed towards the Excon Portakabin. 'I was on radar two minutes before we left and was assured I could be tracked at all times.'

The sergeant who'd confirmed the presence of our Gazelles on the screen was at his keyboard. I chose my words carefully. 'Would you let the Colonel know exactly when we met and what I asked you?'

'Er … yes, sir.' His eyes batted nervously between me and Tommo. He couldn't bring himself to hold the big man's 2,000-yard death stare. I couldn't blame him. Sterner mortals had wilted under Tommo's withering gaze. 'He came in last night to check that his BATS box was working.'

Tommo jumped in with both feet. 'Then why couldn't I see him even once throughout the entire battle?'

'You could, sir. Surely …' The sergeant looked down at his computer. 'One moment.' His face began to redden. 'Oh, he's not there …'

'Make your fucking mind up, man!'

After a few frantic keystrokes, the screen changed. 'Er … here he is at the start, sir, next to the other Gazelle Hotel Two Zero Alpha – see.'

Tommo leaned forward. 'Then what?'

The sergeant tapped away furiously, running the battle at warp speed. The icons began to move. They both examined the screen in minute detail, then Tommo turned and gave me a look designed to kill.

'Well fucking well. You both disappeared together, in fucking unison, the second you got into the exercise area.'

I knew what he was thinking. He was thinking I'd switched off the boxes and gone black.

I needed to get to grips with this, and quickly. 'Why did we disappear?'

'I'm just checking, sir,' the sergeant replied nervously. 'Oh, there you go. Someone deleted you shortly after you took off. It must have been an accident. Lots of callsigns were lost at the same time, see …' He pointed at the monitor. 'We must have forgotten to load you back on with the others.'

At the debrief that followed, I realised that Tommo was impressed by what we'd done. I also knew that he was going to be the last to admit it.

Soon after I got back to the UK I heard that 9 Regiment Army Air Corps would be the first unit to take delivery of the Apache, slated for arrival in September 2003, a little less than three years away. I called Major Tucker, my course leader on grading, who was now the OC of 656 Squadron and asked him if he'd be willing to have me in his squadron.

'You're welcome in Six Five Six,' he said. 'But I won't be here when the Apache arrives, and I don't have the final say-so on this one, Mr Macy.'

'Who does?'

'The CO,' he replied. 'From what I can gather, Colonel Thomson is handpicking the Apache crews personally.'

My heart sank. After our run-in at BATUS, I couldn't see him accepting me in his regiment in a million years, let alone selecting me for the Apache programme.

I called 9 Regiment's only other Apache designated squadron Officer Commanding to hedge my bets. Tommo would be gone by the time 664 Squadron did the Apache conversion course. If I couldn't get into 656 as an Apache pilot perhaps I could go that route. OC 664 told me that the crews would be handpicked from the regiment and anyone not selected would have to do a Lynx conversion course. If I didn't get selected for Apache, I would end up on Lynx and that would end my SAS quest.

ONE ON ONE

From 1998 onwards, I decided I'd amass so much indispensable knowledge about attack helicopters that the Army Air Corps would have no choice but to select me for the Apache when it eventually entered service. I began by reading up everything on attack helicopters I could find. The next part of the strategy was to get myself on an Air Combat Tactics Instructor's (ACTI) course.

A helicopter, by its very nature, is a vulnerable machine. Unlike a combat aircraft, it cannot rely on speed to get it out of trouble over the battlefield. The policy of the British Army, which did not own a dedicated attack helicopter force, was for its pilots to avoid trouble if they possibly could. This entailed remaining covert – flying down in the weeds – or remaining at 'stand-off' engagement ranges: attacking tanks outside the range of their offensive weaponry.

But with the Apache it would be different. The Apache had started life as part of a very exclusive club. Before the Berlin Wall fell, there were precious few attack helicopters in existence. The Soviets had developed a fearsome machine called the Mil Mi-24 Hind and the Americans had developed the Apache and the Cobra. There were other attack helicopters on the drawing board or in development when the Wall fell, but these three were the only ones that mattered.

With their enormous defence budget, the Americans bought the Cobra and the Apache in large quantities. Other less prosperous NATO nations had opted instead for machines like the Lynx, the Gazelle and the German BO105.

The first Gulf War brought things into sharp focus. The utility of the Americans' Apaches quickly became self-evident. In the aftermath of the conflict, NATO nations began to accelerate their attack helicopter plans and numerous competitions were launched across Europe to determine the best machine for the job. The Apache began to find itself in contention with the Eurocopter Tiger and new developments of the Cobra. But it had been massively updated, too, from the 'A' model that first entered service with the US Army in the 1980s, to the 'D' model, which was equipped with the new Longbow radar system.

These machines had an unbelievable level of sophistication that enabled them to fly *over* the battlefield, not around it, looking for 'trade'.

I realised that one of the keys to being selected as an Apache pilot was simply getting to grips with that sophistication. It would force the Army Air Corps into a brave new world of Air Combat Tactics it had never properly had to confront before – not en masse, at least – because pilots of its premier anti-tank helicopter, the Lynx, were taught to avoid battlefield threats, not go hunting for them.

In early 1998, I went to see my OC and persuaded him that we needed an ACTI course at Wattisham, with me and a few other 3 Regiment pilots as its principal pupils. The OC knew as well as I did that the Army Air Corps had some skeleton procedures for fighting and surviving over the battlefield, but no means of teaching it.

'Fine, Staff,' he told me, 'but it you want it, you're going to have to go out there and find it.'

Fortunately, I knew where to look.

The RAF had a Helicopter Tactics course, but the crabs were into a largely different game – ferrying quantities of men and materiel around the battlefield. I was more interested in air combat.

The Royal Marine pilots of 3 Brigade Air Squadron – 3BAS – practised ACT and told me the only way to get a course would be to ask the Senior Flying Instructors' department. Like Aviation Standards – Chopper Palmer's lot – what these guys didn't know didn't yet exist, but where Aviation Standards tested, the SFIs taught.

I'd flown with nearly all of them at some point, all over the world, so I asked whether they would be able to help us out. The short answer was yes.

Our Regimental Qualified Helicopter Instructor selected a handful of pilots – based on the number of flying hours they'd amassed, their standard of flying, their qualifications and a few other factors – and we had our course. The Army Air Corps formally entered the air combat instruction business for the first time.

Our biggest gun-based threat on the battlefield was the Soviet-designed ZSU-23/4, a fearsome radar-guided, turreted beast with four 23 mm cannon barrels, each capable of directing thousands of rounds of ammunition per minute with pinpoint accuracy at low-flying airborne threats. It looked like a tank with a barstool stuck out of the turret. Even a heavily armoured helicopter like the Apache would be unlikely to survive a direct hit by the ZSU-23/4; a Gazelle or a Lynx would be blown to smithereens.

If your helicopter was lucky enough to be equipped with a radar warning receiver, which some of ours were, it told you certain essential pieces of information about battlefield 'emitters': not only what kinds of radar threat were out there, but their distance, bearing and 'mode' (whether they were merely scanning for threats or, more seriously, tracking targets or, worst of all, launching missiles at you).

If your Radar Warning Receiver (RWR) told you you'd been 'locked-up' by a ZSU-23/4, there was only one possible means of survival: diving for the deck in an attempt to put something hard between you and the smoking barstool.

This was chilling enough, but with a radar-guided missile launch – be it from the ground or air – it was even worse. Few British Army helicopters at that time were equipped with 'chaff' launchers – devices that chucked bundles of metal filaments into the path of an oncoming radio frequency (RF) missile in the hope of seducing it away from the target – so, again, your only hope of survival was getting into cover while evasively manoeuvring, trying to break the lock.

The fun stuff was flying and fighting against other helicopters. Here, the baseline threat was the Hind. It was Soviet Cold War-era, but still a fearsome piece of kit – armed with a chin-mounted cannon and an array of unguided missiles that fired 'on-axis' – in line with the nose of the aircraft. You didn't want a Hind anywhere near your six o'clock position; it didn't matter what you were flying, it would simply shoot you out of the sky.

The trick was to keep out of its twelve o'clock position. The Hind was a monster and could stay in the air for a long time, but it was tough to manoeuvre. We had to close in at an angle and keep turning with him, remaining in a tighter circle than he was capable of – we called it a furball – so he couldn't bring his weapons to bear. Then, even in an unarmed Gazelle, we could hold him to a stalemate. With a 'crew-served weapon' – a machine gun sticking out of a door or window – the Lynx was appropriately equipped to take on a Hind; together, we could kill it. In true World War One dogfight style, I might even be able to loose off a shot with my 9 mm pistol.

The point was to stay in the fight – as Churchill said: never give up.

* * *

Meanwhile, my Apache dossier was getting thicker.

I'd discovered something significant. Each Apache squadron was going to need four specialists: a Qualified Helicopter Instructor (QHI), a Weapons Instructor (WI), a Supervisory Forward Air Controller (SupFAC) and an Electronic Warfare Instructor (EWI).

The Apache was more than a gunship; it was one of the most sophisticated EW platforms in the business. Not only was it equipped with radar able to locate and track any threat – ground or air – with a single sweep of its antenna, it also had a highly sophisticated electronic defensive aids system for counteracting enemy missiles. With the Apache just a few years away from delivery, I needed to know about this stuff.

In 1999, I booked myself on an EW foundation course organised and run by the RAF at Cranwell in Lincolnshire. This side of the Atlantic, there was no one better than the crabs at detailing the threat and its countermeasures. The course was chock-solid with all the maths and physics that I'd never bothered about at school. Day One, Lesson One was a '101' on the electromagnetic spectrum.

The threats that primarily concerned us were heat-seeking and radar-guided missiles. In most cases the hottest part of the aircraft was the engine exhaust. A combat jet, which moved at high speed through the air and generated considerable heat friction as it did so, had 'hot-spots' on the parts of its frame that were most exposed to the airflow – the nose and leading edges of the wings especially – and these could also be targeted by particularly sophisticated types of infrared missile.

Airframe heating was not an issue for a helicopter and the missile automatically homed in on the engine exhausts, which, to the seeker, glowed against the cold background of the sky. Once an infrared heat-seeker had locked onto you, there was precious little you could do in a helicopter to break the lock. Salvation was at hand, however, if you had some or all of the following kit: a Missile

Approach Warning System (MAWS) that automatically alerted you to a surface-to-air missile (SAM) launch (its optics scanned the ground for the flash or plume of a missile motor's ignition); an infrared jammer that literally blinded the missile seeker; 'baffles' that dissipated and rapidly cooled the engine exhaust to a level it couldn't be seen; and flares, usually triggered by the MAWS, which fired into the sky around the helicopter in the hope the missile would lock onto them instead of us.

The heart of any system for defeating radar-guided SAMs was the RWR. It gave warning – visually and audibly – that you were being acquired, tracked or launched at by a radar system. It would also tell you the radar's location and type, provided it was recognised by its threat-library.

Because the missile and its radar guidance system had to go through various engagement modes while in the air – all of which involved 'painting' the helicopter with radar-energy for ever more precise targeting data as it closed in on us – the RWR maintained a handle on the one piece of news we really needed: how close we were to being blown out of the sky.

With the foundation phase under my belt, I booked myself onto an EW course and then an advanced EW course. This introduced me to other aspects of the electronic battle – how, for example, jamming platforms like the US Navy's EA-6B Prowler could be employed in a package of attacking aircraft to 'burn' a hole through the enemy's radar coverage. Once this hole had been created – the SAM and air defence operators would see it as impenetrable interference on their radar screens – attacking aircraft, including helicopters, could sneak into enemy airspace and hit their targets without being fired upon.

This was known as a 'soft kill' – temporarily blinding the radar rather than destroying it. For a 'hard kill', I learned about the capabilities of the US HARM and UK ALARM weapon systems.

Launched from their parent aircraft, these missiles would pick out enemy emitters and fly down the beam till they hit the antenna and destroyed it. Both missiles were so sophisticated that even if the radar operator switched off his system, they would have plotted its position by GPS and/or inertial navigation equipment and destroy it anyway.

It wasn't until the last week of the course that I learned about the Apache's own EW self-protection capabilities. By now, details of the Apache's Helicopter Integrated Defensive Aids System had started to emerge. HIDAS was unlike anything that had ever been fitted to a helicopter before. Four RWR receivers – two either side of the nose and two more behind the engines – provided interlocking arcs of coverage; they covered and plotted any radar, ground or air, that emitted a pulse anywhere in the vicinity of the aircraft.

A highly developed MAWS detected the heat plume of any ground or airborne threats – especially important if the helicopter was to stand any chance of surviving in a threat environment where man-portable, shoulder-launched air defence systems (ManPADS) were present. These weapons had developed rapidly since the US Stinger and the Soviet SA-7 had made their first appearance thirty years before. Shoulder-launched SAMs like the Russian SA-14 were highly adept at ignoring all but the most sophisticated flares punched out by an aircraft and were capable of engagements up to 12,000 feet.

The Apache also had a Laser Warning Receiver System (LWRS) – two detectors above the engines and two on the fuselage sides – that would detect if the aircraft had been targeted by a laser-designator, the prelude to it being hit by a laser-guided missile.

All threat data were processed by a central computer which, having computed the type, range and bearing of the threat, would then decide the best countermeasure to defeat it. There were three switch settings in the cockpit – manual, semi-automatic and auto-matic – which allowed the pilot to decide what level of autonomy he wanted to confer on the system. We were assured, however, that it worked extremely effectively in automatic mode and that, by and large, it was best to leave the system, not the pilot, to decide what kind of countermeasures to dispense and when.

Like HAL, the computer in *2001: A Space Odyssey*, the HIDAS's (female) Voice Warning System (VWS) would alert the crew to any given threat. The information would also be displayed on one of the two multi-purpose displays; there were two MPDs in each cockpit – TV screens used to display flight, critical mission data and targeting images. Imminent threats – prioritised at any given moment – were displayed in positions relative to the aircraft.

It was probably inevitable that the VWS had already earned herself a nickname: Bitchin' Betty.

Before I could 'graduate' from the course, I had to take an exam – and it wasn't your average GCSE. We were to mount a national evacuation operation from an island – whose geography resembled Sicily – embroiled in civil unrest. Some Brits had been taken hostage. I was the commander of a force tasked to fly in, free them and fly them out.

Using the knowledge I'd amassed over the previous few months, I decided to mount an operation using Apaches, EA-6Bs, a B-2 Stealth Bomber and a C-130.

I jammed the island's surveillance radars with the EA-6Bs and sent in the Apaches to take out the coastal radars. The B-2, so stealthy that it was largely invisible to radar anyway, then dropped a stick of satellite-guided 2,000-lb Joint Direct Attack Munition (JDAM) bombs on the command centres. Amidst the chaos, Special Forces were airdropped in to rescue the hostages. Once they had safely ex-filtrated the danger zone, I sent in the C-130 low level over the sea, chaperoned by Apaches, to airlift them out.

I now had an intuitive feel for how EW could master the battlefield. Although it wasn't a dedicated EW platform – unlike the EA-

6B – the Apache was stuffed with so much electronic wizardry that it would enable the Army Air Corps to do things with helicopters it had never dreamed of before.

I did my EW instructor's course in early 2001. With the arrival of the first Apaches in-country, there was a buzz about our quantum leap in capability. Even though I'd only ever sat in one once, nearly ten years earlier, I felt I was really beginning to know this machine, to understand how it worked.

I began a war of attrition on 3 Regiment's Adjutant to get posted 200 miles further north, to Dishforth in North Yorkshire, the future home of the Apache. He wasn't up for it and neither were the pen-pushers in Glasgow, but bull-headed perseverance finally got me within reach of the man I'd last crossed swords with during the finale of BATUS, Lieutenant Colonel Iain Thomson.

On the day of my interview, I popped in to pay my respects to the commander of 656 Squadron, who tipped me the wink that Tommo was in ebullient mood; he was still riding high on the news that his regiment had been selected to receive the most important piece of kit the army had procured in years. But while CO's interviews were scheduled to last twenty minutes, I'd be lucky to get ten.

I knocked on his office door. There was a growl from within and I entered. Tommo barely glanced up as I snapped a salute.

'Sit down, Mr Macy,' he said. 'Still bending the rules, are we?'

I said nothing, just prayed he wasn't going to fob me off with a Lynx conversion course.

Tommo got up from behind his desk and strolled over to the window, hands behind his back. This was it: Win or lose time. I had to make every shot count.

I took a deep breath and told him what I'd been up to in the months since I'd last seen him, what I'd learned at every level of my recent training, and the ideas I'd developed about Air Combat Tactics.

There were moments when he responded as if I was talking Swahili, but when I finally shut up his eyes shone. A week later I was making a PowerPoint presentation to the boss of Joint Helicopter Command (JHC), an amalgam of all the helicopter activity undertaken by the British Army, the Royal Navy and the Royal Air Force. Three days after that I ran through the presentation again for the Director of Army Aviation.

We ended up with a plan to establish a 'purple' ACT Instructor's course; a course with a dual objective – to teach pilots of unarmed helicopters like the Gazelle and Chinook how to get into a furball and survive, and to teach gunship pilots the new world order.

THE HUNTER

At the end of 2001, Tommo fired out a questionnaire to all pilots in 9 Regiment: who *didn't* want to do the Apache course and why? Surprisingly, not everybody was keen. I guess some thought, *why do I want to go and learn all this new stuff, when I'm already at the top of the tree? The money's coming in, the wife's happy …*

Not me. I couldn't wait.

The first Apache arrived at Middle Wallop in the summer of 2002 and the list of those selected for the Apache Conversion To Type (CTT) course number one was posted in Regimental Headquarters. My name was on it. There were twenty-one pilots earmarked for CTT1, one of whom would be the new CO, Lieutenant Colonel Richard Felton. So that left twenty operational pilots for 656 Squadron's eight Apaches, enough for five flights: HQ Flight with the boss, Ops Officer and two QHIs, and four more, each manned by a flight commander, a specialist and two others.

With two seats in each bird, the minimum they needed was sixteen; in other words, not all of us would make it.

I knew that ten years' flying experience didn't mean I was a shoe-in. The Apache was an immensely complex machine to master; I needed to make myself indispensable. I had ticked the EW Officer box, but I had my eye on the Weapons Officer's course. It could lead to the sexiest job in Army aviation: Squadron Weapons Officer – guns, rockets and missiles; right up my street – and the more I learned now, the better.

Three of us from 656 were assigned to a bespoke Apache Weapons Officer's course. My old mate Scottie would be there; he was going to become the Weapons Instructor for 673 Apache Training Squadron at Middle Wallop. It was billed as the most in-depth course we had ever attempted. If we managed to jump through every hoop, we'd end up advising on Apache weapons tactics to senior officers, teaching weapons and firing techniques to Apache aircrew, planning and running Apache live firing ranges, and designing and running Apache weapons missions in the Boeing simulators.

Captain Paul Mason started the first day as he meant to go on – grilling us on what we knew. I'd learned shit-loads and was keen to show him. There was no pass mark, thank God; we realised we actually knew jack-shit. I think I got my name right and that was about it.

Paul was *the* Apache weapons guru. A good-looking lad from the north-east, he wasn't physically imposing, but boy, did he walk tall. He'd studied weapons, sights and sensors in the USA and decided there and then to rewrite the rulebook. This horrendously complex course was his baby.

It sounded as though it would take us half a lifetime to develop sufficient understanding to even come within reach of the hardware. He left us in no doubt that to become a weapons, sights and sensors instructor on this aircraft we would need a level of knowledge so comprehensive our brains would feel like they were about to explode. I immersed myself totally and quickly discovered what he meant.

The Cold War had fostered a proliferation of single-role platforms – ships, tanks and aircraft that were each designed for one purpose and one purpose only. The Apache was one of the new breed of multi-role ISTAR asset – a relatively new acronym for Intelligence, Surveillance, Target Acquisition and Reconnaissance. It could be flown from either seat. The gunner sat up front, the pilot in the rear, but the pilot could activate the weapons and the gunner could fly the aircraft. A series of back-up systems ensured that if a critical piece of kit got hit – or even the pilot – the Apache could still get home.

The helmet-mounted display harmonised man and machine. The helmet itself was connected to the aircraft by two electrical leads: the first for comms, the second for the sensors. As soon as you powered up the aircraft, a pair of surveyors behind each seat transmitted pulsed infrared beams and the four helmet sensors let the system know the position of the pilot's head relative to the cockpit.

You then stared down the Boresight Reticule Unit (BRU), a tube on top of the coaming which contained a series of concentric circles, through the crosshair within the monocle over your right eye. When your right eye, crosshair and bull's-eye were perfectly aligned, the aircraft knew precisely where you were looking.

The monocle display could get pretty busy. It showed the direction in which the aircraft was headed, and where both crew members were looking. The pilot would generally have flight symbology – airspeed, altitude and distance to the next waypoint – displayed, and the gunner weapon symbology: to know 'range to source' – the distance to whatever target he happened to be scoping. If either of us actioned a weapon, weapon symbology would automatically kick in.

Behind the symbology, we could view whatever was being looked at by the Target Acquisition and Designation Sight (TADS) System or the Pilot's Night Vision System (PNVS) (known as the 'Pinvis'). It was like viewing a movie, complete with subtitles, projected on a window, while still being able to see through to the outside world.

The TADS day television – DTV – camera image could also be displayed on the monocle, along with the Pinvis or TADS thermal image.

In thermal mode, vehicle engines and people would glow white, day or night; if it was cold enough, we could even trace footprints. The Apache gunner and pilot were now becoming like Schwarzenegger's Terminator: hunting for the target in both normal and thermal vision simultaneously. This took multi-tasking to a new level: your right eye viewed targeting symbology and a computer-generated thermal picture of the world one inch away, while your left scanned the outside world in full colour at infinity.

We had two principal means of detecting targets – via the TADS and the Fire Control Radar. The FCR – the heart of the Longbow system of the 'D' model Apache – was awesome. Its Air Targeting Mode (air-to-air targeting) and Terrain Profile Mode (enhanced terrain avoidance navigation) were impressive enough, but the Ground Targeting Mode's 'RF missile engagement' capacity blew my mind. In a double sweep of its antenna, lasting just three seconds, the FCR could recognise and detect 1,024 targets. Within the same three seconds, it would automatically prioritise the top 256, accurately locate them, automatically store their coordinates in its computer and then display them to the crew. It would display the top sixteen targets to the crew in priority of threat, selecting which to destroy and in what order.

When flying in squadron formation, the lead aircraft could coordinate with the others via a secure datalink – an unjammable, encrypted, wireless modem – to ensure that no two gunships went for the same target. Two Apaches would watch a flank each and cover the rear while the other six would be the attack aircraft. The gunner could break down the display into six 'lanes' on his MPD – the multi-purpose display TV on his instrument panel – selecting sixteen targets per lane. With the push of a button, each attacking

Apache would then receive their own share of the targets. A few seconds later ninety-six missiles would navigate towards their individual targets. Once the missiles had impacted at the point of maximum mass, each Apache sent its 'shot-at' file to the leader with the push of another button: not bad for one minute's work.

The TADS turret was situated in the helicopter's nose, and was the heart of the Apache's day and night sensor capabilities. The Forward Looking Infrared (FLIR) system lay behind a tinted window on the left. The gunner's FLIR and the pilot's Pinvis constituted cryogenically cooled optical cameras, highly sensitive to any heat above minus 200°C. They could find a mouse in a wheat field from a thousand metres.

The clear window on the right contained a laser designator, laser range finder, laser spot tracker, the Direct View Optics (DVO) and the DTV camera. The DVO was linked to the Optical Relay Tube (ORT) – the big metal block that jutted out about a foot from the gunner's cockpit console.

When you placed your forehead on the ORT's browpad and selected 'DVO Mode', you saw a magnified picture of the real world in glorious colour. There were two fields of view: wide and narrow.

The DVO confirmed vital recognition data to a Forward Air Controller (FAC), your crew member or other members of your flight – 'the target building has yellow window frames ...' – preventing fratricide or collateral damage. The DVO was permanently slaved to the TADS; wherever the TADS led, the DVO followed.

On either side of the gunner's ORT were what looked like steel PlayStation hand grips, covered in switches and buttons. They controlled sights, sensors and weapons. Each and every button had its own distinct feel and shape – one was smooth and concave, another was serrated and convex; another was shaped like a Chinese hat. You didn't want to dispatch a missile at your own troops when you really intended to find out their range.

The DTV camera had three fields of view: wide, narrow and zoom. It was called 'low-light TV', but it wasn't really for low light – it worked on a wavelength that allowed it to penetrate 'battlefield obscurants', primarily optimised to cut through dust and smoke.

Everything the TADS DTV, FLIR and FCR could see could be viewed in the monocle for quick targeting, on both MPDs for target detail and pinpoint accuracy, and on a small TV on the ORT.

With the flick of a button, the gunner could switch from FLIR to DTV and back again, depending on how much smoke or dust was in the air and the level of heat contrast presented by the target.

When you gripped the controls either side of the ORT, each of your index fingers found a guarded trigger: the right for the laser, the left for missile-release. Once you were lined up on the target, you pulled the right trigger to the first detent to establish range to target. The second detent gave a constant range readout, accurate to a centimetre or two over several kilometres, and painted the target with laser energy.

The missile 'saw' the laser energy bouncing off the target. Pressing the left trigger launched it off the rail like a whippet after a rabbit.

Shit ... I thought. We really could accidentally demolish our own troops if we got them the wrong way around.

Each helicopter's laser was 'coded' so that missiles didn't get confused in the air. The TADS housed a laser 'spot-tracker' that allowed Apaches to designate for each other – a procedure known as target handover. The laser spot-tracker allowed the TADS to slew instantly to where another Apache within the flight was looking, if you wanted it to do so, at the push of a button. It could also look for targets designated by ground forces. With so much laser energy bouncing around the battlefield, it was a wonder more people hadn't been blinded in the one memorable conflict that had seen action by Apaches: when AH-64As of the US Army had decimated the tanks of Saddam Hussein's Medina Brigade on the Basra Road during the 1991 Gulf War.

The course continued to explore the arsenal in the kind of microscopic detail that I thought would only interest the boffins who'd designed it. Little did I know that the lessons Captain Paul Mason taught me would be put into vigorous practice and have me reading more and more just to stay one step ahead of the Taliban.

In March 2003, while I took a break from the Apache to work on temporary assignment in Bosnia for SFOR (Stabilisation Force), George W. Bush and Tony Blair launched their ill-fated assault on Saddam Hussein in response to intelligence, later known to be highly flawed, that Saddam was harbouring weapons of mass destruction and Al-Qaeda insurgents. It was the start of a road that would eventually see us being assigned to the front line of the so-called War on Terror.

THE KILLER

1 SEPTEMBER 2003
Middle Wallop

The Apache instructors, some still sporting suntans from their US training, were eager to start teaching us, but my first flight was going to have to wait. CCT1 – the first Apache pilot's course – was being paraded in front of the camera; the British Army loved a team photograph.

Shuffling around in front of twelve, brand new, immaculately paraded Apaches were fifty-nine very proud people – the people who were busting their balls to get the Apache into service. With over half a billion pounds' worth of assets behind us, the shot had to look impressive. With any luck, it would capture a team brimming with pride and confidence; never mind the fact that the road to initial operational clearance – the day that the Apache was declared fit for military ops – was still some way down the pike.

While most of the group grinned like chimps, the twenty pilots of 656 Squadron were hoping that the camera would be far enough away not to pick out our faces in any detail. To have our mugshots printed in newspapers and glossy magazines could already prove fatal.

The war against Iraq, in which George W. Bush had recently declared the United States victorious, had unleashed a storm throughout the Islamic world. A crew member of our deadliest attack helicopter was well on the way to becoming a highly valued target. The idea of being taken hostage and identified scared us all, but someone in front of me made light of it with a hilarious impression of our Taliban captor.

Before any of us could fly, we had to go through several weeks of ground instruction. We covered every Apache system in great detail. It had hundreds; we even had to learn about refrigeration in case an air-conditioning unit failed at a critical moment.

We were finally introduced to the sharp end of the Apache 'capability matrix' by the one and only Captain Paul Mason – basic revision of the complex world he had led four of us through the previous year.

We began with the 30 mm Hughes M230 Automatic Chain Gun, the cannon, attached to the airframe in a fully steerable mounting beneath the cockpit. It could be operated by both crew members. By selecting 'G' on either cyclic, or the gunner's left ORT grip, it automatically followed the direction of your sight – TADS crosshair, FCR target or, if you were in Helmet Mounted Display Mode, to wherever you were looking through the monocle. The computer calculated the necessary compensation for the speed of the Apache, wind velocity and drop of the shell during its time in flight; all we had to do was point it at the target and pull the trigger.

The cannon was accurate up to 4,200 metres – over two and a half miles – but was most effective at less than half that distance. It fired ten rounds per second in pre-selected bursts of ten, twenty or fifty rounds – or, if we wanted, the whole lot in one go: 600 rounds a minute. Optimum effect – the 'combat burst' – was set at twenty rounds.

The shell was a 30 mm High Explosive Dual Purpose round, known as HEDP (pronounced 'Hedpee' by pilots) but commonly referred to as 'thirty mil' or 'thirty mike mike' by FACs and JTACs. Its shaped-charge liner collapsed on detonation to create a jet of molten metal that could cut through inches of armour. Fragmentation of the shell created its anti-personnel effect, but once detonated it also torched the target, making it devastating against buildings and vehicles.

US experience had shown that if pinpoint accuracy was required and sufficient time available, the gunner should use the TADS as his sight. When time was a factor the helmet-sighting system was as effective, but with an increased spread.

The stub wings of the Apache held 'hard-points' that enabled the helicopter to carry two air-to-air missiles and four underslung pylons for a range of weapon combinations, depending on the nature of the mission.

One option was to mount four M261 rocket launchers – nearly seven foot long with their black rocket protection devices and carrying nineteen CRV7 unguided rockets each.

We chose the CRV7 – Canadian Rocket Vehicle – C17 rocket motor instead of the American Hydra 70 because it was faster. Being able to hit more distant targets gave us a better stand-off distance. It also had 95 per cent more kinetic energy at shorter distances and 40 per cent better accuracy too. It's a fast spinning, fin-stabilised rocket motor capable of being fitted with and carrying several different warheads up to eight kilometres. They would go further, but we wouldn't need to fire from more than five miles away, we were told.

The most commonly carried warheads were the High Explosive Incendiary Semi-Armour Piercing (HEISAP) and the Flechette. The final choice was the Multi-Purpose-Sub-Munition, which Rules of Engagement (ROE) generally wouldn't support. The MPSM – 'the death from above' – was a multi-purpose rocket, connected to the launcher by an umbilical cord that was hard wired to the weapons computer. It told the rocket how far to go before exploding above the target, whereupon nine bomblets – sub-munitions – would descend, slowed by a small Ram Air Decelerator (RAD) resembling a triangular yellow duster. As the sub-munition struck a vehicle its shaped charge would detonate, sending a high speed molten jet of copper through a tank or APC, killing everyone inside. The casing would also fragment on anything it touched.

Each bomblet would fragment into scores of red-hot, razor-sharp shards of steel, travelling at 5,000 feet per second in all directions. The only warning the enemy would get would be a pop above them; by the time they spotted the yellow RADs, there would be no time to run, drive off or take cover.

It was the perfect weapon for mounted and dismounted troops but had one serious drawback. On soft soil or sand, some would fail to detonate. To an unsuspecting child, the bright yellow dusters would act as an invitation to violent death or maiming. We couldn't fire them without special orders, and even then we'd have to record the impact point and treat it as a minefield.

The HEISAP – 'the beast' – was a kinetic rocket, originally designed to sink ships. Its nose contained a heavy steel penetrator that would drive through the hull. Once inside, a delayed fuse would ignite the high explosive, ripping the ship apart and igniting its incendiary charge, which would stick to the internal alloy structure and other materials; it wouldn't take many to set off multiple inextinguishable fires.

I thought of the fatalities aboard HMS *Ardent*, *Sheffield* and *Coventry* and the merchant vessels like *Atlantic Conveyor* and *Sir Galahad* in the Falklands. The majority of them burnt to death.

The most fearsome of our three weapons, however, was the one that carried no explosive to its target at all: the Flechette rocket – 'the swarm of death'. Its warhead contained eighty tungsten flechettes, each dart weighing eighteen grams. Just less than a thousand metres after firing, a small charge would push two forty-dart cradles out of the nose of the fast spinning rocket. Centrifugal force would spread them into a conical pattern. A pair of rockets would suffice against most targets, but if we increased the distance we would need to fire more to ensure a kill, or 'probability of hit'.

A speed in excess of 1,100 metres per second would see the flechette impact at Mach 3.3 and enter an armoured personnel carrier with ease. Scabs of metal would peel off the inside of the armoured vehicle at high velocity with the contorted flechettes and kill its inhabitants outright.

They travelled so fast that they created an intense vacuum behind them, an unseen and lethal void. In the open, a single five-inch tungsten flechette passing close by you would create a vacuum sucking the air from your immediate vicinity, and ripping muscle off bone. There was no warning that the swarm of death was on its way; it travelled way faster than the speed of sound.

Our new CRV7 rockets were devastatingly accurate – except when the pods were misaligned. Over a range of 5,000 metres, they could spread over a kilometre; not what you'd want if your own troops were anywhere in the vicinity. We were searching for a way of making them align consistently but the solution hadn't been found yet.

It was the AGM-114 Hellfire missile system that had cemented the Apache's reputation as an iconic, state-of-the-art weapons platform. The 'Air-to-Ground Missile, HELicopter FIRE-and-forget' had been developed for the Apache and its new Longbow radar. Five feet eight inches from nose to tail and weighing in at a staggering 105 pounds, it came in two different variants. The AGM-114K Semi-Active Laser, the SAL, four inches shorter and five pounds lighter, was guided onto the target via the TADS laser, while the Radio Frequency (RF) worked in conjunction with the Longbow radar, which was less discriminating when it came to deciding who were the good guys and who were the bad guys on a complex, fast-moving battlefield.

The SAL was our preferred option, for obvious reasons. Each weapon we fired would have to comply with the Rules of Engagement and I couldn't see our government ever allowing me to fire at a target without seeing it physically.

Whether fire-and-forget or laser guided, all Hellfires were equipped with dual warheads for defeating enemy armour. The first, 'precursor' warhead detonated micro-seconds before the main charge; both 'reactive armour' – a layer of explosive bricks designed to detonate and destroy an offensive weapon before it could penetrate the hull – and outer skin would be blown off, making way for the full fury of the Hellfire's main charge: a huge warhead capable of blasting any main battle tank into tiny pieces.

If you fired the SAL missile without using a laser, it would simply hare off into the distance, searching for laser energy, until it ran out of juice and fell out of the sky. When the Apache's laser was on-target and its energy could be seen by the missile's seeker, it became a precision instrument. There were two ways in which to fire the SAL: in Lock-On *Before* Launch Mode – LOBL ('lobel') – and Lock-On *After* Launch Mode – LOAL ('low-al').

In LOBL Mode, the missile was programmed to look for the correctly coded laser energy bouncing off the target while it was still on the launch rail. The moment the crew had confirmation that the seeker had acquired the target – whether it was designated by its owner, another Apache or a ground callsign – the gunner would release the Hellfire and it would fly unerringly to the desired point of impact.

LOBL required the gunner to be able to see the target directly. This was all very well if it was relatively unsophisticated and unlikely to fire back at us. If, on the other hand, it was well defended, we could stand off at a greater distance; it had a range of over 8,000 metres and travelled at just shy of a thousand miles per hour.

The LOAL *Indirect* Mode allowed the pilot or gunner to fire the missile from behind cover while relying on a third-party – a Special Forces team, for instance – to designate the target with their laser; a sneaky way of hitting the enemy without alerting them to the presence of clandestine forces. It could be fired in LOAL Low so it hugged the ground under a low cloud base or LOAL High so it could be fired over mountains too.

You would use LOAL *Direct* Mode – operated with eyes-on – if you believed the target to be in possession of laser-warning capabilities. To maintain the element of surprise you'd fire the missile, wait until the last possible moment, then lase the target a few short seconds from impact so the Hellfire would pick it up in its terminal phase.

We could also fire multiple Hellfires, one after the other, and simply move the crosshair from target to target.

In every case, when the seeker detected the correctly coded laser energy it forced the missile to climb as high as it could before slamming down hard on the target with as much kinetic energy as it could gain in the dive and exploding with a force of five million pounds per square inch. Even in poor weather – when the laser spot could be lost in cloud – its autopilot would correct its flight path to relocate the laser before impact. It was both devastating and surgical, which made it ideal for fighting modern wars – wars in which as many civilians as enemy were likely to be in the vicinity of the target.

The Apache was capable of carrying sixteen Hellfires in any combination of RF and SAL, although it was more likely to carry a combination of SAL and rockets. A typical mix would be eight Hellfires, four on each launcher, and thirty-eight rockets – a mixed bag of MPSM, HEISAP and Flechette – nineteen in each pod.

The moment I selected 'M' on the cyclic or ORT grip to action the Hellfires, the 'missile page' appeared on the MPD screen above my left knee, giving me a graphic depiction of their status. An *R* indicated a missile was ready in LOAL; a *T* showed it tracking the laser spot in LOBL. The same information was also displayed in the monocle.

At this point, the missile was ready to fire. I'd kick the tail rotor pedals, slewing the Apache left or right, a few degrees off centre – depending on which side of the fuselage the missile was to be launched from – ensuring that it didn't fly through the line of sight of the TADS, its exhaust gases saturating and blurring out the DTV image or blinding the highly heat-sensitive FLIR camera. In the complex dynamics of the modern battlefield the gunner needed to maintain eyes-on the target right up until the moment of impact, especially with a missile that covered a kilometre in three seconds.

The news from the Iraq campaign had been full of harrowing details of civilian casualties and we knew we needed to do every-thing possible to avoid them.

Should a child or a 'friendly' suddenly appear near the laser spot on the target, at any point up to impact, all the gunner had to do was move the crosshair elsewhere and the Hellfire would readjust its flight path to intercept the new point of aim.

As I listened to Paul, I realised that the Hellfire lay at the centre of the Apache's lethal, flexible weapon system.

After lessons each day, the four of us that had done the Weapons Officer's Course were given additional instruction on how to teach what we had just been taught. It was a punishing routine, but I knew that I'd found the specialist role I'd been looking for. The machine's full potential lay in its ability to deliver the Hellfire, rock-ets and cannon projectiles with pinpoint accuracy. Only by becom-ing the Squadron Weapons Officer would I be able to make good on the promise offered by this unique platform.

LEARNING TO FLY –
LEARNING TO FIGHT

The day of my first flight started like any other – in one of the lecture rooms of the facility that had been built especially for the Apache at Middle Wallop. After a month of theory, we were ready to put our new knowledge to the test. We were also ready to meet our instructors. Mine turned out to be Scottie, whom I'd been friends with for over a decade and with whom I'd shared many sorties over the Emerald Isle, flying patrol support during the Year of the Sniper.

'Helloo, Ed!' He breezed into the lecture room. 'Are ye ready to go flying?'

I tried to pretend that it was no big deal, but Scottie wasn't having any of it. 'Och, come on, Ed, you're allowed to show a little appreciation. You showed me the ropes in Ireland; now it's my turn. You're going to love this – I guarantee it.'

The lucky bugger had spent a few months learning to be an Apache instructor in the wide open spaces of Alabama, flying sorties from Fort Rucker after finishing the Weapons Officer's Course with me last summer.

We walked into one of the specially revamped hangars. Twelve Apaches lay waiting under the arc lights, each with only a few hours on the clock. The tips of their rotor blades were rigid and interleaved to make the most of the available space. Scottie gave the nearest a reassuring pat on the nose. 'I don't think there is anything I could tell you about this that you don't already know,' he said.

I grinned. 'I could build one in my garage if you gave me the bits.'

He curled his finger and beckoned me to follow him. We walked around the stubby wing on the right-hand side of the aircraft and paused beside the fuselage. I was finding it really hard to remain calm.

What never failed to impress was the sheer size of the Apache; the mighty Chinook that could carry fifty-five troops in the back was only a little over two feet longer than this two-seater. It was twice the length of a Gazelle and considerably bigger in volume. Up close, it was angular and ugly. The hangar was enormous, but getting twelve in was like solving a giant jigsaw puzzle.

My mouth had gone dry.

Scottie pulled himself up onto the wing. I jumped up, too, and watched over his shoulder as he opened up the cowling that shielded one of the two RTM322 engines and demonstrated how to inspect the oil levels – one of the pilot's many duties before takeoff. Satisfied, he proceeded to check that the intakes were free from obstructions and then opened up the gearbox inspection hatch on the wing, just forward of the engine intake.

Back on the ground, he opened up the access panel on the back of the wing that contained some of the communications equipment. We then walked down to the tail and checked the stabilator – the aerofoil wing that sat horizontally below the tail rotor. It was locked and secure, as was the tail wheel below it.

The inspection continued up the port side. Finally, standing on the top of the Apache, above and behind the pilot's cockpit, I watched Scottie spin the radome, perched on the main rotor hub, over sixteen feet above the grey-painted concrete floor.

'Aren't you going to tell me what you're doing?' I said. 'I am here to learn.'

'Och,' Scottie tutted, 'you don't want to be fussing yourself over stuff like this. Not today. Today is for flying, Ed.' He pointed a manicured finger at his wrist, gesturing for me to take a look at the latest addition to his watch collection. 'Though according to Mr Breitling, we've time for a spot of lunch first.'

I was about to voice my frustration when Scottie, knowing how much I wanted to get airborne, put his hand on my shoulder. 'Climb down, Ed. Everything in its own time. This wee machine isn't going anywhere. It'll be ready to fly after we've eaten.'

By the time we returned, the ground crew had towed all twelve gunships onto the pan. Protected by an imposing razor-wire fence, they were accessible only via a set of electronically activated gates designed to accommodate an Apache with room to spare.

They were arranged in two rows of six, their noses pointed inwards like prop forwards about to lock heads in a scrummage. I handed my camera to another student, a guy called Pat Wiles, and asked him to snap away. As I shook Scottie's hand I felt like I'd been preparing for this moment all of my life.

Scottie showed me how to swing myself into the cockpit using the grab handles in the cockpit roof. For today's flight I was in the back seat, which was stepped up to give the rear-seater – the pilot on a normal sortie – visibility over the gunner's head.

When I'd pulled on my bonedome, Scottie showed me how to adjust the monocle. Then, after running rapidly over the cockpit layout, he jumped into the front.

After closing the cockpit and going through our preliminary flight checks, I fired up the auxiliary power unit, a small gas-turbine that supplied juice to the aircraft when it was on the ground. A faint hum was quickly drowned out by the rush of the air conditioning. In front of me, screens and displays burst into life.

By following the procedures I'd become familiar with in the simulator, I bore-sighted myself to the aircraft by aligning my monocle with the BRU on the coaming in front of me.

I threw the engine power levers forward and the blades began to turn.

After a further round of systems checks, Scottie asked whether I was ready.

I'd been ready ever since he'd first bloody asked me.

The Apache was nearly seventeen feet from wing tip to wing tip, but its undercarriage track – six and half feet – was relatively narrow. Scottie warned me that this, coupled with the heavy FCR above the main rotor head, made the helicopter feel unstable while you were taxiing.

I told him I was good to go.

'Right,' he said in my ears, 'we need to pull in a little power. Thirty per cent torque will do.' He reminded me to look for the 'ball' – a solid circular graphic, bottom centre in my monocle. If it was to the left of its kennel when we were on the ground we were leaning to the left. It also acted like a conventional slip indicator in the air.

I lifted the collective lever slightly with my left hand, increasing the power. The Apache began to vibrate. Everything looked and felt good. I checked the monocle: in the top left it told me the RTM322 engines were reaching 30 per cent.

'Okay, that's enough power now – you've got sufficient induced flow to move the aircraft.' Induced flow was the downwash generated by the main blades. Pushing the cyclic tilted the rotor disc forward. I could feel the Apache straining to be released.

'Raise your visor,' Scottie said.

'Why?'

'I need to see your face while you're taxiing.'

I glanced up. His eyes were watching mine in the little vanity mirror above his seat.

'Okay, Ed. Brakes off and remember to keep her bolt upright. If she leans left move the cyclic to the right. Push the cyclic forward to go faster and back to slow down. Got it?'

'Sounds simple enough, Scottie.'

I glanced down to place my feet on the very tops of the pedals.

'Don't look down, Ed!'

'Okay, mate, keep your hair on.'

I rotated the tips of my toes forward and the parking brake handle released with a loud clunk.

I pushed the cyclic a bit more and we started to roll forward. Suddenly, I started to panic. The helicopter felt like it was about to fall over.

I could hear Scottie laughing.

Ahead of me the yellow line curved to the right in a large sweeping arc towards the huge gates and safely away from the Apache parked in front of me.

'Right, I want you to release the tail wheel – but, remember, be careful.'

I looked down for the button on the collective.

'Don't look down, Ed. One more sneaky peek and I'll mark you down for not knowing your controls.'

I'd spent weeks learning where they were but I didn't want to make a mistake and push the wrong button.

'Sorry, Scottie. It's nerves. Mate, I'm afraid to fuck up.'

'Relax, Ed. This is the easy bit. You must learn where things are instinctively. It's for your own good. Wait until you do the bag.'

'What exactly is the bag?'

'You'll find out soon enough. Now, just concentrate on taxiing this thing because you need to follow that line.' He paused. 'So unlock the tail wheel.'

Making sure I didn't look this time, I pressed the appropriate button on the collective. Immediately, and to my enormous surprise, the tail weather-cocked rapidly to the right.

Whoa!

'I have control.' Scottie's voice was reassuringly calm. 'You've got too much left pedal in. There's your first lesson.'

I cursed under my breath. *Jesus. The power of this thing ...*

'You're overcontrolling. With the tail wheel released you have to use the pedals to keep the aircraft straight and the cyclic to keep it upright. Try again.'

I tried to follow the painted yellow line on the concrete that led towards the gate posts, but it was impossible. I'd never flown a helicopter with wheels before – the Gazelle had skids.

'Where are you going?' Scottie asked, as the Apache weaved precariously either side of the line. I was zigzagging all over the place. It was worse than my first driving lesson.

The line was now pointing straight towards the gates but I still couldn't follow it.

'Okay,' he said after several more seconds of this torture. 'I have control.'

I felt terrible. I'd never known anything like it. I was worried that I'd never get the hang of it.

Scottie plonked us bang on the line and manoeuvred the Apache between the gates and lined us up on a piece of taxiway called the 'keyhole' because that was how it looked from the air. It was designed to allow you to take off into wind whichever direction it was coming from.

'I'm not teaching you this bit, Ed. Just sit back and enjoy it.'

With that, Scottie pulled up on the collective. There was a thunderous noise of downwash as the blades coned upwards, battering the air into submission. For a brief moment, as the two power plants fought to provide the torque that the Apache needed, I

ABOVE: Ed going solo in the Chipmunk T10.

LEFT: Ed in the Gazelle.

ABOVE: The Army Air Corps cap badge.

ABOVE: Ed sits in an Apache for the first time ever at Middle Wallop, during his pilots' course.

LEFT: The Northern Ireland Gazelle with its huge Nightsun infrared light next to Ed. The grey TV and thermal camera are on the other side.

ABOVE: Firing CRV7 rockets in the dive.

RIGHT: The Apache firing 10 rounds of 30 mm HEDP every second.

BOTTOM: The Target Acquisition and Designation Sight (TADS) system along with the white Missile Approach Warners (MAWs) and black Radar Warning Receivers (RWR) either side.

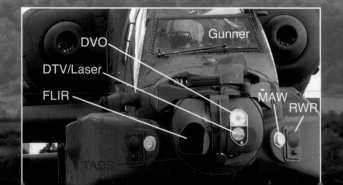

Gunner

DVO

DTV/Laser

FLIR

MAW

RWR

TADS

BELOW: The mighty Hellfire missile.

RIGHT: 656 Sqn patch. 656 were the first operational Apache Sqn in the British Army.

MAIN PICTURE: A flypast on Task Force Availability Day. 9 Regt AAC are ready for war.

BOTTOM: The Longbow Fire Control Radar (FCR) sits on the very top of the Apache. Sticking up either side are the Laser Warning receivers (LWRs).

FCR

LWR

ABOVE: An Apache sits waiting to begin a Combined Air Operations mission (ComAO) with fast jets. Ed flew the Hawk (centre) during FAC training.

RIGHT: Scottie hands over the monocle to Ed before his very first flight on CTT1.

FAR RIGHT: Ed in 'the bag'. Note that black PVC panels cover every window. When the door comes down, it is pitch-black in the cockpit.

LEFT: Ed and his Sqn learning to fly and then fight from HMS *Ocean*. The UK has the only amphibious Apaches in the world.

BELOW: The line-up of the brand new Apaches and those who brought them into service, including Ed's 656 Sqn.

LEFT: Firing rockets outside Thumrait Airfield, Oman.

BELOW: Ed riding an £82,862.08 AGM-114K SAL Hellfire (Air-to-Ground Missile, Semi-Active Laser, HELicopter FIRE-and-forget).

BELOW: A Hellfire page showing four Hellfires is displayed on the Multi-Purpose Display (MPD).

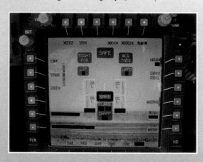

MAIN PICTURE: 2 Fight, 656 Sqn AAC in Oman, the night before firing our first Hellfire. *From left:* Jon, Ed, Jake and Billy.

became aware of just how massive it was. And then suddenly we were airborne and accelerating skywards.

As I looked back over my shoulder, I saw Pat tracking us with his camera. I had no doubt my taxiing efforts would be enjoyed by all that hadn't flown yet well before our wheels were reunited with terra firma.

Over the next two months, I learned how to tame the beast. One of the hugely innovative things about the Apache was the degree of automation built into it. Early on, I was taught about 'holds' – how you could punch a hold button and maintain the aircraft's position over the ground in the hover, or its heading, or its speed, or height or a particular rate of turn. There were so many things you needed to stay ahead of in the cockpit that being relieved of the necessity to fly at certain times really helped to shoulder the load. Soon, I was climbing, descending, turning and doing climbing and descending turns.

I learned to master the MPDs – the TV screens that obviated the need for the Apache's cockpit to be littered with the dozens upon dozens of instruments and dials of its forebears. In fact, the only ones that were common to the US AH64A were four tiny standby instruments in case all of the electrics failed; everything else was requested by the pilot as a page on an MPD. Over 5,000 different information pages could be stored on the computer and displayed on the MPD screens. Learning how to navigate our way through them was like grappling with a new Windows-type software program and we had to know it instinctively. It was the same with the knobs, switches and buttons. There were 227 of them in the cockpit, but most had at least three different modes or functionalities, giving us nearly 700 positions and over a thousand permutations to remember.

We also had to master the monocle. As well as targeting and flight information, it could also display FLIR imagery beneath the data to allow the pilot to see at night. This was all well and good. What wasn't so good was what they called 'monocular rivalry' – it was by far the trickiest task I had ever had to learn.

Basically, your right eye stared at a small glass plate less than an inch from your cornea. Your left eye, meanwhile, was looking at the real world – which could stretch from your cockpit instruments to infinity. Bringing either the left or right image into focus was fairly straightforward, but trying to see both clearly at the same time seemed impossible.

Ever tried it? Which one wins?

The fact was: neither did. Each eye fought the other for supremacy in the brain, threatening to split my head apart. But then, one day, the headaches stopped; my eyes and brain had discovered how to work together. Slowly, I was becoming a part of the machine.

I learned how to do field circuits, hovering, navigation, autorotation and running takeoffs and landings. I then found out how the Apache performed on limited power – i.e. with one engine out. I practised manoeuvring in and out of confined areas – much trickier in this big machine than it had been in the Gazelle – and how to land on a slope; again, not easy in a large helicopter that had narrow wheels for an undercarriage rather than skids.

Finally, I was taught quick-stops, wingovers and high-g turns at max power and performance; how to get to height fast, how to get down fast and how to turn hard.

Then, as 2003 became 2004, it was into the part-task trainers and the simulator again to continue learning how to turn our knowledge into practice. The position and function of every switch and button was supposed to be intuitive by now; as natural as drawing breath. The instructors drilled us hard on this point. The simulator had very little light during this phase and we soon found out why. Everything we'd done had just been a prelude to flying 'in the bag'.

Flying in the bag did not equate to anything I'd ever done before. During my early sorties in the Apache, I'd noticed Velcro strips around the interior of the cockpit. It turned out that they were to hold big black PVC panels over the clear perspex canopy for 'bag flights' – flights in which the student pilot was immersed in darkness. With the PVC panels in place no light entered the rear cockpit. Our only reference to the external world would be via the monocle and the feed from the instruments; the FLIR and the PNVS would be turned off. The thought of flying in the bag terrified me.

It didn't matter what we'd achieved up till then, if we failed the bag, we'd be out.

With the PVC panels in place the rear cockpit door came down and I was plunged into total darkness for my first bag flight. Scottie flew us out to a disused military camp on Salisbury Plain – somewhere we couldn't bump into anything, he told me reassuringly. The Pinvis was switched off and the engines were at full pelt. We were parked on a concrete square, around 100 feet by 100.

'I can do this blindfolded!' Reminding me of what I'd said time and time again over the past eleven years, Scottie continued to mock me. 'Now you are. So let's see, eh?'

I stared at the symbology on my monocle – the only help I was going to get. Scottie wanted me to lift the aircraft ten feet into the air and hold it there. It sounded simple, but I had to do so without the tail weather-cocking and without drifting forwards, backwards, left or right. If I did drift, I had to correct it and reposition the helicopter over my takeoff point.

The symbology would tell me if I was drifting. Instead of the normal crosshair, what I got now was a small circle. This represented the cyclic stick position. Sitting in the centre as it was now meant I wasn't moving. If a line – a velocity vector – started to grow towards the top of the monocle, I was drifting forwards; to the right and I was heading to the right. All I had to do was move the cyclic between my legs in the opposite direction to the velocity line and it would return to its starting point; we would stop drifting. No rocket science there.

In the meantime, the ticker-tape at the top of the monocle gave me my heading – something I could control with the pedals. Pushing down on the right pedal while allowing the left one out would spin me left, and vice versa. A scale running up the right-hand side of the monocle would let me know my rate of climb or descent and my height above the ground.

Today was my first practice, but uppermost in my mind was the bag test we'd have to take in a few weeks' time and the rules were the rules. If we drifted from the takeoff point, I'd fail. If I went above or below ten feet, I'd fail. If my heading changed, I'd fail. I had to go straight up, keep the Apache there and activate the position and height holds.

'Bloody hell,' I said to no one in particular, 'how am I supposed to do all this on one eye?'

'I guarantee you, as soon as you take off, the aircraft will go forwards or backwards, right or left and you'll instantly adjust the stick in the other direction,' Scottie said. 'At this point you'll drift the other way. Don't worry about it – it's natural. You won't be able to keep it at ten feet and you won't be able to keep it pointing in the same direction either. Prepare for sensory overload, Ed. You'll drift all over the place. But when it comes to the test you'll be able to do this – you'll go straight up, hit ten feet and hover and you won't move a millimetre. Remember, it's not scary for me; only for you. I can see out. So, relax, don't overcontrol, and try to take in as much as you can. Are you ready?'

As ready as I'd ever be, I told him.

'Okay, do not fly by your senses, use your symbology. Here goes. Maintaining three six zero degrees and the same position over the ground, I want you to climb to ten feet and put the holds in.'

I raised the collective lever, applying power, and we began to lift clear of the ground. My right eye flicked between the circle at the centre of the monocle, the ticker-tape above it and my height on the right. I could see nothing else. It was like sitting on a hill in a car with a blindfold on and releasing the handbrake and not knowing what the fuck was coming at you …

All three wheels left the ground and the line started to grow out from the centre, towards the right-hand edge of the monocle. I tilted the cyclic as gently as I could in the opposite direction. Too much. Fuck. The line shot out of the other side of the circle. So I overcompensated again. Then I realised my heading was off. I tried to correct with the pedals.

I was stick-stirring and the aircraft felt like it was going all over the place.

Between fits of laughter Scottie told me to put the holds in. I flicked the button on the cyclic in opposite directions engaging position and height hold as quickly as I could and the aircraft became rock steady.

'Okay, Ed. Other than being at forty feet and facing north-east, where do you think we are?'

'I've no idea.' I felt drained. I'd probably only been airborne twenty seconds, but it felt like a lifetime.

'How far do you think we are from the concrete?'

'I don't know. Somewhere near the top right-hand corner, maybe?'

'Is that all?'

My heart sank. It was worse than I thought. 'Okay then, some-where just *off* the top right-hand corner?'

'How many feet from it?'

I was getting bored with this game – and faintly irritated by it. What did Scottie want me to say? I'm a shit pilot? I'm not cut out for the Apache? 'I don't know Scottie – fifty feet, maybe. More …?'

'Okay, Ed, switch on your Pinvis.'

I did as I was told and the outside world suddenly flickered into life in my right eye.

Jesus. I'd hardly moved. I had hardly *moved*.

'We may not have moved,' Scottie said. 'But what were you doing wrong?'

'Flying on instinct,' I told him. Exactly what he'd told me not to do. When you flew by the seat of your pants, using all of your senses, you ended up all over the fucking shop.

'When the velocity vector moves to the edge of your monocle, Ed, it means you're only moving at six knots – that's all.' He paused. 'Now I want you to use your bob-up box.'

The bob-up box, another piece of symbology, would give me unbelievable situational awareness in my black void. It always stayed in exactly the same place in relation to the real world. It represented my initial position over the ground and would move accordingly; it gave me a point of reference – something I'd not had during my first foray into oblivion.

He told me to switch off the PNVS and try it again.

This time when I took off and the line drifted out from the centre I could see that the bob-up box had hardly shifted at all. Moving the bob-up box to the edge of the monocle represented a real-world shift of only six feet.

'The lesson of the bag, Ed, is trust your symbology, not your instincts. If you end up with no vision, in the shit, with nothing else to rely on except what's in your monocle, it's symbology that will save your life – not your skills as a three-thousand-hour seasoned seat-of-the-pants aviator.'

I heard what Scottie said, but could not envisage any situation a helicopter pilot might encounter that would emulate the conditions I'd just experienced in the bag: total blackout with no picture at all.

On that score, however, I would be proved utterly wrong.

Seven months down the line, with my bag test flight behind me, I was back at Dishforth. Sixteen out of the twenty of us earmarked for 656 Squadron who'd gone to Middle Wallop were in the briefing room; 9 Regiment had its first Apache Squadron.

It had been a long, hard road. Wives, girlfriends, children and friends were all happy to welcome us back. The army had expected everyone to pass CTT1 – it was just a conversion course, after all – but the Apache had proved a very difficult beast to master. The lads that failed each had over 2,000 military flying hours – and worse still, we'd lost our QHI.

The rest of us knew all too well that all we had done was learn how to keep the thing airborne and make sure it was pointing in the right direction when it fired its weapons. We were now about to embark on an even more punishing course: CTR – Conversion to Role.

We'd be spending many more weeks away training. Even in barracks the average day lasted fourteen hours. To work a long day was one thing; to be in an aircraft or simulator as complex as the Apache was quite another.

During one night sortie, my front-seater and I were working so hard we became target-fixated. The red mist came down because the target vehicle, a recce car, was moving so unpredictably. Pat was doing everything he could to get a steady crosshair on it, but it was proving incredibly tough. Our cannon rounds always landed just in front of the vehicle. Just as we fired, the bloody thing changed direction. By the time the rounds had flown to the predicted position the vehicle wasn't there.

www.harperplus.com/hellfire

Eventually, we closed to within a thousand metres. Then we heard a huge bang and the seat punched up into the small of my back.

The aircraft lurched dangerously and plunged nose-down. The world was spinning at such a rate I couldn't make sense of the swirling green; attempting to pull out was proving more difficult than I'd anticipated. The nose started to come up but the Gs were getting worse; the Apache began to spin within its own circumference. I'd lost tail rotor authority; I was out of control. There was only one outcome to this and I prayed we would survive it.

As the Apache passed through 500 feet, the low height warner started beeping loudly and the lamps in front of me glowed bright. The airframe was vibrating so badly I couldn't focus.

Then the monocle went black.

It was dark outside the cockpit. I glanced down at the MPD to see we were passing through 200 feet with a 4,800ft per minute rate of descent. Eighty feet per second with enough ammunition on board to win a small war. The MPDs cut out as we lost all electrics. I was now totally blind. I didn't know which way was up. I knew we were coming up for impact so I grabbed the coaming to brace myself and prayed.

The seat crunched into my spine and the windows bloomed bright red.

Total silence …

The silence was broken by a voice in my headset: 'Ed, Pat, that will be a re-fly. See you both in the debriefing room in ten.'

Thank fuck we'd been in a simulator.

The instructor debriefed us on our performance. We had become so engrossed in trying to kill the recce car that we had flown too close to the enemy. A guy with a shoulder-launched SAM-7 had shot us down. The missile had hit us just aft of the engines and taken out the tail rotor. The blast had pitched us forward and the loss of tail rotor authority had given us the spin. Keeping the speed on could have helped us regain control, but it was hard to want to keep flying fast when you were only a thousand feet up, and pointing straight at mother earth. Pulling up had slowed the aircraft's speed, but then I'd lost the tail altogether.

My only saving grace was that I had managed to level the aircraft before impact.

Would I have survived?

Yes, but not without some back surgery – and I didn't want to go there again. Had we crashed at or less than 3,660 feet per second I could have walked away unscathed. The Apache was the most survivable helicopter in the world. Pilots had crashed at multiple G levels and walked away without injury. The cockpits were guaranteed to maintain 85 per cent of their original shape in an impact.

Would my front-seater have survived?

Probably not. Pat's face would have ploughed into the ORT, the metal tube that jutted out of the coaming in front of him.

I felt embarrassed. Both of us should have been aware of the proximity of threat. I was working so hard just flying the aircraft aggressively to keep us on target I'd had no spare mental capacity. I'd become saturated and then I'd drowned in what they called my 'ability reservoir' – a reservoir I was beginning to realise was more of a puddle.

Pat had been trying so hard to hit the vehicle with the cannon that he'd been unable to process any other information. We'd both had classic target fixation and the direct result had been loss of situational awareness.

So, we had failed the sortie – a sortie that had been flown in a simulator. Strike one on CTR. What was interesting about this, when I managed to get past the humiliation, was that I'd grabbed the coaming in a bid to diminish the impact of … well, nothing; it was just a simulator.

I found out later I was not alone. The Apache simulator was so good that you forgot where you were within seconds of taking off. When you were in it, you really did think it was the real thing.

A year earlier, things had kicked off in Iraq. British troops stationed in and around Al-Amarah had found themselves locked in a brutal insurgency war. Armed with AK47s and rocket propelled grenades (RPGs), the followers of Muqtada Al-Sadr had been in almost continuous contact with British Army troops since April 2004.

Things were also beginning to hot up in Afghanistan, where unrest fomented by a reconstituted Taliban – supposedly defeated in 2002 – was beginning to destabilise the nascent democracy of Afghan president Hammid Karzai. To keep the peace, Britain had recently announced that it was due to send several thousand more troops to supplement the thousand or so it already had in-theatre.

It added fresh fuel to our efforts to master the Apache in all its complexity. I was appointed as the Squadron Weapons Officer – the SWO. My workload doubled overnight.

CTR saw us learning how to conduct single-ship ops in the Apache, then two-ship ops – flight missions – then finally whole squadron operations. The squadron, led by our OC, Major Black, was split into three flights and a Headquarters Flight, with two Apaches each. We formally completed CTR on 16 September 2004 and were awarded our Initial Operating Capability (IOC).

The IOC allowed us to deploy four Apaches to a semi-permissive environment for recce and strike but warned the government that we were unable to sustain any prolonged operations. As significant a milestone as it was, we were a long way from being combat-ready. We still needed to integrate with the rest of the British Army and the wider services.

From October onwards we exercised with everybody, starting with the RAF on Combined Air Operations. During ComAOs, Apaches and RAF combat jets learned how to mount escort missions for Chinooks, the RAF's principal transport helicopter. We practised convoy protection missions – keeping watch over the life blood of logistics support operations in Iraq and Afghanistan.

The first six months of 2005 we exercised with 16 Air Assault Brigade, the troops ready to deploy to any hot-spot at a moment's notice. After a particularly gruelling exercise Lieutenant Colonel Felton gathered us together and announced that we had achieved TFAD. The Task Force Availability Date meant we could now deploy as a regiment to conduct operations in support of other units, but under the kind of restrictions that would take a brave government pen-pusher to sign off.

Soon afterwards we joined HMS *Ocean* off the coast of Northumberland for a couple of weeks of ship-borne takeoffs and deck landings. In late summer we joined it again off the south coast. We had learned how to fly to and from HMS *Ocean* in the North Sea; this visit was about learning how to fight from her. Over a month we flew numerous sorties from the helicopter support vessel to the Castle Martin weapons range in Wales, where we carried out attacks in representative combat conditions against targets on the ground. There wasn't a firing range big enough in the UK to safely accommodate the range envelope of the Hellfire – but we shot off just about everything else.

We felt we'd got about as close as we could ever come, short of a real shooting war, to mastering the beast. As it turned out, this was just as well.

Lieutenant Colonel Felton had been briefed on the likelihood of our going to Afghanistan. In October, he was pretty much certain. As the weeks marched towards Christmas, it became the worst kept secret in the army.

www.harperplus.com/hellfire

With our short Christmas break behind us, the CO confirmed that 16 Air Assault Brigade had received orders to deploy to Afghanistan in support of the Afghan government. Along with 1310 Flight from RAF Odiham, 9 Regiment Army Air Corps was to form part of the Joint Helicopter Force (JHF) in support of the legendary 3 Para battlegroup.

The JHF would consist of eight Apaches and eight Chinooks; our brief was to provide four of each per day to whoever needed them, plus a couple of Lynx for good measure.

We were already gelling with 16 Air Assault Brigade. Our problem was that we hadn't live-fired with them – and we hadn't so much as seen a live Hellfire, let alone found somewhere big enough to fire it.

And we were due to deploy in May – just five months away.

DUSTY HELLFIRE

Our imminent deployment changed one very significant aspect of our operations. Up until now we had been concentrating our training in the low-level environment. At less than a hundred feet off the deck we were an extremely hard target to hit. It didn't matter if we were two Apaches or a formation of eight Chinooks and eight Apaches – we blasted across the European landscape as fast and as low as we could.

If someone had wanted to shoot us down they would have been hard pressed. The ground clutter – villages, towns, hedges, trees, woods and forests – would mask our arrival and departure both visually and audibly. By the time we were spotted or heard, we'd be gone. That, at least, was what the manual said – and we now had no reason to doubt it.

We received our briefings on Afghanistan in early January and were given our Area of Responsibility (AOR): Helmand Province – the lawless badlands in the south, the last known hideout of Osama Bin Laden.

We would be operating in a barren wasteland – the Dasht-e-Margo, or Desert of Death. The vast majority of our work would be carried out in this environment, but we were also likely to operate in the mountainous north. If we operated low level out there we would be seen from miles away and have nowhere to hide.

Then we got our threat brief.

Supporting 3 Para's battlegroup would entail escorting Chinooks into and out of austere locations laden with men and materiel. We would also be responsible for protecting the Paras should they get into any trouble. John Reid, the UK Secretary of State for Defence, had just visited Afghanistan and announced to the world that everything was going swimmingly; that 16 Brigade would probably be in and out of the country without firing a shot. Needless to say, anyone with a modicum of military experience ridiculed this statement. We hoped for the best but trained for the worst.

The Taliban, Al-Qaeda (AQ) and the HIG – the Hezb-I Islami Gulbuddin – were not known for their willingness to cooperate. We were briefed that there was a distinct possibility they would stand their ground and fight. Their easiest target – one that would cause the greatest amount of casualties for least effort – would be to shoot down a Chinook stuffed full of Paras. The unholy triumvirate knew that sending body bags home would sway UK public opinion against the war and hoped, in turn, that this might persuade Blair's government to withdraw from Afghanistan.

We expected to have the following weapons fired at us: small arms (SA), machine guns (MGs), heavy machine guns (HMGs), rocket propelled grenades (RPGs), anti-aircraft guns (AA), and Man Portable Air Defence Systems (ManPADS) – shoulder-launched SAMs. Any one of these was more than capable of shooting us down if we stuck to the low-level environment.

If we operated above what was called the 'small arms band' – the expanse of sky where SAs, MGs, HMGs and RPGs were deemed effective – we would go a long way to reduce that risk. The Apache's HIDAS would take care of any SAMs. AA guns were the only remaining threat, but they were extremely difficult to operate, used up lots of ammunition quickly and were hard to maintain. Lack of training and practice since the Russian invasion also meant they were unlikely to be used effectively. It didn't take a genius to decide that flying at altitude would be the safest option – but the big questions still stood: could we fulfil the mission? Would we be able to get through the small arms band safely and do our job at altitude?

As a young Para I learned the art of shooting down helicopters and slow aircraft on Salisbury Plain by practising on target drones. We were shown how difficult it was to hit one if it varied its velocity, azimuth and elevation without warning. And while instructing Air Comat Tactics from 1998 to 2003, I demonstrated how to change direction, altitude and speed to throw off the hostile gunner. The trick was to swiftly recognise the threat.

We flew to Thumrait Airfield in Oman – where it was suitably hot, desiccated and mountainous – for the month-long Exercise Desert Eagle.

Billy was my instructor for dust-landings. We had bumped into each other on a number of occasions since my Basic Rotary Wing Course at Wallop. He'd been to the Apache academy in America before instructing on CTT1, and we were privileged to have him as our Squadron Qualified Helicopter Instructor (SQHI). He was very open and had the knack of getting the best out of people. 'If you've done something wrong, if you've made a mistake, don't hide it,' he used to say. 'Chances are, if you're doing it, others might be too. You'll be dealt with, but you won't be punished; and you might just save someone's life.'

When he wasn't flying helicopters, Billy drove his Lambretta come rain or shine. If his life had been a movie, it would have been a cross between *Blue Thunder* and *Quadrophenia*, with a soundtrack by The Jam.

To perfect a dust-landing, Billy explained, we would need to employ what he called a 'zero-zero' technique: to reduce speed and height simultaneously in a steep approach, and to avoid rolling forward by reaching zero speed and zero height at exactly the same time. We had to trust our symbology because we would lose all external references in the final stage. Dust-landings would be like 'the bag' on speed.

We gave it a spin the following morning. Billy warned me it was going to be alien and uncomfortable, quite unlike anything I'd done before. The dust and sand would disorientate me; if I didn't focus 100 per cent on the symbology, I would crash. If I got distracted, I would lose all sense of my position relative to the landing zone. Any drift would end up, at best, with the Apache rolling onto its side, and thrashing itself to pieces. At worst, we might end upside down.

No pressure then.

Billy took the reins and selected a solitary rock in the otherwise featureless landscape to land beside. It scared the shit out of me. Forty feet up, I couldn't see a thing outside the window and my PNVS had gone as blind as I had. I only knew we were down when there was a thump as we hit the ground firmly on all three wheels. When the dust cleared I could see he'd parked the Apache right next door to it.

'Happy with that, Ed?'

'You must be having a laugh. I want to see you do that again to make sure you weren't using the Force ...'

Billy fancied himself as a bit of a Han Solo, but he shook his head. 'Stop being a wuss.' He grinned. 'Your go.'

Second time around he talked me through the final 100 feet.

'Concentrate on the symbology and digital readouts, Ed. Watch your speed and height readouts and keep them coming down in tandem. You need to make constant cyclic, collective and pedal adjustments to maintain an accurate countdown. We can't afford to come into the hover or have any speed on when we hit the ground.'

Righty-fucking-ho ...

Then, suddenly, it was like a bad day out with Lawrence of Arabia.

'I'm losing all references, Billy.'

'Me too, mate. Not a drama. Just hang in there and concentrate on the symbology. Passing forty-six feet, keep driving her forward … keep driving her down … I'm totally blind now …'

It was a fucking nightmare out there. I forced myself to focus on the velocity vector, heading and height in my monocle rather than the dust cloud billowing around us.

Billy's calm voice helped me to stay in the zone.

'While maintaining your scan on the heading and height and using control inputs, watch the symbology. Look at the velocity vector, Ed.'

The velocity vector – the line that told me my speed and direction of drift – edged back towards the centre circle in my monocle.

'Keep it coming back towards the middle, but *do not* let it move out to the side. If you do, we'll roll over. Keep bringing the velocity vector back using the cyclic and the height down with the collective. At the same time, keep an eye on the heading tape and adjust the pedals to make sure she doesn't turn off heading. We're getting into the ground cushion now, so force it down with the collective and keep her moving forward with the cyclic, constantly reducing the rate on both. You okay?'

I couldn't see a fucking thing outside. 'Five feet to go …'

'Critical time, Ed … Any drift and we're crashing this thing.'

Bloody marvellous.

I felt a bump as the Apache's struts absorbed the impact.

'And we're down,' Billy said as if we'd done nothing more arduous than reach the ground floor in a lift.

We sat stationary as the dust began to dissipate.

'You've just got to trust your symbology, Billy,' I said with new-found bravado.

Billy laughed. 'Easy, eh?'

'Easy enough, despite the last fifty-odd feet being totally blind.'

'Okay, smartarse, where's the bloody rock, then?'

The air had now cleared sufficiently for me to have a good look around. I couldn't see the bloody thing anywhere. We took off again and spotted it some distance from our wheel marks on the desert floor. I'd landed about forty feet too long.

'If that was a landing point, you'd have missed it. It's okay here, where there's miles and miles of nothing, but if that was the only place to touch down – if it had any obstacles or worse still other aircraft around it – we would have crashed. Now let's see how easy it really is when you have to touch down somewhere a little smaller than the Oman. I want you to land right next to the rock this time. Let's go.'

An hour or so later, I was still at it. Each landing got harder and harder. I began to hit my spot, but had to pull away before touching down or we would have crashed. I could land okay elsewhere, but doing so where I wanted to in a dust storm proved to be ninja.

It took every last ounce of mental ability and skill I'd ever been blessed with to land next to our rock, but I managed it in the end.

When day turned to night, I had to do it again. I knew that darkness wouldn't make a jot of difference to the shit conditions, but I still found myself hesitating. Billy rammed home the point. 'Ed, it doesn't matter if it's daytime, night-time or the world's turned pink. You're blind the second you get into dust, and we fly by symbology alone. Got it?'

Now I knew why we'd spent so long flying the bag.

'That's right, mate. If you can't pass the bag, you can't land blind. Simple as.'

'And they say the conditions here are a peach, compared to what we're going to get in Helmand.'

'Want to give it another go?' Billy said.

It was one thing to be shot down by the Taliban, quite another to die by my own hand. I didn't want that on my tombstone; and I didn't want it on the tombstone of the other guy either – the guy I'd be flying with.

'Yes,' I said. 'Just to be on the safe side, let's give it another go. One more for the road …'

We were confident that we could now get safely from the desert floor to altitude and back, but could we operate there?

We fired the cannon and rockets on the ranges outside Thumrait with the FACs so they could get used to calling in Apache fire. We practised firing from altitude instead of low level until we became proficient at the new height.

After each session, I viewed every inch of gun tape and debriefed the crews on every rocket and just about every round they fired. I did this in more detail than they'd ever wanted, but it was worth it; our accuracy improved dramatically. It was all a part of my responsibility as the squadron's Weapons Officer and it was one I took extremely seriously. After two weeks of nothing but cannon and rocket firing we were hitting targets first time, every time.

The main event, however, was yet to come.

One of the principal reasons for coming to the Oman was to launch the Hellfire. There simply wasn't enough space on any UK proving ground to accommodate the weapon's danger-area envelope.

I was very proprietorial about the Hellfire. Call me obsessive or compulsive – which some of my mates were starting to – but I saw it as a make or break. We'd fired rockets and cannon for nearly two years to get to this standard, but we had one shot to get the Hellfire right. We'd trained in the simulator for hours but now we would actually fire it for the first time. And since each weapon cost the equivalent of an Aston Martin or a mid-range Ferrari, I wanted us to get it right.

The Air Manoeuvres Training and Advisory Team oversaw our instruction. AMTAT were a bunch of senior instructors with expertise in multiple disciplines who were there to see that the Apache was worked up to its full fighting potential prior to being declared fully operational. They'd been teaching us since we started CTR and now hovered around us like bees around flowers, keen to collect every bit of data they could from the Omani experience.

When it came to weapons training – and the Hellfire, in particular – they were all over us like a rash. They wanted to make sure that we could do our job, and that the missile did what Lockheed Martin had said on the tin.

The AMTAT opted for the lottery approach. They wrote down every conceivable way of firing the Hellfire on a series of cards that we of 656 Squadron then drew.

Each of us had to fire two missiles apiece and because Billy and I were qualified to fly in both seats – front and back – we were told we would have to swap. It was all about getting ticks in boxes. I had to fire from the front seat and so did Billy.

The cards were spread out on a table. The firings would range from the hover to 140 knots, from low altitudes to extremely high. We would fire autonomously and we would fire remotely; we would fire single missiles and two at a time – two in the air at once, from the same aircraft, at two separate targets. We would also fire some in LOBL Mode, and others using LOAL Direct, LOAL Low and LOAL High. We would go through the whole sequence by day; and to cap it off, we'd repeat it all by night.

This was to be the culmination of two and a half years' training, two of which were spent under the guidance of the UK's greatest attack pilots. The stakes were high; no one wanted to miss with an £82,862.08 missile. And the coppers on the end weren't an accounting error; the bean-counters had worked it all out, down to the last penny.

I drew my cards and was given two missiles to fire and three missions in which to destroy three targets.

My first was a maximum range, high-level, autonomous daytime shoot against a small building with the Apache at maximum speed.

My second was to fire a missile by night as a pair of us ran in at 100 knots with an FAC lasing the target.

My third was to gather another crew's missile in mid-air and kill an armoured personnel carrier at night while maintaining a high altitude hover. This tactic was straight out of Paul Mason's weapons lecture, to be employed if I was out of missiles and could detect a target equipped with laser warning receivers. By the time the LWRS alerted the APC crew to the threat, the Hellfire would be one second from impact. Goodnight, Vienna.

Becoming increasingly less popular with the crews, I ran through every engagement technique in detail.

The following morning we flew out of Thumrait Airfield for the weapons range, ninety minutes away. A selection of old vehicle hulks and the odd building – our target 'sets' for the next few days – were the only notable features in the otherwise barren landscape.

We set up our tents, cooked some food and sat around under a full moon shooting the shit.

'You've something on the bottom of your shoe, Simon,' Jake said.

Simon lifted his heel and dropped his shoulder and was instantly embarrassed.

'Ooh, hello sailor,' we chorused.

Simon was a navy exchange officer. Being the only matelot among us, he was always getting stick – but dished it back with interest.

'You'll all get AIDS, you know,' he said.

'But only if you mess around,' Jake waved an admonishing finger.

We rolled around laughing.

'He means Apache Induced Divorce Syndrome, Jake,' Billy said. 'You catch it from being on operations or exercises for the duration of your flying career.'

'I've nothing to worry about; my wife is used to me being away at sea. But you Pongos are prime candidates,' Simon said. 'Not that you need any help from the Apache. You seem to be doing a fine job of it all by yourselves. Isn't that right, Billy?'

Billy had just been on a romantic holiday with his wife. When they got back his car had been nicked. What upset her was that he'd left his house keys and the address in the glove box. Their insurance wouldn't pay out for any losses.

I was next in the firing line.

'I think Ed's a prime candidate, after his performance at the Mess Christmas ball. What do you reckon, Jonny?'

Being officers, Simon and Jake hadn't yet heard about this. Jon quivered with excitement at the prospect of a fresh audience.

'Picture me, Billy, Ed and the wives sat around a large table with wine waiters and silver service waitresses pampering to our every whim …' He was now positively wriggling with pleasure. 'Ed, ever the gent, pulls back Emily's chair just as she goes to sit on it. She falls flat on her back; her legs shoot up above the table and she wallops her head on the wall.'

My cheeks burnt bright red as the hilarity increased. She'd looked like she'd been in a car crash – her dress ripped so high she could have auditioned for Spearmint Rhino.

Jon's eyes sparkled. 'I reckon Ed is more likely to get AIDS if he stays home than if he disappears for months on end.'

Jake came to my rescue by telling a story about 'Bus Stop Jonny'. Jon – being ginger – was always being accused of stinking of piss, hence the nickname.

Which, predictably enough, brought the ribbing straight back in Jake's direction. He was no stranger to this. As a young lad with a wife and his first baby on the way, no one got as much stick as Jake – at least partly because he could take it on the chin and chuck it back in buckets. Jake was from an affluent family and was brought up in Antigua; his relaxed Caribbean outlook sometimes made it hard to believe he was legally allowed to vote, let alone fly an attack helicopter. He got the nickname Floppy at Sandhurst, for being a 'fucking laidback overseas person' – and the piss-taking didn't stop when he was awarded the Sword of Honour.

As dawn broke, we watched our ground crew load four Hellfires onto our aircraft. Billy and I inspected our missiles and gave the machine a thorough walk around before saddling up.

We picked up the FAC's transmission as we crossed into the range.

'Apache, Apache, this is Bravo Two Zero. Firemission, over.'

'Bravo Two Zero, this is Outlaw One. We are a flight of two Apaches – callsigns Outlaw One and Two – with eight Hellfire missiles on board. Ready for Firemission, over.'

The FAC came back loud and clear. 'Firemission … Target grid: Four Zero Quebec, Charlie Hotel, Seven Zero Eight, Zero One Eight.'

After a brief pause, he continued: 'Target elevation: Four Five Eight feet … Target Description: Small building.'

Another pause: 'Friendly forces: Three thousand seven hundred and twenty-five metres south …

'Laser code: One, One, One, One …'

And his final call: 'Read back, over.'

I'd punched the grid and altitude data into the computer with the keyboard on my left as he spoke. When he finished I pressed the 'slave' button on the ORT. I found myself staring at a ten-foot square building on the TADS.

I read back the Firemission: 'Firemission; Four Zero Quebec Charlie Hotel, Seven Zero Eight Zero One Eight, Four Five Eight feet; small building; friendlies Three Seven Two Five metres south; Laser One One One One. Over.'

'Correct. Call when visual. Over.'

Bingo. The guy was good.

I'd done this in the simulator loads of times. I replied to his last message immediately. 'Outlaw One is visual. The target is a small building to the north-west of an east–west track with one building to the south of it and one building to the north of it.'

'Correct. Your building is the middle one. Call when ready. Over.'

I'd now identified the FAC's location – in a trench with about fifteen other guys, south of the target.

'Ready.' I'd already locked up the target with the Image Auto-Track (IAT). The missile was spun-up and ready on the rail.

I lased the target and the FAC called: 'Clear hot.'

Distance was 8,225 metres away and counting down fast. We were at 5,000 feet and Billy was doing nearly 140 knots.

The LOBL box appeared in my monocle and I knew that the missile could now see the laser energy reflecting off the target.

'Outlaw One firing.'

A second later, the missile slipped off the left rail with a barely perceptible whoosh. Our helmets, the two engines, the slipstream and the environmental control system drowned out all other sound.

The Hellfire climbed into the deep blue sky. I lost sight of it after about two miles. My aim was to hit the target by manually tracking it, so I disengaged the IAT and held the crosshair over the centre of the building.

It looked like some kind of dwelling; the sort of thing I imagined peppering the Afghan hinterland in large numbers.

Our run-in was nice and smooth. The Apache was built to attack and this was about as much fun as we could have with our pants on.

The countdown timer on my symbology clocked the final few seconds and then I saw a black needle – a barely distinct smudge – dropping fast from the top of the screen.

The Hellfire. Two seconds … It was creaming down … One second … It was homing onto the crosshairs – bang on my laser energy spot.

There was a big black cloud. Debris and timber spiralled through the air.

'Outlaw One, this is Bravo Two Zero,' the FAC called. 'Delta Hotel, Delta Hotel. End of Firemission.'

Direct hit.

As the dust cleared, we saw that he wasn't wrong. The building had disintegrated. A black scar on the ground was the only sign it had ever been there. Scattered around the edge of it were wood splinters and nothing else.

'Outlaw One, Delta Hotel. Target building destroyed. End of mission.'

The remaining Hellfires did exactly what they were supposed to. I collected the statistics and handed them over to the AMTAT. We'd demonstrated that the Hellfire could be fired by day or night in every conceivable way thought out by those devilishly clever people at Boeing and Lockheed Martin. 656 Squadron Army Air Corps was now ready for war.

There was only one question left. Could we do it for real on what we called a 'two-way range' – firing while being fired at?

The name of this range was Afghanistan. In less than eight weeks, we'd be up close and personal in the Desert of Death.

MOOSE TIME

30 APRIL 2006
Dishforth

An Intelligence Officer (IntO) from 16 Brigade briefed us on what
we could expect when we got to Afghanistan – a move, my diary
had been telling me for several weeks, which was earmarked for
tomorrow. I had to force myself to listen, not because it wasn't
interesting, but because there was a lot going on in my head.

The day before we made our move to Afghanistan happened to
be Emily's birthday, and I was trying to work out what I was going
to say to her over dinner.

We had been going out for almost five years. Emily was a nurse
– a midwife – Scottish and sassy. She'd be putting on a brave face
tonight, and so would I.

Both of us hated goodbyes, but this one was especially poignant.
We'd just returned from two weeks' diving in Egypt, during the
course of which I'd spent every waking moment that I wasn't fifty
feet beneath the surface of the Red Sea reading books and journals
on Afghanistan and in particular the Mujahideen. Anyone that said
we'd be back without a shot being fired was talking bollocks, and
she knew that as well as I did.

The worst thing was that I was excited to be going and Emily knew that too. It didn't make either of us feel particularly good. All in all, she was getting a pretty raw deal – as shitty a birthday present as you could get. This wasn't what I wanted for our last day together.

I forced myself to concentrate. The IntO had come to the bit about hearts and minds – how we'd be helping the people of southern Afghanistan get back on their feet. Perhaps some of this might come in useful during the awkward silences that we'd try to fill tonight.

'Our mission – 16 Brigade's mission – is to support the Helmand Provincial Reconstruction Teams. The PRTs will be operating in a triangular area between Camp Bastion, Gereshk and Lashkar Gah.' He pointed to a section of the map that covered about 150 square miles, 70 per cent of which was open desert.

He went on to give us the big picture. From Camp Bastion our boys would support the PRTs as they went out into the surrounding countryside, establishing contact with the local village elders. The Afghan government wanted us to help them rebuild the infrastructure and become self-sufficient. The job of 16 Brigade was to provide the muscle to stop the Taliban killing the PRTs as they waltzed around the place promising all the good things Tony Blair had to offer.

Most villages had a police station that could act as a focal point for resistance. Part of the British mission was to train Afghan National Army (ANA) recruits and to work with those in the Afghan National Police (ANP) who hadn't been totally corrupted by the Taliban until they could take over responsibility for the protection of the surrounding landscape.

'The upshot,' he said, 'will be that the neighbouring villages will see how these guys are living the good life and they'll want to join the party. The Taliban won't be welcome. Our goodwill will spread like an ink spot on blotting paper; eventually it'll turn the whole map blue.'

He didn't mention narcotics once. I was gobsmacked.

I knew that we were part of a UN mandated programme, the International Security Assistance Force (ISAF), to reinstate a democratic government that could sort out the entire country, not just Kabul, properly train the ANA and ANP, rid the place of terrorists – and halt opium production.

While the US was tasked with destroying the Taliban, HIG and Al Qaeda, the other NATO participants had been given different roles in the reconstruction process. The UK was tasked with ridding Afghanistan of the poppies that made the heroin that accounted for between 90 and 95 per cent of the UK's smack market, the majority of which were grown along the banks of the Helmand River.

Weaning the farmers off this most lucrative of crops was not going to be easy; the lion's share of the profits ended up lining Taliban pockets, but their very survival was at stake. It didn't matter how many bridges, hospitals and schools the PRTs built; the Taliban, HIG and Al-Qaeda didn't want anything to get in the way of the drugs trade. In Helmand, the farmers were under increasing pressure to scale up heroin production and any village elder dim-witted enough to turn down Mullah Omar and his cronies would be beheaded in front of the very people he sought to protect.

As things stood, there was no one around to stop them. The ANA and ANP seemed to be completely incompetent (and smacked out of their heads) or in the pay of the Taliban. Not unsurprisingly, this was just how the Taliban liked it. In recent weeks it had sent a message to Tony Blair: if he sent British troops to Helmand, we'd come back in body bags.

I stuck up my hand. 'I'm sorry, sir; I must be missing something here. What is our objective exactly?'

I wanted to know if I was on a UN reconstruction mission, a NATO anti-terrorism mission or the unstated anti-narcotics mission.

'Our objective?' The IntO looked surprised.

'Our role, sir.'

'We are not in a warfighting role. We're going to support the Afghan national government – to help the place function as a normal country again.'

'But would I be right in thinking that the Americans *are* there in a warfighting role and the UK *has* signed up for the anti-narcotics role?'

'I can assure you we ... er ... 16 Brigade ... are *not* there to rid the country of narcotics, and the Americans ...' He paused. 'Well ... the Americans are the Americans I suppose, but that won't affect our mission.'

Won't affect us? The Americans are part of the NATO force and the Taliban had said they'll send us home in body bags; I could hardly see them making a fine distinction between us.

I sat back in my chair. The whole thing sounded totally fucked-up, but that wasn't my problem. All we had to do was support our troops on the ground – pretty much what I used to do in my Gazelle in Northern Ireland – and the odd Chinook escort flight.

The IntO – and we'd heard a lot like him before – made it all sound breathtakingly simple. But, of course, everyone knew that it wasn't.

The thing we needed to cling to – the thing to tell Emily – was that we were there to help. This wasn't Iraq, where our military presence was based on a dodgy premise and false intelligence. In Afghanistan, we'd be bringing peace and security to a people who badly needed it, we'd be ridding the world of some seriously bad hombres, and we'd be stopping the drugs trade in its tracks.

When I got home, we both managed to put on our brave faces. I'd been on deployment enough times to know the signs: the small talk, the thin smiles, the succession of reassuring glances ...

We'd decided to go to Emily's favourite restaurant, a quiet French one with subdued lighting. I'd called the manager, a friend of ours, to secretly lay on a birthday cake.

God, I thought, let's get this torture over with.

We were standing by the door, poised to step out into the spring evening, when the house phone rang. I checked the display.

'KEOGH'.

Captain Andy Keogh was the squadron's Ops Officer, the guy who was tasked with getting us out to Afghanistan. He was a universally popular workaholic.

'Hi buddy,' I said. It was typical of Andy to wish me well on the tour, and to let Emily know he was there if she needed anything.

'I've got some bad news, Ed. You're not going, I'm afraid.'

I looked up. Emily must have seen the expression on my face. She was watching me expectantly. 'We're not going?'

'No,' Andy said. 'The squadron's going. But you and Jon are staying behind.' Jon was part of my flight, and a SupFAC – a Supervisory Forward Air Controller. My stomach felt like lead.

'Why?' I still hadn't taken it in.

'Not enough places, apparently. Two people are going to have to stay behind.'

'For how long?'

'I don't know. A few days, perhaps. Probably something to do with Jake, but I don't have all the details. We'll sort it, Ed. I'm sorry. I know it's the last thing you need right now. I'll call you in the morning when I know more.'

I put down the phone. Jake was my flight commander; his wife Chloe was about to have a baby and he was going to join us after the birth.

I tried not to look disappointed. It was Emily's birthday. This was her day. I'd be able to spend more time with her. I did my best to make it look like good news.

She started to clap her hands. 'You're not going?'

'Jon and me are staying back for a few days.'

'Why?' She was beaming from ear to ear.

'I don't know. I'll find out in the morning. Andy said it was something to do with Jake.'

Emily's expression reminded me that there are some birthday presents money can't buy. But there was something else there too; something just behind her eyes.

I smiled and took her hand. She put her arms around me and gave me a squeeze.

'Still want to go out?' she asked me.

I nodded and smiled back. 'Wouldn't miss it for the world.' I meant it too. I had never known a woman like her and not a day went by when I didn't thank God she'd walked into my life. But we knew what that look meant. We were just delaying the evil moment. In a few days we'd have to go through the same process all over again.

At the squadron, I found out that Jon and I had fallen foul of the rules governing the number of fighting personnel each nation was allowed to have in-country at any given time. The UK had exceeded its quota; even though Jon was the SupFAC and I was the Squadron Weapons Officer we had to wait until some Brits shipped home.

To keep ourselves busy, we flew the simulator and practised our weapons drills; then, when there was still no call to head for Brize Norton, we nipped over to 664 Squadron and asked if we could borrow one of their Apaches so we could stay current. Very obligingly, they said yes.

On 5 May there was still no sign our departure was imminent. I decided to head for Catterick Camp; 664 Squadron were doing their Annual Personal Weapons Test – something everyone in the armed forces had to go through to ensure that we knew the pointy end of a gun from the butt. I decided to take the opportunity to test out an idea I'd been toying with for a while.

We carried a personal weapon in addition to our sidearm in case we were shot down on operations. The short-barrelled SA-80 carbine was the only rifle allowed in an Apache, but because its handle jutted into the cockpit, restricting our escape route in an emergency, we had to remove it and screw it back on if things went pear-shaped. This had always struck me as certifiable. If I were lucky enough to survive a crash, the last thing I'd want to do was fumble around with my carbine handle while the Taliban were launching an action replay of Rorke's Drift.

My idea was simple – fire the weapon without it. And today was the first chance I'd had to put it to the test.

I arrived at the range and was immediately confronted by a huge staff sergeant with a shaved head, straight out of Central Casting. *Listen in, you facking lot! Watch and shoot, watch and shoot! Bring me my facking brew …*

I unscrewed the handle of my SA-80 and dropped to the ground, facing the pop-up targets in Lane 6. A long shadow fell across me. I squinted against the sun to see Staff Sergeant Tank, hands on hips, looming over me.

'You can't fire your weapon without a handle,' he boomed for all to hear, adding 'Sir' as an afterthought.

Patience, Macy. 'Staff, this is how I'm going to have to fire in-theatre,' I replied as courteously as I could manage.

'The rules clearly state that you are not allowed to fire it without a handle.'

'I know what the rules say, Tanky, I'm a Skill at Arms Instructor too,' I said, marginally less diplomatically. 'Do you know *why* you're not allowed to fire it without a handle?'

He looked as if he'd just been asked to solve differential calculus on *University Challenge.*

He mumbled something incomprehensible.

'So, you're telling me not to do something but have no idea why ...'

Staff Sergeant Tank stood there grappling for an answer.

'The reason they insist that you fire this thing with a handle is because it has a short barrel, so, as there's nothing to grip, you might end up shooting your fingers off. Let me assure you, however, that it's not going to happen to me. Take a look at this ...'

Ten minutes later, I'd done the business. The handle made no difference at all. I'd rested the rifle in the crook of my left arm, taken aim and fired. I tested the method on targets at 50, 100, 200 and 300 metres, in the prone, kneeling and standing positions. I placed the bullets squarely where they were supposed to go and listened for the tannoy.

'Lane 4. Fail.'

'Lane 5. Pass.'

'Lane 6. One Hundred Per Cent Awarded Marksman.'

'Lane 7. Pass.'

I'd not dropped a single round. Tanky had his back to me now, but I didn't need to rub it in. The important thing was that I knew I could fly minus the handle and, if the shit did hit the fan, count on taking some of the fuckers down if I found myself in my own private version of *Zulu Dawn*. I'd broken a few rules, but so what, I figured the rules were supposed to be there to protect me.

A few days later, on 9 May, we got our first message back from the boys via MSN-Messenger. They were still at Kandahar Airfield, which I now knew as KAF.

Bastion isn't ready. No one is doing any tasking.

We don't expect to do any for a while. Everyone is ground running the aircraft. Then we'll airtest them.

It was all routine stuff, but it did nothing to ease my frustration. There was still no word on when Jon and I'd be leaving. I felt as if we were participating in our very own Phoney War – lolling around in a deckchair waiting for the Hun to attack.

It wasn't long before he did.

On 17 May, there was a newsflash on Sky. Fighting had broken out in southern Afghanistan and British and NATO troops had been involved. The details only came through the following day. Ninety insurgents were reported dead in Helmand. There was no news of any British casualties. Jon and I felt like a couple of caged tigers.

It wasn't until later in the day, when a message came through on MSN from Chris, a member of 3 Flight, that we learned Apaches had been involved.

I've used up two of my nine lives!!!

Canadian soldiers went out today and hit the hornets' nest with a baseball bat. They encountered RPGs and small arms.

My TADS was u/s. We went, but couldn't fight.

Hornet not afraid of AH. ROE didn't support firing.

Did a show of force at 125 feet. Heard RPG miss the cockpit. Black smoke trail. Couldn't return fire.

Pat didn't see the RPG, so he couldn't shoot back.

Another RPG passed between our aircraft. I couldn't ID which man fired it, so I couldn't return fire. Climbed back up.

Fight died down. RTB.

There was a lot of information to absorb here. The guys had seen action. Serious action. A 'show of force' normally meant a fast jet streaking over a bunch of troublemakers at low level as an implicit warning: next time, it would be a bomb. Low level for a jet was low enough to be seen but still above the SA band. A show of force by an Apache at 125 feet – no wonder he'd been fucking shot at, I thought. What happened to high level?

I couldn't understand why they were in Panjwai either; it was in Kandahar province, thirteen miles west of Kandahar City, well short of the eighty miles to Helmand. Chris was a small bloke with a big sense of humour. This was no joke, though. I could read his excitement between the lines as well as the relief. RTB. Return to base. We'd been lucky – on the squadron's first outing, I'd nearly lost a couple of mates and we'd damn near lost a helicopter.

As I reread Chris's message, one line in particular filled me with a combination of excitement and trepidation. 'Hornet not afraid of AH (Attack Helicopter).'

So, the Taliban wanted to mix it with us. Then bring it on. But please let me be a part of it. It sounded mad, irrational, even to me, but I had been twenty-one and a half years in the armed forces, with half a year left to go, and this was what I'd trained for.

Later that day, I read that a Canadian JTAC had not been so lucky. She'd been killed in an RPG attack when the Taliban launched an assault on their position after the Apaches, low on fuel, had been forced to fly back to KAF. She had been the first female NATO soldier to be killed in Afghanistan.

Within a few hours, the news channels reported the crowing response of Mullah Omar, leader of the Taliban. 'The Taliban consider themselves at war with British troops in Afghanistan,' the Mad One trumpeted. 'There will be a wave of suicide attacks as we step up our fight against the government and its allies.'

According to Mullah Omar, there were people queuing around the block to don explosive vests and pick up Kalashnikovs, he had twenty-five mid-level commanders in southern Afghanistan, and his forces there were armed with anti-aircraft weapons.

Well, this was shaping up to be a ding-dong tour.

Several thoughts popped into my head. I wondered what John Reid was making of all this. What about our reconstruction mission? The Mujahideen tactics I'd read about in Egypt seemed to be alive and well. And when the fuck were Jon and I going to get our marching orders?

I got the answer to the last question later that day. Jon and I were due to leave on 20 May, in two days' time. Whatever the ins and outs, we were on our way at last – and not a moment too soon. The Brits were engaged in heavy fighting down south and the Americans were doing their bit by sending the bombers in – big heavy B-1Bs armed with 2,000-lb GPS-guided JDAMs; bombs would do a whole lot more than rattle the bars of the Taliban cages.

The night before I left, Emily was on night-shift at the hospital again, hoping to deliver Jake's baby, and I was at my desk doing some cheerful last-minute admin – signing my tax forms, upping my military life insurance and checking the details of my will – when the phone rang. I raised it to my ear.

'Andy ...' I said cautiously.

'Just checking that everything's okay for tomorrow and wishing you well for the tour, Ed. Remember, if Emily needs anything, she only needs to pick up the phone.'

Transport had been laid on from the base to Brize Norton, a journey of around six hours. From Brize, we'd fly to Kabul. It was going to be a long day.

I went to bed early and slept so soundly that I never heard Emily return from her shift.

The next morning we got up, ate breakfast and drove straight to Dishforth. Neither of us said much and the weather wasn't helping – it was tipping it down.

The car that would take us to Brize was already waiting.

I chucked my bags in the boot and turned to say goodbye to my girl. She was sitting at the wheel of her car, window down. The wipers were doing their best against the rain and I could see that Em was struggling too. God, I hated this. We both did.

I leaned in and gave her a kiss. 'Love you,' I said.

'Love you too. I suppose there isn't any point asking you not to do anything stupid ...'

I kissed her again. 'See you in three months.'

I watched her go until I lost sight of the tail-lights in the rain.

As we started our final descent, the loudspeaker told us to get our helmet and body armour ready. Ready for what? Nobody told us and it didn't seem to matter much because somehow the threat – whatever it was – seemed a long way away.

As we banked I got my first real look at Afghanistan. The mountains looked majestic beneath us. Kabul itself looked dusty and exotic as it swam in and out of the heat haze. Smoke from a number of fires hung listlessly at the edge of the city. I thought for a moment that it might have been the result of some kind of attack, but an old RAF hand behind me said that it was always like that. Carbon emissions legislation wasn't high on Hammid Karzai's agenda; the 'Mayor of Kabul', as he was known, had more pressing problems to solve.

We landed in Kabul at 0615 Local – 0245 in the UK – and joined the queue to get processed into theatre. Jon and I joshed about the place we now found ourselves in; the airport was a cross between a junkyard and a high-tech arms fair, with rusting Soviet-era transport aircraft mixing it with gleaming F-16s and NATO and UN helicopters. Neither of us could believe how hot it was, or the smells that assaulted our nostrils.

When we got to the head of the queue we were ushered into a tent and, after showing our ID cards, were pointed towards a cargo trolley where our bags from the UK flight awaited us. From here we'd board a C-130 Hercules to Kandahar, where the rest of the squadron was assembled.

We took our seats in the Herc and waited for it to take off. The rear ramp remained open to allow what little ambient air there was onto the aircraft.

We weren't the first on board. To our right was the fattest bloke I'd ever seen in the armed forces, a Territorial Army captain, awash with sweat. Next to him were two other members of the TA: a skinny major – Little to his Large – and a female sergeant major unenviably close to a small open urinal that was bolted onto the bulkhead that separated the flight-deck from the cargo area.

A loadmaster appeared and handed out 'white death' boxes containing our rations for the flight.

The big bloke was eating out of it almost before the box had left the loadie's hand. Jon and I watched in amazement as he stuffed two whole muffins into his mouth, holding his helmet beneath them to catch the crumbs. He then fell asleep.

Upon being woken by the loadie a short time later and told the plane was about to take off, the captain slapped on his helmet and ended up with so many crumbs clinging to his sweat-soaked skin that he looked like he'd suffered an outbreak of scabies.

A moment or two after we were in the cruise, a Para corporal celebrated the fact that the train had left the station by climbing over everyone to get to the urinal. He beamed at the female sergeant major as he vigorously relieved himself. This, I imagined, was not contained in any in-theatre threat brief she'd ever attended. A few hours in Afghanistan, poor thing, and she looked like she was ready to go home.

The rest of the flight was relatively normal, except for the fact that the two loadies stood by the side doors during takeoff and landing, watching for missile launches. In their hands was a 'pipper' connected by a bungee cable to a box that controlled the flare launchers on the Herc's fuselage. It was all very Heath Robinson.

Unlike Kabul, Kandahar was flat. The first thing that assailed us on landing wasn't the heat – although it was like a furnace – but the stench. The smell of excrement in the air was unbelievable and it forced its way into the aircraft even before the ramp opened.

As we made our way onto the concrete, a bus drew up. It was painted in garish greens, reds and yellows and was festooned on the outside and inside with chains, from which a bizarre assortment of pendants dangled and jangled.

As we took our places, the bus seemed as if it might collapse under our weight as the driver, an Afghan with very few teeth, revved the engine noisily to signal his impatience. An RAF warrant officer, the guy who'd told me about Kabul's fires on the earlier flight, noticed my expression and told me to relax. The bus had no first or second gear, but he promised it would get us there.

I was about to ask where 'there' was when I saw a huge tented city through the windscreen.

We pulled up by a marquee-like structure alongside a sign that said, 'Cambridge Lines'. We went in, got processed again – 'Had we had the mine-threat brief, the medical brief and several other kinds of brief?' We had, thank God, back in the UK – before finally being released through a flap on the opposite side.

There, we were greeted by the cheery sight of Pat, the 3 Flight Commander, lolling behind the wheel of a Land Rover. He was brushing flies away with his cap, but fighting a losing battle.

We piled into the vehicle and set off towards our accommodation. As we wove in and out of the tents, the smell that had greeted us on landing seemed to be getting worse and worse.

'What *is* that?' I asked eventually, as Pat ground through the gears.

'What's what?' he said.

'That smell.'

'It's shit, Ed. What else can I say?'

'Where's it coming from?'

'You'll find out soon enough.'

Five minutes later, we screeched up in front of a white, semi-permanent, single-storey structure, approximately twenty metres wide and sixty long. As aircrew, Pat said, we were fortunate to be given 'hardened accommodation' – ours was one of the 200 identical tin hutches lined up in this part of KAF.

Jon and I grabbed our bags and prepared to enter our new home, but before we got as far as the door a gust of wind, stoked by the fires of hell, blew through, bringing with it a smell that eclipsed anything we'd experienced so far.

With my hand clamped over my face, I asked Pat again: 'What the fuck *was* that?' And this time, to shut me up, he offered to show me.

After threading our way through several alleyways we found ourselves facing a huge circular shit-pit. The giant 150-metre pond – filled with gravel and God knew what else, and fed by a giant revolving arm – was right next to our accommodation block. It was that fucking big we could spot it on Google Earth before the camp itself.

There was a huge sign:

SWIM AT YOUR OWN RISK
NO LIFEGUARD ON DUTY

'So now you know,' Pat said, with a resigned shrug. 'Either of you sleepwalk?'

Safely inside the hut, though still not entirely removed from the smell, we were led to our room. I was greeted by Billy and Mick, an old ex-Para mate, now the Regimental QHI.

'Ed, Jon,' Billy said cheerily from the edge of his bed, to the right of the now firmly closed door. 'Come and wave hello to Andrea.'

'Are you delusional?' I asked. Andrea was Billy's wife.

Billy pulled a face. Only then did I notice the laptop beside him. 'She's on MSN, you idiot.'

I dropped my bags and peered around the edge of the screen. Andrea beamed at me. She gave me a fuzzy wave then the ticker tape flashed.

'Hi Ed.'

I leaned over Billy.

'Hi Andrea.'

While Billy and Andrea cooed sweet nothings at each other, Jon and I settled ourselves in. The room was cool and comfortable, with only the merest hint of Eau de Shite to spoil the ambience. There were Glade air fresheners everywhere. My bed was back left; Jon's back right.

When Billy had finished his chat, he and Mick filled us in on the latest news. Although the squadron hadn't yet fired a shot in anger, it had loosed off a Hellfire. The day before, a French Special Forces convoy had been ambushed – they'd suffered one KIA, two MIAs and had been forced to abandon three vehicles in the desert. One of them, ironically, had been stuffed full of Electronic Counter Measures (ECM) equipment. It could not fall into enemy hands, so Pat had been dispatched to take it out with a Hellfire and Chris finished it off with a hundred rounds of 30 mil. Other than that, in the wake of them dodging RPGs and Chris using up two of his nine lives, things had settled down a bit – apart from the odd bit of bitching that some of the guys were getting more flying hours than others.

Billy then said he had to nip out, but suggested I got online to tell Emily I'd arrived safely.

Ten minutes later, my girl's face crackled into view on the screen of Billy's laptop.

She took one look at me and promptly burst into tears.

Knowing that something radical was required, I stuck my hands up on my head and moosed her.

How to explain 'moosing'?

Some years earlier there had been a dare going round the squadron. In the midst of a shag, the bloke had to place his thumbs on his forehead, fingers upright and splayed like antlers, then take a look at himself in the mirror. That was it. The trick was not to get caught; the girl was never supposed to find out.

I failed dismally, and had a great deal of explaining to do. Emily found it so funny that, from then on, we used it as our special greeting. If I was out and about and happened to spot her, I'd moose her and she me.

Through the graininess of the connection, I saw her raise her hands to her head, give me a couple of shaky antlers, and break into a brave smile.

I moosed her back and then, together, we both pressed the button that severed the connection.

There are times when antlers speak louder than words.

WILDMAN OF HELMAND

MAY 2006
Kandahar Airfield, Afghanistan

Work had always kept me focused and at KAF there was a hell of a lot of it to be done. There were six Apaches in-theatre and all needed time, love and attention to get them into full operational shape. The Apaches had been flown to Afghanistan in RAF C-17 transporters – giant four-engined aircraft that reminded me of International Rescue's lumbering Thunderbird 2 – and then offloaded and reassembled. Once they were back together again, they had to be tested on the ground then airtested before they were deemed safe enough to fly and ready to fight the Taliban.

While Jon and I had been in the air between the UK and Afghanistan, the first Apaches had flown out to Camp Bastion. The CO's plan in the early days was to keep half the aircraft stationed at Bastion and the remainder at KAF, because you never quite knew where the threat was going to develop next. As Squadron Weapons Officer, my focus was now on ensuring that the aircraft could fight as well as fly and I'd already heard there were problems. The rockets had proven horrendously inaccurate when tested on a nearby range, but to anyone who knew the foibles of that particular

161

weapon system when coupled to the Apache, it didn't come as a huge surprise.

I'd spoken to the IPT about it after Oman. The Integrated Project Team – a multi-disciplinary band of experts drawn from the armed services, the UK MoD and the defence industry – was brought together in the 1990s to bring weapons into service and maintain them as efficiently and cost-effectively as possible.

US Hydra rockets were so inaccurate that American Apache crews didn't generally fire theirs at any targets in excess of 1,000 metres. We used different rockets, but shared some of the same problems. If the pod wasn't correctly aligned, you could get a wide dispersal of rockets – they could go low and to the right from one pod and high and left from the other. When I broached this with the IPT, they gave me a pat on the back and told me to stop fussing because the CRV7 rocket was an 'area weapon', to which I'd replied: 'Yeah, but which area?' I didn't want to be responsible for a blue-on-blue – a friendly fire incident – our worst nightmare.

The cannons also needed to be aligned correctly to each Apache airframe. They slipped out of alignment for a variety of reasons and needed, every so often, to undergo 'dynamic harmonisation' – a little like getting the wheels of your car balanced down at Kwik Fit.

I'd slept badly; it hadn't helped that Mick had snored like a pig all night and KAF still stank like a sewer. But the cookhouse brightened my day; it served some of the best food I'd ever eaten in a military camp.

Jon, Billy and I strolled over to the Joint Helicopter Force Afghanistan (JHF(A)) Headquarters, a Nissen hut where the CO and his team were busy working out what needed to be done to bring the squadron up to ramming speed. With Apaches still rolling off C-17s inbound from the UK, the priority was still to ensure the aircraft were performing as they were supposed to after reassembly.

The aircraft were put together by the technicians in concrete bays, protected by rows of Hesco Bastion barricades, a kilometre away, close to the north threshold of KAF's main runway. The five given over to our aircraft sat in the full glare of the Afghan sun; temperatures routinely reached forty-seven degrees, although working in the cockpit, where the rays were magnified, they generally exceeded fifty.

Over the next week, the race was on to get the aircraft ready before the Taliban got busy again. 'Hot and high' was bad news and Afghanistan had both – heat that could fry your brains and mountains that stretched towards the sky.

Helicopters hate heat and most do not perform well at altitude. We used a temperature and pressure chart to come up with a daily 'density altitude' that we adjusted according to the conditions. Thank God for the 30 per cent additional power our British Apaches got from their Rolls-Royce engines. The Americans had to remove the Longbow radar from their Apaches and still lacked the power to get above 10,000 feet with a full range of weapons.

Some of the peak temperatures still pushed us extremely close to our limits. The Apache was initially cleared not to exceed forty degrees. On most days, we'd seen the needle creep closer to fifty. We were in uncharted territory. It would be bad enough to lose an aircraft due to enemy action; it would be criminal if we lost one because we'd just not paid enough attention to the climatic conditions.

Getting the weapons aligned was a slow, methodical operation. I'd devised the method myself after the IPT gave us a no-show on a solution. In one particular Apache, the left launcher was found to be one and a half degrees low, which would have resulted in its rockets falling almost 700 metres short of their target. The right launcher, on the other hand, would have dispatched its ordnance more than 300 metres long; the total dispersal area would have been a kilometre wide. We would have been inviting catastrophe every time we fired: a blue-on-blue of headline-grabbing proportions.

The technicians were losing weight fast and getting blacker by the day as they struggled to push out as many hours as possible. I joined them in the sweltering bays, working side by side to ready the gunships. Getting the weapons sorted was no picnic in this heat and I eventually took a break in the groundies' tent beside the flight line. Sheltered by a Hesco Bastion wall, it was a twelve foot square affair with no ends, a table and a few well-carved benches.

'All right Taff? Mind if I grab some warm water?'

'Get it quick,' he said. 'There'll be none left when this lot finish.'

Four of the team were stuffing multiple king-size muffins into their mouths.

'What on earth are they up to?'

'Ah …' His eyes gleamed. 'That would be the Spunk-muffin Challenge, sir.'

Taff saved me the embarrassment of inquiring.

'The boys get free Otis Spunkmeyer muffins from the MWR, don't they? And bring them back here by the truckload. They were about to hit their "best before" date, so I'm making them eat 'em, see, for being greedy. That'll learn 'em.'

The challenge was to eat five as fast as they could. The winner dropped out and the remainder had to do the challenge again. The numbers worked out perfectly.

'When I was at a Navy Seals base in the States they had something called the Subway Challenge.'

'What's that?' Gifted asked.

A blond lad with boyish good looks, he was the youngest member of the team; every mother's dream. Fresh from school he turned up on his first day in the army wearing a T-shirt with 'GIFT-ED' emblazoned across it. The name stuck because he wasn't.

I began to regret opening my mouth, but they pushed me for an explanation. Little did I know I'd just inspired them ...

Lieutenant Colonel Richard Felton stood at the far end of the bird table and sucked thoughtfully on a cigarette. How anyone could smoke in this heat was beyond me, but it was the way the CO did it that cracked me up. He pinched the tab between the very tips of the index and middle fingers of his right hand, keeping it as far as possible from his lips until the moment he seemed to force himself to take a drag, face contorted, as if it was a freshly lit fuse that might detonate at any moment.

'The Rules of Engagement, gentlemen ...' Legs crossed, left hand on his hip, he started to outline, in that soft, well-spoken way of his, exactly what we could and could not do while we were in-theatre. If it wasn't for the seriousness of the brief and the fact that Felton was one of the youngest, toughest, no-nonsense colonels on the circuit, we'd have been forgiven for thinking we'd walked into a sketch for *Comic Relief*.

The ROE briefing was always going to be a bitch; I'd need to keep my wits about me. So far, our enemy were armed with little more than small arms and RPGs. But we already knew they weren't afraid of the Apache, the weapon system that had been billed as a quantum leap in the way the British Army would fight future wars. The Taliban were medieval in their fighting methods – but also in their brutality. The boffins called it asymmetric warfare. All we knew was that with a handful of rudimentary weapons the bad guys had levelled the playing field.

Lieutenant Colonel Felton took a last drag of his cigarette before dropping it into the dregs of his coffee. I checked the battery level on my digital voice-recorder and placed it on the edge of the bird table, next to the map that depicted our area of operations. The temperature in the long metal tube that housed the CO's HQ was unbelievable. I glanced at the blokes propped around the table. Simon, Billy, Pat, Tony, Carl, Nick and the others seemed to be taking it in their stride. If I was the only one suffering, I didn't want them to know.

'I know how much you've been looking forward to this,' Felton said. There was a groan from the floor. 'There are basically two different scenarios in which the ROE apply. The first is where we're told to go and destroy a target deliberately – a known Taliban HQ, for example. Deliberate Attacks are covered under a document called the "Targeting Directive". It's for pre-planned targets only and will have been cleared by government, with signatures all the way to the top. So, if the Intelligence community find a Taliban set-up at a particular location and we confirm it's definitely there, and the authority is given from Whitehall, then that is a legitimate target under the current guidelines. Is that clear?'

Billy nudged me and muttered in my ear: 'They're giving with one hand and taking away with the other.'

Yup, I thought. Legitimate, maybe, but once all those checks and balances had been attended to, it wouldn't be us who'd be inflicting the damage, it would be fast air in their Harriers, B-1Bs and A-10s.

But the fun and games had only just begun.

'Fast air don't have it all their own way,' Felton continued, 'because the target set also has to conform to the collateral damage matrix. Each of the nations out here has different ideas over what constitutes collateral damage.'

Someone opened the door behind us and a blast of air from the furnace outside blew through the HQ, scattering the ROE sheets across the bird table. Beads of sweat dripped from one lad's nose. I forced myself to focus on what the CO was saying.

'The second scenario and the rules that affect you basically fall into two categories: self-defence and when you want to take specific action against a target for a reason other than self-defence.' The second category was obviously the hot potato.

If, for example, the enemy below was about to lob a mortar round at our boys on the ground – we would be allowed to engage without consulting the chain of command, as long as we had 'reasonable belief' that the person in our sights was the enemy.

Somebody next to me made a choking sound. If the CO heard he didn't show it, but the civilian in the chair behind him clearly did; I saw him glance up sharply from his notepad like an eagle-eyed schoolteacher. We were never told who this individual was, but in his conspicuously smart clothes, God bless him, he might as well have had 'Whitehall' stamped across his forehead. He was probably a lawyer of some description; maybe the pen-pusher who'd drafted this nonsense in the first place.

How the hell were we meant to know who had hostile intent when just about every male in Afghanistan carried a weapon. In the middle of the Green Zone a primitive house and a few livestock was all that most could afford, but they were never without an AK47 and a moped. How were we to know the difference between a farmer out patrolling his crop or the Taliban out patrolling? With a distinct lack of uniforms it was impossible to distinguish the enemy from the Afghan Army, Afghan Police, Afghan Security Forces and some other *discreet* security forces.

An unsettled feeling started to gnaw at my stomach. I stuck up my hand. The man from Whitehall peered at me over his glasses. The CO paused and gave me an encouraging smile.

'Yes, Mr Macy.'

Lester W. Grau, a CIA analyst who'd studied the tactics of the Mujahideen against the Soviets, had been high on my reading list. As the Squadron Weapons Officer, I was expected to know every-thing about the Taliban's capabilities, but I'd also wanted to get inside the heads of these bastards. What I'd learned was simple and frightening. We were up against an astute, resourceful enemy that would never give up. In the 1980s, a handful of armed resistance fighters had gathered the populace and had seen off the mightiest army in the world. And no Soviet general had had to pussyfoot around under a set of unworkable guidelines.

'How do I demonstrate they have hostile intent?'

'Very good question, Mr Macy.' The CO reached for another cigarette. He was clearly in no hurry to answer it.

My hand stayed up. 'And what happens if they're still armed, but looking for cover? How do I know they're not going to continue the fight after we've run low on fuel and buggered off? How do I know whether they're farmers scared out of their wits looking for somewhere to hide, or Taliban looking for defensive positions from which to continue the fight?'

I paused and looked around the bird table at my fellow pilots before turning back to the CO. 'What then, sir? What do I do?'

The CO lit his cigarette and took the smoke deep into his lungs. He shook his head. 'Your call, Mr Macy.'

My call?

The existence of hostile intent would be judged on evidence presented via our TADS camera footage and the camera didn't always see everything.

Jesus ...

As I walked back to our billet I thought about the nightmare we now found ourselves in. It wasn't the CO's fault; he was just the messenger. This was down to the politicians. They were sending us to fight their war in a bird that cost £46 million a pop; a bird that was on trial every bit as much as we were. We were both expected to perform flawlessly – with our arms now tied behind our backs. And if I put so much as a foot wrong, because I didn't have crystal balls and couldn't read the enemy's mind, I'd find myself court-martialled for not knowing whether the enemy had hostile intent.

No one else was subject to this level of scrutiny.

As they prepared to rain shells on a position ten kilometres away, the artillery boys weren't asked to file a report stating that their enemy had hostile intent.

Nobody would ask 3 Para to explain themselves.

The fast-jet pilot who dropped a bomb on a grid wasn't called to task if he made a mistake – his authority came from a guy on the ground.

But we were well and truly in the crosshairs.

If we got it wrong we'd find ourselves in a court of law and the first-ever deployment of the British Army's Apache weapons system would be judged a complete failure. We'd be crucified by the media, the politicians and the Whitehall bean-counters. The Apache would be branded a white elephant – a £4.13 billion mistake.

The press hadn't helped by spouting shite about the Apache programme since the outset. Every time the attack helicopter programme came across a hiccup they would wade in and blow it out of all proportion. It was just an excuse to have a go at the politicians for spending more money than ever before on a single piece of hardware, but Joe Public had swallowed it hook, line and sinker. Due to the bad press, it had already failed in their eyes.

When I'd joined the army twenty-two years earlier, this was not how I'd imagined it would be.

But fuck it, I'd come this far, and the people around the bird table were my mates. Some of them – Billy and Geordie, for example – had been with me damn near the whole time I'd been on the path.

One way or another, we had to find a way of making this work. Or else the Taliban, who didn't know the meaning of the word 'rules', would shoot us out of the sky and decorate their caves with our entrails.

For the past seventeen years I'd bent the rules every which way to get to where I wanted: here, on Ops, with the greatest weapons system in the world, in the stinking heat of an Afghan summer.

Why the hell should I stop now?

Later that evening, as the sirens went silent after a rocket attack, the groundies came bursting into my room.

'Sir, sir, you've got to come quickly.'

I dived from my bed thinking we'd lost a man or an aircraft. Then I was told they were about to start the Subway Challenge.

'You and your big mouth.' Billy smiled and grabbed his pistol.

'Wait for me,' Jon shouted.

Inside one of the huge US-built relaxation facilities was a gaming area, movie area, coffee bar, games area and a 150-feet-square music room jam-packed with instruments. We entered the music room to see the groundies gathered enthusiastically around three six-foot tables, arranged in a triangle.

Half a dozen foot-long Subway sandwiches had been laid end to end in front of each of the competitors.

Airtrooper Howson – Challenger Number One – was your typical prop forward and played rugby at club level for civilian teams as well as the army. He looked as if he could have swallowed every one of his Subways without pausing for breath.

Gifted looked at the contents of his table as if they were a series of incoming Hellfires.

Which just left Tiny, who looked as though he was about to try to eat several times his own body weight.

'My money's on Howson,' Billy said before Jon or I could wage a bet.

I bagged Gifted.

'Three, two, one, go,' Taff called.

They all started at a nice slow pace. Facing each other; matching each other bite for bite. Tiny was being advised not to drink anything because he wouldn't be able to fit a single Sub in.

They had an hour in which to eat their own height in Subs. The winner would be the first to finish, or the one to have consumed the most when the clock chimed. Anyone that barfed would be instantly disqualified, unless he ate what he'd just thrown up. I'd seen a Navy Seal eat seven feet of Subs in thirty minutes in Atlanta.

They were all finishing their third Sub with thirty minutes to go. Everyone had placed their bets. The music room had glass windows and curiosity got the better of everyone who passed them. The place was packed with Brits, Americans, Canadians, Italians, French; you name it, they were there. The banter was ear-splitting, but Gifted, Howson and Tiny continued to match each other munch for munch.

Forty-five minutes in, Gifted was fading, halfway through his fourth Sub.

'Gifted's going,' the opposition shouted.

He grabbed the bucket from under the table and chundered explosively to a chorus of laughter and a flurry of fresh bets. Howson was now the favourite by a country mile.

The two remaining tables were pushed around to face each other as the noise got louder and the contest became ever more gladiatorial.

Five minutes away from the final bell, both reached for their sixth and final Sub. They'd clearly begun to tire.

Tiny threw down his Sub, folded his arms and looked Howson in the eye. Realising he too was unlikely to finish the whole two yards, Howson followed suit and took a slurp of Gatorade. There was uproar; both of them looked as sick as pigs.

'Two minutes to go,' Taff shouted.

A sprint finish was now a dead cert.

'One minute.'

Howson moved his Sub, positioning it for the perfect draw, but Tiny kept his nerve and barely blinked.

'Forty seconds to go.'

Howson picked up his Sub, almost in slow motion, and held it a foot from his mouth, directly in the path of Tiny's steely gaze.

'Thirty seconds.'

They were locked in complex mental calculation. If they started too soon and had to stop, they'd lose the contest.

I knew which way Howson's pendulum was swinging. He reckoned that he'd easily out-bite Tiny.

The second the prop forward looked up at Taff, Tiny swiped his Sub and went at it like a termite on speed. Howson rammed his down his throat and removed three inches in one go.

The noise was deafening.

'Ten seconds,' Taff bellowed.

Howson was doing his best to swallow and Tiny was still going the chomp-swallow-chomp-swallow route.

'Five …'

Tiny had another eight inches to go.

'Four …'

Howson swallowed hard and tore off another three inches. His cheeks looked like an overpumped airbed.

'Three …'

Tiny was seven inches away from glory.

'Two …'

Tiny grinned and gave Howson a cheeky wink.

As Taff called, 'One', Tiny took a huge three-inch bite of his Sub and placed the remainder on the table.

The crowd went crazy.

'STOP,' Taff yelled.

Knowing Tiny only had to swallow his last mouthful to win, Howson lost the battle to keep his last couple of Subways down. His head disappeared into his bucket.

A huge roar and a round of multinational applause egged Tiny on to finish and set the new Afghan Subway Challenge record: one hour and six minutes.

'Gee!' an American girl shouted. 'What does he win?'

'He gets his Subs paid for by the losers,' I said. 'And they pay for their own.'

VISITING THE SHRINE

A couple of days later, I found myself on a mission to Camp Bastion. I'd familiarised myself with the area around KAF; an airtest or two had given me glimpses of the mountains and the desert, but the trip to Bastion was my first foray into the Helmand region.

Our tasking was to escort a Chinook, callsign Hardwood Two Two, to Lashkar Gah, where it would drop off some personnel. From there we'd fly directly to Bastion where another Chinook, Hardwood Two One, would lift off and RV with us. All four of us would proceed first to Now Zad, then to Musa Qa'leh, with the Chinooks dropping off and picking up men and materiel along the way. After the round-trip, we'd land at Bastion and remain forward-deployed there for six days. We'd been getting wind of some kind of operation – the reason for calling us forward.

We were two Apaches, callsigns Wildman Five Zero with Simon in the front and Jon in the back, and Wildman Five One, with Billy in the gunner's seat and me behind him.

'Wildman Five Zero Flight are two Apaches and one Chinook, ready for departure,' Simon said as we lined up on Foxtrot taxiway.

'Wildman Five Zero Flight, you are clear to depart Two Three Foxtrot,' the American controller replied.

The Chinook lifted off first and we started to roll down the taxiway. I quickly tucked in behind it, our Apache hanging off to the back left, Jon to the back right. All three of us hugged the desert floor till we were away from KAF, then the Chinook shot up to altitude.

I turned to Billy. 'That'll change when we get back.'

'What will?'

'That procedure: the Chinook going up first.'

'I see what you mean,' Billy said after a moment's thought. 'That was all wrong, wasn't it?'

Had someone fired at the Chinook while it was climbing to altitude, our two Apaches, supposedly its escorts, would never have seen the threat – and the Chinook, which had no armour (all Chinooks received their armour later in the tour), would not have withstood the shot.

One of the Apaches should have popped up to altitude first, to maintain a hawk-like vigil for the second Apache's climb to height. Once we were both up, we could then provide cover for the Chinook's ascent. The Apaches were built to take small arms fire and they could handle a missile launch; the Chinook couldn't. And we all knew that the Taliban would have given their eye teeth to shoot down a 'Cow' – their name for the big, lumbering RAF helicopter.

Well, not on my watch, I swore to myself. We'd need to talk to the Chinook boys and fix that procedure at the first available opportunity.

I looked down. We were crossing into the Red Desert – so named because of the colour of its remarkable three-hundred-feet-high dunes. From the air they looked like rust-coated waves rolling inexorably north from Afghanistan's border with Pakistan and threatening to engulf the south-eastern city of Kandahar.

The desert was impassable by foot, almost impossible to cross by vehicle, and was uninhabited except by nomads who only ventured onto its fringes in winter. As far as NATO pilots were concerned, the

Red Desert was a friend; being devoid of people, it was also devoid of threat.

We ploughed on at altitude until a pale strip appeared hazily on the horizon. As I peered at it, the outline of a sprawling city began to emerge.

I checked the navigation page on my MPD. Lashkar Gah: the first stop on my cook's tour of Afghanistan.

The Chinook's nose dropped sharply. Jon and I eased our Apaches left and right to take up station above and to each side of it as it swooped low over the desert towards the base nestled in the north-east quadrant of the city.

All the bases in Afghanistan were programmed into our computer and with a punch of a button the crosshairs in my monocle shot away to rest squarely over the one at Lashkar Gah.

The cueing dots directed me to look down and to my right and, as if by magic, there it was in my line of sight: a large compound filled with two-storey buildings surrounded by a fortified wall with sangars built into it as watchtowers.

Except for the dust and the heat haze it didn't look a whole lot different from some of the set-ups I'd overflown in Northern Ireland.

Even from two miles away, I could see the helicopter landing strip (HLS). The Chinook was bombing towards it at full-throttle.

I checked what Billy could see with the TADS. Bisecting the screen, pointing like an arrow towards the army base, there was a long straight street, one hundred metres wide and a kilometre in length. Leading off it were little alleyways and housing blocks. With the DTV camera in the TADS on zoom, it was as if we were only twenty-five metres away from the teeming throng of people on bikes, women with pots on their heads, kids running about, trucks and mopeds grinding along in low gear, dogs nipping at their wheels. It was all happening in Lashkar Gah.

The Chinook suddenly cut into the bottom of the picture. In a remarkable piece of flying, the pilot took it straight down the street. I would have expected the women and the kids and the dogs to have scattered, but none did, used as they were, perhaps, to a generation of machines that had brought conflict to their country.

At the last second, the Chinook pulled up its nose, bled off speed, dropped over the wall and disappeared in a cloud of dust.

We started to wheel over the city, keeping our eyes peeled, but didn't have to wait long. Less than twenty seconds after it had vanished there was a 'click-click' on the radio – the only signal we would receive from the CH47 boys on the Chinook flight-deck, and the Cow suddenly emerged out of the muck. Batting low over the rooftops, it pulled up clear of the small arms belt. We crossed into the Green Zone as soon as it resumed station alongside us.

The strip of fertile land was irrigated by the Helmand River, glistening through the trees below us. Around two kilometres across at its widest point, its lush foliage provided plenty of cover, not just for roaming Taliban units, but for anti-aircraft guns and ManPADS that could shoot us down.

We passed on into the dusty air above a parched, sand-coloured desert that stretched south, west and north as far as I could see.

'Twelve o'clock, fifteen kilometres, Camp Bastion,' Billy said.

I peered out of the cockpit and saw nothing except for tyre-tracks criss-crossing the barren wastes below us. Billy still had the TADS set to DTV zoom and I could see Bastion starting to take shape in black and white on the screen. First some tunnel-type tents in the south-east corner of the base, then other features sprang into view: the berm bulldozed up around the perimeter, the sangars with their tin roofs and sandbag fortifications and numer-

www.harperplus.com/hellfire

ous vehicle parks brimming with Land Rovers and various types of APCs. A Chinook sat at the northern edge, blades milling, on one of two square pads that marked out the HLS.

There were two stationary Apaches on the other pad. The HLS was tiny compared to the luxurious concrete-lined complex we'd become used to at KAF. Technically, we were supposed to be able to fit four Apaches at a pinch on one pad, but I wondered, from up here how that would be possible. I didn't have time to dwell on it, because Hardwood Two One, the second Chinook, lifted off its square. When it popped out of its own dust cloud, I could see its underslung load: a bunch of crates in a low-hanging net. The Chinook hugged the ground for several hundred metres then rose to meet us in a zoom climb.

As soon as we RV'd, we set course to the north and our next destination: Now Zad.

The two Chinooks flew in formation about a thousand metres apart. Billy and I took up station above and around two kilometres behind and to the left of them; Jon and Simon did the same to their right.

We could see the Chinooks from our vantage point, and more importantly the ground beneath and behind them. Our primary concern was a SAM launch. Unlike us, the Chinooks didn't always have an integrated defensive aids suite. If the Taliban did fire on them, they'd have to rely on the good old Mark 1 Eyeball – ours as well as theirs – to spot the launch plume. After that, it would be down to good judgement and their 'pippers', hand-held controllers like the ones I'd seen on the C-130 flight from Kabul to KAF, to launch flares to seduce the missile away from the aircraft.

The only place where the threat was deemed at all likely on this segment of our journey was the point at which we crossed Highway Zero One, which looped around most of Afghanistan. You never quite knew who was going to be on the road as you roared across it – on this occasion we were fortunate; it was empty – and we always treated it with respect.

Shortly afterwards I saw a pockmarked town, smaller than Lashkar Gah. Surrounded by hills and mountains Now Zad sat in a basin, with a rough road running north–south for around 500 metres through its centre.

Houses spread back for 300 metres on either side of this road, with smaller streets and alleyways running east–west. The place looked medieval in its chaos. The houses were ramshackle and built to no discernible pattern, the majority constructed on one or two levels, with access to the flat roofs via a staircase from within. The roofs of the handful of three-storey buildings gave the Taliban some excellent fields of fire direct into the District Centre.

The DC was located to the west of the potholed main street. It had been a police station and its compound had recently come under some very heavy fire. Surrounded by a high wall that was still remarkably intact, it had a big metal gate at the front and a sand-bagged watchtower turret at each corner, manned by sentries round the clock.

Billy told me that forty-one Paras were stationed there and that the threat level was judged to be so high that they were in 'lockdown' – they went nowhere except to collect ammo and provisions from their Chinook replen flights using their quad-bikes and WMIK all-terrain vehicles – stripped down Land Rovers fitted with a Weapons Mounted Installation Kit that allowed a GPMG and a .50 cal to hang from its frame.

All the inhabitants to the west of the road were friendly towards the Brits and had a good relationship with us. Everyone to the east had taken to their heels as the Taliban moved in.

A few hundred metres to the south-west, just outside and a couple of hundred feet above the town perimeter, was a hill, easily identifiable from the air, occupied by the ANP and known to us as 'the Shrine' because the slope facing Now Zad was a burial ground, full of fluttering flags and streamers.

If the Shrine went down, Now Zad would too. From here, the ANP and a few British troops kept a watchful eye on the area and directed fire out of the DC onto the Taliban. The DC was too small to accept a Chinook within its compound, so flights landed to the south-west of the Shrine, under its garrison's protective gaze but out of sight of the town.

The landing site (LS) was approached across flat desert and through a wide opening in the mountains. The town extended for a further 500 metres north-west of the DC, and was occupied mainly by Afghans intent on living a normal life.

'They bring no bother to this area,' Billy said, 'so we try to patrol out that far to reassure them we're friends.'

The town stopped abruptly at the western edge of the built-up area and turned to desert. Two kilometres further on, steep hills rose to form the edge of the Now Zad basin.

The dodgy area of town stretched a few hundred metres east of the main road before entering a small wadi, used as a route out through the Green Zone, filled with orchards, crop-fields and tree-lined groves and bordered by a huge mountain ridge, only a few hundred metres wide, but climbing a thousand feet above Now Zad and stretching north as far as the eye could see.

The so-called Green Zones were christened by the Russians in the late seventies. Southern Afghanistan was not naturally fertile but the mountains were so high they generated their own micro-climates. Clouds often obscured the tops of the ranges and produced rivers that meandered during the summer months and thundered down in winter. The Helmand was the largest of these, stretching for hundreds of miles through the southern deserts.

The Afghans had mastered irrigation, and the river banks were lined by fields that spread back from ten metres to a couple of kilometres on each side.

The Taliban lived in and where possible fought from the Green Zones. They didn't have the numbers, equipment, weapons, logistics or support with which to do so in the open.

The richly fertile area provided a latticework of concealed approaches and escape routes. It was so dense in some areas that you could barely see thirty metres. They built hides and underground tunnels, disguising the entrances so they couldn't be seen from the ground or air, and the irrigation system, channelling water from field to field, made their movements virtually impossible to detect. In many places, the only way through was on foot. The soft-earthed labyrinth was often inaccessible to tanks, APCs and vehicles of any description.

The Taliban didn't want us anywhere near Now Zad, and saw the DC as a big threat. The Paras had come under intense fire, morning, noon and night the entire time they had occupied it. In the recent upsurge of violence the town had been mortared by what the threat-briefers called a 'hard core' of Taliban. The Green Zone on the eastern edge of the town was the place to watch; it was where they'd mounted their last attack – principally with rockets and mortars.

Simon's voice came over the radio. 'Widow Seven Three, Widow Seven Three, this is Wildman Five Zero, how do you read?'

Widow Seven Three was the JTAC who coordinated all air-to-ground activity in this area.

With no acknowledgement from him, Simon tried again. I suddenly spotted blue smoke below. I checked Billy's TADS image. It was coming from the grid-reference we'd been given for the LS. Billy increased the zoom and I was able to make out a couple of vehicles at the base of the Shrine – a quad-bike and a WMIK. Blue smoke meant that the LS was secure.

The Chinooks were beating their way across the desert approaches from the south-east. Jon was already wheeling his Apache above the streets just north of the Shrine to allow Simon an unrestricted top-down view of activity in the alleyways and the compounds below. I was doing the same above the area of Green Zone to the east. The danger was a mortar strike on the LS during the few brief seconds that the Chinooks would be on the ground. My responsibility was to keep an eye on them as well as on my wingman.

The Chinook with the underslung load disappeared in a pillar of whirling dust; the second went to land just outside this cloud and promptly disappeared as well.

Seconds later, we heard a double-click on the radio and first one machine then the next reappeared.

The Cows veered away to the south, keeping low, then pulled up to join us at altitude. Within moments we were back over the desert, cruising at a safe height en route to Musa Qa'leh, our last RV before heading back to Bastion.

The Musa Qa'leh drop-off went without incident. We saw one of the Chinooks descend into a wadi to deliver a vital supply item, the identity of which was on a need-to-know basis (which meant we had no need to know), to an American patrol operating in the area, and then we turned for home.

As we flew high over the desert towards Bastion, I thought back to the ROE brief and, for the umpteenth time since I'd heard the CO deliver it, how crazy it was.

What if I went down in this hell-hole? How would I protect myself?

I glanced across at my SA80. I had three magazines with thirty rounds of 5.56 mm each, and an unusually short mag packed with twenty 5.56 mm tracer rounds in case of emergency. It jutted out from my carbine in the seat frame to my right. Strapped to my right thigh, inside an Uncle Mike's Sidekick holster, was my 9 mm pistol for which I had four magazines, thirteen rounds in each, with one inserted – ready – into the grip.

Three days earlier, I'd visited some Para mates. In exchange for some AAC patches and badges, I'd been given two hand grenades. Needless to say, it was absolutely verboten to fly with grenades – I'd be drummed out of the corps, most likely, if they were discovered in the aircraft. But the way I saw it, they were only dangerous to those unfamiliar with them. They sat in my grab bag to my right-hand side with my spare magazines and two smoke grenades. I was out there flying against the Taliban and the rule-makers weren't, so the grenades flew with me.

If it ever came to my *Black Hawk Down* moment, the grenades would allow me to take as many of the bastards down with me as I could – my final two-fingered salute to the ROE.

We cleared Highway Zero One and prepared for our landing at Bastion.

The patrol commander always landed first and I saw Jon's nose drop as he readied to take us in. I lowered the collective, ensuring that I retained a bit of power to keep the clutch from disengaging, and kept the nose up, bleeding speed. Then I lowered the nose, accelerating and jinking left and right – shades of the lessons I'd learned as a young Para when trying to shoot down drones on the range at Larkhill. I could hear Captain Mainwaring shouting at me now. It was damn difficult to hit an aircraft that was manoeuvring unpredictably …

'Jon's going to dust-out massive,' Billy said. 'I know it looks like he's heading for a hardened landing site down there, Ed, but trust me, in a moment he's going to disappear from view.' He paused. 'Do you want me to take this one for you?'

I grinned. 'I'm going to have to do this at some point. Just follow me on the controls in case I fuck up.'

I'd already been told that landing at Bastion was a nightmare. Helicopters hated hot and high – that had been drummed into us from Lesson Number One. Add dust to the mixture and everything threatened to turn to ratshit.

To get around this problem at Bastion, they were planning on building a hardened aircraft landing strip (HALS); a short runway, in effect, that would allow us to do rolling takeoffs and landings. Rolling takeoffs not only allowed us to get airborne with more ordnance, they also ensured we didn't get lost in our own sand-storm.

The trouble was, the HALS hadn't yet been built at Bastion; instead, we had to land on a square pad – there were two of them – a raised area built from builder's rubble that the Chinook and Apache boys had robbed from the engineers constructing the camp.

The pads had originally been built as a vehicle park. This was all well and good, except that the omnipresent dust settled in among the rubble. Only 'dust' didn't really do this stuff justice – at Bastion, apparently, it was like talcum powder, and it went fucking every-where. The makeshift landing pad I was heading for, Billy had warned me, was barely safe to use.

Terrific.

'Billy?'

'Yes, mate?'

'You still there?'

'Following your every move.'

'Good. Just checking.'

I continued towards the pad. I needed to carry out a 'zero-zero' landing. I didn't want to end up in the hover, because I'd find myself still in the air in a dust-out and that's where crashes begin; and I didn't want any forward speed when I hit the ground either or I'd roll into the two Apaches that were already parked ahead of my landing spot. The only way to crack this was to fly forward and down, forward and down, in one steep smooth approach, until we banged onto the pad.

My fears were confirmed when I saw Jon bringing his Apache into land ahead of me. One moment I could see him, the next he just vanished along with the whole pad and the two Apaches already on it. There was no room for error. If I drifted left, I'd collide with Jon and Simon. If I drifted right, we'd hit uneven ground and roll over. If I rolled forward, I'd hit the two stationary aircraft.

Oman had been bad, but at least it had been sand, not dust, and there'd been nothing else to hit.

I continued towards the pad bringing back the speed with the ground 100 feet below. Billy advised me to slow down some more to allow the dust from Jon's landing to settle.

'Yeah, copied mate.' I did as he said. Trouble was, dust was also blowing in from the two Chinooks that had landed a hundred metres or so to the south; a roiling, billowing cloud of dust, 150 feet high and hundreds of metres wide, was blowing across the camp.

I began my zero-zero descent. The world as I knew it immediately disappeared.

'Fuck me.'

'Don't worry, just trust your symbology.'

Suddenly, through the dust, I saw the dim silhouettes of aircraft – two directly in front of me and one forward and to my left. I was bleeding speed off and dropping down towards them, forward and down, forward and down …

'You're doing good, doing good,' Billy said. 'Trust your symbology …'

If I bottled it and attempted to go around again, I'd hit the aircraft in front of me. I was getting to the point of no return.

I glanced left and saw two faces – Simon's and Jon's. You always watched somebody coming in to land because there was every chance it would go wrong. It wasn't a morbid curiosity, it was just plain dangerous, and they were watching me like a pair of hawks.

Any second now and I'd have to commit.

'Stand by,' I said. 'Three ... two ... one ... committed!'

The aircraft was slowing, the ground still rising to meet me. I fought the instinct to pull power, but in the end I couldn't help myself. I tweaked some on – just a fraction – and the dust came up. Oh God, I thought, here we go ...

'I've got the toe-brakes, mate,' Billy said.

Thank fuck – one thing less to worry about. Billy would pop the brakes the moment we hit the ground.

We passed through sixty feet and I made the big mistake of glancing down to my left.

The dust was blowing away from me in rivulets – the ground, wherever it was, looked as if it had turned to liquid. I had lost all sense of terra firma below me. Anything and everything that represented solidity had disappeared from view and been replaced by a rippling carpet of liquid mush. This sea of dust moving left made me feel like I was side-slipping right at speed. I fought to trust my symbology.

The Apache on my left began to disappear from my peripheral vision and then, wham, the dust started recirculating down through my rotors, and my peripheral vision disappeared entirely. I was still fifty feet off the ground and totally blind.

'Forward and down,' Billy continued. 'Forward and down ...'

I kept my head still, not moving a muscle, as I stared into the monocle. It was in hover mode. The velocity vector line moved ever so slowly back from the top of the monocle towards the centre; I knew I was doing six knots. I had to get the vector back to the centre – zero speed across the ground – at exactly the same time as the height also hit zero.

I didn't know for sure if I would hit my point on the pad and took a quick peep out of the right-hand window.

Mistake …

The line drifted to the left.

'No further left!' Billy yelled.

'I've got it, I've got it …' I shouldn't have fucking looked. I was concentrating so hard to fight the urge to stop a drift that wasn't even there.

I brought the stick back to the right to compensate for my error and – smack! – we hit the ground and I felt a reassuring lurch as the struts stroked downwards and the undercarriage took our full weight evenly.

I had no idea if I'd landed where I was supposed to, but was ecstatic that I'd not rolled over or hit anything. I looked to my left. After a few minutes the dust thinned and I caught sight of Jon and Simon, arms above their heads, giving me a slow theatrical hand-clap. I should have acknowledged with a little bow, but I was too damned drained to do anything. I slumped back in my seat.

I glanced up and saw Billy's face in his mirror. He gave me a cheeky smile and a thumbs-up.

'Fucking hell, that was scary,' I said.

'Well,' he replied, 'I did offer …'

We were bounced over the rough terrain to the main camp in a Land Rover. On the ground, Bastion was smaller than I imagined and it only took a minute or two of driving in our own dust cloud before we reached the accommodation area, a tented compound surrounded by Hesco Bastion barriers. The Portakabin luxury we'd known briefly at KAF was markedly absent but, on the plus side, so was the stink of shit. Bastion was still in its infancy and very austere.

After dropping our kit off in our tent, Billy and I walked over to the north side of the compound, past a couple of Paras manning a gap in a Hesco Bastion wall, and entered the Joint Operations Cell. The JOC was run by the 3 Para CO, Lieutenant Colonel Stuart

Tootal, a short, wiry man with several masters degrees under his belt and, rumour had it, a PhD or two for good measure. Tootal was passionate about the men under his charge and just as determined to fulfil his mission in Afghanistan.

The JOC was a very long tent with a walkway down either side. Men and women in uniform sat at long tables staring at computers, some with their heads jammed to radio handsets. Every unit operating in Helmand, including ours, had a desk here. During an operation, Major Black would move into the JOC and act as liaison between us and Tootal.

One of the most important areas in the JOC – Billy pointed to two adjacent positions on his left – was given over to the JTACs, the 'Widow' callsigns who acted as liaison for air operations. The JTACs out in the field had a special radio for communicating back to this Widow Tactical Operations Cell (TOC), Billy explained, and this was the hub, where it all happened. He directed my attention to some large tables in the middle of the room, covered in maps that depicted the Helmand Area of Responsibility (AOR). The maps were covered with plastic laminate and ringed in places by red chinagraph.

'ROZs,' Billy said pointing to the Restricted Operating Zones. 'If the shit hits the fan and there's a battle, no one is allowed to enter a ROZ without permission from the relevant JTAC on the ground. The JTACs are all-important. Without them, nothing would happen here.'

I noticed that there was a large red ring over Now Zad.

'It looks like something's going down there,' I said. Several members of Tootal's staff seemed to be paying particular attention to the place.

'After the trouble a few weeks back, there are persistent rumours that the Taliban are going to strike at Now Zad next,' Billy said. 'When I ask anyone who should be in a position to know, they shrug and give me the brush-off, which means, almost certainly, that the rumours are true. B Company 3 Para moved into Now Zad about a week ago and found the place deserted. Everybody had buggered off, including the ANP.'

If the Afghan National Police had left, it was a fair indication of trouble.

I thought back to my time in Northern Ireland, to the indicators I'd been trained to look for – dumper trucks parked where they shouldn't have been; a dustbin out on a non-collection day; upper windows open to prevent them being blown in by the pressure wave of an explosion; kids not out playing when they should be ...

Here we go again, I thought.

We left the JOC and walked next door. The 'JHF(A) Forward' was our Ops centre, known to us as the 'Ops tent'. There was a desk manned by a corporal where visitors checked in and out. Otherwise, it looked like a smaller version of the JOC. There was a desk for the OC, Major Black, a desk for the Ops Officer, a couple of positions for our signallers and watchkeepers and a few other spare desks for people like us to use when we needed them. In the middle, again, were two tables, one given over to a 1:50,000 map of Helmand, the other to aviation maps of Afghanistan.

Two-thirds of the way down the tent was a screen – a large white board that separated the operations area of the Ops tent from the administration area. The admin area, Billy explained, also doubled as a place where pilots on readiness could hang out, away from the frenetic activity that would kick off next door if and when the shit hit the fan.

In the corner, a flat-screen TV was tuned to Sky News – quite how, I didn't know. On a table next to the TV was a laptop where we could send and receive emails to and from home and pull data from the internet. On the opposite side of the tent were two mission planning stations – computers where we could sit down and map out our sorties.

Mission planning had reached new heights with the Apache. Everything from weapon parameters to frequencies and codewords was input into the laptop before we flew. Once we were happy with the way the mission looked, we pressed 'save', downloaded the data to a data transfer cartridge then took it down to the aircraft and plugged it in. The mission was then uploaded into the Apache's own computer and we were ready to fly.

After the Ops tent, Billy led me back to 'tent city' where we went and grabbed some nosh from the 'Para kitchen'. The Regimental Sergeant Major of 3 Para, flanked by a couple of burly mates, was checking to ensure that everyone washed their hands with anti-bacterial scrub before they sat down to eat. It was like being back at school. But Bastion was such a tight ship, and so stretched, Billy explained, that nobody could afford a bunch of rogue e-coli to sweep through the camp. And the capacity for transmission of this or any other disease was breathtaking, as I was about to find out.

It had been hot in the JOC and the JHF(A), but the cookhouse felt like a sauna. The heat was so bad that people came in, grabbed their food, sat down, shovelled it into their mouths and left. I don't sweat easily – it's not something I do even when out running – but in less than a minute at the table, I was drenched. Rivulets ran down my arms and onto my plate. My plastic bucket chair was like a swimming pool. It didn't take me long to figure out why nobody hung around to chat. I did what everybody else did: stuffed my meal into my mouth and got off and out – total elapsed time, three minutes. Talk about fast food.

Our tent, my new bedroom, was fifteen feet wide and thirty long and filled with eight camp beds: four on the right and four on the left. A giant plastic duct pumped cool air in from a huge exterior air-conditioning unit, but it was fighting a losing battle against the heat. The talcum-like dust – that had so nearly done for me during my landing – covered everything.

After my various exertions, I was exhausted. I took a shower, threw my sleeping bag on my cot and crashed out, my head buzzing with thoughts of the 'bag' and dust-outs; so much so that I found myself dreaming about an Apache flight in which Billy had been replaced by my old instructor, Chopper Palmer. Palmer was bollocking me for the way I was attempting to land my aircraft in a dust-out. While I was trying to concentrate, Chopper reached forward and shook me by the shoulder, which was fucking annoying because I was trying to concentrate on not killing us. But still he kept on shaking ...

I opened my eyes and there was Billy.

'Ed,' he said, slightly freaked, no doubt, by the wild look in my eyes. 'We've got to get on back to the JOC. Now.'

'Why?' I said, wiping away the thin film of dust that had settled on my face in the couple of hours I'd been asleep.

'The mission's on,' Billy said. 'It's Now Zad.'

THE 7 PS

FRIDAY, 2 JUNE 2006
Camp Bastion, Afghanistan

Billy and I headed for the duties board with a spring in our step. We'd heard whispers about the upcoming operation over the past few days, and been told we'd be on a deliberate mission.

Sure enough, Op Mutay was up there, lined up for the fourth. But our flight was marked HRF and IRT. We'd be on standby; we'd been taken off the mission.

As Helmand Reaction Force and Incident Response Team we needed to be ready for anything, and that included supporting the Deliberate Ops Apache pair. We'd be the next to fly, responsible for replacing Pat and his crews if needed. How on earth could we do that if we'd been kept in the dark?

Pat told us it was because we weren't a constituted flight – we hadn't operated together. The OC had his two flights up and running, under Pat and Dan. He wanted to keep it that way because they'd know what they were doing.

'Why do you need constituted flights?' I asked.

Pat shrugged. 'Flight procedure.'

Billy beat me to it. 'There's no such thing.'

www.harperplus.com/hellfire

He wasn't wrong. The only flight procedure was that any one of us could jump into any aircraft with any wingman and mesh in seamlessly. Pilots were matched in an aircraft and kept together until they operated as one, but periodic changeovers stopped errors creeping in.

'Well, our flights are constituted,' Pat insisted. 'We've practised together.'

I couldn't believe what I was hearing. They'd flown together on a handful of missions in Afghanistan, that was all. We'd trained together for years.

We left, knowing only that Op Mutay would take place around Now Zad. Even the broadest brushstrokes were being kept secret from other aircrew.

The alarm bells kept ringing in my head. I turned to Billy and Jon. 'What if it goes tits up and the rest of us have to step in?' We hadn't been here long and only had four Apaches up and running.

Keeping the circle of knowledge to a minimum was normal and necessary. A lot of locals worked at Camp Bastion. The Taliban could infiltrate their ranks, or intimidate them into handing over information. That was why we only ever discussed a mission in the secure Ops tents and briefing areas.

The OC and Pat – who commanded the only Apache flight designated to the mission – had taken this to extremes. They had attended the preliminary mission orders along with Dickie Bonn, the new Operations Officer, and decided not to allow any other crews into the planning process.

We discovered that confirmatory orders were going to be at 0700 on the morning of the mission – two days' time – and knew we had to be there.

This was going to be 3 Para's – but more importantly to us, the British Apaches' – first ever deliberate operation in Afghanistan. We'd spent over two and a half years training for this, and by hook or by crook, we'd have what it took to make it work.

Back at the tent, 3 Flight's lights were out. A quick shower and I was into my doss bag on my camp cot. It wasn't particularly comfortable, but then again, I wasn't in the pissing rain in the middle of Dartmoor in December with a hunter force tracking me down with dogs and dragging me away for interrogation.

When the artillery temporarily eased up my mind still wouldn't let me sleep. I'd been plagued by the fear of failure or rejection all my life; I didn't want to be remembered as one of the bumbling idiots that fucked up our very first mission. Worse still, if we left a gap in the support to 3 Para and someone died we'd be dismissed as a shambles and never be trusted again. If the papers got hold of the details the whole Apache programme would be seen as a big white elephant.

Billy and I skipped breakfast the next morning and headed over to the Ops tent for a coffee. We had an escort mission – to insert the Gurkhas into Now Zad – but when we weren't flying we kept pushing.

We finally decided to brief for the operation ourselves, late in the evening when the Ops room was quiet. We knew jack shit, but we could at least do a detailed map recce, and settle on a strategy if everything did go pear-shaped.

We crisis-planned. We went through all the what ifs. What if one of them was sick in the morning? What if the plan changed and they needed four Apaches? What if they crashed on departure, en route, in the target area or returning to base? What if they got low on fuel and 3 Para were in a firefight? We planned for every eventuality we could think of.

We were in the Ops tent bang on time the following morning. I'd had nightmares about not being able to start the Apache, about the CO of 3 Para shouting through the cockpit window that it was my fault his men were bleeding to death in Now Zad.

The boss barked, '3 Flight we need to get over for the JMB now.'

We asked our Ops Officer yet again if we could attend the Joint Mission Brief. Dickie Bonn finally relented; we could squeeze in if there was room.

We were off before he finished speaking. We didn't even have time to make a brew.

The tent was packed and stiflingly hot. The briefing team stood in front of an array of maps and satellite photography. Most of the guys were seated, but for late arrivals and the officially uninvited it was standing room only, at the very back.

The 3 Para Ops Officer began the orders. The mission was a cordon and search operation of a known Taliban house and grounds. The commander of the operation was Lieutenant Colonel Tootal. The CO was an extremely astute man. He had delegated mission command to the lead Chinook for the insertion and extraction phases. The lead Chinook callsign, Hardwood Two Five, was captained by Nichol Benzie, a polite, dark-haired, highly capable naval lieutenant.

'The Taliban commander is located at grid Papa-Romeo Four-Zero-One Eight-Six-Three. That's Papa-Romeo Four-Zero-One Eight-Six-Three in Now Zad.'

The Ops Officer pointed to a satellite photograph – a house approximately twelve feet high, with ten-foot walls around the perimeter. The target was using it as a bomb-making factory. It was also a safe house for local fighters and an arms cache.

He and his associates were likely to have small arms and RPGs.

The 3 Para battlegroup was to fly into the Green Zone east of Now Zad, under the shadow of the mountain spine, between the town and the main wadi. It would use four Chinooks to land in three sites at exactly 1100 hours.

The first LS, codenamed Green One, was just to the north of the house. The second, Green Two, was one field to its south-west, and

Green Three one field to the south. There were four alternative LSs further from the target in case it was too hot or unacceptable to the crews following a 'boiling' call.

'Meanwhile,' the Ops Officer said, 'the troops in Now Zad DC will have moved out in their WMIKs to collect Haji Muhammadzai, the District Chief of Police.'

He'd only find out what was happening as the troops touched down on the LSs, so no warnings would be sent to the occupants by anyone. As they set up a cordon around the grounds, he'd be driven to the house by the troops from the DC, arriving before we went into the compound to confirm that the search and lift was done in a dignified manner with no harassment to any locals. Other troops from the 3 Para battlegroup would have secured the perimeter to ensure that no Taliban escaped and no reinforcements could infiltrate the target area.

The Patrols Platoon was going to move into and block the western side of the Green Zone. They had two JTACs, callsign Widow Seven Zero, qualified to bring in air support and with a secure radio giving direct communications to the jets.

The Ops Officer tapped a map with a long wooden pointer with an orange tip. 'Ten Platoon of the Royal Gurkha Regiment positioned themselves in the DC yesterday and are going to secure the eastern perimeter. They are going to route north initially, under the normal watchful eye of the Apaches, to give any Taliban dickers the impression that this is a routine patrol.'

If they came under any trouble they'd get Widow Seven Three to command the air support onto the target. It was becoming pretty obvious that 3 Para's offensive support would be from whatever fast air they had on standby while the Apaches took a back seat.

Nichol took over for the aircrew brief when 3 Para's second in command (2i/c) had done his bit. The Chinooks would be supported by 3 Flight. Pat was flying with Tony in Wildman Five Two and Chris with Carl in Five Three.

I looked at the other three invisibles standing alongside me. I still found it hard to understand why we weren't officially part of the briefing and there was no mention of Apache contingencies.

'Deconfliction: the Apaches will operate below 5,000 feet over the target until their fuel has been used up. After the drop-off the Chinooks will hold *not below* 5,000 feet.'

'Plan: on arrival the Apaches are to assess the target and LSs. If they think the LSs are hot – under imminent threat or under fire – they will give the codeword "boiling" to the Chinooks. If the LSs are cold – no threat and safe to land – they will give the codeword "freezing".'

'If the Apaches are in contact when the Chinooks arrive the Apache crews will give the codeword "sausage" followed by either One, Two, Three or Four, depending upon which sector they are engaging into. The Chinooks will then be able to adjust their flight profile and route, choosing the best sector to approach and depart without the fear of flying into the Apaches' fire.'

'Let's go sausage side and give them what's for!' was the age-old Tommy refrain when doing battle with their wurst-loving German enemy.

'Once the Chinooks have deposited 3 Para they will lift, egress the target area and hold above 5,000 feet for the guys to get in, find their man, search the place and call for their pick up. If the operation is taking longer than expected they will return to Bastion and wait on thirty minutes' notice to move for a call to collect the troops.

'If all goes to plan, the Apaches will cover the Chinooks in low level and then provide protection to us, finally returning to Bastion where they will wait with us on thirty minutes' notice to move, ready to escort us back in.'

I couldn't help smiling. Unlike us, the Chinook crowd could switch off their machines, go and have a drink in their air-conditioned tent, and still be off the ground within thirty minutes of the shout.

Apache crews wouldn't get out of their aircraft. They'd be on the Auxiliary Power Unit, main engines off but with all systems running, ready to go. The APU hardly used any fuel, so time was on our side. I'd once sat in the bird for six hours without taking off, my arse as numb as a dead man's.

It was swings and roundabouts, though. The Apache was air-conditioned and generally very comfortable to fly; the Chinook was boiling hot inside and filled with dust and sand.

Jon gave me a nudge as Nichol concluded with the extraction details. 'It looks to me as if the Apaches are only trusted to escort Chinooks.'

I nodded. If it all went to ratshit it would be the Jet Jocks that would be mixing things up with the Taliban.

Our Intelligence Officer stepped up to the plate and briefed us on the specific threats to aircrew – which basically amounted to Stingers and an anti-aircraft gun that had been sighted in the area. 'If the reports are true, it'll be fitted to the back of a pick-up truck. This weapon system *is* a significant threat, especially if the operator is competent. Better have the radar ready to detect vehicles.'

Most of the operational detail had been thrashed out in our absence over the last couple of days, but I reckoned we'd now picked up enough to allow us to take over if all went tits-up.

At the end of the brief I brought up the million-dollar question: what was deemed 'hot' and 'not'? Hostile fire would be obvious, but what if there were male adults – or of mixed ages – in the tree lines or the general area, with or without weapons?

We decided that there were four different levels of 'hot' – but knew that only Nichol could make the LS call.

*   *   *

We went and had a brew then corralled Dickie Bonn again.

We needed to know what would happen if one of the Apaches had a malfunction prior to arriving at Now Zad. Would the whole mission be postponed until its crew came back and changed aircraft? That would mean forty minutes in transit, twenty to swap aircraft and a further thirty to get it started – an hour and thirty minutes in total, assuming no snags. If the mission went ahead in the meantime, who would give the boys on the ground their Intimate Support? If we'd been read into the mission (fully briefed, prepared and ready to fly) we could be on the APU, waiting to go, a mere twenty minutes from being on station.

Worse still, what would happen if they got shot down and couldn't return to the fight? Would they be sending out an unbriefed crew?

Dickie promised he'd have another word with the boss – when the boss had a minute to spare.

Nick was the squadron pin-up. He'd graduated from university, then Sandhurst, joined the Army Air Corps, and gone straight onto the pilot's course. From there he'd been streamed directly onto Apache CTT1 and joined 656 Squadron. He was young, energetic, infuriatingly good-looking, and an enthusiastic and highly capable aviator.

He was to command our flight during this mission, despite being our least experienced pilot. It was the way the AAC worked. Jon – who had thousands of flying hours – would captain the aircraft from the back seat. While the commander was responsible for the success of the mission, the captain was responsible for the safe conduct of the sortie and the safety of the airframe and crew.

Jon had been a tank commander before training on the Lynx. His ability to interpret a battlefield was second to none, making him the perfect person to show Nick the ropes – even if he hadn't been in combat with the Apache before. He was also our SupFAC.

Supervisory Forward Air Controllers trained and coached the squadron's pilots in the art of controlling fast jets and guiding their bombs onto targets.

Their callsign was Wildman Five Zero, and they were currently part of the IRT. If there was an incident in our AOR – in this case Helmand province – a road traffic accident, mine strike, injured personnel or even a compassionate case that needed to return home to their family, the IRT would respond. A Chinook did the ferrying while the Apache provided support. If the location the Chinook was bound for was deemed hostile, the second Apache, the HRF cab, would also go.

Apaches in combat were always flown in pairs – or more – for mutual support. Billy and I were in Wildman Five One.

Billy was the most experienced Apache pilot in the squadron, with more than twice as many Apache hours as any other pilot when we turned up in Afghanistan. Originally from the Royal Corps of Transport, he'd been driving vehicles on the ground and in the air for the best part of twenty years. He was qualified to fly both seats, and did so with immense gusto. Today he was captaining from the rear while I'd command from the front.

But for the time being we just had to sit it out.

Billy turned to me and said, 'Do you think we'll get away without firing a shot?'

I shook my head. 'When was the last time you saw a plan surviving contact with the enemy? Prior preparation and planning …'

'… prevents a piss poor performance,' Jonny kicked a stone across the ground in front of him. 'The seven Ps. Let's hope you're wrong.'

With just over an hour to go the mission timings slipped by an hour; 3 Para would now land in Now Zad at midday. We still didn't have access to the spot maps of the area, the callsigns, the positions of the troops on the ground or the Chinooks and the fast air above.

We begged to at least be on the APU.

The answer was still no – if we were needed, we'd be given everything we'd requested 'in sufficient time'.

3 Flight walked to their Apaches at 1030 hours.

We'd run out of road. We were into crisis management at the slightest deviation from the plan.

GO-GO-GO

SUNDAY, 4 JUNE 2006
Camp Bastion, Afghanistan

1030 hours local
10 Platoon D Company RGR leave Now Zad DC heading north towards Haji Muhammadzai's residence in WMIK and Pinzgauer vehicles. There are thirty Brits and ten ANP in the convoy. After collection they are to continue to secure the eastern perimeter of the target by the wadi.

1115 hours
Patrols Platoon depart on their way to secure the western perimeter of the target to prevent the Taliban from reinforcing and to capture or kill any insurgents attempting to escape.

1120 hours
10 Platoon is contacted in a wadi just to the north of Now Zad, way short of Ali Za'I where they are supposed to inform Haji Muhammadzai of the planned cordon and search op. They are pinned down and can't get back into their vehicles. The firefight becomes a furious battle in which they are fighting for their lives in true Gurkha fashion.

1130 hours
Patrols Platoon is in a fierce firefight in close country, totally unsuited to their vehicles. They too are trapped and fighting for their lives.

Two Apaches headed for Now Zad from Camp Bastion at 1130 hours on the dot, with no idea of what lay ahead. Exactly five minutes later, the Chinooks took off with the first elements of 3 Para on board.

The battle was being run from the 3 Para Ops tent – the JOC – so we could only listen to 3 Flight's transmissions in our own Ops tent. And their scant sitreps gave us little sense of the full battle. Worse still, the CO 3 Para would be flying high above Now Zad, and the Chinooks' insecure radios would only transmit when absolutely necessary for fear of compromise.

The mountains around Now Zad and the distance between us meant that even if we tuned into the ground troops' frequency, we wouldn't be able to hear a thing. The Apaches had good comms back because of their altitude.

We gathered round the radio operator to pick up whatever crumbs we could.

The air-conditioning pipe was on overdrive but the tent was roasting. It was like trying to chill a bucket of warm beer with an ice cube.

The first we heard back from them was that they had arrived on station. The place looked quiet. It wouldn't take long to discover how wrong they were.

1155 hours

A Company's 2 Platoon, the Engineer search teams and the A Company HQs led by Major Will Pike land in two Chinooks 100 metres to the north-east of the target on the intended LS and come under contact immediately. Their JTAC is Widow Seven Two.

*A Company's 1 Platoon land in their Chinook 350 metres west of their
intended LS just east of the alternate LS, Green 6. They come under
horrendous fire and have to fight through the Taliban's defensive positions to stay alive. Once they get the situation under control they still
have to make their way to the target compound, which entails climbing walls with ladders and trudging through swampy irrigation
ditches under fire.*

*CO 3 Para remains airborne to direct the battle from above, protected
by the two Apaches of 3 Flight.*

1200 hours
*3 Flight orientate and try to locate all the troops. It's mayhem on the
ground and the CO instructs them to assist his men in returning some
semblance of order to his plan.*

*3 Flight are called by Widow Seven Zero to help Patrols Platoon break
clean from the enemy. 3 Flight pour 30 mm into the warren of alleyways. Patrols Platoon are hugely grateful for the respite in enemy
action and break clear after forty-five minutes of hell in what they'd
thought was going to be a never-ending firefight.*

1205 hours
'Providing covering fire,' Chris called.

It must have been madness on the Mission Net because he was
speaking to Pat on the Apaches' inter-aircraft frequency. They
couldn't follow transmissions from Bastion on this one, but for us
to be able to hear them was a real bonus.

'I can't see into the compound they said the firing is coming
from,' Chris said. 'I'm going to fire a witness burst into the next
field.'

At that point we knew they had joined the fight.

We listened intently for any sign that we should be cranking up the next brace of aircraft. The boss was following the battle in the JOC next door. We tried to get in but it was already heaving. He told us to wait in our Ops room.

Everyone gathered in our tent to find out what was happening. After two and a half years of hard sweat the squadron was finally doing what it had trained to do. We'd been bashing our heads against a brick wall for the last few days, and were bursting to join the fight. The ground crews wanted to load up Apaches and welcome them back empty. The signallers wanted sitreps to pass onto command and the techs wanted to patch up bullet holes and send the gunships back into the ring.

The next voice we heard was Pat's. He was picking off Taliban in the alleyways of Now Zad.

Jon and I exchanged a glance. I grabbed Dickie Bonn. He reached for the phone and spoke to the OC. 'Suggest we stand to, sir.'

The OC instructed us to wait. 'The battle's being run from Now Zad and a stand-to hasn't been requested,' Dickie relayed.

'No one in Now Zad's going to be thinking about this. We need to—'

Pat interrupted my gripe over the loudspeaker.

'Wildman Five Two. Sitrep as at twelve-twelve hours. Taliban contacts all over the place. Engaging to the south-west of the target area. Out.'

A quick glance at Jon and Billy and I could see they were as uncomfortable as I was that we were still in the Ops tent.

Jon could never remain motionless at the best of times, he just physically couldn't. When he was standing, his hands were always tapping or altering the position of anything within reach. When he sat, he constantly lifted his heel and flexed his toes. Even when he was in his camp cot in complete darkness I could still hear him twitching in time with the music from his iPod. At least I hoped that's what it was.

He was tap dancing like Gene Kelly right now, and checking the time every sixty seconds. I wasn't much better. My watch was closer to my nose than it was to my wrist. If I bellyached, bleated, commented, complained, griped, grumbled, objected, protested, remarked, whined or whinged one more time, I would officially become the Grumpy Old Man of 656.

Over the Common Tactical Air Frequency (CTAF) we heard, 'Wildman Five Two this is Saxon Ops. Send endurance. Over.'

I nearly gave him a round of applause. There was no reply to the boss's request, but we knew how much gas 3 Flight had; we needed to move.

We were dying to get out and mix it up with the Taliban. And if we weren't scrambled soon the boys on the ground would end up taking casualties.

Both Apaches were now involved in separate contacts. The place seemed to have gone berserk.

Billy had finally had enough. He went up to Dickie Bonn. 'Look, we've got to mount up and we've got to have the spot and target maps. We need to walk *now*.'

I nodded. 'It'll take us ten minutes just to reach the aircraft and get in, and a minimum of thirty to start it up.' On top of that, I told him, Now Zad was a twenty-minute flight away and it'd take us another ten minutes to RIP (Relief In Place) so the boys received seamless firepower from the Apaches.

'Pat and his men should be breaking station at about 1330,' Billy said. 'That means we need to lift at 1300 latest.'

Dickie tried again but we were told to wait.

1230 hours

*1 Platoon has managed to link up with A Company HQs and 2
Platoon. The target is now quiet and they set about searching the
empty property.*

*The Gurkhas are holding the enemy firm but 3 Flight are called by
Widow Seven Three to assist in 10 Platoon's recovery to their vehicles
and extraction. Protected by a shower of 30 mm rain, the Gurkhas
return to the Now Zad DC.*

Billy was beside himself with frustration. Jon looked close to
exploding. Nick was thumbing through *FHM* and letting us know
that we worried too much.

1258 hours

Major Black came running into our Ops tent. He went straight to
the signaller. 'I want to know 3 Flight's endurance.'

He turned to us. 'How long until you're ready?'

He hadn't once warned us to be ready. But he wanted us to go
and he wanted us to go now.

We were the IRT and HRF crews on thirty minutes' notice to
move so he could have answered his own question.

Nick – until that moment preoccupied with the challenge of
tautening his torso in twenty-eight days – gave a pretty convincing
impression of a coiled spring. 'We *are* ready; we just need spot maps
and a detailed brief.'

Smart of him to step in before one of us exploded.

The OC's reply made our jaws drop. 'There aren't any left.'

The red mist descended in front of my eyes. In the time we
had spent waiting we could have had a couple of sets made up.
We would be the only players on the battlefield not having a clue
what anyone meant. We were going to look like a bunch of

complete twats. Jon dragged me away a second before I went into meltdown.

As we ran out of the tent we heard the signaller shout, 'Sir, they need to pull off at thirteen-thirty.'

We weren't going to make that, and I hoped the Taliban weren't listening because 3 Para were about thirty minutes away from having no Intimate Support.

We sprinted for our Land Rover.

'Fuck the RIP,' Jon shouted. 'Let's just get off the ground quick. We need to be in the air by 1310.'

1303 hours

My head whacked the roof of the Land Rover with one hell of a thump then I was thrust violently back onto my seat. The engine was revving so fiercely I could barely hear myself think. The door wouldn't close properly and dust filled the cramped space. I was thrown to one side, and before I could protect myself I was lifted clear of the seat and my head hit a large nut on the underside of the roof bars. This time it really did hurt and I was seeing stars.

'For fuck's sake,' I snapped at whoever was driving in the front with Nick, 'I know we're in a hurry, but I want to get there in one piece.'

The outside temperature was ludicrously high and it had turned our hard-topped Land Rover into a furnace.

To add insult to injury, Billy and Jon were laughing like drains.

I felt the lump on top of my head and wished my hair wasn't shaved so close to the bone. A thick pelt of hair might not have cushioned the blow, but it would have soaked up some of the blood.

My eyes were watering and the dust swirling around the cabin clung gratefully to any available moisture. I must have looked like a clown.

A few seconds later, Jon was catapulted upwards and cracked his head on the bare steel.

'What goes around comes around, Jonny boy.'

We all burst out laughing. The tension was immediately released; and boy, did it need to be.

There was no made-up road from the Ops tent to the helicopter LS; it was just a stretch of desert that now resembled a mogul field. Each time a heavy vehicle transited round the outside of the camp, it carved an ever-deepening track into the compacted sand. It made for one hell of a ride.

We'd debated the best way to cross this sea of ruts last night.

'I've done shit loads of off-road driving,' I boasted. 'Jungles, deserts, savannah, bush, you name it. The best way across is to go max chat.'

Jon took a more methodical approach. 'If you go really slowly the vehicle will last longer.' He had a calmer variation on most themes. As an ex-tanky, he didn't fancy fixing another vehicle in a hurry.

I disagreed. 'A fast rattle and a few sharp bumps are kinder to the vehicle than huge changes of angle or bashes against the rocks – not to mention the risk of getting stuck.'

Jon's min-speed theory was definitely not going to be tested on this occasion because 3 Para were being shot to bits by the Taliban and we needed to expedite.

Unfortunately, months of traffic had turned the fine sand to talcum powder and the breeze was coming from behind us at its usual 10–15 mph. We needed to drive faster than the wind to prevent being engulfed. Driving blind, unable to see the end of the bonnet when there was around 200 million pounds' worth of helicopters strewn all over the HLS, was unthinkable. So was driving over two-foot-high speed bumps at 20 mph, but the choice was simple: hold on.

The Land Rover came to a sharp but spongy stop. We waited a couple of seconds for the dust to settle before running the final forty metres to the Apaches.

I took the first available opportunity to cough up a lungful of dust. The light wind blew some of the remaining powder from my body, but it was too hot to cool me down.

1308 hours

Taff, the Arming and Loading Point Commander, was ready and waiting. The ALPC was in charge of the Apache all the time it was on the ground, even when the aircrew were onboard. It was his responsibility to load and unload all its weapons and fuel, and to check that the aircraft was safe during starting and shutdown. The helicopter was under his safe and ever-watchful eye until he disconnected his intercom lead from the wing.

Taff had a big smile, an eight-man arming team, many thousands of cannon rounds, hundreds of rockets, over twenty missiles, two Apache pilots and over forty million pounds' worth of helicopter under his command and control. It was a lot of responsibility for a corporal who got paid the same as our squadron clerk.

'All the blanks are out and the tee-fifty pin is stowed, sir.'

The small metal T50 pin sat under a cover on the Apache's nose, just in front of the co-pilot gunner's window. It had a long red and white flag attached to make sure we didn't take off with it still in place. With the pin removed, the yellow-and-black, dog-bone shaped initiation device – the same as the ones in both cockpits – was automatically armed. Their job was to initiate the detonation cord threaded round the side windows, blasting both canopies fifty metres. In an emergency, it would be Taff's job to initiate the explosion if we couldn't.

Billy yelled his thanks.

'I'm going in the front, Ed – jump in and get her started.'

Billy began to run round the Apache checking that all the blanks that kept dust and debris from every orifice had been removed and she was ready to fly.

I was still trying to take in what he'd said. We had fully briefed the mission, monitored whatever we could of the battle and authorised the flight, gearing everything towards me being in the front seat as the gunner and commander, and Billy in the back seat as the pilot and captain.

Every military flight required prior authorisation signed by both the aircraft captain and the authorising officer. It declared the exact conditions of the flight: which Apache was being flown, the flight date, who was captain, who was in which seat, which survival jacket they were wearing for escape and evasion purposes, the ETD and the ETA. It then outlined the mission: takeoff location, route, landing location, mission number, outline mission details, any limitations (like the minimum height), and if there were any fuel restrictions. If any of these details were altered, the authorising officer had to be informed and the authorising sheet amended before the flight.

I was puzzled by the late change, but the flight was on Billy's authorisation as he was captain. I wasn't in a position to order him into the back seat as briefed. I could have refused to fly until we went back to Plan A or changed our authorisation – but the time for that had long since passed. I wasn't being anal. If we got shot down, the authorisation sheet would wrongly identify which of us was where – and that could have serious repercussions in the post-crash, escape and evasion phase.

I knew Billy would have some reasonable justification – but that didn't stop me wondering if he just wanted to go in the front so he could do the shooting. Either way, there was no time to argue. We needed to get off the ground asap, then tell Ops and have the appropriate discussion when we got back.

It was only early summer, but the weather was unbelievably hot and taking its toll on our troops. Everyday tasks appeared a hundred times more difficult and ten times slower to perform. The sun only seemed to have one goal – to punish us for being somewhere we couldn't call home.

My combats were already damp with sweat and clung uncomfortably to my body. As I climbed up the blisteringly hot skin of the starboard side of the aircraft I noticed that Billy was also struggling. Grape-sized beads of sweat tumbled down his face, which was contorted with concentration.

I felt much older than my forty years in this heat, but my brain felt like an eighteen-year-old's, buzzing with adrenalin and fired up by the prospect of the impending battle. I knew Billy felt the same; we didn't need to discuss it. We were both WO1s and had a shit-load of military experience between us.

656 Squadron Army Air Corps was the first and currently the only Apache squadron in the British Forces capable of deploying to a combat zone. We lived to outwit the enemy and survive to fight another day. It was utterly addictive and nothing could compare to it. At that moment I genuinely believed it would be better to die today at the hands of the Taliban than to rot into old age, swapping war stories in my retirement home.

Today would be fun.

I heaved open the door and clicked it into place above the entrance to the rear cockpit. I stretched across, inserted the ignition key and twisted it to On.

The beast began to stir as it sucked life from the battery and the relays kicked over. The Up Front Display sparked up and confirmed that there was full fuel – no faults so far.

The UFD also had a digital clock fed by two GPSs:

13:10:08 … 13:10:09 … 13:10:10 …

LATE

SUNDAY, 4 JUNE 2006

1310 hours local
CO 3 Para lands in his Chinook at the now quiet and well-protected target compound. He orders Patrols Platoon to get out of the close country and move south-west to more open ground where they can employ their .50 cals without the restrictions of alleyways and orchards.

Still kneeling beside the cockpit, I bellowed, 'Pylons … stabilator … APU clear?'

We were now officially late. I hoped 3 Flight could push their fuel a bit longer.

Taff checked there was no one near the weapons pylons, the slab-like stabilator, or within range of the hot exhaust gases the Auxiliary Power Unit would be spitting out very shortly.

In his broad Welsh accent he reported back, 'Pylons, stabilator and APU clear – clear to start the APU.'

The APU was the Apache's third engine, only used to get all the systems up and running and to provide compressed air with which to start the main engines.

Back in the UK it used to take us about an hour to start an Apache and be ready to taxi. It could take as little as forty-five minutes if you cut corners and all went well. Out here, in a rush, on a good day, with no snags and if the TADS cooled quickly enough, it could be done in as little as twenty minutes, but between thirty and forty was more usual. With the APU running, to all intents and purposes the Apache was ready to go. We could sort out any problems and get the TADS and PNVS ice cold so it could see properly. All we needed to do then was switch on the main engines and pull power – a two-minute job.

Stretching back across the cockpit I lifted a small clear cover and pushed the recessed button beneath it. The APU was startled into life. Within a few seconds the acronym on the button glowed green, and it was soon screaming away at full power.

I flipped my helmet onto my head, making sure my ears weren't folded, and then buttoned the chinstrap tight. A bent ear now would drive me to distraction later.

I grimaced as the internal harness pushed down on the weeping egg on the top of my head.

I dragged my life-support jacket from my seat and pulled it on. It felt cumbersome and tight as I zipped it up, and became even more uncomfortable when I slipped a triangular armoured plate into the sheath on the front.

The 'chicken plate' was designed to shield the vital organs within the chest cavity from bullets and shrapnel. As I pulled up the outer zip holding it in place, it pressed heavily on my bladder, making me even more uncomfortable and irritable than before.

It fitted so tightly that it was impossible to take an extra-deep breath. But if it were slacker it would become a snag hazard if I had to be dragged from the cockpit in an emergency. I tried to look on the bright side: it would stop my organs spilling out if I were shot. The pressure would stem the flow of blood and keep me conscious for a few more valuable seconds.

The heat was getting to me good style; I could actually smell it. The cockpit stank like a workshop. The wiring, glues, resins, metals and a whole host of other materials came under immense temperatures in the glass cocoon.

I took hold of the grab handles above the seat and pulled myself inside, arching my back so I didn't catch the magazine jutting from my stubby carbine clipped to the right side of the seat.

I adjusted the position of the pistol strapped to my right thigh and began to clip on the five-point harness that would save my life in the event of a crash. You couldn't help but feel a moment of omnipotence in the rear seat of an Apache on operations – master of a £46 million boy's toy with everything you needed at your fingertips, elevated above your surroundings, looking down on everyone working their arses off to get you into the air.

1313 hours

'*Bastard!*' I let go of the cyclic stick and winced.

I made a mental note for the second time in as many weeks: do not touch black objects in the Apache until you've put on your fucking gloves. To add insult to injury I'd smacked my funny-bone on the carbine magazine as I pulled away. Taff grinned like a maniac and held up his hand. He sported a cracker of a blister on his palm that made mine look pathetic.

I strapped my black brain to my left thigh and opened it to read the A5 mission information sheet. The brain also contained vital operating information. Not everything could be committed to memory.

I grabbed a fresh sheet of paper, ready to scribble vital grids in the heat of battle.

The web between the thumb and forefinger of my right hand had whitened; I could already see the beginnings of a blister. I wondered what temperature the cyclic must have been after baking in the midday sun.

The heat in the cockpit was still insufferable. Every breath seared my nasal passages. It was the hottest part of the day; the sun sat directly above me and beat down through the cockpit glass, turning it into a pressure cooker.

Within a matter of seconds, the inside of my helmet was saturated with sweat; it gathered in rivulets beneath my browpad and ran into my eyes and down my nose before cascading onto the front of my survival jacket.

My eyes stung like hell, but there was no point in wiping it away. It would instantly replenish itself, and my hands were too busy sweeping around the cockpit, getting this highly complex flying computer up and running and ready for takeoff.

Taff firmly closed the cockpit door and I switched the air conditioning to fifteen degrees. It was a constant battle to bring the ambient temperature down a single degree. There was a lot of metal radiating a great deal of heat.

1315 hours
Patrols Platoon come under fire as they attempt to set off once more. 3 Flight continue in support. No sooner have they started firing than Patrols Platoon break clear and begin their move to safety again.

We spent the next fifteen minutes getting all the systems up and running. We didn't need to speak to each other. Our hands were a blur as they moved around the plethora of switches, buttons, levers and controls.

On this occasion our Apache had started swiftly and with no snags, but Nick and Jon were having severe comms problems. They could only get a single inter-aircraft radio working, which fell well short of our normal four.

In the mission critical equipment section of today's briefing we'd stated that a minimum of two radios were required for IRT/HRF, but it wasn't like they could just conjure up a spare. We only had four Apaches in-theatre, two of which were already out on the mission.

According to the rule book, Wildman Five One was the only Apache in Afghanistan capable of launching. Theoretically, the mission should have been aborted. Billy and I were unable to perform alone. We relied on each other for mutual support and to keep a seamless stream of fire. But there were guys out there on the ground depending on us. I'd rubbed up the boss too much lately; thank Christ it wasn't my decision to make. As mission commander of our pair of Apaches that weight fell squarely on Nick's perfectly formed shoulders.

His call came through the helmet earpieces.

'Wildman Five One, this is Wildman Five Zero. As I see it we don't have a choice.'

'Nick's going to abort, buddy,' I muttered to Billy. 'He doesn't have the experience to go against the abort criteria for the benefit of 3 Para.'

'I agree. He'll follow protocol.'

Nick had literally just finished his pilot's course when he joined us on our Apache conversion. He was full of enthusiasm but had zero experience.

Nick came back, 'I'd rather relay messages between us than leave the lads without cover. In the meantime, we'll try and fix the comms en route. What do you think?'

Inexperienced he might have been, but he was learning fast. We backed him to the hilt; 3 Para was in a fierce firefight and needed our support.

I replied, 'Wildman Five Zero, this is Wildman Five One. Roger that, we can talk to the ground troops.'

If their comms couldn't be fixed by the time we got there, then we'd coordinate the fire from our aircraft, directing Wildman Five Zero by the only radio they had available.

1330 hours

I blinked rapidly to flush my eyes of salt, but aggravated the lump on my head in the process.

I imagined my daughter looking at me and rolling around the place, hardly able to contain her giggles no matter how stern a face I tried to maintain, and my son reciting my overused response to him whenever he hurts himself: 'Man-up, Dad!' I smiled, misfortune forgotten.

The radios were teeming with transmissions from what sounded like the entire British Army. I could make out Chris's voice intermittently, then the same nagging question from Ops: 'How long is it going to take to get airborne?'

I wanted to yell, 'As long as it always takes, which is why we should have been here hours ago', but I managed to button my lip. At any minute now 3 Flight would be breaking station, while 3 Para were about to be deprived of Apache cover. We were pushing every envelope to get off the ground as soon as possible.

By now 3 Flight must have been down to zero combat gas – the quantity of fuel required to fight to the very last minute before returning to base direct. They must have been eating into their reserves to provide cover by now. We called it 'chicken', as in 'chickened out': the very last possible safe moment to return using a straight line, A to B, flying the glideslope from your original height to land with the very minimum fuel allowed.

If they stayed out for another twenty minutes there was a real probability they wouldn't make it home. Eat into your chicken fuel and you lost your wings for ever if the vapours in the tank didn't hold out.

I glanced across at the other Apache as our rotor blades started to spin.

What a wonderful sight: Beauty and the Beast all wrapped into one. To my eye, at least, its lean profile was beautiful. Not an inch of fat, not a superfluous nut or bolt. Everything had been designed with everything else in mind, to produce a perfect flying, killing machine. Warheads and cannon barrels bristled menacingly from its sleek, perfectly honed surfaces; just seeing one of these things coming at you was enough to chill most of our enemies to the core.

I called 'Ready' to Nick and Jon, and we got a two clicks back, two quick presses on the transmission button to indicate the message had been heard and understood and he was going to comply. We were not truly ready, but if push came to shove we were in a safe enough configuration to lift.

The air conditioning was finally winning its battle against the blistering heat and the temperature slowly dropped. Sweat no longer dribbled down my face.

It was time for the Weapon Op checks. I actioned the gun and felt the thud under my feet as its hydraulics sprang to life.

'Gun coming right, Taff,' I warned him before I turned my head. The gun had enough power to jack the Apache completely off its wheels if you looked down with your right eye without the safety in place. If I looked quickly right it could break Taff's legs.

As I moved the cannon around Taff told me where it was. 'Fully right … twelve o'clock … fully left.'

As long as it had full movement I could sort out any other possible snags in flight; the rest of the gun checks could wait. The rocket and missile launchers would have to wait until we were airborne too.

My left hand swept round the cockpit checking the switch settings while my right gripped the now much cooler cyclic. I flicked down a rocker button with my right thumb, changing the symbology being projected into my right eye to hover mode.

I repositioned the cyclic and trimmed it so that the velocity vector in my right eye was smack bang in the middle on takeoff. If I could keep it there I wouldn't need any external references to keep the aircraft over the same point. I didn't want a repeat of the drift I'd managed on landing here. I needed to trust my symbology, despite the fact that every instinct still recoiled from it.

1333 hours
We were positioned slightly ahead and to the right of Jon and Nick. We waited for them to lift first.

'Wildman Five One this is Wildman Five Zero. Ready. Lifting.'

'Copied. Will lift as soon as your dust clears.'

The blades on their Apache coned upwards and they disappeared into their own dust cloud. The vortex stopped just short of our blade tips, held back by the light wind and our rotor wash.

I watched them emerge into clear air like a giant conjuring trick.

Taff finally unplugged himself, stretched out his arms and took a good look around. Satisfied that we weren't about to climb straight into any £46 million obstacles, he lifted his arms like a cricket umpire signalling a series of sixes, giving us the signal to lift off.

As my hand moved to the collective lever, I caught the end of a conversation between the aircraft of 3 Flight. They were at chicken fuel. They had to return now or risk landing below the legal limit. I heard myself begging them to eat into it, but knew they couldn't hold out for more than another five or ten minutes even if they did.

I removed the collective friction lock with a single twist of my left hand. Keeping my head perfectly still, I glanced up at the torque reading: 21 per cent; normal with MPOG – minimum pitch applied on the ground. With my right eye still focusing on the torque reading, I watched a pinker-than-usual Taff with my left.

I raised the collective lever, pushed my left pedal down and allowed my right to come up to prevent the Apache from spinning, left eye glued on Taff and right eye on the torque reading, now counting towards 30 per cent.

I shifted my perspective between the torque and the balance ball bottom centre of the monocle. As the torque passed 31 per cent, the ball was being displaced and my right hand instinctively corrected the roll of the aircraft by adjusting the cyclic so the Apache remained upright. As my right eye tracked the ball heading towards the centre, my left saw the dust cloud beginning to build.

I must trust my symbology ...

With my right knee bent high and my left leg nearly straight my feet rotated forward, depressing the tops of both pedals simultaneously until I could hear a light thud. My left eye flicked down to confirm that the parking brake handle had retracted and then back to where Taff was still standing in front of us.

Billy completed the final checks. 'Tail wheel and parking brake?'

A quick glance at the UFD confirmed the tail wheel lock command had been selected. The green TAIL WHEEL UNLOCKED light was extinguished on the panel by my left hand. Torque was passing 50 per cent.

'Tail wheel lock selected,' I replied. 'Light out. Parking brake off and the handle is in.'

As the torque increased Taff disappeared inside a thick blanket of dust. I knew he'd be leaning forward to prevent himself being bowled over by the colossal downdraught.

Billy sat six feet in front of me and a couple feet lower. I could see straight over his head. His gloved hands took a firm grip on the handles in the roof either side of his head. He wasn't bracing himself for a bad takeoff. We were about to lose all external references, we'd have very little power, we were thirty feet from a huge stack of live ammunition – so holding tight was the best way to suppress the urge to grab the flying controls.

The torque reading nudged past 85 per cent as the wheels lightened. I couldn't see a fucking thing outside the cockpit.

My right hand made minute adjustments to the cyclic stick then pushed the trim button when the velocity vector in my right eye was central. My left hand gradually increased the pitch on the collective lever; my feet balanced the pedals, slowly correcting the balance ball and preventing the tail from spinning. My left eye tried to ignore what was happening outside the cockpit.

We were now in complete brown-out conditions. It looked like the windows had been the target of a dirty protest.

'Takeoff 1335 hours,' Billy said.

EMBARRASSINGLY LATE

SUNDAY, 4 JUNE 2006

1355 hours local

'Symbology … symbology … symbology …' I kept repeating it to myself, over and over again, like a tribal mantra to appease the helicopter god.

The heading tape was stationary in my right eye. We weren't turning or spinning. The velocity vector was centred. We weren't drifting into Taff's ammo.

The torque nudged past 96 per cent. I checked our height reading: thirty feet – just enough to be clear of obstacles. Our big problem was that we weren't climbing any higher.

My arse was telling my brain I was drifting right, towards Taff's fireworks store, but the symbology was perfect. *Trust the symbology …*

'You happy with me transitioning out of this on symbology, Billy? I have no external references, but we're clear of obstacles and I have her under control.'

Billy came back cautiously: 'Just don't over-torque it.'

That was what I wanted to hear. 'Going for it.'

With no outside references at all, the Apache was being flown solely by the symbology beamed into my right eye. With a gentle push forward and a trim, the velocity vector indicated that we were drifting forwards and not sideways – so far, so good.

Symbology … symbology … symbology …

Suddenly the radar altimeter began to count down. I couldn't see the desert floor but I knew we were heading towards it. I topped up the power with the collective until we were at maximum torque. I had nothing left to pull and we were still dropping.

The powerful, precision-built Rolls-Royce Turbomeca RTM322 engines were coping easily, but the torque they generated would rip the Apache apart if I demanded more of them.

Billy called out height and speed. 'Twenty-five feet, four knots … twenty-three feet, five knots … twenty-one feet, eight knots … Watch your torque, Ed.'

'I am.'

Billy must have been unnerved as we got dangerously close to over-torquing the aircraft. We should have been getting some translational lift by now to stop the descent and reduce the power required to fly.

'Nineteen feet, still eight knots, Ed.'

'Come on, come on – fly!'

'Twelve feet, nine knots.'

We were now below the height of the berm that had been 100 metres in front of us.

The chant continued in my head: *Please fly … symbology … symbology … symbology … please fly … please …*

There was a small waver in the tail and I knew we were passing translational lift. I had no idea how far from the berm we were. All I knew was we were forward of our takeoff point by some considerable distance.

Billy called, 'Eleven feet, eleven knots.'

The torque dropped off 5 per cent as the blades caught the cleaner airflow in front of us.

'Got it, Billy. She's flying.'

As I topped up the torque back to maximum, Billy called, 'Fifteen feet, fifteen knots ... sixteen feet, eighteen knots ... nineteen feet, twenty-two knots ...'

With the most gentle of corrections aft on the cyclic, the speed was maintained and the aircraft started to climb.

Just as Billy finished saying, 'Twenty-nine feet, twenty-eight knots', we popped out of the front of the dust cloud into a deep azure sky.

'Well done, Ed. Have you got them? I'm blind.'

'Not yet ... yes, got them – right one o'clock, 250 metres, same level.'

'Visual.'

'Your ASE, Billy,' I prompted.

A touch of the right thumb set the trims in place then I flicked the radio button. 'Saxon Ops, this is Wildman Five One. Five Zero and Five One wheels off your location now, over.'

'Saxon Ops, roger, out.'

Ops now knew exactly what time we'd taken off; they could predict what time we might need replacing if we got into a fight, and more importantly what time to start overdue proceedings if we hadn't called them or landed when we reached our endurance point.

Billy set up the Aircraft Survival Equipment so we were protected against surface-to-air missiles.

'Okay, Ed, CMDS armed.'

The ASE CMDS indicator lamp shone bright yellow.

'Armed in the rear,' I replied. 'Bring on the SAMS.'

The Apache's Counter Measures Dispensing System was now armed, its chaff and flares ready to frustrate an incoming missile.

'CMDS set to semi-automatic, your button pushes,' Billy said.

'My button pushes, ignoring everything from the camp, buddy.'

If a missile was launched against us, Bitchin' Betty would be straight on the case, telling me what it was and where it was coming from. Her voice had supposedly been chosen for its combination of firmness and reassurance, but she sounded to us like a cross between a dominatrix and a vindictive ex-wife.

In this mode, my already-busy right thumb repositioned itself over the recessed button to punch off flares if the Bitch sparked up. I'd elected to ignore the camp because each flare burnt at in excess of 1,200°C, to have her drop a fistful onto a collection of tents and fuel stores wouldn't have won us any popularity contests. I also didn't want to use up valuable kit I might need later.

We were now seventy-five feet above the desert floor, in trail with the Apache in front and the perimeter fence of Camp Bastion 200 metres behind and to our right.

'CMDS now set to automatic, Ed.'

'CMDS auto – thanks, buddy.'

A quick trim with the right thumb and we were accelerating to 120 knots, offset slightly to the right and about 500 metres behind Wildman Five Zero. If a missile came at us now, the Bitch would both alert me and pump out flares. With a bit of luck and no misfires, the greater heat source would lure it into exploding harmlessly once it had passed through the flare, leaving me free to spin the beast on her heels and take out the foolish man with the launcher on his shoulder.

I accessed the navigation page with three button pushes on my left MPD, then route information and route review. It was set up for Now Zad and my monocle display told me that – at this speed – we had eighteen minutes to arrival.

Nick called Pat to let him know.

Pat was quick to respond that he was breaking off in a few minutes because they were both fuel critical.

A picture paints a thousands words, so a Relief In Place should be conducted over the battleground and include sufficient time for every significant factor of the battle to be described and understood by the replacement crews. Most important of all was to exactly identify the locations of all friendly forces. As one pair of Apaches ceased firing, the relieving pair should be taking over the baton and engaging; a seamless transition maintained the tempo of the battle.

No chance of that now. We just had to get to Now Zad as soon as we possibly could.

Jon transmitted: 'Wildman Five One, this is Wildman Five Zero, high-high, five-five, and six-zero.'

'High-high, five-five, six-zero,' I replied.

The lead aircraft wanted us to climb to 6,000 feet. We should be okay at this height as the Chinooks had returned to base, and having them 500 feet below us should eliminate the risk of air-to-air collisions if we lost a visual lock on each other during a fight.

Billy glanced up from punching grids into the computer. 'Clear above.'

I hit a button on my left MPD and brought up the weapons page, then selected the pilot's helmet sight as my acquisition source. I could now command the Longbow Fire Control Radar to search for targets wherever I turned my head.

As we left the general flying environment and entered the battle phase, my left hand moved to the upper part of the collective, the mission grip.

My left thumb selected the FCR as my chosen sensor then switched it into radar mapping mode. The Apache began to climb. I looked to the right and pulled down on a rocker switch.

Eight feet above and four feet behind my head, the Longbow radar suddenly kicked into life. The large, Edam cheese-shaped dome began to sweep back and forth, scanning the ground along the line I was looking, searching for anything unnatural in shape up to eight kilometres away. If it detected any object that was trying to hide or didn't match the terrain it would classify it, prioritise it, and display it on my MPD and in my eye.

The unusual objects I was interested in were mopeds, cars and trucks.

The average local owned a donkey and, if they were lucky, a tractor. If he owned a car it would be a very old sedan – and he'd have been off his rocker to attempt a crossing.

There weren't that many all-terrain vehicles in this neck of the woods. To own a 4x4 or a good pick-up required money, of which only drug tsars and the Taliban weren't short.

A horizontal ticker tape appeared next to my torque reading, warning me I was reaching an engine limitation. I reduced collective power a tad to avoid buggering up the engines before I got a chance to investigate.

I adjusted the collective with my left hand to ensure I didn't blow up an engine while my right pulled the cyclic towards my groin to initiate a steeper climb. I could see Jon doing the same about 1,500 metres away. The airspeed was washing off; as it passed sixty knots I pulled the cyclic to the left. The Apache banked and changed direction.

Billy didn't look up. The front seater's primary job was to fight the aircraft. It was my job to defend it. It was no use being able to kill the enemy if we got shot down in the process.

If there was a gunner out there ready to shoot, he'd be having problems now. It may have been sixteen and a half years ago but Captain Mainwaring's words of wisdom echoed in my mind. To have any chance of hitting us, he needed to aim in front of the aircraft. If his range was correct and he estimated that his shells would take four seconds to reach us, he needed to be able to predict where we were going to be. Reducing my speed just after he fired should mean they'd pass in front of us. Climbing faster just after he fired should mean them passing below.

I'd increased the rate of ascent but slowed the Apache down. I couldn't keep slowing without becoming an easier target. He'd only have to lead me fractionally to score a direct hit. The minute I flew a constant speed, rate of climb or in the same direction, we were fucked.

I pushed forward on the stick and eased it to the right. The Apache rolled and accelerated. As the speed increased the rate of ascent decreased, but we were still climbing nicely. The distance between me and any potential gunner should be changing too, sparing me Billy's wrath as we tumbled to an almost certain conclusion with full military honours.

I swung my head rapidly from left to right, searching for gunners and SAM operators and suspicious vehicles; anyone or anything that might take a shot at us.

I was also keeping my distance from Jon. Too close together and a missile would be spoilt for choice. The Bitch would spring into action, but if the missile was fitted with a proximity fuse, it didn't even need to hit us; it would explode when it got within its prescribed distance and blow shrapnel into our airframe, blades and cockpits.

As it was, the SAM operator would be able to target only one of us. The other would be able to engage and kill him before he loosed off any more missiles.

That was the theory, anyway.

Though the Apache had a particularly low heat signature and was thus very hard to lock-on, the threat of a SAMbush – two or more operators working together – was always on my mind when we climbed or descended through their threat band.

We levelled off at 6,000 feet. I pulled in what remaining power we had until the Power Margin Indicator (PMI) warned me that I was within 10 per cent of an engine limit.

I selected the engine page on my MPD. The Number One engine on the port side was eating vigorously into its sixty-minute timer at this torque setting and Number Two on the starboard side was taking regular nibbles. Neither could be reset until we landed. Once I'd used up all sixty minutes, that power setting would not be accessible again without damaging the engines.

Did I keep the speed on and have nothing left for later? The decision was fairly straightforward on this sortie; the transit time to Now Zad was now fourteen minutes. Once there, I'd be slowing down and using less than half of what the engines could produce. For the return journey I would be a lot lighter – most of the fuel would have been burnt off – so as long as I saved twenty of my sixty-minute timers I could travel back at max chat. If they needed us somewhere else at short notice, I'd have to think again …

Fuck it. It was a no-brainer. We were going to Now Zad because our lads were being badly shot up. Nothing else in Helmand was going to be a higher priority. Not in the next few hours, anyway.

Watching the engine page like a hawk, I called, 'Head's in.'

Billy acknowledged. 'My head's out.'

Last thing we wanted was both of us looking in at the same time; that was how mid-air collisions and smacks into terra firma were triggered.

I pulled through gradually until the five-minute timers kicked off.

We couldn't eat into these without fear of retribution. If we lost an engine, we'd need the five-minute margin to touch down and save the good engine for another day. To use it up now could mean trashing the thing on landing. Not something I fancied explaining to the brass, even in an emergency.

I backed off a fraction on the collective. I was now coaxing this puppy for all it could give without going into the red.

The Apache was cruising at 132 knots fully laden with munitions and fuel at 6,000 feet when Billy called, 'Twelve minutes to run.'

North of Camp Bastion lay a huge expanse of nothingness we called the GAFA. The Great Afghan Fuck All was an ancient, rocky sea bed with a thick covering of salty sand as fine as talcum powder, saturated by the rains the last time there had been a wet season several years ago and now set solid. It was as flat as a pancake until it approached Now Zad, where the mountains began.

Nothing grew in this harsh terrain save the odd bush that had miraculously survived floods, sandstorms and salt. There was no shelter from the elements, no reason to live here even if you could. Only the nomads set up their temporary shelters here in the winter to feed the goats on the meagre green stubby bushes that popped up when the rains came. But now, in the height of summer, even the masters of survival found this place inhospitable.

No wonder they'd named it Dasht-e-Margo, the Desert of Death.

The mountains in the far north rose steeply towards the Hindu Kush, with little if any habitation away from the rivers that cut through them.

The foothills, on the other hand, had good access to water. For thousands of years they had supported life. The Afghans had once irrigated the desert for food crops, but drought had shrunk their fields by 90 per cent. Cultivated land no longer stretched far from the major river wadis before it became unsustainable.

The mountains meant the only way of travelling east or west at any speed in northern Helmand was south along the desert floor. A few miles north of Bastion was the only substantial east–west road, commonly known as Highway Zero One. The surrounding towns and villages needed to access it to get into the neighbouring provinces of Kandahar and Nimruz.

The surface was so compact there was no need to turn the steering wheel to get to Highway Zero One. You just had to point your vehicle in the direction of your destination – north or south – and drive in a straight line.

Two large hills stuck out of the desert floor in front and either side of us, like a pair of shark fins. The sea of sand just stopped at the foot of a sheer rock face which had been gouged into for shelter and to store the harvest. The big difference these days was that the caves and tunnels contained Taliban, weapons and ammunition.

As I scanned the barren, featureless landscape below us, an icon flashed across my monocle – a stationary wheeled vehicle icon 5,700 metres away, prioritised by the Forward Control Radar as the next target to shoot.

The powers-that-be had wanted to remove the Fire Control Radar to save weight. The Taliban didn't drive about in armoured vehicles and tanks, they reasoned, so it would be of no use to us. Without it, they said, we could add more weapons and achieve a better performance. I begged to disagree; the best possible performance depended upon us detecting the Taliban as quickly as we could. The Longbow was proving to be a real winner in Afghanistan. It could even target a lone figure in the middle of a huge expanse of desert.

My right eye placed the icon in the crosshair of the monocle while my left scanned the real world.

Going by its size and shape, the vehicle was probably a 4x4.

'Gunner – target – FCR – wheeled vehicle – stationary – range: five point seven – possible a 4x4.'

'Stand by,' Billy said. 'Sensing.'

Less than four seconds later: 'On.' He had the target visual in sight and no longer needed the FCR.

I glanced at my right MPD. A white Toyota Landcruiser. Even at this range, it filled my five-inch black and white screen. It had stopped in the middle of the desert – not to launch a SAM but to change a punctured tyre. As Billy zoomed in a little closer we identified its occupants.

'Good spot, Ed, disregard – 4x4 Landcruiser broken down with women and children in it.'

A good spot, indeed. The FCR had said it was a wheeled vehicle and that it was stationary, and it was right on both counts. When it came to finding needles in haystacks, the FCR was the king of kings.

On one of my first flights across the desert it had detected a camel. The classification it gave to these ships of the desert remains a closely guarded military secret.

The secure radio sparked up: 'Wildman Five Zero Flight this is Wildman Five Two Flight. We are RTB.'

No longer could 3 Flight hold on.

'We're out of gas and I think the Taliban are onto us. They kicked off big style at our chicken fuel point. I think they may have been listening to the CTAF.'

Nick: 'Copied.'

'I can't give you any grids because everyone is moving around so fast and the enemy are everywhere. They'll be useless in the few minutes it'll take you to get there. Good luck; we'll be ready to RIP when you call for us.'

The sudden escalation in hostilities at the time they were due off-station might not have been a coincidence. The Taliban listened to coalition transmissions on the Common Tactical Air Frequency. The Combined Air Ground (CAG) frequencies were also insecure; anyone on the ground could use them to talk to any air asset – or vice versa – in an emergency. They hadn't ever been changed, as far as we knew.

OPERATION MUTAY

SUNDAY, 4 JUNE 2006

As we flew through the hills twelve miles to the south of Now Zad, the distinctive bowl around it materialised through the dust and heat haze.

'Holy smoke, look twelve o'clock, Billy.'

'Oh my God.'

Columns of black smoke towered into the sky, spreading to the east as they met the winds above the ridgeline. The town was aflame. A fast jet sent out a series of orange flashes, each one higher than the last, as it broke off its attack and pumped out flares as it climbed back to the safety of the ether.

The fight or flight instinct kicked in and the metallic taste of adrenalin flooded my mouth. I fought the urge to urinate. My body was preparing itself for battle. My grip tightened on the controls. This was my first proper mission in an Apache, not just my first in Afghanistan.

Time to rock and roll.

Bring it on.

With Nick's mission radio down, we had taken the lead. It was not something we'd discussed in the air. It had been briefed during the planning phase and kicked in when necessary.

I was the JTAC in our aircraft, and until Billy got used to FAC speak, I would be the one in communication with the JTAC on the ground.

FAC speak was used to portray the ground, circumstances and type of attack required. Although not coded, it employed vernacular protocols with definitive meanings. Our training in Canada and the Oman had enabled me to get the best out of even the worst JTAC and with a bit of luck I could now show Billy the ropes.

Widow Seven Two, in the main body of the attack, should have been alongside the attacking commander Major Pike and the CO Lieutenant Colonel Tootal. All I could hear between the hoarse breathing and the loud ruffling of the mic were the words, 'Wait out.'

I switched to Widow Seven Zero. Judging by Pat's calls, they had been in the thick of it. I couldn't raise them on the secure radios, but eventually managed to on the insecure CTAF. Now I understood why we'd heard so much earlier. Widow Seven Zero was breathless, too, as he told us they'd called in a US A10. It must have been the one I'd seen climbing away from the battle, coming in now on its next run.

The jet screamed towards the ground, waiting for final clearance. The Taliban were firing out of the woods; despite their proximity, Widow Seven Zero decided to prosecute the target. They ordered the A10 'hot' – the executive command to fire live munitions – turned around and sprinted.

The JTAC still had his mic on; my earpieces filled with the rippling, ground-shaking blast of the wood line exploding behind them. I felt my blood pulsing through my veins and every one of my senses on hyper-alert.

We were still a couple of miles south of Now Zad when Widow Seven Zero finally caught his breath. 'Wildman Five One, this is Widow Seven Zero, how do you read?'

'Wildman Five One, Lima Charlie,' I replied. Lima Charlie was FAC speak for Loud and Clear. I whacked the holds in so I could go hands free and grabbed my pencil.

'We are receiving heavy fire from our south-east and need you to suppress the buildings at … standby for grid …' He kept his mic open and I could hear someone reading it out as he relayed it to us. 'Grid Forty-One-Sierra Papa-Romeo Three-Nine-Six Eight-Five-Two, copy?'

Billy punched the coordinates into his non-qwerty keyboard as I scribbled. 'Wildman Five One, Forty-One-Sierra Papa-Romeo Three-Nine-Six Eight-Five-Two.'

Widow Seven Zero was asking for us to engage the buildings beside the smoke. I was pretty sure what he meant but Now Zad was now full of the bloody stuff. My training had drilled into me: never assume; assumption is the mother of all fuck-ups. I needed more information.

'We need to positively identify your location. Confirm you're on the west side of the Green Zone, over.'

I guided the Apache into an orbit over the western edge of the Green Zone and began to search north-west.

We flew through a shaft of incredibly bright sunlight into the shadow of the biggest smoke column. Our world dimmed and I banked too tightly, taking us into absolute darkness. For a moment I felt as though we'd been swallowed whole; then we emerged from the belly of the beast once more, into the blinding sunlight.

The stroboscopic progression of light and shade made it almost impossible to operate the TADS, but within a couple of seconds I found friendly vehicles with the naked eye, about a klick west of the grid.

Billy confirmed and drove the TADS to the tower of smoke east of the vehicles, in an attempt to ID Taliban.

Widow Seven Zero wasn't with the vehicles – I'd gathered as much from his breathless running – and I couldn't ID him anywhere near where the A10 had laid down its fire.

The Widow attempted to describe his position but neither of us could identify it. My cueing dots led my gaze back towards the smoke; the acquisition source crosshair hovered over the burning building. Open fields stretched to the north-west; empty fields bathed in sunshine and criss-crossed by irrigation ditches.

I asked if they had a mirror and, if so, to signal to me with it.

A flicker of light immediately glinted in one of the ditches 250 metres away.

'Visual standby.'

The ditch ran north–south between two fields, one of which was black and smouldering from an earlier fire.

I called, 'Confirm that you are in a north–south irrigation ditch, in the middle of fields with a triangular compound to your west containing friendly vehicles.'

'That's correct. We're pinned down, taking heavy fire from an area to the south and south-east of us. I need you to fire into a compound to the south-east of me by a couple of hundred metres.'

I was in no doubt that they were in receipt of some heavy fire. I could hear the crack of the bullets flying over their heads on the radio, above the sound of their own fire. I relayed the Widow's position to Nick and Jon and instructed them to watch out for the troops while we attempted to ID and prosecute the enemy.

I walked the Widow onto the target I thought he meant. 'Right in front of you I can see a burnt field …' pause '… in the far corner of the burnt field is a compound with a smoking building in it …' *pause* '… confirm that is the compound you want us to fire into.'

'Negative. It's south of there; it's south by fifty metres.'

The next compound down was the last to have line-of-sight with them before a densely wooded area. Another plume of smoke drifted slowly upwards from one of its buildings.

I was flying an odd orbit just to keep eyes on the area. Jon was flying a much larger elliptical pattern below us, in the opposite direction.

'Reference the compound just beyond the burnt field ... directly on its southern edge ... is one row of east–west trees ...' I paused long enough for Widow Seven Zero to get his head up out of the ditch and process my information.

'To the south of the row of trees is a high-walled compound ... it has a raised wall on the northern edge ... there's a building behind it ... this building – which may look like a high wall to you – is smoking ... confirm that is the target.'

The Widow responded in an instant. 'Correct.'

'Where's the target, Ed?' Billy wanted to be 100 per cent sure. We were both keen not to fuck up our very first offensive action.

I instinctively placed the crosshair in my right eye over the target building and called, 'Gunner – Target – HMD – Target building low left.'

Billy had already switched his acquisition source from the previous grid to my Helmet Mounted Display and pressed the slave button. Following every movement of my right eye, the TADS swivelled itself towards where I was focused. Billy scanned the picture the TADS was giving him on his MPD; I couldn't look away until he was happy.

'On ...' he said. 'De-slaved.'

The TADS was back under his control and not slaved to my eye; my gaze could now sweep wherever I wanted. I glanced at my MPD to confirm he had the correct target.

I kept in tight to the target, a trick I'd learned in Northern Ireland. Whenever a helicopter circled directly above anyone who was in the wrong, they assumed the helicopter crews could see everything they were doing. They weren't always right. The sky had very little in it, so a helicopter was blatantly obvious. The ground, on the other hand, was full of clutter: buildings, trees, walls, bushes, high ground, alleyways, low ground, deep avenues of trees, you name it. It was a huge expanse from our perspective, and pinpointing the enemy was like finding the proverbial needle in the haystack.

'I'll increase the radius of the turn to make it easier on the TADS,' I told Billy. 'We'll fire a witness burst into the compound, just as we clear the smoke, starting ninety degrees out from the boys and finishing at the forty-five.'

I was still nervous about this first shot. It was dangerous practice to fire over the heads of your own troops – or even point towards them in case the range information was wrong and the rounds went long or short of their intended target. That was why we were offsetting.

Billy placed his crosshairs on the centre mass of the target building and I confirmed on my MPD that he had the correct target. 'Widow Seven Zero, Wildman Five One, target identified. Ready with thirty mike mike.'

'Widow Seven Zero – fire as soon as you can so we can extract to the west, over.'

'We'll kick off with a witness burst. I need you to confirm that we have the correct target. If we do, we will cover your extraction.'

He acknowledged.

Billy scoured the target for innocent civilians, but could see no one in the compound at all.

'Clear to engage, Billy.'

From a standing start to full speed in a quarter of a second, the M230 cannon thundered away beneath our feet.

'Firing,' I called. 'Confirm splash.' I wanted the JTAC to confirm that the rounds were landing in the right place.

The cannon fired all twenty rounds in two seconds but I could still hear and feel every single one. The sheer brute force of the thing pushed the Apache's nose to the right and twisted us, ever so slightly, left wing low. She regained her perfect orbit the second she stopped, with me following her on the cyclic.

I called Camp Bastion. 'Saxon Ops, this is Wildman Five One, engaging compounds with covering fire, out.'

I looked out of my cockpit, low and left. The twenty rounds went straight into the middle of the compound, with no collateral damage. Billy's firing was absolutely accurate, and more importantly still, so was the gun's. The rounds kicked up enough dust to obliterate the view inside the compound but the Widow couldn't see them land behind the wall.

I asked Billy to change to a ten-round burst and go for the building instead.

I transmitted, 'Stand by for a further witness burst.'

Then to Billy: 'Clear to engage.'

Billy squeezed the trigger again until the cannon had dispensed its ten rounds.

I transmitted, 'Firing now.'

The rounds impacted on the target building, ripping holes in its roof and gouging into its sides. Even from this height I could make out slivers of rock and adobe blasting all over the place.

'Negative, negative.' Widow Seven Zero shouted. 'Go fifty metres south-west. The enemy have moved; go fifty metres south-west.'

As we flew over our troops I spotted a square compound with one single single-storey building hidden in the trees fifty metres further south-west.

'Confirm the very next compound south-west of our fire is the compound you want us to attack.'

'Yes, yes,' came his urgent reply.

'Stand by while we set up.'

I lined up the Apache to the east of the target, heading north, so I could keep an eye on the Widow's position.

Billy called, 'Ready.'

He let go with another ten-round burst onto the wall facing the Widow so he could observe the splash they made through the trees.

'Firing now,' I informed the Widow.

The Widow shouted, 'On target, on target' the second we saw the rounds impact on and around the compound wall.

Billy changed the burst rate back to twenty and unleashed two further onslaughts into the building on the north-western edge of the compound. I watched the boys break from cover then looked at the MPD to see what Billy could see.

The rounds exploded with a ferocity I had never imagined. The training ammo we used was inert; these High Explosive Dual Purpose (HEDP) rounds were the real McCoy. I knew what they claimed to be able to do, but I was completely unprepared for what I saw. They were far more deadly than their name suggested.

I saw the heat haze swirling behind the succession of little black dots that flew up the image and dropped onto the building. Each one produced an almighty flash as the armour piercing punched its way through roof and walls. Once through the building's skin, the incendiary set the interior alight. Thick black smoke billowed from a small window like steam out of a pressure cooker. I could only guess at the effectiveness of the HEDP's fragmentation. The blast should have sent red-hot shards of metal winging their way into every corner.

Chunks of rock and adobe flew off the exterior and the court-yard entrance remained empty. Either there was no one at home or the frag was working big time. My money was on the latter; the Patrols Platoon had been able to get the hell out of that field without being engaged again.

I lost my visual lock on them in the plantation to the south for longer than I was comfortable with. I couldn't raise the Widow.

Then I spotted them moving fast into an orchard to the south and south-west of where they'd been pinned down.

The boss should have been extremely thankful that they'd managed to hold out. I wouldn't have wanted to explain why we hadn't been ready to Tootal. Without Apache cover they'd been sitting ducks, out in the open, nowhere to go.

When I finally got hold of them they were moving through the orchard 200 metres west of the compound Billy had just annihilated. Widow Seven Zero informed us that they had broken contact and were going to search the area they'd come under fire from. 'Report any movement in the target compound.'

Saxon Ops at base gave us grid 41S PR 3957 8673. The target was a suspect white pick-up in the north of Now Zad. With the threat brief earlier, this target was deemed to be a direct threat. Billy handed it over to Nick and Jon because they couldn't speak to the ground troops.

I kept a close eye on Jon as he peeled away to the north.

We couldn't see anything moving or leaving the compound or the wood alongside it. We covered the lads through what seemed to be a cross between an orchard and open parkland.

They looked like ants from my vantage point, but I could see them employing good FIBUA tactics as they entered the compound. No surprises there; 3 Para were masters at Fighting In a Built-Up Area. Once inside they reported loads of blood and blood trails all over the place, but no human life.

'They must have dragged the injured and dead into the trees, undercover of the dust and smoke,' I said.

'Lesson identified, lesson learned,' Billy replied. We wouldn't make that mistake twice.

Base told us intelligence was indicating a target in the north, grid 41S PR 3980 8648. They must have been listening to Taliban transmissions. While I looked out for Patrols Platoon, Billy checked the map. It was only 300 metres from where Nick and Jon had gone to search.

I told Saxon Ops we'd need a RIP in an hour. 3 Flight would be on the APU on thirty minutes' notice to move. They'd have more than enough time to throw their engine power levers forward, taxi, fly out to us and do a full RIP. We were on an insecure radio, but we'd maintain full Apache cover. Better to risk keeping the Taliban up to speed than to leave 3 Para in the lurch again.

I spoke to all three Widow callsigns to see if they needed assistance. Our covering fire had quietened the Taliban down and our presence was keeping them at bay.

I told Widow Seven Two that base had given me intelligence on a target west of their target compound, because he was with the CO. We couldn't wander off on our own little mission without confirming with the ground commander; we were here to assist him, after all. Widow Seven Two informed me that they had the same information and 2 Platoon of A Company 3 Para were already routing to the grid from the east.

Nick and Jon were still hunting for the white pick-up. They were over the area of the grid, knowing that this posed a greater threat to the boys on the ground than they perhaps realised. If it knocked us out of the sky, they'd have a helicopter rescue mission on their hands.

With that in mind we moved fractionally north, leaving them to hunt for the pick-up. I still maintained a wide-enough orbit to pass over our lads every couple of minutes; with a bit of luck it would keep the Taliban diving for cover.

Billy looked into the intelligence grid; all we could make out was the edge of a field, a north–south track bordered by a wall, and a compound about fifty metres due east.

We had no other information about the target. The obvious feature was the compound; the only fire we'd encountered in our short brush with the Taliban in Afghanistan was from a compound, and the blood trails must have led somewhere.

The area was totally enclosed, with a double wall on its eastern side bordering a wood which stretched 500 metres to the main wadi – our perimeter. Opposite it was a large white steel gate, the only access point to the compound. What appeared to be five open garages ran along the northern wall. I saw shadow movement in the furthest east, but couldn't identify it. I needed to tell the CO's men, and find out where they were.

Widow Seven Two said he had a few hundred metres to go; I requested another flash from his mirror.

The signal was easy to see; they were in a sunlit clearing in the wood, closer to the target than we'd anticipated, tracking directly to the intelligence grid. They'd break out into open fields if they continued. I instructed him to continue west then turn south ten metres short of the wood line and contour the edge of the wood until they reached the double wall. It should give them the element of surprise and afford them whatever cover was available.

Widow Seven Two called when he was at the wall. I talked them round the perimeter until they were on the track just west of the compound. They gathered by the gates and studied their maps.

I saw the JTAC look up.

'Wildman Five One, this is Widow Seven Two. The grid we have is some fifty metres west, in another compound.'

'Wildman Five One, there isn't a compound fifty metres west. The wall you're looking at isn't a compound wall; it's just got a track on the other side of it, and then a field. The field stretches about 100 metres to an orchard and that's it. No buildings or compounds.'

Billy had called Nick and Jon to join us as the pick-up was nowhere to be seen and there was little else happening. Jon and I flew contra-rotating orbits around the whole area, with us high on the inside and them lower on the outside so we could both fire at the centre point without hitting each other.

I told Widow Seven Two that if they wanted to check out that area they'd have to follow the wall north initially then turn back down the track for fifty metres. From there they could look west and see the empty field for themselves.

We gauged our fuel and reminded Saxon Ops that we would need 3 Flight to leave in the next five minutes. I was pleased with our performance. We hadn't killed anyone we weren't supposed to and 3 Para felt safe enough to patrol around Now Zad looking for an intelligence target.

Saxon came back to me a minute or two later.

'There will be no RIP, I spell, Romeo, India, Papa. On your return to base you are to refuel, rearm and go back to Now Zad immediately.'

Something must have flared up elsewhere in the AOR; 3 Flight must have deployed to support other troops in contact. We let Nick and Jon know. I felt a hollowness in my gut at the prospect of the ground troops being without Intimate Support again.

Nick and Jon hadn't spotted anything suspicious and nor could we. I took advantage of the lull in activity to inform the CO of our predicament and asked Widow Seven Two if we should break station now and come back asap or wait until we'd reached chicken fuel. He told me to wait out while they asked the CO.

The Paras moved down the wall in single file. Billy scoured the area for Taliban while I maintained overwatch of the troops. I could see the lead soldier; he wasn't much more than a boy. As he reached the end of the south wall he'd be able to see across open ground towards the orchard.

I heard Widow Seven Two's microphone click open to reply as the lad and his immediate successor stepped clear of the wall. I saw the wall explode and heard a massive weight of machine-gun fire over the JTAC's radio.

Dirt, rock and soil erupted from the trail and wall. I saw a figure tumble back towards the wall. A pair of legs shot up out of the dust. I knew it was the young soldier I'd just delivered to the Taliban on a plate.

SIGNED, SEALED AND DELIVERED

SUNDAY, 4 JUNE 2006

I yelled across to Nick: 'Contact. They've been contacted.' I thought for a second. 'There are no troops further west than the north–south track; watch and shoot.'

Someone shouted from the ground, 'Contact. Wait Out.' Someone struggling to make himself heard above the explosions hammering their position.

My mouth was dry. I had the sick feeling in the pit of my stomach that comes the second you realise you've done something extremely bad. My mind raced. I couldn't see enough through the dust to know if the boys were still alive.

Was it me?

I could see men taking cover behind the wall as it disintegrated above their heads.

Was it my fault?

No one was moving a muscle down there.

Why did they break cover by walking straight around the corner? I'd lulled my own men into a false sense of security. I couldn't see any fire coming from the orchard. Where were they being contacted from?

I flicked my attention between the orchard and my fallen soldier. He'd been catapulted backwards at such a rate he must have been badly hit.

I needed to get on with my job or there'd be more blood on my hands.

Billy searched desperately for the enemy firing position.

The wall our boys were behind was still being smashed to smithereens. The fire could only be coming from the orchard, but where?

We could have hosed down the whole wood with rockets and cannon but we were not in the business of indiscriminate fire, and we'd raise such a dust storm we'd not know if we'd actually hit anyone.

'Widow Seven Two, this is Wildman – can you see the firing point?'

'Stand by to watch our tracer.' The mayhem I could hear through my earpieces was outrageous. Why couldn't we see anyone firing at them?

'Standing by.'

I told Nick and Jon to watch out for the tracer indication.

I could see a couple of our guys firing through holes in the wall but couldn't see a hint of tracer. Those that weren't firing were down on their belt buckles, some in the foetal position.

I suddenly realised why we couldn't see the tracer. They were less than 100 metres from the orchard. Tracer started to burn at 110.

'Widow Seven Zero, this is Wildman. I cannot see your tracer or any enemy. Can you see the firing point?'

'It's 100 metres to our west.' The sound of incoming was as ferocious as ever.

The orchard frontage was a few hundred metres long and we were running out of fuel. I still needed a clearer description. If we could pinpoint the Taliban position we could deal with it. If we simply hosed the place down our boys could be targeted again as soon as we broke station.

'From the bottom of the wall …' I said, 'go 100 metres across the field with a couple of bushes in it … there's a low wall on the forward edge of the wood … where's the firing point from this wall?'

'That *is* the area of the firing point.'

'Gunner – Target – HMD.' I brought Billy's TADS into position.

Billy slaved to the area and quickly identified the wall. It was deep in the shadow of the trees and the enemy could have been hiding behind it. We asked Jon and Nick to keep eyes-on as we fired onto the target.

We were happy with the cannon's accuracy but really concerned about the proximity of our lads. Any rounds that failed to explode could ricochet from the wall and the frag could also hit them at ninety. We decided to fire from behind our lads' right and over their heads. All the rounds would be travelling away from them, blowing any frag or rock in the opposite direction. Or so I hoped …

Billy needed to make sure his range was stable and accurate; any miscalculation and our rounds would fall short. We were about to do what I had nixed in the simulator – unless there were absolutely no other options.

Without hesitation, Billy called firing and I broadcast the call.

'Firing now … confirm splash.'

We were about 1,200 metres away as the cannon ramped itself backwards and the first few rounds pumped from the barrel. From this point onwards it was in its optimum position. The remaining seventeen HEDP rounds exited without pause and streaked towards the wall.

At the bottom of the MPD image by my right knee I could see the wall and our lads hiding behind it. The wall Billy was aiming at was at the centre of the screen; the top half of it covered the sunlit trees. I stopped breathing as the rounds flew in towards the target in an untidy conical pattern, in what looked like slow motion, each maintaining exactly the same distance from the next.

They exploded bang-fucking-on, hurtling rocks and soil twenty metres into the air.

The radio burst into life. 'One hundred metres north, 100 metres north.'

As we followed the JTAC's instruction Billy adjusted and opened up at the tree line with another twenty-round burst. The wall had stopped further south.

'Firing now.'

By the time the nineteenth and twentieth rounds were reverberating through my feet the first were impacting the dry soil and dirt at the edge of the orchard.

A dust cloud mushroomed out of the trees at the edge of the field.

'Fifty metres further north, fifty metres further north, that's where the firing point is.'

Jon came up on the radio, the pitch of his voice higher than normal: 'We've picked up the Taliban firing point, just north of your last burst.'

I barked, 'Put down a burst and I'll confirm with the Widow that you're in the right area.'

This was getting better. The Widow and Jon were talking about the same place. I looked down at the boys. They hadn't moved and the wall was still being blown to bits. Whoever was in this wood wanted protection and had the means to do it.

Billy moved his sight fifty metres further north and Nick and Jon's rounds impacted right over his crosshair.

'Good rounds,' The Widow shouted back. 'Good rounds.'

'Wildman Five Zero, Wildman Five One, we're going to fire into the same area with you.'

I had the fleeting image of two men lying in the shadows behind the shit Nick had just kicked up, then Billy and Nick opened up in a coordinated attack. They took it in turns to pound the target, with no let-up between bursts – one, then the other.

My eyes darted between the devastation and A Company's 2 Platoon. They weren't going anywhere fast but I made out some movement between bursts onto the target. I counted four individual movements in the same vicinity before the dust storm closed in; they were either rolling or trying to crawl.

It dawned on me that we hadn't updated Ops on our mission.

'Saxon Ops, Wildman Five One. Both callsigns engaging Taliban in tree line as troops withdraw, out.'

After spitting 120 bundles of hell into the tree line, both Billy and Nick stopped when Billy transmitted, 'Watch and shoot.'

The entire field and wood had disappeared under a dust cloud a hundred feet high. But the lesson we identified earlier was now a lesson learned. No one down there would live to crawl away this time. There would be no rescue party to drag them to safety.

I looked towards the end of the wall, expecting the worst.

'Look at that!' I pointed my crosshair at the lads as they got up, brushed off the dust and began to saunter back up the track. I couldn't make out any stretchers, but I couldn't see everyone from this angle.

Jon and I kept our orbits tight around the orchard so Nick and Billy could look for leakers – Taliban trying to escape – but we were hampered by low fuel.

'Widow Seven Zero, this is the Wildmen. We're going to have to RTB to get some gas. We'll be back as soon as we can to assist in your withdrawal.' I thought they might want to hang fire until we got back, considering what happened last time the Apaches left.

'Widow Seven Zero, good shooting. Thanks, but we're bugging out and look forward to your return.' Jesus, these men were made of stern stuff.

'No problem. Were there any casualties from that contact?'

'No. Thanks to you we all got out okay.'

'Thanks, we'll stay on this frequency to relay any messages on our way back and will call you inbound later.'

'Copied, safe flight.'

I was wondering how on earth the young soldier had survived. He must have been a bloody acrobat; those legs were upside down. Lady Luck must have been on our side.

The Taliban could not have escaped north or south because we would have picked them up. They had not egressed through the orchard. The rear of it was too open and they would have been easy to spot in the light cover. They must have died where they were hit, but we couldn't wait around long enough to find out.

Our troops were safe.

Billy and I only had 510 pounds of fuel left and needed to get back asap.

We turned for home.

I flicked the MPD onto the performance page: 'RANGE SPEED 117 KTS'. The computer had calculated the optimum speed to maximise our remaining fuel. I set our speed to 117 knots, put Bastion on the centre of the heading tape, triggered the height and attitude hold and let her fly us back home. As Scottie had taught me on my CCT course, she was a much better pilot than I was.

On our approach, we were confronted by the sight of the 3 Flight Apaches still on the ground. I confirmed with Ops that they wanted us to return to Now Zad. We were told to return asap.

When I touched down on the dusty HLS I had 350 pounds of fuel remaining – fifty pounds below the minimum, but what the hell. If I was put in the same position again, I'd bust my limits once more.

When we owned up to our misdemeanour during the debrief later that day, Jon announced he'd landed with just 200 pounds, half the absolute minimum. The price you could pay for preventing our troops from dying was an engine-off landing back at base if you were lucky, in the middle of the desert if the gods were against you. The chances of both crew members surviving one in an Apache were extremely high. Whether or not the Apache would fly again was another question altogether.

The problem with this job was that if you got it right after taking a risk, you were 'reminded' that you took a risk and got away with it. If you didn't get it right, it was aircrew error – and you would be constantly reminded that you cocked up as you flew a desk for what remained of your career.

Taff plugged into the wing and announced that one of the other Apaches had been shot straight through the tail during the morning's activities. He said that Pat had begged to go back but had been turned down.

After a quick suck of gas and a rearm we were ready to depart again.

We took off first with Jon and Nick slightly after us.

We'd caused an almighty dust cloud. Billy screamed at me, 'Come hard left *now*.'

I threw the stick over and banked round, my head shifting to align the crosshairs. Whatever he'd seen had got him very excited very quickly.

I saw Jon's tail at about forty feet, disappearing into his own dust cloud. They were headed straight for the camp.

My stomach lurched. There was a moment's silence and then I heard Billy's voice.

'They've crashed,' he said in an I-don't-believe-what-I'm-seeing kind of way.

'Oh my God,' I said. The dust suddenly became much darker. They must have gone in hard.

We circled for a few seconds, waiting to see how bad it would be. Both of us knew better than to try to talk to them. They would speak to us if they could. But I wasn't counting on hearing anything.

We did two complete orbits before the dust cleared.

'How the fuck did they end up like that?' Billy asked.

'No idea.'

'I'd better see if they're all right,' Billy said. 'Wildman Five Zero … Wildman Five One. Are you both okay in there?'

No answer.

Then a rather quiet voice came over the ether. 'Give us a minute,' Jon said. 'We're a bit shook up.'

No shit.

'Are you okay?'

'Wildman Five One has had a bit of a heavy landing,' Jon said.

'How hard?' Billy said.

'Not hard enough to stop us from protecting 3 Para,' Jon replied. 'Five Zero is lifting'

We watched them take off, successfully this time.

On the route out to Now Zad Nick asked us to check the aircraft over. I flew up beside it and dropped slowly back, sliding down their right-hand side. Billy and I were looking for damaged antennas or weapons. I flew around their whole aircraft but couldn't see a single dent.

The boys had extracted to the east of the wadi where they were going to be pulled out by Chinooks. The extraction of 3 Para was going without a hitch until a US B1 bomber did a show of strength.

The CO wanted to warn the Taliban against following them across the wadi and decided to let them see what he had waiting for them if they tried it on. The B1 was a huge aircraft with great big engines, designed to fly at altitude. Down here it would be a SAM magnet for any ManPAD operator.

Jon and I were on the southern edge of the town. The B1 would fly between our positions and we couldn't wait to see it up close.

When it appeared, it flew over the mountains at 5,000 feet and crossed Now Zad from south to north. It passed between us with little drama until it nosed up and exposed its engines to the town. The second it opened them up to climb away I nearly shit myself.

'Missile launch short range left eleven o'clock,' Bitching Betty screamed at me.

'Missile launch,' I shouted to Jon over the radio.

'Missile launch too,' he shouted back. My mouth turned to liquid aluminium and my scrotum shrivelled.

'SAMbush ...'

The second the Bitch said it, I started counting down. Flares were pouring off both sides of my Apache; my eyes were peeled, scanning the sky for streaks of smoke heading towards me.

Five ...

I knew not to manoeuvre until after five. I could see Billy highlighted in the glow of the flares.

'Widow Seven Two, this is Wildman Five One. Did you see a missile being fired at us?'

Four ...

I was trusting in the Air Warfare Centre's reassurance that we'd be okay, but I was fucking shitting it.

'Negative.'

Three ...

'Did you hear a bang over Now Zad that could be a misfired missile?'

Two ...

'Negative.'

One ...

And with that I flung the Apache onto her left side to change my profile relative to the ManPAD operator.

Jon and I climbed, looking for smoke trails.

Nothing.

The Chinooks appeared on my radar and we went back to what we were supposed to be doing; we concentrated on getting the men out.

The extraction went like clockwork from this point on, but all four of us remained very spooked.

We were diverted to pick up a US casualty in the middle of the desert on the way back but other than that the trip was uneventful.

On our return the lads were eager to hear how many Taliban we'd killed. The honest truth was we didn't know and never would. I vowed from that point onwards never to count. Killing didn't bother me; to me it was part of the job. My countrymen voted in a government. That government had sent me here under strict ROE. I complied with these ROE and that meant killing bad people. End of. I got paid at the end of the month and if I was lucky, I might even get home to spend it.

During the debrief, it became very clear to us that we had killed whoever had been in the woods. The boss told us that the intelligence hit to the north, the one we had just shot up in the woods, was actually 3 Para's target. We wondered why he hadn't told us this at the time. The boss claimed he didn't want to divert our attention from the primary task of protecting 3 Para.

I was fuming inside. Had we been armed with that knowledge we could have got Nick to leave the area, fly over the top of 3 Para and use the TADS to observe and ID the guy from a distance. That way 3 Para would have got a bit of protection and we would have been able to report what we saw. We could have ambushed him on the CO 3 Para's orders, instead of the target sitting in a wood waiting for me to deliver a young Paratrooper into his sights. The thing that made me most angry wasn't his meddling from a distance; it was his complete lack of trust in our ability to do the right thing.

We never did find out if a SAM was fired at us. I was comforted to know that Jon shared my faith in the system, even if all four of us admitted to being terrified in those few seconds.

Billy did have a good reason for sticking with his seat, and he was quick to apologise. He knew it would only take thirty seconds to swap, but couldn't have lived with the thought of a soldier dying if we arrived even ten seconds later.

The boss never did thank us for saving the day; not that I expected it. The only thanks I needed was knowing that the guy 3 Para were chasing hasn't been heard of since. One way or another, he must have ended up dead.

SCRAMBLE

SUNDAY, 16 JULY 2006
Camp Bastion

0325 hours local
My watch alarm went off and I forced open my eyes. It felt like only minutes since I'd crashed out.

I was shagged out, absolutely ball-bagged. We all were. We'd finished Op Augustus a couple of days before, and had been out the whole of yesterday. We hadn't got more than a couple of hours' sleep.

I strapped my head torch round my wrist then pulled on some shorts and a pair of desert boots. My flying suit was at the aircraft.

I joined the others at the Burco boiler. There wasn't much chatter. What was there to talk about, except how completely fucked we were? I had my own coffee maker. I threw in some ground coffee Emily had posted to me, poured on boiling water and pushed down the plunger without waiting long enough.

It was pitch-black outside, but as warm as an English summer's day. You could wander about in no more than a T-shirt and there was no chill to your skin. The nights were also absolutely, totally still, not a breath of wind.

We blundered our way to the Ops room, across ditches and berms. The Chinook IRT/HRF pilots and loadies fell in alongside us. Brews in hand, everyone was quiet. We'd got to the point where we didn't really want to wake up. We were going through the motions, following where our exhausted bodies led.

Simon and I now flew as one pair and Jake and Jon the other, in what had become the newly constituted 2 Flight. Jake had turned up several weeks earlier following the birth of his first child, a little boy, Finn, at the end of May.

His arrival had coincided with a squabble over which flights were getting the most action. Dan's 1 Flight and Pat's 3 Flight had gone head to head, with 2 Flight – us – left on the sidelines. Some form of organised rotation would have sorted things out in an instant. It was all a bit ridiculous.

Jake's response was typically phlegmatic. 'I don't care how many hours I fly or how many missions I do or don't go on,' he'd said, when we told him the score. 'I'm not here to indulge in a load of bitching about who gets the plum jobs and which flight is the boss's favourite. I only care about two things: doing what we're asked to do, to the best of our ability, and getting home safely. And now I'm ready for a brief.'

Between then and now the Taliban had seriously raised the stakes.

We knew they were planning a spectacular; they'd set their hearts on either taking a District Centre or shooting down a helicopter.

Now Zad, Sangin and Musa Qa'leh were all under increasing levels of Taliban attack. Our lads were barely holding their own, and at considerable cost. The bases were grandly named District Centres – but, in fact, each held no more than a platoon, so the CO 3 Para was constantly forced to shift troops to whichever location was in most imminent danger of being overrun. We were forever chaperoning Chinooks, moving men between one DC and the next.

A Company 3 Para had moved into Sangin on 21 June, right on the doorstep of what our most secret order believed to be the Taliban's southern headquarters. They were ordered to hold it at all costs. They were under heavy fire morning, noon and night. The cost was high. Five British soldiers had been killed in nine days.

Our job had been to pound the few hundred metres around the DCs pretty much 24/7. The troops on the ground were knackered, we were knackered, and the Chinook crews were two steps beyond zombie mode. They were having the toughest time of all.

Where they'd failed in Now Zad, the Taliban were succeeding in Sangin and Musa Qa'leh. They had good fields of fire onto the DCs and were hitting and killing British troops on a regular basis.

We were at our most vulnerable when flying casevac sorties, as the enemy well knew. The risk evaluation to the flight and medical crews on board the Chinooks was now so extreme they were only cleared to go into Sangin or Musa Qa'leh if an injured soldier would die unless he got to hospital in an hour. Now Zad was heading in the same direction. Even with the Shrine shielding the LS, we were running out of ways of getting safely in and out. The minute that happened, the troops would go without resupplies – like those holed up in Sangin and Musa Qa'leh.

In the meantime, intelligence had picked up plenty of Icom chatter between Taliban commanders about taking a helicopter out. There were reports of at least one shoulder-launched missile and possibly an anti-aircraft gun in the area.

We'd flown supporting missions throughout, even though the air temperature was regularly near 50°. Our operating limit of 44° Celsius was finally increased to 49° on 5 July, so at least we wouldn't have the book thrown at us if we fucked up while flying beyond the Release To Service (RTS).

Now Zad, Sangin and Musa Qa'leh had been under sustained Taliban attack for a month solid. Because we'd been flying our aircraft around the clock, we'd been ordered to 'slow-fly' them for a week or so – cut the hours right down – but that was easier said than done; it was like the Alamo out there.

Jake glanced at his watch and groaned. 'This timetable is killing me.'

'Three and a *half* hours ahead of the UK?' I croaked. 'Where the hell did the half come from?'

It was common sense that 3 Para were on local time: they worked with the locals. Seven in the morning was 0700 local, and bingo, breakfast was served. Fast air worked differently. A B1 bomber from Diego Garcia, a Nimrod from Lossiemouth, an F15 from a ship in the Arabian Gulf and a pair of Apaches from Bastion could all be working together, so we all worked on GMT. To airborne assets there was no 0700 local; it was 0330 GMT and breakfast arrived in the middle of the night.

We still had to integrate with ground units, of course, so 0330 local was midnight to us, and that was when the codes changed and all the frequencies flipped over. It was barking mad. The codes changed, we were briefed, and we went back to bed again. It made sense that the changeovers took place at the quietest time; most attacks were during the day, it was heavy on the aircraft, and it was hot. But months passed before some bright spark worked out we could simply change over at the 1900 evening brief and everyone could get a solid night's sleep.

However, for now, this was just the way it was.

The Ops tent was lit up like Wembley Stadium. We stumbled in and gathered round the map table. I was starting to wake up.

One of the Chinook boys checked the weather computer and came back with the forecast min and max temperatures, wind speed and direction. It was going to be red hot, a ten knot westerly blowing dust.

Kenny, one of our watchkeepers, told us what had happened in-theatre over the last twenty-four hours. 'Now Zad's being fired at again regularly. Half an hour after last light, the rounds started once more.'

The Taliban waited till it was dark, extracted their weapons from wherever they hid them, set them up, and started firing into the base. Half an hour of mortars and rockets then they'd stop. They knew our reaction times. They'd wait another hour or so then start again. Ken said Now Zad was also receiving accurate fire from a sangar that they were calling the Turret.

Then came briefs on Kajaki, Musa Qa'leh, Sangin, FOB Robinson and Gereshk. It always followed the same order – clockwise around the DCs and Forward Operating Bases – ending up at Helmand's HQ in Lashkar Gah. We learned what had been happening to them physically on the ground, the routes, callsigns and timings of any patrols due out.

We then went on to the J2; intelligence. Jerry, our IntO, gave us his interpretation of any reports that had come through.

We were taking over IRT/HRF tonight. Jake and Jon were the IRT, callsign Wildman Five Zero. Simon and I were HRF, Wildman Five One; he and I were qualified in both seats and swapped regularly to keep up our flying and shooting skills. For this duty Simon would be in the front, I'd be in the back.

Brief over, it was always the same routine on a changeover night. We had to load up the aircraft and check them over. Brew recharged, the four of us wandered down to the aircraft. It was still pitch-black, and there wasn't a single light out towards the flight line because it fucked with our night vision goggles (NVG).

The Milky Way arced in front of me, a swathe of cosmic confetti. I stared open-mouthed at Orion's Belt and every one of the Seven Sisters, stars I'd never seen with the naked eye before. A couple of satellites drifted across the heavens. It was breathtakingly beautiful.

I suddenly felt achingly lonely, and a long way from home. I'd have given anything at that precise moment to have been lying on my back with Emily and the kids, heads touching, gazing up at the night sky, making up our own star signs from the shapes we could see.

A stumble on a rock brought me back down to earth, literally. I was on my knees, mouth full of dust, vaguely aware of a tired chortle from Simon, Jon and Jake somewhere nearby.

A few minutes down a rough track brought us to the hangar. Only the duty technician was awake; all the rest were sound asleep in various odd corners. They worked longer hours than we did, with precious few breaks. They'd only just finished and would be up in a couple of hours, so we crept past them like cat burglars.

We headed for our F700 books and checked how many flying hours we had available, any new restrictions or limitations, and what faults the Apache was carrying.

I signed the aircraft out. It was now on my flick.

I placed my most recent letter from Emily in the drawer of my locker. I sanitised myself, searching every pocket for anything I shouldn't be carrying. I took out my NVG-compatible torch. It took two runs to get all my kit to the aircraft.

The HRF aircraft was always in the second bay – Arming Bay Two – but I still checked the tail with my torch to make sure it was ZJ227. The IRT cab sat to our left in Arming Bay One; it saved time and confusion on a scramble.

I took the starboard side and Simon took the port as we walked around the fuselage. The inspection was essentially what Scottie had taught me back at Middle Wallop, but now, instead of just noting there was a gun under the chin of my chariot, I inspected it carefully – that it was clean, it moved okay, the electrical connections were made, and most important of all, that it had big, dark yellow-banded HEDP cannon rounds leading down the feed chute.

The Hellfire missiles always impressed me. The seeker on the front was a work of art; I could see the precision engineering through the glass I polished with my sweat-rag. 'AGM-114K' was stencilled in bright yellow down the side of each. I made sure they were securely latched down before moving on to the rocket launchers, checking that their black noses were securely in place. I shone my torch down each tube. There were twelve HEISAP rockets, with their tiny but unmistakable six-spoked silver tips, and seven Flechettes, which just had a plain nosecone to protect the darts. All the blast paddles were down at the back of the launcher. The rockets were held securely in place, electrical contacts made. The Hellfire's strakes – that enabled it to climb, turn and dive – all moved freely.

I lifted the little triangular panel behind the APU to the rear of the starboard engine and checked the pressure. I unclipped the eighteen-inch pipe, stuck it onto the spigot and gave it about fifty pumps, adding more pressure to the accumulator. I wanted the needle deep in the green. Unlike other aircraft, the Apache started on air pressure; it didn't need an external electrical source. No matter where we were in the world, you could start this aircraft. I replaced the pipe in its bracket and closed the panel.

I dropped to my knees and opened the bottom hatch, which we called the boot. I always had my kit set in the same order – chest webbing on the bottom, flak jacket next and battle bowler perched on the top – with a bungee stretched over the lot so it stayed exactly where I wanted it. If we crashed behind enemy lines, I'd go straight under the wing, wrench open the boot and cut the bungee. I'd remove my escape jacket, don the helmet, flak jacket, webbing and replace the escape jacket over the top. Then I'd be off.

The flare dispenser was packed full; I would have woken the boys up there and then if even one had been missing. Along with the Bitch, these puppies were top of the list of things keeping me alive at altitude.

I walked down the tail, scanning every square inch to make sure it hadn't been bumped into. I made sure that the tail wheel was locked so the wind – if it ever got up at night – wouldn't blow her around. The position of the huge horizontal stabilator was even more critical. We always forced the aircraft to leave it in the horizontal position before closing down; if we didn't, it would drop down at the rear. The Americans had once had a bit of a problem in strong winds. The wind caught them and flipped over a whole row of aircraft.

'Your side okay, Ed?' Simon asked.

'Yep. Just check my cowlings and catches on the way down. I'll do yours.' It was easy to leave a panel open so we always checked each other's work after the inspection.

I opened the cockpit, attached my carbine to the seat bracket and put a magazine of tracer on it. I threw my grab bag – what I referred to as my ammo bag – next to the seat and jumped in. I pushed the Data Transfer Cartridge (DTC) into its housing, pulled on my helmet, and fired up the APU. I made sure the aircraft was set up for night, turning down all the levels so I could barely see a thing. I pulled forward the coaming cover on top of the dash, flipped up the left batwing and Velcroed it to the top of the cowling. No light would leak from the left of the cockpit. I couldn't do the starboard side right now because I had to climb out of the door.

I uploaded my information from the DTC and checked that the new codes had uploaded into the radios. We couldn't afford another cock-up like we had on Op Mutay. The Apache's radios were temperamental and we were learning the hard way.

Jon was the comms guru and reckoned he'd now fixed the radio problems we'd been plagued with since our arrival. I set them up ready for him to put them through their paces.

'Wildman Five One, Wildman Five Zero,' he called. 'Check on one ...

'On two ...'

I followed him through each one, making sure I could hear him. I flipped to radio three.

'On three …'

I heard the beep confirming that he had sent his aircraft's position digitally via the Improved Data Modem over the fourth radio.

I looked down. His icon appeared next to mine on the MPD's Tactical Situational Display (TSD) page, confirming the IDM and fourth radio both worked.

I called, 'Good data', meaning I could receive and had his icon, but we were only half done. The system was so complex that hearing and receiving data didn't mean you could transmit and be heard. And we needed to prove my IDM could send too.

I repeated the procedure in reverse and pushed the Present Position button on my MPD.

'Good data, closing down.'

Once I was sure we had no snags I set the stabilator to horizontal and powered everything down again. I wedged my Flight Reference Cards between the coaming and its cover, put one of my gloves on the cyclic to remind me not to touch it with a bare hand when it was hot, then put my helmet on the dash. I climbed out, threw my escape jacket back on the seat and closed the door.

Simon and I wandered back up to the Ops room and let them know we were off to bed. Then it was back across the road, kit off, and into our scratchers.

The four of us were in the Apache IRT tent instead of our normal accommodation. It was closer to the Ops room. The Chinook crews were next door. We had a couple of camp cots lashed together as a sofa in front of a big TV with magazines strewn all over the place. This was where the guys on IRT/HRF spent most of their down time. If you weren't in there, you had to make sure the Ops room knew where you were going, and take a walkie-talkie with you.

I was mostly writing requirements at the back of the Ops room in our admin area, where the Sky TV was playing next to the brew-making kit. I fired off memos about all kinds of stuff: for the rocket parameters to be lifted, in defence of using Flechettes, to justify buying a different type of warhead for the Hellfires – and a policy document for dynamic harmonisation for the gun.

When I wasn't writing I was studying gun tapes I hadn't caught up with from the previous day. There were a lot of battles going on, so hours and hours of tape. Every inch of it needed to be viewed so I could collate the data and send back my reports as well as advise crews on their techniques.

The four of us struggled awake again at 0700 local – 0330 GMT. I usually skipped breakfast, but these were crazy days and you never knew when you were going to eat next, so I grabbed a big bowl of porridge and a piece of fruit and washed it down with half a gallon of coffee.

I wasn't part of Operation Daz today, so since all was quiet, a few hours later I let the Ops room know that Simon, Jon and Jake were taking the Land Rover on a laundry run and I was legging it across to the satellite phones. It was 0800 on Sunday morning back in the UK; there was a good chance of catching Emily at home. The phones were at the opposite end of the camp, just over a kilometre away, so I grabbed a radio and set off.

I'd only been chatting away with Emily for a few minutes when the Motorola chirped into life.

'Mansell … Senna … Top Gear … Silverstone …'

Mansell was the call for the IRT, Senna was the HRF crew.

Top Gear meant go fast, it's an emergency.

Silverstone was the Ops room. That's where I needed to be.

Bloody Nora: I was at the wrong end of the camp, without a vehicle – but I didn't want to alarm her.

'Who was that?' she said.

Jon acknowledged the call before I got time to turn the volume down. 'Mansell … Top Gear … Silverstone.'

'Oh … er … some F1 advertising thing. Listen sweetie, you won't believe it,' I said, 'but I'm desperate for a poo.'

I was right. She didn't. 'But you only just got on the phone …'

'You know what I'm like …'

'You'll call me straight back?'

Oh bollocks.

'I'm not near the toilets. If I don't call it'll be because the queues are that bad on a Sunday.'

I made my call the moment I put down the receiver.

'Senna, Top Gear, Silverstone.'

It was 1145 local and as hot as an oven. Apart from my flying suit, I was in full gear with my pistol strapped to my right leg and roasting like a pig. I sprinted through the camp as fast as I could go. When I got to the end of the main boardwalk it dawned on me that Emily may have spotted that Senna was dead and Mansell hadn't raced in years.

As I ran across the road I bumped into Jon coming from the other direction.

'Straight to the aircraft,' he yelled. 'Now Zad is nearly Broken Arrow. Simon and Jake are getting the details.'

This was bad. The base was close to being overrun.

We left the Land Rover for Simon and Jake. I ran alongside Jon, up and down the berms, until we finally split between the two hangars, Jon going left and me going right.

Taff, Gifted and the boys were all over the aircraft, blitzing the blanks and covers and bunging the last few into their wooden storage boxes.

We had the Hardened Aircraft Landing Strip installed now, so we were off the engineering park and could do running takeoffs. The HALS, its taxiways, the refuel pads and arming bays were made of thick click-together corrugated steel and our boots slapped the metal against the sand as we ran across it.

An arrangement of eight-foot-high concrete bollards, open both ends, protected each Apache. You drove in one end and straight out onto the runway from the other. The bollards were just low enough for the back seaters to be able to see each other.

Finished with our two, the lads raced to clear the spare aircraft in Arming Bays Three and Four in case either of us had a problem on takeoff.

Still on the run, I scanned the back of the Apache to make sure the engine exhaust blanks were out. As I rounded the starboard wing, I checked all the covers were off the TADS.

Taff shouted, 'Tee-fifty pin's out!'

I clambered up and yanked open my door. One glance on the way up had told me the blanks were all off. I craned my neck out of the far window to check the other side of the fuselage.

I gave the key a twist.

'Pylons ... APU ... stab clear ...' I grabbed my jacket.

They weren't hollow warnings. The hydraulically powered pylons could cut a finger clean off when they jumped into position and the lads were always checking weapons as they powered up. The hot exhaust gas would soon be blasting out as the APU fired up and it wasn't stifled like the main engines because it didn't need to be: we didn't fly with it on. When the stabilator got its hydraulic power it would bang straight down with enough force to kill anybody in the way.

'Pylons, APU and stab are clear,' Taff barked back.

From arriving at the side of the aircraft to being settled in my seat with my chicken plate in had taken six or seven seconds. Simon would probably be no more than fifteen or so behind. I flicked the MPDs and other settings to daylight while I put my harness on and powered up his TADS so it cooled the FLIR.

Simon ran round the side of the aircraft.

Taff had plugged his headset into the side of the starboard wing now I had my helmet on. He opened Simon's front cockpit door. Simon climbed up beside me and shuffled forward along the IEFAB (pronounced eefab) to his cockpit. A bulky Improved Extended Forward Avionics Bay (IEFAB) sat either side of all Longbow Apaches. He jumped into his seat and pulled down the door. Mine was already closed.

He plugged in.

'What's the brief, mate?' I said.

'Now Zad are under attack. They're trying to get into the base. Harriers are on their way from Kandahar. Soon as they turn up we've got to pull off, to save hours.'

'Have we got launch authority?'

'Yes.'

'Brilliant.'

Mindful of Mutay, as soon as the aircraft came alive, I needed to check that the new codes hadn't dropped out of the radios.

'Good data,' Jon called after the comms check.

We now knew we were talking on four radios, and we could send data between the aircraft.

The second Simon was ready I pulled forward and banged on the toe-brakes; I'd need them on landing. The nose dipped to an abrupt halt. As soon as the first aircraft was ready, it would pull forward to let the other one know. I rolled the Apache right onto the HALS runway.

I tracked down a bit and looked over my shoulder. Jon's nose dipped. As soon as I saw him move again, I unlocked our tail wheel, spun the aircraft 180 degrees, locked the wheel up again and waited. I was slightly to the right of the centreline on the very end of the HALS, pointing towards Now Zad.

Saxon Ops gave us: 'Hold – hold.'

Jon continued onto the runway and taxied towards me. He spun the aircraft around, ending up about ten feet forward and left of me. We both had maximum runway for takeoff.

Jake came on the radio: 'Saxon, Wildman Five Zero, send update.'

'They're copying at the moment. Just stay on the APU.'

We brought both aircraft onto the refuel point, got pumped up, turned back and parked up in our bays. I was just about to switch off the main engines when Ops came back to us.

'Don't shut down. They're under attack again.'

I was sure the Taliban had been studying our reactions. Aircraft hadn't turned up after the first attack, so they knew they could give it another go.

We took off and Jake asked Saxon Ops for another update as his wheels lifted.

'They've got right up to the compound and are trying to break in.'

We'd been expecting this. Ever since Op Mutay they'd been getting closer to the DC. They'd tunnelled their way through all the buildings to spring an attack on our doorstep.

'Do you have exact locations?'

'Negative. We don't know where the Taliban are on the ground. All we know is the DC is getting hit hard.'

We gunned it low level across Highway Zero One and started climbing the instant we were over the desert.

Jake was straight onto the radio. 'Widow Seven One, this is Wildman Five Zero.'

No reply.

'Widow Seven One, Wildman Five Zero …'

Nothing. We were out of range. There was no point in us having a go now, but we would when we were closer, in case Jake's radio was on the blink.

Jake ordered the patrol to keep climbing. If we could get line of sight we might get comms from further out.

About sixteen klicks from the town, we got eyes on Now Zad. At first glance, it was hard to see what Ops were on about. The town looked more peaceful than I'd ever seen it.

Jake tried again. 'Widow Seven One, how do you read?'

'Lima Charlie.'

'Send update.'

'We're under heavy attack from all sides. The sangars are smashed and we can't fire out. We think they're trying to break into the compound from the south. We can't get any men in the sangars. We need you to stop the attack on the south side. The Taliban are in the building ten metres south of the DC and close to breaking through.'

BROKEN ARROW

SUNDAY, 16 JULY 2006
Now Zad

The sky over Now Zad was cobalt blue, a stark contrast with my first view of it during my initiation six weeks ago. There wasn't any smoke or sign of battle. The place looked like a ghost town.

'Widow Seven One,' Jake called, 'this is Wildman Five Zero and Wildman Five One. We have 600 cannon, seventy-six rockets and four Hellfires. Five minutes to run to the overhead. Confirm all friendly forces are in the DC and the Shrine?'

'A-firm affirmative; hurry up *please.*'

Shit. The short hairs rose on the back of my neck. It wasn't protocol to use 'please' in fire control orders, even in the opening calls. Widow Seven One was a top JTAC; for him to say please, the situation must be desperate.

'Wildman Five Zero,' Jake said, 'any civvies in the area?'

He got a nervous laugh. 'You must be joking. They all moved out long ago.' I could hear loud bangs in the background but none of the gunfire we were used to when the troops were in contact.

'Copied,' Jake replied.

The Shrine momentarily blocked my view. As we closed in I saw the bright white building beside the DC. It looked brand new.

'Widow Seven One, this is Wildman Five Zero. Four minutes to run. Where are they attacking from?' Jake asked.

'Widow Seven One. We're getting smashed to pieces from the north. They've tunnelled between the terraced houses and every house on our east is firing at us. Stand by for more ...'

I could hear the distinctive cracks and snaps of bullets passing the JTAC and sporadic pops and bangs.

'... and we think they're trying to get through the southern wall,' he continued, 'but we can't really tell because the sangars have been taken out.'

Bloody hell, he had no men on lookout. They must be under some horrendous fire.

'Copied. Three minutes to run,' Jake said. 'I can see a white H-shaped building just to your south.'

'Widow Seven One. A-firm. Hurry up. We're having a grenade fight over the southern wall.'

The Harriers had been crashed at the same time as us. We were still supposed to hand over to them when they arrived. It was just as well they hadn't. Harriers with their bombs and rockets can't shoot anywhere near this close to our own troops; they would have been unable to help them.

Fuck, neither can we really ...

My view of the white building was improving. It was orientated side-on to us and shaped like an 'H'. Just behind it was the base. It looked like they were virtually joined together. I knew they weren't, because I'd looked down there on a few occasions. There was a tight alleyway.

When the troops came out for a resupply run, they would turn right and then right again to go down the alleyway between the white building and the southern wall of the DC. This was going to be tight.

The Taliban had been changing their tactics ever since we kicked off on Op Mutay. Prior to 4 June they had engaged Apaches in the open and had little respect for them. They rushed around taking potshots at us and then laid their weapons down.

After we'd spanked their arses in Now Zad they'd do anything to attack when Apache cover wasn't expected. Now they only fought hard from concealed cover. They were tailoring their attacks to our reaction times. Thirty minutes of fighting followed by a break then thirty minutes of fighting, on and on until the early hours. This war of attrition had gone on, day and night, for weeks. It was wearing the troops down.

The Taliban were so wary of us, they'd tunnelled through buildings to get as close to the DC as possible. They'd bluffed us earlier with a half-hearted attack to test Apache cover, and when we didn't turn up they went for it.

We'd now arrived with the battle raging and we stood a chance of catching the scumbags with their pants down. My only worry was proximity. Too close and we'd either shoot and risk killing our own troops or hold fire and film their deaths instead. I needed a piss badly now.

I looked down at the screen by my knee. Simon's TADS image gleamed in the midday sun. There was no sign of activity in the main street.

We kicked left of the Shrine by about a kilometre, as if to go round Now Zad. Jon kicked right. We were separated by about a kilometre and getting into combat attacking positions on the DC's southern flank.

Our sights and sensors zoomed in the white building. Puffs of smoke blossomed along its rooftop.

We tracked west of the town, and came in perpendicular to the alleyway between the DC and the white building; the area of interest. The place was heaving with Taliban, whirling like dervishes as they lobbed grenades over the fifteen-foot wall. Our guys in the DC were flinging back their own.

They had been forced out of their sangars at the south-east and south-west corners of the DC by weight of fire, so had no idea their grenades were exploding ineffectively on the enemy's roof.

Robed figures moved backwards and forwards between the alleyway and the building, rearming with grenades.

'Bring me onto them,' Simon snapped.

I dragged across the cyclic and buried it in the inside of my right thigh, throwing the aircraft into a steep banked turn. I rolled it out again, facing the DC, then leaned us over so we moved crablike until I'd lined us up with the alleyway.

At this point, Jon and Jake were still wheeling round to our left.

I brought them up to speed. 'We've got Taliban in the alleyway to the south of the DC and PIDd them as hostile. Tipping in on a gun run, but it's danger close so call for clearance quickly.'

'I've seen them, stand by.' Jon broke off to speak with the JTAC. Positive ID lobbing grenades was sufficient for ROE to engage but the proximity wasn't. It was scary. Danger close was a major league understatement.

'Widow Seven One, this is Wildman Five Zero. We've PID'd them. They are danger close. Repeat, danger close. Confirm you want us to fire.'

Widow dropped his callsign to make the calls quicker. 'How accurate is your thirty mil?'

'I can put them through the window if you want,' Jake replied, 'but I repeat, they are danger close. Danger close. Get your men under cover with body armour and helmets on if you want us to engage.'

That was brave. He *could* post them right through the window in theory. In practice, I wasn't so sure. Neither of us had fired this gun and we didn't have time to test it either.

I'd pulled the stick back and dropped the collective to slow our approach until we got permission to fire. I could see the Taliban still criss-crossing the five metres between the alleyway and their building.

The JTAC came back to us within thirty seconds.

'A-firm. Clear hot.'

Jon jumped in: 'Checkfire! Don't fire!'

'Checkfire,' I called back.

We were running in. I threw the stick left and slowed her right down. Then I crabbed her to the right, hugely reducing our closing speed, so Simon could keep the TADS on the enemy, ready for the call.

Come on! We need to get the shot in here! The Taliban had seen our approach and run for cover.

'Acknowledge danger close with your initials and your clearance,' Jon said.

We didn't have cockpit recorders. If there was a board of inquiry, Jon wanted to be able to say: 'He knew we were danger close because he said danger close. To confirm it, here are his initials.' That was what made him one of the best SupFACs around. He was way ahead of the game.

'A-firm, Charlie Alpha – Charlie Alpha – that's a danger close, danger close. Clear hot, clear hot. Acknowledge.'

'Charlie Alpha, danger close. Clear hot,' Jake copied, cool as cucumber.

'Running in,' Simon called to Jake.

I could see everything on the MPD. Simon placed his crosshairs where the roof stopped and the wall facing us began. I turned us head-on to keep his sight as steady as it could be.

'Only go for ten rounds, buddy.' I didn't want to cramp Simon's style, but I didn't want things to go horribly wrong.

'I've already set it to ten. And I'm only going to pull a few of them off.'

Good call. He wasn't going for a normal combat burst of twenty. The longer the burst, the greater was the chance of accidental movement. If you fired a fifty-round burst, it meant five seconds of holding that crosshair absolutely dead still with an aircraft that's swooping towards the target. I was going to have to hold her steady and point straight at them to give Simon a fighting chance.

'Do you think it's accurate enough?' he said.

The slightest accidental movement of his thumb would shift the TADS and moving at that speed the weapons computer would assume he was tracking the target.

We were flying at thirty knots. The Hughes M230, single-barrel, externally powered 30 mm chain gun had a three-millimetre error. At this distance – 2,000 metres – that equated to six metres.

And the gun wasn't the only variable. I doubled the figures in my head – make that as much as twelve metres at this range. So some of our rounds could land in the compound. One thousand five hundred metres should bring the fudged error down to about nine metres – clear of the compound – if Simon was a good enough shot. If not, we'd have an authorised blue-on-blue.

'Mate, this is it. Three mil error, double it to six for the wife and kids. Two thousand metres is twelve mils and that's inside the compound. We need to be at a maximum of 1,500, which gives us nine. You don't want to fire before fifteen, buddy.'

I had to hold this thing 100 per cent steady, Simon had to perform flawlessly, and we didn't even know if the cannon was capable of hitting the target he aimed at. We both knew that if our rounds zapped into the compound, we'd be highly likely to kill or seriously injure our own troops. We would also be putting ourselves right in the Taliban's engagement zone; we'd be sitting ducks.

Whatever we did, it was going to be a nightmare down there.

We were busting every rule, doing everything our training told us not to do.

But what choice did we have? If the enemy broke through it would be like a knife fight in a bar. We'd be useless.

We had a JTAC under such immediate threat that he was prepared to risk bringing rounds down on his own men to save the majority and hold the base. To them, surrender was not an option; the Taliban would skin every one of them alive.

We had one shot and this was it.

I accelerated to sixty knots so I had speed to manoeuvre if we were shot at.

I called down the range. 'One point nine … One point eight …'

'Nice and steady, Simon. Any movement will throw those rounds.'

'I fucking know that, Ed.'

Of course, he did. But just saying it made me feel better.

I saw figures spilling out into the alleyway again. They moved towards the DC wall with what looked like a wooden cross in their hands.

Simon had his TADS on the same point – he had no choice but to hold it perfectly still – and I was still counting down. Simon had zoomed in to make sure there was no error on trigger pull, and when you zoomed in at that range, the image on the screen was massive.

The figures moved out of the frame and I looked up to see what they were up to. They'd got to the base of the wall.

'… One point six … one point five …'

A split second before Simon pulled the trigger, they bomb-burst away from the wall and ran back towards the building, dragging the cross with them.

The gun pumped. My feet vibrated. Simon's crosshairs never moved a millimetre. I saw the counter on the MPD drop quickly from 300 to 295 as the rounds swirled away, but didn't need to look; I'd heard and felt five distinctive thumps.

RIGHT: Ed aligns the rocket launchers to make them accurate so that the Apaches are ready to fight.

BELOW: The technicians work in the sweltering heat to rebuild the Apaches.

Pizza Hut

Shit-pit

My Room

ABOVE: Kandahar Airfield looking east. The Apache bays are on the far side of the Shit-pit.

RIGHT: Escorting Chinooks.

BELOW RIGHT: Loading up 30 mm High Explosive Dual Purpose (HEDP) cannon rounds into Ed's Apache under the watchful gaze of Taff before the spunkmuffin challenge. Ed's carbine rifle sits in a bracket on the right side of seat without the forward grip! His chicken plate sits on the seat, with his escape jacket and helmet on the Improved Extended Forward Avionics Bay (IEFAB).

ABOVE: Flying west with the M230 cannon actioned. The patrol skirts the Red Desert as the Apache passes south of Panjwai.

ABOVE: The monocle that sits over Ed's eye beams everything he needs to know to engage the enemy with a glance and the flick of a button.

MAIN IMAGE: The Red Desert with its 300-foot-high rolling sand dune spans as far as the eye can see south to Pakistan.

LEFT: The dust cloud of a Chinoo landing at the Task Force HQ.

LEFT: Lashkar Gah: the sprawling Provincial City of Helmand. From the bottom right is a 1km-long and 100m-wide road – known as sniper alley – which heads up and to the left, ending a a square grey compounc the Helmand Task Forc HQ. Beyond the city is the Helmand River and the Green Zone and beyond this, the GAFA Great Afghan Fuck All.

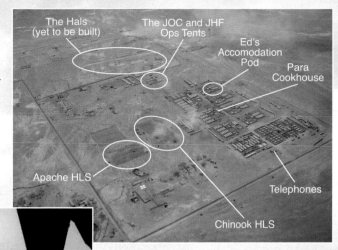

RIGHT: Camp Bastion in the early days. The layout has completely altered since.

BELOW: At the top of the drop before descending into Bastion ahead.

The Hals (yet to be built)

The JOC and JHF Ops Tents

Ed's Accomodation Pod

Para Cookhouse

Apache HLS

Telephones

Chinook HLS

LEFT: Ed's bed space with his pistol hanging from the fluorescent light above his cot.

BELOW: Large map tables in the JHF(A) Forward Ops tent. The aircrew area is at the back behind the white screen.

MAIN IMAGE: The Green Zone provides the Taliban with cover to approach the troops then melt away after any contact.

LEFT: Ed's flight ready to lift on Operation Mutay.

ABOVE: A Chinook extracting 3 Para.

BELOW: Patrols Platoon vehicles with JTAC stuck in the irrigation ditch ahead, during Operation Mutay.

LEFT: 30 mm HEDP rounds waiting to reload Ed and Billy on their return.

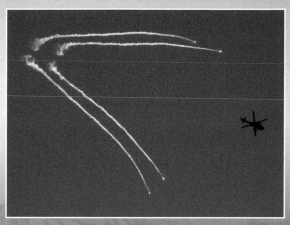

ABOVE: Having gone back to Now Zad, 'Bitching Betty' screams MISSILE LAUNCH and punches out flares to attract any missiles away from Ed and Billy.

ABOVE: Rockets being fired at dawn into Sangin to protect a Casualty Evacuation (casevac) Chinook whilst it pulls out seriously injured troops.

RIGHT: Ed's flight.

RIGHT: Groundies with a 100lb Hellfire missile.

MAIN IMAGE: Looking south over Now Zad town.

Banana building

Turret

LEFT: Hellfire laser seeker.

LS

——— Shrine

Clinic

DC

ABOVE RIGHT: A Hellfire slips off the rail.

ABOVE: A Hellfire being fired in anger.

RIGHT: Damage from a Hellfire.

ABOVE: The youngest air trooper officially opening up Camp Bastion's flight line.

BELOW: Musa Qa'leh showing the route of the convoy. The puffs of smoke are where Ed fired two bursts to initiate an improvised explosive device (IED). Billy dropped us ultra low level and skirted under the artillery shells saving us vital time.

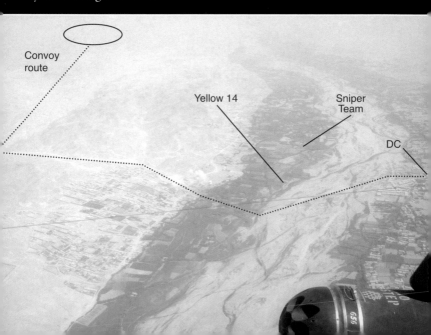

Convoy route

Yellow 14

Sniper Team

DC

After throwing their grenades, the last three Taliban returned to what they thought was the safety of their building, just as the rounds ploughed into the wall and roof. I saw all five rounds impact. Three bored small black holes in the roof and the two that hit the wall head-on made a much bigger splash. To the casual observer it must all have looked pretty insignificant, but to me it meant one thing: the gun was on. It was Deadeye Dick.

I called Delta Hotel – Direct Hit – on the JTAC's frequency.

My jubilation was swept aside by Widow Seven One. 'Stop! Stop! Stop!'

I broke hard right with the cyclic and ripped up the collective from the floor, climbing away from the building. We'd descended to 1,000 feet and were now 1,000 metres away from the Taliban. I'd been trying to keep the same aspect all the way, and I didn't want to change the profile of the aircraft while Simon was fighting to keep his crosshair still.

I flew the death profile, straight into their eyes. If they stood their ground now and decided to fire, they could shoot us just as easily as we could shoot them. I shouldn't have been doing it. But there was no one looking up at us – the men I'd seen on the street had run back. My only concern was that these rounds had gone into the compound. I'd witnessed the damage they did to buildings and the men hiding within.

'STOP STOP STOP,' the JTAC repeated. 'Your rounds are landing inside the DC. Copy?'

Simon yelled, 'Fuck!'

'Wildman has stopped,' I called back. I craned my head over to the left as the DC came into view. No one was firing up at us; it was just dust billowing in our own courtyard.

Fuck, had Jake blown it and hit the compound? I couldn't see Wildman Five One. They'd continued round the wheel and would have set themselves up to cover us. I knew Jon would be right behind me in my six o'clock position, with Jake's cannon at the ready. As we broke off our attack run, Jake would fire straight down to cover our sharp break. Setting up the racetrack, we called it, or setting up a pattern – one shooting, one setting up, then one breaking off, one running in.

Jon came through: 'Mate, you hit the DC.'

What the fuck was he thinking?

I guess he thought we'd just fired a ten- or twenty-round burst, only saw a few splashes on top of the building and assumed the rest had raked the compound.

I flung the Apache onto its left side as we hit altitude and spotted Jon and Jake off to the west, where we'd begun our attack run.

I flipped onto the inter-aircraft radio and pressed the mic button on the cyclic while Simon scoured the target and DC for enemy and friendly fire. 'We didn't. Every round landed on the building. Did you fire to cover our break?'

This wasn't a bitching contest. I just needed to confirm my theory.

'Negative,' Jake said. 'We did not fire.'

'I thought not. I'm 100 per cent sure that it *wasn't* our thirty mike mike in the DC. They were grenades, not thirty mil. I saw them being thrown from the alleyway just before we fired.'

I switched back to let the JTAC know what had happened.

'Negative, negative. That's not us. That's grenades coming into your compound. We had a Delta Hotel on the building to your south. They're trying to break into the DC. Copy?'

'Widow Seven One, copied. Re-attack … Re-attack.'

I thanked God that as the SWO I'd been watching the rounds like a hawk. I'd been studying the effects of weapons on different buildings so I could improve our effectiveness. I'd looked at every single cannon round fired in-theatre to learn how they impacted on different surfaces, and had taught the tactics accordingly.

If you had a man running along a boggy track in the Green Zone and there was a wall behind him, you didn't aim down at him and the ground. If the rounds missed, they were going to explode harmlessly in the earth. Smack the wall next to him as he was running and the frag would get him first time. You didn't even have to hit the guy.

'Wildman Five Zero, running in with ten rounds of thirty mike mike.'

Brilliant – they were on ten rounds as well.

I'd levelled off and turned the aircraft so we were on the opposite side of the target from Jon. The white building was orientated east–west. I'd run in from the west, fired the cannon rounds, kicked off south-east, then climbed, constantly turning the aircraft left so I could keep an eye on the compound. I didn't want to fly away from it; I wanted to keep it in sight.

Simon was concentrating on his target and I was concentrating on the landscape around it. I looked for leakers so I could call Simon onto them. Exactly the same was happening in the other Apache.

Simon zoomed in to see if there was anyone in the building. He studied doorways and windows.

With a final jink we were now turned head-on. Looking down on the compound from the east, I saw Jon flying directly towards it from the west. He was much closer than us.

We were facing each other and Jake would shoot straight ahead. It wasn't a problem; I knew the rounds were going downwards. But I had a job to do in a few seconds. There was no chance the enemy would go one-on-one with an Apache, but when we turned tail on them they'd send a heat-seeker up our backside or loose off some RPGs.

We needed to cover each other.

As soon as Jon and Jake had finished their run, I had to be in position for Simon to fire his cannon rounds at the building to cover their break – or if I saw any hostiles outside the building, to shoot them myself. By the time I'd talked Simon onto it, it would have been too late; platform protection was a split second win or lose decision.

I could see Jon tanking in towards the target.

We were 2,500 metres out and closing slowly. We were pointing nose to nose. They were closer and faster. When they turned to get away, Simon would have his crosshairs ready to go and I would be looking through the cockpit window; looking at the alleyway and the main street in front of the building for any leakers or Taliban trying to shoot up Jon's bird.

Either of us could fire – whoever had control of the gun last. We both had weapon controls. He had the gun up and it was now slaved to his crosshairs. But if I saw something I'd call, 'My gun', press 'Gun' on the cyclic and it would jump to my eye and be under my control instead.

It was Simon's job primarily to attack the target; to achieve mission success. He was this aircraft's mission commander. It was mine to defend the aircraft; to maintain platform protection. If I spotted a threat to my Apache or Jon's that took higher priority than killing a Taliban any day. It was all about mutual support. That was why we always made sure we could see and defend one another.

Simon had popped his screen out one field of view, expanding the image so he could see the whole of the white building. He could now push the crosshairs onto whatever target he wanted, steady them, and pull the trigger as and when.

I scanned the area for anyone taking a pop at my wingman. The gun wouldn't do anything until it was slaved to my eyes. But the moment I saw something it would be: 'My gun!' – bang – gone. As I made the call, I'd flick up with my thumb and pull the trigger. Within a split second, rounds would pour off the aircraft.

We were running in, but still slowly. Jon was hammering down. When he passed the target he was going to have to climb and turn back as soon as possible to cover our attack run. I was holding back to give him the time to do this; he'd be doing the same on our attack run. We didn't want two aircraft with their tails towards the target.

'Firing,' Jake called.

I saw a grey smudge appear under the nose of their Apache, either side of the barrel, as the cannon's propellant hit the air after being spat out by the muzzle break. Simon scoured the building for leakers. I was primarily looking out for Jon.

'Breaking,' Jon called.

They broke off their run and I watched the rounds impact all along the top of the northern wing. He broke south-west, as we'd done. I watched him climb away and waited until he came up level. Their gun was smack on too. Jake's shooting was spot on; this was going to be our day.

'Stand by.' This time I wasn't going to dive. I didn't want to drop my height. With an accurate gun and TADS Simon would cope with deadly precision. I flew level, Simon's cannon aiming progressively lower.

Again, Simon had his crosshairs on the junction between the roof and the wall.

'Covering.' Jon was letting us know they were in a position to attack if we should be fired at.

'Wildman Five One, running in with twenty rounds of thirty mike mike,' Simon responded on the JTAC frequency.

I accelerated and as Simon pulled the trigger I called on the inter-aircraft. 'Wildman Five One, engaging, twenty rounds, thirty mike mike.'

Rounds thumped along the wall and the roof.

Jon came on the inter-aircraft radio: 'Not sure we're having much effect on it.'

I said, 'Small holes on the roof mean they're penetrating before exploding. It'll be devastating in there.'

'Copied.'

The HEDP rounds were exploding against the wall. That was okay, but the frag was on the outside. The ones that hit the roof looked innocuous, but they were penetrating. I wouldn't have wanted one joining me in the room with a thousand shards of frag and a big flame and shock wave.

'Breaking!' I pulled up as hard and fast as I could, flying south-west, straining to find my wingman as I came round. They were all set up.

Wildman Five Zero thundered in once he saw we were ready. He fired all over the roof. There was still nobody out in the street. They must all have been inside.

We turned back in. Simon aimed his crosshairs up a little from where he'd fired last time. As he went to pull the trigger, he called, 'Engaging!' and moved his line of sight slowly upwards as he pulled off a twenty-round burst. The thirty mike mike stitched their way along the roof.

No one had left the building yet.

Widow Seven One called: 'We can hear screaming. Keep it up!'

It would have been Armageddon inside those walls.

Wildman Five Zero said, 'I'm going for the doors and the windows – you go for the other wing.'

That made sense to me. If I'd been hiding in that first wing, I knew where I'd be trying to run. We'd repeat what we'd just done on the last run, the length of the other roof. Jake had the doors and windows covered in case they were thinking about making a break for it.

Jon and Jake drove in. I didn't see their rounds as they ripped across the far elevation.

We ran in seconds behind and blasted another twenty-round burst along the second roof.

Smoke curled from the entrance holes and billowed from the doors and windows.

Jon and Jake fired another twenty-round burst into the main elevation of the second wing.

After several of these attack runs we'd stripped both tops and both exposed sides. The only bit we hadn't engaged was the central, linking span of the H.

Simon said, 'The final hiding place.' He aimed his crosshairs at the central section of roof. Below it was a steel door. He pulled the trigger and punched rounds through the roof, the door and down to the base of the building.

Jake said, 'Watch and shoot and look for leakers. Copy.'

We were heading west, within 1,000 metres of each other. We wheeled around, looking for movement. The only thing coming out of that building was smoke.

'Widow Seven One, this is Wildman Five Zero. How are things now?'

'Widow Seven One, the grenades and shooting stopped when you started attacking. And the screaming's stopped. Did anyone escape?'

After a brief pause Jon clicked his mic. 'Did you see anyone?'

I said over the intercom, 'Simon, you see anything, buddy?'

'Negative. Not a soul.'

'One hundred per cent no from this aircraft.'

Jake replied, 'Widow Seven One, this is Wildman Five Zero – that's 100 per cent negative. We'll stay around for as long as we can.'

We didn't want to leave them. If anyone had survived, they were going to have to run out of this building at some point, and when they did, we were going to nail them. Either that or they would choke to death.

We swarmed and waited for a breakout. They would have to run across the main road or head for the Shrine.

'Widow Seven One has now got our men in the sangars again.' The watchtowers could now see and kill any leakers themselves.

A Harrier turned up, callsign Topman, and we spoke to the Widow.

'Widow Seven One, this is Wildman Five Zero. With Topman on station, we're sorry, but we've got to break off.' We were under orders to save aircraft hours.

'Thank you very much. I'll see you tonight.' He sounded 100 per cent more cheerful than he had when we'd turned up.

'If it was down to us, we'd be here every night. Good luck,' Jake replied and he meant it too.

'Wildman Five Zero … this is Topman … You got anything for me?'

'Negative, the place looks quiet. Speak to Widow Seven One for AOR update,' Jake said. 'We're breaking for homeplate.'

We couldn't tell Topman any more. All we'd done was turn up and hammer the white building, and we were now about to clear off. We didn't really know anything else.

After the JTAC read out the AOR brief – what had happened and what the threat was – we headed back to base.

We fuelled up and taxied into the bays. After shutting down the engines, the lads went to work replenishing the 30 mm and the techs checked the aircraft.

We were loaded up and ready to close down before Jon and Jake so I got on the radio.

'Saxon this is Wildman Five One, permission to close down?'

'Saxon. Close down.' This was a good sign. It meant that Now Zad had calmed down for the time being. Otherwise we would have been told to stay on the APU ready to take over from Topman.

Jake's grin stretched from ear to ear as we walked into the Ops room. 'Hey, guys! How *you* doin'?' He was quite proud of his Joey impression.

Everyone looked up. There were no smiles.

'Oh look, it's the murderer.' Chris shook his head.

Jake was always having the piss taken out of him royally, but not this time. This time, something was badly wrong.

'President Karzai wants to know why we've slaughtered innocent Afghan nationals.' The OC glared. 'You do know what that building was, don't you?'

Jake looked worried.

'Did it look nice?'

'Well … Yes …'

'Nice white building? Didn't see any red crosses on it, did you?'

'What?'

I trawled my memory at warp speed. I suddenly felt very uncomfortable.

'You shot up the fucking hospital.'

'No!' Jake went white as a sheet and glanced anxiously at the rest of us – his flight.

'It's called The Clinic. It's a hospital.'

Our jaws dropped.

Jake leaned forward and pressed his hands on the Ops table to steady himself. The room remained deathly quiet.

I piped up to give him a bit of support. 'You complied with ROE, mate. I saw Taliban running out with mousehole charges too.'

Chris burst out laughing, followed quickly by everyone else.

'It is a clinic,' he said. 'But everyone left ages ago.'

We had a quick brew after the debrief, in place of the lunch we'd missed. We seemed to have lost our appetites.

'Do you know what was worrying me most when they told me it was a clinic?' Jon said. 'They heard loads of screaming.'

I nodded.

'I pictured little kids and all sorts,' Jon said.

'My stomach did a Fosbury Flop,' I said.

The Taliban went to town before we'd even got our wheels back on the ground. They sent a message to Kabul to say that the Apaches had shot up a clinic and killed scores of sick and injured people. Karzai had swallowed it.

We passed the clearance issue straight to Widow Tactical Operations Cell. The JTAC said he had no choice, and that we'd done what he'd asked. Everyone who'd been to the Now Zad DC knew the building was empty and that it posed a threat to them but it didn't stop the shit from Kabul.

There was a big debate. It went back to the ROE.

Could he see the target? Yes he could. Was that it in his sphere of influence? Yes it was. Could he have stopped the attack using a much softer approach by escalating the level of force to match the attack? No he couldn't; they were about to go Broken Arrow. Our Charlie Alpha JTAC was off the hook, but the buck didn't stop with him.

Kabul still wanted answers and that meant sending the tapes to the CO in Kandahar so he could judge for himself before answering up the chain of command.

With the UK government breathing down his neck, Lieutenant Colonel Felton needed some answers and fast. He rang up and made it perfectly clear that he trusted us, and if something was amiss he would still defend us when the time came. He wanted to know if we had seen anything that could have prevented the attack on the clinic, and did we use proportionality?

We saw everything and it was perfectly clear that the Taliban were using the building as a vantage point to attack the DC. They were not afraid to continue their assault in full view of us and used the building as a refuge between attacks. If we hadn't fired and ended up leaving Now Zad after running low on fuel, they would have continued their attack.

Any fast air on call could not have dealt with a target this close to the DC. Our men there had a one-shot chance of survival. Their final chance was an Apache attack – no other airframe would have worked – to destroy all of the Taliban in the adjacent building before they either broke into the DC or we ran out of fuel.

The CO thanked us and the tapes were to be dispatched by Lynx to Kandahar for him to look at later on.

For weeks afterwards, Jake still shuddered when people walked up to him and muttered the word clinic. And many did.

THE PLAN

SUNDAY, 16 JULY 2006
Camp Bastion

I wanted an immediate debrief with our Hi-8 tapes. I gathered Simon, Jon, Jake and the Ops Officer round the little Sony hand-held to go through them and review the rules of engagement. I wanted to make a particular point about our rounds.

Jake and Jon knew by now that we hadn't fired into the compound, but I still felt it was important to show them exactly what I'd seen.

All weapon engagements seemed to play out in slow motion to me. I'd been watching gun tapes over and over since 2003. I no longer tried to see if rounds were hitting. I looked at where the line of sight was moving, to see if the range was stable. I looked at all the tiny little things that others didn't take in because they were too focused on the excitement of targets exploding inside the crosshairs.

On the tiny 4x3-inch screen we saw exactly what we had described to the CO. I pressed the slow motion button as soon as I saw the counter change from 300 to 299. Simon had been record-ing his TADS image and we were looking at what we'd seen in the

Apache, only frame by frame. The round eventually struck and exploded. I let it continue frame by frame for all five rounds.

You couldn't see the individual rounds, just their heat swirls – and then the explosions. They were separated by 1/10th of a second. It took half a second for all five rounds to impact on the building. Not one of them landed inside the compound.

'Look at the splash here.' I repeated the film of the rounds hitting the roof. There was a small hole where each of the shaped charges had gone clean through. 'Hardly anything,' I said. 'But look where this one hit the wall. An impressive splash, but it didn't penetrate the side of the building.'

I pressed fast-forward and there was a wisp of smoke through the holes in the roof, but nothing from the holes in the walls. Smoke billowed from windows and doors nearby.

'When you fire at something look at the effect it's having; only then will you know if your weapons are—'

The canvas curtain parted and the Chinook boys rushed into the Ops tent. They'd just had a call out. They came over to join us at the bird table. The flight had been saved from me rewinding once again.

The Ops Officer ran in from next door, shaking his head. Dickie Bonn was normally so cool I wondered whether he had a pulse. But normal had flown out of the window. 'It's Now Zad,' he said.

The Chinook boys stared at him in disbelief. On their last outing, the Taliban had only missed them by a whisker. They didn't let it show, but they must have been shitting themselves.

'Is there a time frame?' one of the pilots asked.

'We don't know that yet.'

Nichol Benzie, on a navy exchange with the RAF, looked at us and grinned ruefully. 'Here we go again.'

We knew them all by name and got on well, but didn't really socialise. Everyone pretty much kept themselves to themselves. We'd have a bit of banter when we saw them at Ops, but they tended to stay in their tent and we stayed in ours, even though they were right next to each other.

Partly, we were ashamed to invite them over. The Army Air Corps had a TV set with an old PlayStation underneath, a few books and a couple of magazines; they had stereos, a widescreen surround sound TV, Xbox, Playstations and every game going. We had camp cots lashed together; they had a real sofa. We had cots; they had beds. We had a cool box; they had a fridge. When it came to home comforts, the RAF didn't fuck around.

We occasionally sat together at mealtimes, but not often. Maybe we didn't want to intrude. They were at the pointy end of the stick. They got shot at and shot up on a daily basis. There was no slack with them. When they chilled out, we left them to it.

Their mission now, Dickie said, was to take two Chinook loads of troops and ammunition into the DC. Ours was to protect them.

The critical question for us both was when? Could we do it at a time of our choosing? If so, how were we going to skin the cat? Was there a way of catching them on the hop?

The question we were asking ourselves was how were we going to protect them? The short answer was that we couldn't. We bluffed it last time and the mortars had missed them by no more than a minute.

We were now going to have to search every inch of Now Zad for a mortar base plate, a dish just a metre across with a tube sticking out of it. Thermal was no good: the tube wouldn't be hot until they fired it, and it was too late by then. We were better off zooming in with a camera, but even then, it was like looking for a needle in a haystack. There were just too many warren-like streets and back-yards and alleys.

Where was the obvious place for a firing point? It couldn't be right on top of the Shrine – that was too close. If they took it away into the Green Zone, we had no chance. They could be sitting under a piece of hessian, listening in to our radios. When they heard a crackle, they'd throw off the cover, fire one off, and throw it back over.

We could do prophylactic firing to try to provoke a response, but we weren't allowed to fire at targets we hadn't seen threaten us. We could only fire into empty desert or somewhere we knew for sure was safe.

Nichol shrugged. 'Right, then, how are we going to do this?'

We could dump the guys in the desert a good distance from Now Zad, and let them make their way in. But they'd have to lug tons of ammunition. They could take vehicles out, but in doing so they'd alert the Taliban to their destination. The Taliban would have bags of time to get into the new firing points and hose the lads to pieces when they tried to get back to the DC.

The only viable option was to land close to the DC. And when it came to LSs, the only remaining option was south-west of the base, protected by friendly fire from the Shrine.

The one thing we knew for sure was that we couldn't go in daylight again. The Taliban had been fed the Chinooks' exact grid last time round, and only missed them by seconds. We'd even had a close shave at dusk.

We grabbed the Intelligence Officer. Jerry had catalogued every firing position and every time the Taliban had engaged the DC.

'When exactly does the firing kick off in Now Zad?'

'About half an hour after total darkness.'

'If you were the enemy, and you were trying to set up a firing position into the DC, where would you choose?'

'Except for today, their firing positions have nearly always been from the north through north-east to the east,' Jerry said. 'Never too far out; just around the main town, where they know we can't follow up.'

'Okay, so if you're firing from the north or north-east, how and when are you going to do it?'

'Taking down an aircraft is still their number one goal. They'll have weapons in place throughout the day. They'll only move them if they think you're not coming. I reckon they'll drop their weapons just after dusk, as they shift their attention back to harassing the boys on the ground.

'It's all part of the same agenda. They want to grind them down, in the hope of ramping up the casualty rate. They know that if they succeed, you guys will have to come in, giving them the opportunity to shoot you down.'

'They won't hang around with a weapon system set up,' Jerry said. 'They maintain sporadic fire 24/7, but only start hammering the DC after dark. They're unlikely to move into the town during daylight because they know they'll be spotted from above, especially with a heavy weapon.'

The penny dropped. They must have assumed that by knocking out six watchtowers – we found out about the other two sangars in the debrief – and lobbing over all those grenades, we must have taken loads of casualties. As it turned out, none of them were serious enough to warrant a casevac.

They'd have been waiting to ambush us all day long, and would expect us again before it got too dark.

The two best times to attack were dawn and dusk. It wasn't quite day, it wasn't quite night. Dusk was a great time for a drop off, but also for escaping after an ambush. The eyes hadn't yet adjusted to the darkness so errors in judging distance and recognition were rife. The crews were safer because the Taliban would struggle to pinpoint their exact location when they were at their most vulnerable – the thirty seconds to a minute on the ground. But it was also prime time for an ambush; perfect conditions for having a shot and then melting away because any follow-up would be hampered by darkness. Or so they might think.

We had a FLIR system that didn't care whether it was day or night. As dusk fell and they moved back from their mortar or gun emplacement to the DC, the Taliban would be our perfect quarry.

Once we failed to show up for our wounded after last light, they'd assume none was critical enough to be flown out. They'd pick up their heavy weapons and carry on smashing away at the DC, as they had the last three nights on the trot.

All the combat indicators over the last few weeks signalled that they were determined to take Now Zad before the infidels changed the rules and brought in reinforcements.

We'd already tried a dusk drop off and now knew that dawn could be too late, so agreed that we'd let last light go then get down on the ground twenty minutes into darkness, when the enemy were most likely to be on the move. We'd get in and out after they'd dismantled their heavy weapons and before they'd set them back up again. A short window of opportunity – but the only one we had.

So we knew when. We just had to decide how.

The Apaches would have to sit back. There was no point in flying ahead of the Chinooks to look for weapons; we might as well use a loud hailer to warn them of their impending arrival. We'd done the arrive-and-cause-a-deception-then-bring-in-the-Chinooks-at-the-last-minute plan; the Taliban weren't about to fall for it twice. And they knew the Apaches would only be on station a couple of hours. They'd be set, ready to fire the mortar the minute the Chinooks arrived.

Best to let the Chinooks go in first; at least they'd have no warning. The Chinooks needed to be in, drop them off and pull pitch within thirty seconds. The troops would literally have to hit the ground running.

One major worry was that the Taliban had knocked out all the generators in Now Zad; it was deathly quiet. The Chinook was not exactly stealthy, and your hearing is better at night. If they thundered across the desert as they normally did the game would immediately be up. The best way of getting them in quietly was to screen their noise behind the mountains.

The plan was coming together. As the Chinooks crept in from the west and hit the deck twenty minutes after dark, we'd punch up straight and high. Hopefully they'd be in and out before the Taliban clocked on. If they hit a Chinook, we'd lay down fire so the troops and downed crew could extract into the DC. We had to try to bolster the District Centre, whatever it took. There was no alternative. We all agreed it was our best chance of getting in and out alive.

Now we had to push it past the CO 3 Para, Lieutenant Colonel Tootal.

Dickie Bonn was away for the best part of an hour.

'It wasn't easy,' he said. 'He wants his men in there right now. He's worried about another attack. But he appreciates our plan, and it's a Go.'

We aimed to set off forty minutes before last light and take a wide, circuitous route. We'd fly up through the mountains, where we knew there were no occupied villages. We'd go out to the west, up to the north, and approach Now Zad from behind the ridgeline.

Then we'd come in low level, limiting the run-in so the Chinooks could only be heard on the final two klicks. Keeping close to the ground, sheltered by the Shrine, would muffle some of the noise. We reckoned they could be at the LS by the time they were heard. In the meantime, we prayed for a north-easterly wind ...

As they thumped down onto the ground we would climb and separate, one going right, one left. If they landed bang on plan, twenty minutes after dusk, it would just have become pitch-black.

Plan set. Route set. We programmed it into our equipment. We were ready.

The Chinooks would fly ahead of us, as normal, on Night Vision Goggles. We would remain low too, sitting back about one kilometre so we could react to any ground fire.

No time for dinner again. Jon brought out the chocolate bars and we walked back to our aircraft.

Jon realised it must have been at least an hour since we last took the mickey out of Jake.

'I hope your new baby boy doesn't join the Paras, Jake. That would be most unfortunate.'

'And why might that be, Jon?' Jake's grin told us he knew this was the price he had to pay for munching on one of Jon's choccy bars.

'He'd be called Paraffin.'

Jon always managed to lighten the mood when things were getting fraught.

We took off exactly forty minutes before last light on a completely silent departure. We wanted to give the Taliban as little to chew on as possible.

THE ANTI-AIRCRAFT GUNNER

SUNDAY, 16 JULY 2006
West of Now Zad

Whenever we went back to Kandahar we usually headed directly south into the desert then climbed and eventually turned east. No one would know any different until about an hour later when the Taliban reported us landing in KAF.

Camp Bastion was monitored by the Taliban's informers and we wanted them to think this sortie was entirely routine. By lifting this early, taking that route, and not turning up at one of the bases at dusk they would assume – we hoped – that we must have gone back to Kandahar.

We approached the ridgeline to the west of Now Zad at very low level, the two Chinooks up front, engines glowing on the PNVS thermal image in my right eye, us two behind. Their tails picked up and their engines glowed brighter as they ramped up the speed round the final corner. Once round, the tails settled and their heat signature dimmed as they dropped the power back, so the blades were coasting, deadening the noise as much as they could on the last two kilometre run-in.

I silently begged the enemy not to fire.

One klick to run

Please don't fire ... please don't fire ...

Both aircraft flared, and then disappeared in a dust cloud of their own making.

At that point, Jon and I pulled up hard and separated. I went right; he went left. As we climbed, we both looked straight down. I had my gun actioned, and knew he would too. My finger was on the trigger. I had my range already set up. All I needed to do was steady, and fire.

My left eye was peeled for a burst of tracer, or a flash on the ground from anywhere around Now Zad, my right hunting for small thermal blobs or heat from a fired weapon so I could warn them of imminent incoming. The JTAC had been warned that we wouldn't ask for an AOR update or permission to engage. We knew that our men were in the base and there were no friendlies out there. We still didn't make communication. Even secure radios gave a telltale squelch.

Widow Seven One had been warned of our arrival time, but the information had been kept tight. He would call us once the game had been given away by our arrival. They believed that one of their resident ANP was a Taliban informer. To put them off the scent of an inbound flight over the last few weeks, the boys had periodically jumped into the vehicles, ready to roll. 'Let's mount up, let's go and meet the Chinooks.' The main gate never opened though and they all burst out laughing as they went back to what they were doing, Even the ANP saw the funny side of it.

Another variation was for Dan Rex, the OC, to have all the men chilling out, not a care in the world. They knew what time they'd be going out, but the policemen didn't. At exactly three minutes before the go, every man would jump up, whack his body armour on, clamber onto the vehicles, and roar off to meet the helicopters.

They had to do a lot of that stuff to confuse the touts. At that time, nobody trusted the ANP. It was an awful situation. They couldn't even have guys watching for the helicopters, because their body language would broadcast what they were up to. The commanders could only go by timings or sound. As soon as they heard the aircraft, the men piled out of the base and tanked it to the LS.

The PNVS had an awesome picture tonight; it looked more like a two-tone TV picture than an IR image. I could see the boys coming out in vehicles, under cover of the sangars. I knew they'd be as anxious as I was. There was a lot of ammunition and men to offload, and a Chinook was the biggest target going.

Now that the Chinooks were landing and the game was up, the Widow finally called us.

'Wildman Five Zero this is Widow Seven One. How do you read?'

'Lima Charlie.'

'We've got patrols going out on the ground right now. Stand by.'

We were looking down. I was visual with Jon, and he would have been with us.

I keyed across to him on the inter-aircraft.

'We're visual with the patrols going out. Confirm you've got four vehicles.'

'A-firm, four vehicles coming down to the north of the Shrine.'

Almost immediately, the Chinooks rose out of the dust and pegged it out of there to the south-west.

We'd done it, less than thirty seconds on the ground, a truly amazing feat from the loadies and disembarking soldiers. The Chinooks hadn't received any fire and were now too far away to come to any harm from Now Zad. It didn't mean that the boys on the ground were in the clear, but the prize the Taliban really wanted was a big cow.

All we had to do now was provide cover for the patrols while they got everybody back to camp and then home for a rest.

My heart raced as tracer streamed out of the base, aiming north-west. I thought north-west was a safe area. A village extended from Now Zad in that direction, but I didn't have it down as holding Taliban. Within seconds it was like *Star Wars* down there.

'They're taking fire – I can see tracer,' Jake shouted.

I clicked the mic. 'Negative. That's not incoming.' All of the tracer was coming from the DC and it was now heading north-west, north, north-east and east.

Widow Seven One jumped in. 'We're under attack, we're under attack. We're taking heavy fire from the north-east. Can you see a firing point to the north-east?' The north-east tracer trail had stopped.

'Wildman Five Zero will cover the patrol,' Jake said. 'Wildman Five One, you help Widow Seven One.'

'Copied, Wildman Five One ready for talk-on.' We were ready for him to direct us onto the target.

'All I know right now is the north-east sangar is pinned down from a building 200 metres north-east.'

It must have taken a heavy weight of fire to pin the sangar down. And it meant we couldn't use their tracer to locate the firing point.

At least we had something to go on. We needed to start looking in the area of the bakery. A long street led east off the main one, a couple of hundred metres north of the DC, then south-east, past a drop-off point for the jingly wagons the locals used as buses, to a wadi we called the M25. The wadi was a main supply route for the Taliban, out of sight of the DC.

We'd had a look round to orientate ourselves a few days earlier, because the ANP and Taliban were fighting over who owned the bakery. We'd picked up the offending building quite easily because it was one of only a handful of three-storey buildings in the place. Actually, it just had a little breeze block and hessian-roofed hut on top, but that qualified as three storeys in this town.

I looked down but couldn't see movement. It was pitch-black in my left eye and my right was looking at a thermal picture.

I released the gun back to its stowed position.

Simon scanned the streets with his FLIR camera.

'Five One's looking but nothing seen. Confirm tracer?'

I still couldn't see any incoming. Normally there was a lot of tracer fire from the Taliban, but not this time.

'Negative. He won't give his position away.' Bright bloke. There was an aircraft above him. He was going easy on the tracer.

We were now to the east of the town, directly over the Green Zone, heading north and looking west.

The JTAC tried to steer us onto the gunner's firing position, 'He's on the—'

I saw what he was about to describe in horrifying detail with my naked eye before he had time to finish the sentence – a red glow shooting up from the location he was in the process of describing.

My right eye had the thermal picture, but there was no light in it whatsoever.

Fuck, it was tracer. My right eye only saw heat. Tracer burnt, but from the back. You didn't see tracer on thermal.

The glow in my left eye extended towards us like a long red laser beam. The point it appeared to start from wasn't the muzzle of the gun. Tracer only begins to burn 110 metres out.

If tracer grew in length, it indicated longer bursts. This was a sustained, continually growing line of red light. The gunman wasn't in the business of spraying. He was in the business of killing.

So far, the solid red line was going to miss us. It was way forward of the aircraft. The radio sparked up: 'Being engaged.'

No shit, Sherlock …

I hoped the JTAC was about to tell me which building the gunner was in.

Then the red beam started to curve towards the aircraft. I had no time to react. At 1,000 metres per second, it was approaching far too fast.

We were only 1,500 metres away now, and the stream of tracer had aligned itself to us within one and a half seconds of the trigger first being pulled. I lifted my shoulders and buried my neck low, waiting for the impact, eyes narrowed to stop any shit getting in them at that point. The bullets flew straight past my left window, appearing to mesh through the blades. How it failed to smash pieces off them I had no idea.

Fucking hell …

I'd never had tracer fired accurately at me in the air before. The bending phenomenon was a new one on me.

'That nearly hit us!' Simon's voice had risen a couple of octaves. I knew just how he felt.

My mind raced. Our assailant's range was a fraction too long, which was why it went just over the top, but his lead was perfect. That hadn't been a bend. Tracer only bends with gravity. He'd been firing straight and I'd been moving forward at 110 mph. He'd anticipated where I was going to be one and a half seconds later and only missed by a whisker.

I flung the stick to the right, pulling back hard on the cyclic to wrench the aircraft round.

The tracer continued to shoot past on my left. Had it gone behind us he would have been using the ambush method: fire in one place and wait for the Apache to fly through it. Not this fucker though. He was tracking me. I had less than a second and a half to move before he dropped his aim slightly and cut us in two.

So far it was only luck that had saved us.

I tipped the blades and threw the Apache right, onto its side. When you turn a helicopter through ninety degrees and pull power the thrust drags you horizontally; you are pulling yourself sideways across the sky. But the weight of the aircraft takes you diagonally downwards.

I didn't want to go down in the Green Zone.

I pulled back hard, keeping the Apache on its side, the radius of the turn getting tighter and slower as I adjusted the cyclic, moving the thrust arrow up enough to keep me level.

I held the tight, level turn and shot a quick glance vertically upwards over my left shoulder – left eye, tracer; right eye, nothing – then right, vertically down – left eye, black as a witch's tit; right eye, the Green Zone.

I'd taken about three seconds to roll her halfway around when the tracer stopped. I needed to get eyes back on the gunner, and fast. I didn't want to lose sight of the next onslaught. My mind flicked back through my Air Combat Tactics Instructor training. The length of burst meant only one thing: this wasn't anything less than a proper grown-up anti-aircraft gun. We were facing an AA gunner, one-on-one, and he was holding a better hand than I had. I pulled the stick as far back into my left groin as I could. I needed to change the odds.

I'd virtually turned the Apache on a sixpence by slapping its belly into the air. I'd pulled in all the power I could, which had reduced my speed massively. If I'd just flung it around I'd still have been doing the same speed. Instead, I'd spun the aircraft and slammed the brakes on at the same time.

Simon couldn't help. I'd turned away from the gunner and his TADS was way out of its limits. I'd had no choice.

As we compressed round the final forty-five degrees, I could feel the whole weight of the aircraft push up on me. I was rammed back into my seat. My helmet suddenly weighed a ton and I had to fight to keep my head up. The chinstrap dangled below my chin and the monocle's heavy metal mount on its right lifted the cup over my left ear clean away. The noise of the aircraft's engines deafened me. My monocle was the only thing stopping the helmet from tilting further down on the right. It dug deep into my eye socket, cutting into my skin just below the lid.

I began to groan out loud. My jacket and chicken plate were pressing me ever deeper into my seat.

I was terrified he'd get his range right next time and second guess my speed. If he did, he was going to smack his 23 mm shells straight into our flank. And these weren't AK bullets that would simply bounce off. They were the same kind of exploding cannon rounds that we fired. If they hit us, my misery would come to an abrupt and permanent end.

As I approached the 180 degree point I threw us the right way up and dumped the collective lever. I didn't want to gain any speed. The Apache was a clever bugger, and I was taking full advantage of that. It automatically scheduled the big stabilator on the back to keep the aircraft level. If you threw the stick forward it would begin to nose down, but the stabilator would shift and bring it back up again. As I dumped the lever and pulled back the stick, I was using the stab as a big fuck-off airbrake, the size of a barn door.

We were now facing south, still over the Green Zone, with Now Zad to our right. My eyes were glued to the area where the tracer had been fired. Only eight seconds had elapsed since the first burst, but it felt a lot longer. I knew the gunner was judging my every move, waiting for the right moment, and I was shitting it.

We'd already lost a lot of speed in the turn and it soon dropped through sixty knots with the stab down.

'Keep your speed on,' Simon urged. 'Speed is life.'

Simon was a Qualified Helicopter Tactics Instructor (QHTI). He'd done the RAF's version of my ACTI course. He knew as well as I did that the faster the aircraft was going, the quicker it would respond. A helicopter isn't like a jet, where you flip down an aerofoil and instantly shed a shit-load of Gs. If you're hovering in a helicopter and you throw the stick forward, it takes a while to respond. An Apache could manoeuvre fairly fast at max speed, but not fast enough, as we'd just discovered. The anti-aircraft rounds had appeared from nowhere in the space of a second. The gunship didn't respond in that short a time. We were at this guy's mercy.

I said, 'Not if he gets his range and—'

The AA flared up at us again.

This time, I knew he could get us. His first burst had been a fraction above my line of sight and continued just over the top of us. Not this time though. It began on the line I was looking down. He had his range 100 per cent bang on; the 23 mm wouldn't go above or below us this time. To make things worse, as the finger of red began to reach up in the first half a second it started to bend sharply towards us. He'd got it right; he'd seen me slowing.

'MAN STAB,' I yelled as I flicked the stabilator into manual with my left thumb and rammed it down.

I'd hit the brakes like a full-on emergency stop. I took a sharp breath, and then just held on.

This is it, this is it ...

Over the radio: 'You're taking incommmming!'

The next voice was Simon's. '*Fuuuuuuck!*'

The line of tracer grew and came forward, arcing ever closer, straight towards the nose of aircraft. It was going to take Simon out first.

I wanted to close my eyes. I was terrified.

The very beginning of the jet of hot metal passed so close in front of the aircraft it lit up the cockpit. Simon held onto the handles above him and I could see the silhouette of his helmet, arms and hands in the ghostly red glow.

I forced myself to look down, to try to follow it to its source and pinpoint the gunner. There was no point in Simon using the TADS.

I'd not sat still for more than a second and it would've taken a lot longer than that to get it under control.

I thought, 'I'm going to fly straight into this lot.' But there was nothing I could do.

I watched the tail end of the burst climbing towards us. It had about a second to go.

There seemed to be about a metre between the rounds lighting up Simon. That was closer than I'd have expected, and they weren't all following the same line. It had to be a double-barrelled weapon.

The last one's going to hit …

My mouth flooded with the metallic taste of adrenalin. Fight or flight – and I could do neither.

'FUCK!' I screamed. '*FUCK!*'

I felt my heart pounding against my chicken plate and pulsing through my thumbs. My teeth clenched so hard I thought my jaw would pop.

Simon still gripped the handles. He was fighting the urge to grab the controls and try to fly us the fuck out of here.

The business end of the red snake whipped past our nose and Simon was plunged into darkness as it rose high and to the left of us.

Thank fuck I'd braked. Ten or twenty knots faster would have put us right in the middle of his fire. Only three or four rounds would have killed us.

The gunner was good, too bloody good.

His range was smack on and his lead was too. The stab had braked us quicker than he could have anticipated. We wouldn't get away with it a third time.

Something wasn't right.

He wasn't just sitting there in a tea towel, keeping his fingers crossed.

'He's got NVGs,' Simon and I called in unison.

If we were going to survive once more I had to do more than change direction and speed and distance again. And we couldn't just fly off; he'd shoot us up the arse in a heartbeat. I had to change height. It was all I had left.

I didn't want to lose sight of him, even for a split second. I stared at the area the tracer had come from like a rabbit at a set of oncoming headlights.

Is this my destiny? Is this going to be what happens to me?

It wasn't philosophy; it was pure fear.

But something inside me decided I wasn't going to let him get away with it again. I needed to find him. So far I'd been flying for our lives. I wasn't in a position to fight. I'd have loved to have put a burst straight down, but I didn't know precisely where he was. I could have fired randomly into Now Zad, but that was against the ROE, and wouldn't achieve a hell of a lot. The Taliban didn't do scared. If you missed them, they just kept shooting – and the muzzle flash of our cannon would just give them a clearer target to aim at.

I would have to hit him to stop him. And in the process I was going to have to change direction, speed, distance and, worst of all, height.

It had taken me about two seconds since the last burst for me to think it through.

'Hold on ...'

With the collective lever still low, I slammed the cyclic into my right thigh.

'Here we goooo,' I yelled.

The disc rolled over to the right and the Apache dropped right wing low, like we were creeping over the top of a giant rollercoaster. If I pulled back and into my left thigh, I could keep the nose up. My speed was down to forty knots. At full power it would keep the height.

I left the lever down.

We headed downwards, gathering speed. I let nature take its course. We dropped faster and faster. Eventually the tail would follow the nose, weather-cocking behind it. I didn't pull back on the stick or pull in power. I'd need that power later.

The aircraft side-slipped towards the ground until the stab dragged up its sorry arse and pulled down its nose and whipped the tail around behind us. In a few seconds we'd spun through eighty degrees horizontally and ninety vertically. The Fire Control Radar pointed north, the wheels south and the nose straight down into the Green Zone. I wanted to give our gunman a bigger headache than he'd given me – and fucking with his range was a good place to start.

Our speed built up fast. The loudest sound in the air-conditioned cockpit was normally the swish of the gaspers blowing air. But we could now hear the rush of air flowing noisily over missiles, wing tips, even the angles of the windscreen wiper.

The engines weren't screaming because I had the collective lever down, but their time would come. I was using the energy of the aircraft and the speed and the weight and good old gravity to get it going as fast as I could in the shortest space of time. My head was gyroscopically stable in space, keeping the monocle's crosshair over the same point on the ground. The Apache was effectively rotating about my static right eye.

When he fired I needed those rounds to pass behind us; that meant achieving a speed he wasn't expecting or thought we weren't capable of. Instead of shooting at me high in the sky, I wanted him to try to track me towards the ground. The perfect crossing, dropping, accelerating, distance-changing challenge Captain Mainwaring had caught me out with all those years ago.

In a perverse kind of way I was hoping the gunner would fire, to see if his rounds passed behind me. He had to try to get them ahead of where I was, but I was really starting to motor. He needed to get ahead of his aiming mark – he'd be aiming low and trying to shift. I needed to change angle and keep increasing my speed.

The noise rush grew. I could see 80 in my monocle.

'Have you been hit?' Jon shouted.

Then 90 …

He'd seen the rounds and thought they'd hit us, and now he was seeing the aircraft fall on its side and dive towards the ground.

'Not yet!' I shouted over the inter-aircraft radio.

101 …

I started to pull back on the cyclic and applied a little power on the collective to regain full control.

112 …

Simon came on: 'Height, Ed … height, Ed … *Pull out!*'

'I WILL,' I shouted.

120 became 121 …

Jake yelled, 'Watch your height!'

We were pulling up through seventy-five degrees, nose down and still dropping fast.

I knew my height; Simon did too. He was trying to look out at the world through a TADS camera which may or may not have been slaved to his head. He was targeting, so it probably hadn't. All he'd be able to see in his monocle was the speed building and the height dropping. It was pitch-black, he was blind and hanging on for dear life.

Jake and Jon could see my aircraft plummeting towards the ground. Because I'd said, 'Not yet', Jake was probably thinking, *Why the fuck's he flying towards the ground?* A lot of people had crashed in combat simply because they'd been too busy trying to evade fire. Most of them would have survived if they'd just flown the aircraft rather than tried to avoid the fight. But I had no option. This guy was shit-hot. He'd fucking nearly killed us.

131 top left.

1100 on the right. We were only one thousand one hundred feet above the Green Zone and closing fast.

'Height! *Height!*' Jake's warnings were becoming more strangulated by the second.

'I've got it!'

If he replied, I didn't hear him. The low height warners had triggered. Lights blazed above the console and a siren started to wail. I'd bust my limits and the systems were doing their best to get me to stop. It was as if the Apache itself was yelling at me, 'It's going to crash, mate!'

140 … 141 … 142 …

I was accelerating at 10 mph per second.

510 … 502 … 486 … I was pulling back on the stick as hard as I could, but we were dropping so fast the four-figure digital height reading couldn't keep up. Inertia was still winning.

And then, the final nail in the coffin. The 23 mm fired up again. It came straight at me, as straight as straight could be, like someone was aiming a laser straight into my left pupil. The fire came from a bunch of buildings clustered together in the shape of a giant banana.

I wasn't sure if it was the G force, the tracer coming directly at us, or both, but Simon gave a long, despairing groan over the intercom.

I was transfixed. It was absolutely awesome. For a split second, I could see straight down this luminescent red pencil with my left eye. My right was glued to the thermal world. Then they were superimposed. My crosshair sat over the centre of it. I could make out the banana and another block immediately west of it. The firing came from its roof. I was in no doubt. I knew exactly where this guy was.

I also knew what was about to happen. As half a second turned into one and the tracer rounds looked as if they would cut right through the canopy and into my forehead, the red line bent backwards and up.

I was beginning to level off. The stream of rounds was now well behind us and a couple of hundred feet above.

My crosshair hadn't moved. I could see an elevated square block on top of the target building.

You fucking dancer, I have you!

I pulled up hard on the collective to top up the power to maximum torque. I knew exactly where he was; I had him at ninety degrees to my left.

'My gun,' I shouted.

I pushed my thumb up on the Chinese hat. The gun came straight up. We'd fired the cannon earlier that day, and it was Deadeye Dick. Wherever I put the crosshairs, the rounds were going to land. I was going to put a burst right down both his barrels.

The weapon display gave me 300 rounds and my range was set to 1,500 metres.

He was roughly 1,000 metres away. I was going to have to aim half a reticule down to hit him. I had a warning message.

'LIMITS' appeared across the bottom of my monocle.

Bastard …

We were still at ninety degrees and going full pelt. The barrel had reached its left stop and couldn't point any further back. I'd need to turn towards him a fraction. His tracer rounds were tracking behind us now.

I'd outwitted him, but we were over the Green Zone at 300 feet, a perfect height for small arms to take us down.

What now? My primary role was to defend the aircraft. I could make a break for the wadi – or we could do what it was designed to do: protect the lads out on the ground by hunting and killing their enemies.

I hoped he wouldn't be able to correct. If we stayed in the same profile he would certainly have another go. I needed to do something different.

I pulled back hard and left on the cyclic. The manoeuvre pulled a loud involuntary groan from both of us. The aircraft had been shifting in excess of 140 mph, and the Apache's nose came shooting up, tilted to the left, still pulling and topping up the power.

The height warners extinguished and then the LIMITS message disappeared. I kept staring down and to my left. I wanted to get to the top of the climb, bump the aircraft over, level it, and pull off a burst. We were screaming straight up. It wasn't a manoeuvre helicopters were famed for as they soon ran out of speed, so I hoped the gunner hadn't bargained on it. The power margin indicator came on to warn me I was within 10 per cent of trashing the engines.

Then it started again. The tracer came pouring out. I hadn't taken my eyes off him since I made that first desperate turn. This time it began low and behind us. I'd changed aspect and was climbing straight up, and he was well behind the curve. I made his position a familiar-looking shelter about thirty to forty metres along the flat roof of the building beside the banana.

Enough was enough. He'd started with the best hand possible, but now I had one or two trump cards of my own.

I ignored his fire and steadied the crosshairs.

I called Jon. 'Where are you?'

'South of the town.'

That was all I needed to know; he wasn't anywhere on my line of sight. I pulled the trigger.

'Engaging.'

The soles of my feet vibrated as the twenty-round burst of High Explosive Dual Purpose rounds began to pump out of the cannon barrel. I couldn't see them in flight; I could just feel the airframe shudder. I knew the AA gunner had stopped firing because the jet of red light was now way behind and below us.

The Apache was still climbing, but I hadn't once moved my crosshairs off the target. I held my aim with my right eye as my left watched the first HEDP rounds impacting with a series of bright orange flashes. I had to hold a steady aim because the cannon was still disgorging rounds at a speed of 800 metres per second. I lifted my finger from the trigger after it fell silent.

'Look at the target,' Simon called.

'I am.'

'On,' he said, allowing me to move my head.

I looked down at the MPD by my right knee. For the first time since we'd been engaged Simon was in a position to use the TADS.

I called Jon: 'Did you see the firing point I just hit?'

'Negative, we have men on the ground, and they're firing tracer all over the place.'

The building lay at forty-five degrees to us then straightened up as I bunted over the top of our rollercoaster arc.

Simon zoomed in. There were splashes of heat all along the rooftop where my cannon rounds had exploded but the box-shaped, brown-topped structure I was aiming to destroy remained untouched. At first glance, it looked as though it covered the staircase leading to the top of the building, but I was now sure it concealed something much more sinister.

I levelled off pretty much where we'd been when we were first engaged.

Jon had been keeping an eye on us while Jake watched the troops on the ground. The tracer fire could be a distraction tactic.

'Wildman Five One, this is Widow Seven One – my north-east sangar confirmed that was a Delta Hotel on the Turret. Re-engage.'

The fucking Turret ... *Of course.* It was the thing we'd seen on top of the bakery a few days before.

'My gun,' Simon called.

'Is that raised block the firing point,' he said. His crosshair was bang over the Turret.

'A-firm.' I never got to say anything else; the roar of the M230 thundering up my legs and into my arse told me everything I needed to know.

'Engaging,' he called.

I looked closely at the TADS FLIR image. The cannon was chewing great chunks off the Turret and scattering them across the surrounding area. But I wasn't sure it was doing a good enough job.

I was pretty much convinced now that we were up against a ZU-23-2 anti-aircraft mount. The Russians left plenty behind when they threw in the towel. It was the smallest and simplest twin-barrelled AA gun the Taliban could get their hands on. They mounted them on pick-ups and flatbeds – and on top of buildings.

Until we destroyed it, they'd continue to pound the life out of the DC.

We needed to finish it off good and proper – and there was only one weapon to do that.

'Let's stick a Hellfire into it, Simon,' I said.

HELLFIRE

SUNDAY, 16 JULY 2006
Now Zad

We both studied the target carefully. We could see heat sources around its three-metre-square perimeter. Small objects, not human beings: empty shell casings. They couldn't have been ours; our cannon rounds exploded when they hit and the spent casings would have fallen into the Green Zone a klick to the east. They were still hot enough for us to know they were the remains of the tracer that had nearly knocked us out of the sky.

The ZU-23-2 – if that's what it was – must have been hidden under what I could now confirm was not a roof but a hessian cover. The gunner must have hammered it good style, then disappeared back under the hessian. That's why we hadn't seen any points of impact. Our rounds had gone clean through the loosely woven material.

'Delta Hotel, Delta Hotel,' Widow Seven One called after watching Simon's rounds pummel the Turret. 'Destroy the building.'

'I agree, Ed. It's got to be a bomb or a Hellfire – and there are no jets here.'

The Widow continued to build the picture. 'We've been under attack from there for the last three days.'

'Wildman Five One, copied. We'll put a Hellfire into it.'

'We're close to chicken, so expedite – the men are now in the base.' Jake confirmed and authorised on the JTAC's frequency.

'Widow, copied.' He knew we were off after this.

'Five One, copied,' Simon said.

We were now to the north-east. We could see the Turret quite easily.

The Hellfire missile had a double-shaped charge. If we fired from the north-east, it would direct its energy towards our troops. The blast would throw debris their way, and if we had a malfunction, the Hellfire could carry on and land anywhere along the line of aim, depending on its reserves of propellant. And if it had a potted coil failure it would nose dive into Now Zad.

Our boys were to the south-west; I wanted to keep them at ninety degrees.

'We're going to run in west to east,' I told Jake and Jon on the inter-aircraft radio.

That way we had a clear view of the street in front of the building. If the gunner legged it we could adjust the crosshair and whack him in the street.

'Copied – expedite,' Jon said. They wanted us to get our skates on.

We kicked out to the west and I brought the aircraft round. We lined back up with the target. Now all we needed was clearance from the JTAC.

Simon zoomed in with the TADS.

'Widow Seven One, Wildman Five One. Confirm clear to engage with Hellfire.'

The Widow shouted: 'Stop, stop, stop. My men need to get under hard cover.'

What?

We were three klicks out. I turned ninety degrees left so Simon could maintain eyes on the Turret and the street. We didn't want to orbit back over the town. I weaved between north and south, always keeping the target in view.

Jake and Jon were silent. I used the Longbow radar to keep tabs on them to the south of the Shrine.

After a few minutes we were pretty sure our boys would be under cover; they were used to being mortared and it never took them long.

We started our attack run again. Simon identified the banana, then the bakery.

'Wildman Five One. Confirm we are clear hot on that target?'

'Widow Seven One. My ground commander wants to know the safety distance.'

I cringed.

I carried the safety distances for bombs on a small card in my black brain, but there was nothing for Apache munitions.

Simon muttered, 'We don't have one, do we?'

'No. Stand by, buddy.'

I switched radios. 'Widow Seven Zero, Wildman Five One – there isn't one. Just get your north-east sangar to wear a helmet; it's not that spectacular.'

'Stand by.'

We were still running in, but I was slowing up. I needed his green light.

Come on, let us go!

Jake came on the inter-aircraft: 'We're chicken and they're not happy. Don't fire without clearance. Break off.'

'Does he really think I'm going to fire without clearance?' I snapped.

'He's just doing his job, mate,' Simon said quietly.

The JTAC finally came back to us.

'We're less than 200 metres from the target and more than a little bit concerned about the safety distance.'

'You sure they'll be okay?' Jake asked on the inter-aircraft frequency.

My frustration bubbled over again. 'For crying out loud, mate, I'm the army's Hellfire guru!'

'And he's the patrol commander,' Simon replied.

I got a grip on myself. 'Yeah, I know.'

I switched radios.

'Wildman Five Zero and Widow Seven One this is Wildman Five One breaking off.'

I leaned the stick and we flew a graceful arc that would take us back over the DC on the way south.

Simon said, 'It's the right call, mate. It doesn't look as though they want this to go down.'

'It's going to have to happen some time, buddy.'

Jon and Jake were circling to the south. I picked up their heat source in my monocle.

'Wildman Five Zero, roger. Widow Seven One, we're out of gas and we're RTB.'

Widow Seven One came back on, his tone urgent: 'My commander wants that firing point destroyed.'

There was an overly long silence. No one knew what to do. They didn't want a Hellfire and we had nothing else that could do the job. Jon was critical on fuel and we were running out fast. We were just passing south of the Shrine and needed to decide if we stayed or ran.

'This is becoming farcical,' I said to Jon and Jake on the inter-aircraft radio.

'What's the risk to them?' Jake asked.

'There isn't any risk.'

'Go for it then, but be quick.'

'Widow Seven One, Wildman Five One. Trust me, you'll be fine. If you're worried, get your men under cover. I will attack south to north, so the blast is away from you. Do you want it destroyed?'

In other words, make your bloody mind up: you either want it taken out or you don't.

'Widow Seven One. A-firm, clear hot.'

Fucking brilliant!

I turned the aircraft hard round and rolled it out. We were running in. We were pointing straight at Now Zad's centre. The DC was low and left of us on my thermal picture. We were going to fire the missile long of the base.

I glanced down at my MPD. I wanted Simon to fire from as far away as he could and that meant as soon as possible. We had to turn 180 degrees after firing to begin the journey home. We'd already hit chicken fuel and every minute in this direction was an extra minute getting back.

Simon said, 'I can't ID it.'

I nodded at the screen. 'It's about thirty metres along the top of the building.'

Then I realised: Simon hadn't been with us when we orientated to find the bakery the other day.

'Keep coming right, keep coming right – ON!'

The Turret looked completely different from this angle because it was sited at the front of the roof. The thermal contrast on it was very poor too. From the east or west it stood proud of the roofline; from here it merged with the buildings behind it.

'Are you sure, Ed?'

'One hundred per cent. I can see the bakery and the banana to its right. It's the only three-storey set-up here.'

Simon tried to lock it up with the Image Auto-Track (IAT) but was struggling to capture the image against the backdrop.

We were getting closer and closer.

'Break off and run in again, Ed. I'm not doing this manually,' Simon said. 'I need this locked up. He's freaking about it as it is. If we miss we'll never get permission to use a Hellfire again.'

'Okay, mate. No problem.'

I didn't blame him for wanting to lock the target up properly. Neither of us had ever fired a Hellfire out of training. We already had people shitting themselves on the ground. So if we were going to make this happen, it had to go like clockwork, no matter what the fuel gauge read.

I broke off right to come round again.

The IAT was an awesome TADS tool which grabbed the target and held it. You looked for a thermal contrast and centred the crosshair on the brighter or darker constituent. When you engaged the IAT's gates they closed in on the contrasting shape and centred the crosshair on it. From then on, no matter what you did with the Apache, the gates would hold that target dead centre.

You could fire the missile without locking up the target by holding the crosshair over it with your right thumb, pulling the laser with your right index finger and squeezing the trigger with your left, keeping the crosshair and laser in place throughout the missile's flight. But if something momentarily interrupted your aim, you'd have to fight to get the crosshair back on what was already a difficult target to ID. And this wasn't a stationary vehicle or a remote outpost in the middle of nowhere that we had all the time in the world to hit – and no worries about where the missile might go if we fucked up. This was a hard target to ID, close to troops, in the middle of a town, at night. And we were rapidly running out of fuel.

It was also going to be the first Hellfire that had ever been fired in anger – but nothing angered me more right now than the AA gun sitting in the Turret.

I broke off and set up. Jake came on the radio as we turned. 'We need to RTB *now*; we're short of gas.'

'One more run ... Setting up ...' I didn't quite know whether I was asking him or telling him.

No answer; he wants us to fire

I banged it around. 'We're running in.'

I begged he wouldn't say stop.

We were a lot further out this time and Simon needed every available second to ID the target.

The thermal contrast on the Turret was poor. The gates wouldn't hold the centre of it. Simon moved his crosshair to the left, where the edge was dark enough to engage the IAT. The gates grabbed on and the crosshair centred itself on the left extreme.

Simon flicked the offset button which gave him a certain amount of authority over his crosshair when it was held by the IAT. We were closing fast and virtually running on air. I kept quiet. Simon was doing a brilliant job. As he applied pressure to a thumb-force-controller the crosshair moved to the centre of the Turret while the gates still held the lock to the left. He'd done it.

'It's the right-hand missile,' I said, 'and I've stepped on it so it doesn't break your lock.' The nose was pointing slightly right so the Hellfire wouldn't fly across his TADS image.

'Confirm we're still hot,' he barked. He was right to call it one more time. Everyone was jumpy as hell. He wanted to make sure the Widow hadn't changed his mind.

'Wildman Five One,' I said over the radio, 'confirm we're cleared hot.' Simon couldn't change frequency; he was using every finger and thumb to hold his aim. I bet he hadn't blinked either.

'Clear hot.'

'Fire, Simon!' I yelled.

And then he must have pressed the trigger.

I heard the *whoosh* from the right-hand side of the aircraft, and the missile glowed as it shot off the launcher, clearing the aircraft without cutting through Simon's line of sight.

'Climbing.' My job was to build Simon's mental image of what was happening every step of the way. If something odd happened –

like a woman or child suddenly appearing beside the target – he needed to know where the missile was, not just how much time remained before impact.

'Climbing ... Levelling ... And dropping.' I glanced down. Simon still had his crosshair smack in the middle of the target. I looked back up.

'Dropping,' I confirmed. I watched the glow of its heat source shrink to a pinpoint as it sped towards Now Zad.

'Three ... Two ... One ... Impact ...'

The whole MPD screen went white and Simon's IAT gates lost their lock in the blossoming explosion.

Simon immediately zoomed the FLIR picture out to the widest field of view. All I could see was 500 metres of Now Zad town and this big ball of heat in front of it. A second later everything was black again.

I looked through the front of my window and saw an orange glow give way to darkness.

'Breaking off,' I called to Jake and the JTAC on the Mission Net. I threw the aircraft onto its right side and brought it round hard.

'Wildman Five Zero and Wildman Five One are RTB, send BDA.' Jake was all over it like a rash. He was keen to get out of there.

I could see Simon manually tracking the target for as long as he could to get the Battle Damage Assessment himself. As we passed 120 degrees, his TADS hit its left stop. He couldn't get any further back. We'd lost it. The last image was of intense heat and a devastated building.

'Widow Seven One – stand by.'

We were running back and once again the Apache told me exactly what speed to fly at to maximise our distance. Jon was forward and right of us by about four klicks. He'd set off before the impact so I could only guess he was on fumes.

'Widow Seven One – Delta Hotel, Delta Hotel, firing point destroyed.'

I tried hard not to give out a whoop.

Jake asked: 'Wildman Five Zero – was there any collateral to you?'

'Widow Seven One – negative, just a bang.'

'Wildman Five Zero – pass that information onto the rest of the JTACs and copy.' He wanted tonight's *lessons identified* to be *lessons learned*.

'Copied – and I hope not to see you again tonight.'

Jake, ever the cool guy, replied: 'Don't hesitate if it kicks off again.'

We headed south over the desert and past the mountains. I felt fantastic. We'd fired our first Hellfire. But I also felt drained. We couldn't go through this nightmare again. I resolved to go and debrief the Widow Tactical Operations Cell when we got back. We had to be clear about this on future sorties. The guys on the ground could say what effect they wanted: I want that man killed. I want that building destroyed. I want that area suppressed. But how any of those things were achieved had to be up to us. We were the only ones qualified to know which weapon matched the target. I didn't ever want to go down this route again. We called it the long screwdriver; someone else, detached from us, tinkering with what we were doing in the cockpit, fine-tuning our attack.

We knew the risk to the troops on the ground and we'd tell the JTAC if it wasn't safe to fire. Normally it was the JTAC's responsibility to make sure there was separation and distance, but he worked with fast jets that dropped bombs. They had all the distances worked out – Apaches didn't. We'd been firing just ten metres from our own troops this morning and we'd swapped initials, so surely they must know that if we were prepared to do that, we weren't talking danger close?

I could understand this ground commander's concerns. He'd never seen a Hellfire go off before.

I could understand the Widow's concern too. Charlie Alpha had been out in Oman with us, staying miles away from the target in case something went wrong. Now all of a sudden he was just 200 metres from it, shitting himself.

The dropping of a bomb is a fine art. JTACs work with the expectation of a hit, so they have all the safety distances worked out. With an Apache, it was more fluid. We'd bring it as close as we needed to without killing our own troops. And we'd always let them know how bad it was going to get.

This was another evolution in the rules of engagement, in how we employed our weapons and integrated with the ground force with intimate fires. We could get in close, like we had in the run-in earlier, to narrow down our arcs. If need be, we'd fire 100 metres from them. We'd do whatever we could to help them, but they had to understand they couldn't tell us which weapon to fire. They just had to tell us what the target was, what effect they wanted, and we would do the rest.

We were not Close Air Support. We were Intimate Support.

I admitted to Simon on the way back that I was dog tired. He was too. We weren't getting much sleep, we weren't eating regularly, and we were taking far too many risks. They were escalating with every sortie. No matter what we planned for, we would always get something blindside that we didn't see coming.

We'd gone up there and we'd achieved our objective. Now Zad was resupplied with men and materials. Above all, they'd taken us on with a double A and we'd won.

We refuelled, rearmed with 30 mm and Hellfire, and called Ops for permission to shut down.

We were about to go in and debrief the sortie. As the Squadron Weapons Officer, I was becoming increasingly unpopular, debriefing every shot, but it was a very steep learning curve for everyone.

I wasn't there to be popular and I was going to have to tell our Apache pilots that they were responsible for their own weapons and there were no guidelines. We must have had the only weapon system in the UK arsenal that didn't have any safety parameters.

I gathered them all before we went into our debrief to explain what I meant.

'Simon. How close to our own troops can you fire a Hellfire?'

'I've no idea,' he said.

I asked a few others and they were just as stumped. I told them what we'd just done and explained about the angles we used to limit collateral.

'In the end it's down to you to decide what you think is safe,' I said. 'If you blow it, if you shoot too close and kill someone, the MoD will hang you out to dry. A board of inquiry will acknowledge that you didn't have sufficient guidelines or safety distances in which to operate the weapon system. But it will find that the cause of death was aircrew error. No matter what the operational risk, you shouldn't kill someone you are trying to protect.'

I asked the boss his position on the safety distances. His reply was typically politically correct. If in doubt, you don't take the shot.

'Then what *is* too close, sir?' I pressed.

'I don't know, Mr Macy,' he replied.

'Two hundred metres, sir?'

No answer.

'One hundred?'

Still no answer.

'The pressure is on, lads. You need to be 100 per cent sure 100 per cent of the time, and that's why every cannon, rocket and Hellfire shot will be viewed in slow time by everyone. Any questions?'

'Yeah,' Chris said. 'So what are we going to do about the rockets?'

The rockets were notoriously inaccurate. I had a system of aligning them so they were absolutely smack on but couldn't get permission to use it. I was using it on my own aircraft when the boss wasn't around. I wasn't going to fall foul of the system and didn't care what he, the IPT, the JHC or the MoD thought. There was no way I was going to cause a blue-on-blue.

'What do you think?' I said.

'Take 'em off and stick more Hellfires on instead. I won't be using them.'

I could see the concern etched on everyone's faces. We were weary, bone weary, and fighting a war with no umbrella to protect us from above. If we fucked up, shit would come up and shit would come down and we would be hung out to dry.

We went to watch the video of our weapon releases. Jake flung his arm over my shoulder and we walked in side by side. He gave me a manly hug.

'Well done, matey,' he said gently. 'I wasn't stepping on your toes when I told you to break off. We were seriously low on gas and I genuinely didn't think he was ever going to give you clearance to fire that Hellfire.'

'I know, mate. I'm sorry,' I said.

'You don't have to be sorry to me, Ed. Ever.'

Jake was just too nice for his own good; he didn't know what I'd apologised for. I 'fessed up.

'I'm sorry because I was bumping my gums to Simon about you thinking we might shoot before getting clearance and—'

'Stop it. It's okay.' He hugged me tighter. 'We just need to save as many lives as possible and all get home safely to our families. Now let's enjoy that Hellfire shot.'

We recounted the sortie from start to finish: the boys on the ground; the fact that the mission was a success; the fact that we couldn't do it the same way again. We were running out of ways of getting in and out of Now Zad.

We talked about getting fired at, and how we avoided it. I ended up having to write that episode up for the Air Warfare Centre and send it to them explaining how our manoeuvre had worked. It wasn't rocket science. Pilots had been doing that sort of stuff since the very first aircraft was fired at. This was just the first time it had been used by a helicopter in combat.

We considered ourselves extremely lucky to have got away with it because, whoever the gunner had been, he was bloody good. Jake and Jon said they thought we'd been taken out – they'd seen the rounds go up; they'd seen the aircraft tumble out of the sky.

I admitted I'd pulled out of it far too low. I'd put us in a really poor position against small arms, but it wasn't a small arms threat that worried us right then, it was an AA threat.

I tried to convince Simon I'd known how low we were. 'Like that'd stop me crapping myself,' he said.

We had no footage of our aircraft being fired upon. The TADS moved around and was recording, but we couldn't see a thing. Jake, ever the professional, had been concentrating on his mission and was already heading back to Bastion when the Hellfire hit.

We had caught the mayhem of the missile impacting. Frame by frame proved we had had a direct hit. It had hit the Turret inch perfect. There was a huge and instant heat source and a cloud of dust and debris, then Now Zad was plunged back into darkness. I forwarded it a few frames and froze it. We could make out what looked like the structure's skeleton. The Hellfire had blown the thing to bits.

Jon and I made our way next door to tell Widow TOC what they were and weren't qualified to do. If they were in doubt, I said, they just needed to confirm by calling the aircraft and asking them: 'Are we safe here?'

The JTACs moved around a lot. There were only a handful of them, and they were in demand all over the theatre. The one I was speaking to that evening was pretty much the senior JTAC at the time.

Jon as the SupFAC explained what had happened. It was nobody's fault, he said. You must let your lads know what to do: tell us what they want, where they want it and when. We'll do the rest.

The JTAC listened and nodded, and then explained that his guys had strict ROE guidelines to follow and some of them worried about just telling an aircraft to crack on.

That was that. No ruckus. Lessons taken onboard. New policy implemented. The learning curve was getting steeper for everyone.

'Just one thing,' he said, 'before you go …' He pointed at my cheekbone. He thought I'd been fragged.

Action Man figures had their trademark scar down the right cheek. Apache pilots did too. If the monocle were to move one millimetre it would be disastrous for our ground troops. One millimetre at about two centimetres equated to a 150 metre error at three kilometres. We couldn't risk even 0.1 millimetre, so we dug it into the cheek bone and locked it tight. The weal normally took about half an hour to disappear.

The protective ring was missing on my monocle and the high G had cut an arc under my right eye.

'Nice work, Ed,' Jon said. 'Looks like you've had some much-needed cosmetic surgery.'

Four days later, when Charlie Alpha was back in Bastion, we found out they'd had their first full night of peace after we'd fired the Hellfire. Icom chatter had been detected and a Taliban commander had been heard saying that the mosquitoes had a weapon that is silent and deadly. It comes from the sky without warning and kills everything.

The DC hadn't been shot at again from that vantage point, and for the next three nights there was no sustained fire against the DC.

The Taliban had got smacked up a treat. The tables had truly turned in Now Zad.

The troops hadn't been able to patrol into that area to see what had happened to the AA gun, but between us we reckoned he'd fired somewhere in the region of eighty rounds per burst. It wouldn't all have been tracer – it'd probably have been every other round – and he'd loosed off four of them. That was an absolute shed-load of ammunition, and he might have stopped firing simply because he'd run out. I liked to think it was because the rounds that I fired back made him run for cover.

Because we never had proof we'd hit the gun or the gunner, we had to assume that they were both still operational. He wasn't a known player, so intelligence couldn't confirm if we got him or not. From that point onwards, everyone dreaded getting caught over Now Zad. If the gunner was still alive, he'd had his warm-up. He would have analysed what went wrong, and he wouldn't make the same mistake twice.

The truth was that we'd got away with it by the skin of our teeth. The guy was better than anyone could have imagined. How he got to that level was beyond belief. I certainly didn't want to fly over him twice.

The Intelligence guy confirmed our suspicions about the night sight. In other words, we could be seen day or night, wherever we were. It was open season on Apaches.

Now the pressure was really on. We knew that they wanted to bag one. They were constantly shooting the Chinooks on the ground but had failed to kill one … so far. They'd been taking potshots at us as well; Pat and Tony had two holes in their fuselage to prove it. Tony went on to collect a lot more too.

Now they'd brought in the one weapon system that we couldn't defend against. RPGs we could survive, assuming they were lucky enough to hit us. SAMs we prayed the aircraft could deal with. The geeks at RAF Waddington said it could, but it was yet to be proven. But an anti-aircraft gun could kill us.

They could now do so, day or night. The Taliban wanted a spectacular – to break into a base or to take down an aircraft. They'd come within inches of both today. The charred remains of an Apache would do nicely, as far as they were concerned. We'd got away with it this time, but there was still a weapon out there that potentially had our name on it.

Uppermost in everyone's mind was the fact that, because the sun was so bright in Afghanistan, you couldn't see tracer by day at 1,000 feet. We wouldn't know the blind death was heading in our direction until it hit us. If our encounter with the AA gunner had taken place in daylight, the first clue to his presence might have been when we were hurtling out of the sky, breaking into small pieces as we went.

SIEGE

In March 2006, 16 Air Assault Brigade's elite, twenty-five-strong Pathfinder Platoon deployed to Helmand province. Their primary role was to pave the way for the 3 Para battlegroup's forthcoming deployment. The last time the Parachute Regiment had been involved in heavy fighting was during the Falklands conflict in 1982 – two years before I joined up – and they weren't expecting much of a ruckus this time round. Their only task was to provide security while reconstruction got under way …

Travelling in heavily armed WMIK Land Rovers with Pinzgauer 4x4 trucks as support, the Pathfinders put in long-range patrols across the province. They were attacked almost immediately by Taliban, and engaged in virtually continuous combat for the rest of their tour. By the time they left the province, the 3 Para battlegroup had suffered the loss of fourteen soldiers, one interpreter and another forty-six badly injured.

In June, US forces moved out of Musa Qa'leh and the Pathfinders, who had already spent some days in the town, were ordered to relieve them. What was meant to be a six-day occupation until relief by A Company 3 Para turned into a six-week nightmare.

The compound they shared with local police came under daily attack from small arms, machine guns, snipers, RPGs, mortars and a sangar-busting 82 mm recoilless rifle. A Company were ordered to hold Sangin and CO 3 Para informed the Pathfinders that he did not have the resources to relieve them.

Living conditions were grim, with dust, temperatures of nearly 50°C, and dwindling supplies of food and water. Even the rules of engagement were against them. They were prevented from firing until they had physically seen a weapon being raised against them. To make matters worse, some of the ANA and ANP they were working with were either high on drugs or tipped off the Taliban, the Americans had a habit of carrying out operations they didn't tell their allies about, and directives kept coming back from the top brass in Northwood that they were using too much ammunition.

The Pathfinders must have thought we were on a bungee cord. I lost count of the number of times I'd been crashed out to Musa Qa'leh. I had every firing point committed to memory and knew the place as intimately as Crossmaglen. The fighting was just as ferocious as at Now Zad and Sangin but luckily for the Pathfinders, they never had that many serious injuries; lucky, because it was impossible to get in and out safely by air.

One Chinook trying to pull out injured lads was shot up four times and the crew had to go back for another bird. It was so dangerous the lads were told to ration themselves because they would not be resupplied by air.

Finally, after over a month and an average weight loss of a stone each, they were reinforced by a bunch of Danes in armoured vehicles. The Danes took five days to get into the town because of the tenacious resistance of the Taliban. Unfortunately, the Norsemen brought a new problem with them. Once they were in they couldn't get out, and they began to eat the Pathfinders out of house and home.

A huge operation to resupply Sangin and to build up its defences was mounted by 3 Para. Once this was complete all efforts were directed towards pulling out the now emaciated Pathfinder Platoon and replacing them with two platoons of Royal Irish.

Yesterday that mission failed badly.

We lost three soldiers trying. Musa Qa'leh has a high concentration of Taliban and a long Green Zone in which they could move virtually at will. It was in the Green Zone that the Taliban ambushed the armoured recce cars, killing a JTAC and two members of the Household Cavalry. We flew our arses off in support of the beleaguered troops. Jon and I had to swap aircraft because we had flown the arse off the one we started in.

After firing the Hellfire just over two weeks ago, we were sent to KAF for three days to sort out the broken aircraft. The technicians worked us hard at KAF. The Apaches were getting a bit ragged and the techs needed us to test them morning, noon and night. It wasn't without risk either.

We had a four-hour lull late one night and decided to go for a pizza instead of having a late dinner at the all-night American Dining Facility (Dfac). We stood outside the arctic-trailer that was Pizza Hut on the boardwalk – a large wooden walkway with trailers scattered around it acting as shops.

The place was mobbed with soldiers of every nation. Weapons were being handed over to each other so photographs could be taken – *this is me with an Armalite* – and it all seemed a bit surreal.

'It's like leaving the jungle in Nam and going to Hanoi on R&R,' Jake said as he waited to be served. As he did so I heard something that reminded me of my days as a paratrooper in remote outposts of Northern Ireland. It came very quickly and the pitch change made me squat before throwing myself under the Pizza Hut trailer.

'Hey dude, it's not—' Jake was cut off mid-sentence as I covered my head in the foetal position.

There was a huge crash followed by two more in rapid succession only a couple of hundred metres away.

I crawled to the edge of the trailer and as I started to get up everyone else was diving for cover.

'I think you've got it the wrong way around, lads,' I laughed. 'You're supposed to take cover before the rockets hit.'

The sirens sounded and everyone ran off to the air-raid shelters. To me it was all a bit too late really. I was left alone except for a shadowy figure about fifty metres away, sitting on a bench, smoking a cigarette.

'Nice Para-roll, crap-hat,' he shouted.

When I moved closer I realised he was an ex-Para mate now working for the boys in black.

We shot the shit for thirty minutes until the sirens sounded the all clear. We'd missed our pizza but I felt lucky that the three Chinese 107 mm rockets had missed me. Not by far, but they had; they'd landed in the Dfac a couple of hundred metres away, killing and injuring late diners.

On our return to Bastion we flew relentlessly every single day and I was feeling physically and emotionally drained.

Colonel Wild came out to visit us and was shocked by what he saw. I'd flown for him when he was a major in charge of AAC's Special Forces Squadron. We knew each other well and he couldn't get over how haggard and old I looked.

He made direct references to the fact we were killing – within the ROE – without blinking an eye, and treated death and destruction as a part of daily life. What shocked him most was the level of stress we were experiencing, from ROE to shooting far too close to our own troops to being shot at and shot up. 'At times you have to play God,' he said – a very poignant statement from a dedicated practising Christian.

This leap into attack aviation took a lot of the top brass by surprise. I don't know what they thought Apaches did, but Billy's account of his introduction to the US Apache course should have been shared with the army's high rankers: 'If anyone here doesn't think they can look a man in the eye and kill him stone cold dead, then he'd better get up and leave. This course is for *attack* pilots.'

Wild had come out to explain the factors that were causing more and more battlefield helicopters to crash every year. He went home with a brand new agenda: to brief the AAC, JHC and MoD on how kinetic, fluid, ferocious and tiring being an Apache pilot was in the Helmand.

It didn't pay to think about the sleepless nights, or being crashed out to platoon house after platoon house, or the stifling heat of the tents. I was never one for counting down the days; that only made the tour seem longer. I threw myself into paperwork and kept myself busy unless there was something more interesting to do, like a good old knees-up.

WEDNESDAY, 2 AUGUST 2006
Camp Bastion

We held a ceremony to claim ownership of the flight lines. We christened it Chinthe Lines after the squadron symbol on our flying badges, the lion-like creature that often guarded the entrance to holy places in South-east Asia. In local mythology, chinthes almost always travelled in pairs, and served to protect the pagoda or temple.

After curry, poppadums and soft drinks, the youngest air trooper in the squadron, Emily Leggett, was to unveil the sign. All the boys sang the theme to *The Stripper* as she unwrapped the plaque in a fit of giggles.

CHINTHE   LINES

AH/SH   LS

Lieutenant Colonel Tootal, the guest of honour, was presented with a flechette rocket mounted on a board. A rocket had misfired in one of the tubes so the lads had got the Ammunition Technical Officer (ATO) to remove the explosives and pull the flechettes out as trophies. Tootal gave us a few words.

He said he'd been an outspoken critic when the MoD first bought the Apache, and didn't mind who knew that he thought it was a waste of money. We should have bought something cheaper and we should have bought a hell of a lot more of them. The Apache was too role-specific and wouldn't have the flexibility needed for modern warfare. He'd had no idea how he was going to employ it in this theatre, and had been totally in favour of buying armed Black Hawks instead.

He was now converted, and made a point of telling every visiting military and parliamentary dignitary. He described the Apache and the crews who support and fly them as valuable assets that he couldn't do without. They'd saved his men's lives on many occasions. His men were always confident when the Apaches were above them. He also congratulated us on our jointery; the fact that we were purple air – joint service – and worked seamlessly together.

It could easily have been mistaken for a sweetener for the nightmare to come, but he was much too genuine to play games. We would be going back into Musa Qa'leh in three days, and this time the Taliban wouldn't stop us.

We had our squadron, flight and aircrew photos taken, and then got stuck into a game of floodlit volleyball. The Apache crews opened up a can of Whoop-ass on their Chinook counterparts.

FRIDAY, 4 AUGUST 2006

The day started with bad news.

Our IntO interrupted a briefing for a Special Forces job. A walk-in source had tipped them off that the Taliban were ready to bring down a helicopter with an anti-aircraft gun at Musa Qa'leh.

The ANP in Musa Qa'leh had gone out on patrol in the Green Zone and came back unscathed. They should have been under fire within 100 metres of the gate. It didn't add up; they were traitors in the eyes of the Taliban.

The Pathfinders reported Icom chatter suggesting the Taliban had been reinforced to twice their original strength, and the newcomers had brought forty more 107 mm rockets with them.

The penny began to drop; they were being tipped off. The Taliban now knew that Musa Qa'leh was off-limits to helicopters and that the men were so desperate they had taken to drinking goats' milk. They knew they had to be resupplied at some point, and it would have to be by road. They knew vehicles were an easy target in Musa Qa'leh because of their limited movement, and had had great success against us three days ago. They were preparing to defend Musa Qa'leh.

Taliban morale was very high.

SATURDAY, 5 AUGUST 2006
0730 hours local

Straight after breakfast, all aircrew were summoned to the briefing tent.

The mission orders would be slick and make a point of everyone knowing what everyone else's part would be. The tent was jam-packed. However, as big as it was, there still wasn't room for all the participants, so only the head sheds appeared; for us that now meant all of the aircrew on the mission and everyone likely to support it on IRT/HRF.

A lectern had been set up at the front, next to the usual briefing boards containing satellite images and the all-important scheme of manoeuvre – every individual's part in the mission at any given time.

We went and sat at the back with the Chinook boys. In front of us were the Mortar Platoon and Patrols Platoon commanders, a couple of company commanders, their platoon commanders, platoon sergeants – anybody, in fact, who had some control and could affect what was going to happen on the day. There was a buzz in the air. Everyone knew this was our last chance at getting into the DC at Musa Qa'leh. If this failed, we would have run out of options.

'Yes, we're going to attempt a resupply of Musa Qa'leh.' Lieutenant Colonel Tootal nodded at the sea of expectant faces. 'It will be codenamed Operation Snakebite. We have tried to get in there before, and failed. We must make this work at all costs.'

He described the enemy. There were two distinct groups of Taliban, he said, with forty to fifty men in each, operating either side of the wadi on the approach to the town. Many of them were Arab fundamentalists who'd infiltrated through Pakistan. With these well-trained fighters there would be an untold number of additional fighters. We could expect a hard fight.

Everyone would have his or her part to play. We had to push a convoy through so they could get in thirty DoS – Days of Supply – ammunition, fuel and food; enough to withstand any onslaught the Taliban could muster. We would pull the Pathfinders out and put in two platoons of Royal Irish. They would be backed up by more ANA and ANP, who were going to form the Afghan National Security Force (ANSF).

The Danes were going to stay in place. They would be responsible for securing the LS and providing the additional firepower.

Tootal sat down. The Ops Officer of 3 Para got up and stood by the maps.

'These are the orders for Operation Snakebite. It's a resupply convoy mission into and back out of Musa Qa'leh on Sunday, 6 August. Tomorrow.' He pointed at the map. 'This is Musa Qa'leh town …'

On its western edge was a huge north–south wadi. We'd need to cross it to get into the town. The wadi was wide open and we'd be very vulnerable crossing it.

Bordering the western edge of the wadi was a north–south strip of Green Zone, about 200 metres wide, where the Taliban moved freely, fought and hid. We'd need to fight through this to reach the wadi.

Just to the west of this Green Zone was an urban area about a hundred metres wide, where the Taliban would be waiting for us. We'd need to clear it before we could get into the Green Zone.

To the west of the urban area was a long, forward-facing slope up to a plateau. The Taliban would have good fields of fire across it from the urban area, and we needed to advance down it.

On top of the plateau was an empty desert and except for one wadi it spread as far west as the eye could see. This area was heavily mined during the Soviet invasion. We lost a vehicle when it drove over a mine in this piece of desert only four days ago during the first attempt at getting into Musa Qa'leh.

'This is where we will start the operation,' he said.

You could have heard a pin drop.

'Today, the Patrols Platoon and the mortars, with callsign Widow Seven Zero as their JTAC, will move out and overnight in the middle of this desert to the west of Musa Qa'leh, in preparation for the following day. At the same time, India Battery with their three 105 mm guns, and the convoy with the resupply, will move out into the desert too, and they will occupy their lay-up position.

'Early doors Sunday the sixth, tomorrow morning, the convoy will leave the gun position and route to a safe area north-west in the desert, in preparation for being called forward to pass through a safe passage.

'The Patrols Platoon and the mortars will move forward simultaneously through the known minefield, to find, clear, prepare and secure an area for the LS. It will be as close to the plateau as possible and capable of receiving all the Chinooks.

'There will be three levels of support. We will have indirect support from the guns and the mortars. There will be Close Air

Support from nine airborne CAS sorties, giving us a seamless supply of fast air. Finally, there will be Intimate Support from British Apaches. There will be a permanent flight of Apaches overhead from insertion and these will be under the control of Widow Seven Zero, as will all CAS.'

'On L Hour – the set time when the first Chinook touches down – four Chinooks containing B Company 3 Para and CO 3 Para's tactical headquarters will land at the LS cleared by Patrols Platoon.'

'On landing, the guns and the mortars will set up and register so they are accurate and ready to provide support,' he continued. 'This will also cause a slight diversion but we do not need the element of surprise. We're not going to hide from the enemy or pretend we don't have artillery. We're going to let them know what we have and that we're coming whether they want to fight or not.' Guns and mortars within range would be a show of force.

'On landing, B Company will get out of those Chinooks, and they will go to ground.'

The Chinooks would scoot back to Camp Bastion and pick up D Company then wait at Bastion until called forward.

'With everybody on the ground, the convoy hidden so the Taliban don't know where it is, the guns and mortars zeroed in, Apaches above us and CAS above them, B and D Company will prepare to move.'

Both fighting companies would move to the edge of the forward slope and take up positions ready for the advance to contact.

He indicated the map with a long stick.

There was a track leading from the ridge at the edge of the desert, east down the slope, through the urban area and through the Green Zone to the wadi.

'Everything north of the track belongs to B Company, everything south, D Company.'

D Company would stay firm with their weapons trained on the urban area as B Company advanced to contact down the slope in a 500-metre extended line, oriented north to south. The track would be their southern border.

If they came under contact, D Company would fire into the urban area at all targets to cover B Company. Widow would call the Apaches to hit the enemy hard and fast from above, tracking any survivors. They would use artillery to suppress them wherever they were then smash them with CAS.

'B Company will then systematically clear or assault every compound from east to west 100 metres up to the edge of the Green Zone, then south to the track, capturing or killing any Taliban that want to fight. They will refer to this list of building numbers.'

We all had a satellite image showing the outline of every compound 300 metres north and south of where the track ran through the urban area and into the Green Zone. Each compound had a designated number.

'The numbers will cut down on the time it takes to get the Apaches to fire and will negate any errors induced by incorrect grids.'

This was a far cry from the escorting role we'd played during Op Mutay.

Once all the compounds had been cleared, D Company would do exactly the same on the southern half. As they cleared these areas a small force would be left behind, covering arcs, to maintain the security and integrity of the convoy route.

B and D Companies would then move the 200 metres through the Green Zone, west to east, systematically clearing 300 metres north and south of the track, fighting any Taliban that got in their way. They would keep one foot on the ground and move slowly to ensure the line was watertight until they reached the wadi.

'In this area,' the Ops Officer said, pointing at the wadi and the Green Zone surrounding the crossing point, 'we will refer to spots from the Op Snakebite Spot Map.

A spot map had been produced as a one-off for this mission, dotted with coloured numbered spots for quick identification to speed up fire control commands from the Widow.

They would go firm at the wadi with a long string of men left behind, covering north and south.

'During the move to the wadi, the engineers will be clearing the track to ensure there are no mines or IEDs waiting for the convoy.'

With the area sanitised and interlinking arcs all the way back to the plateau there would be no way any Taliban could get access to RPG or IED the convoy. The Taliban had buried a triple mine in the road a week ago and remotely detonated it under a Spartan. Then they RPGed the Scimitar trapped ahead of it. The occupants had had an almighty firefight to get out alive and then back in again to save their horrifically injured comrade. The IED killed three of them outright and left two burnt-out vehicles behind.

'Once B and D are firm on the other side of the wadi, the Pathfinders and Danes will exit the DC on foot and in their vehicles. They will patrol the 350 metres west along the Bazaar road to the edge of the town where it meets the wadi. They will fan out and take up defensive positions. So now we have both sides of the wadi covered. If anybody tries to attack the convoy, they will have troops on either side ready to attack them.'

The convoy in the desert would be told to move out if they hadn't moved forward already. They would make their way to the plateau, follow the route cleared down the slope by the engineers, through the urban area, through the Green Zone. The final push would involve darting across the wadi, the most dangerous part of their mission. The track across the wadi kicked left forty-five degrees when it left the Green Zone and cut across the wadi at this angle for 700 metres before kicking right forty-five degrees onto the Bazaar road leading to the Musa Qa'leh DC.

This angle meant that they were still vulnerable from the north and south, either side of the wadi, but it afforded them the best protection 3 Para could provide.

'Once secure in the DC they will unload thirty DoS, deposit the men and then start to make their way back out of Musa Qa'leh the same way they came in. Patrols Platoon will jump into those vehicles, leaving the Danes, the Royal Irish and the newly formed ANSF behind.'

They would then do the dirty-dash back across the 700-metre wide wadi, under the protection of the Danes on the east, D Company and B Company on the west, until they reached the Green Zone.

'From there they will backtrack through until they are safely back inside the desert; the mined desert.'

B Company and D Company would then fall back through the Green Zone to the urban area. D Company would move back to secure the high ground with B Company covering them until they finally moved up themselves.

'The Chinooks will be called forward and everyone will fly back to Camp Bastion with the Apaches escorting the Chinooks. Job done. That's the format and you all know your piece. Any questions?'

All of the what ifs, questions and answers had already been hammered out. We knew that we were Intimate Support, 3 Flight would go in first, and we would RIP them. We also knew the extent of the threat to us: anti-aircraft guns, RPGs, small arms, SAMs, snipers, even mortars. You name it; the Taliban had it. Our two trump cards this time round were artillery to keep the enemy's head down, and a relatively small area to work in, just a couple of hundred metres wide.

All that remained was the Rehearsal of Concept (RoC) drill. The tent emptied and we went to the side of the secure area where 3 Para had set up a fifty metre by fifty metre scale model of the whole operation. The ground was scattered with minetape – a two-inch white or orange plastic ribbon used to cordon off mined areas – sandbags, rocks, cardboard and empty Coke cans.

Bastion and the LS were Coke cans, the white minetape tracked down the slope – and they'd made a slope too – through the urban area with compounds made of cardboard. It stretched through a sandbag Green Zone to an orange minetaped wadi into a rocky Musa Qa'leh and ended up at the DC Coke can. The convoy's lay up point (LUP) was marked too.

'Okay, Patrols Platoon and the mortars are going to be leaving shortly with Widow Seven Zero ... so the commanders will go along here, and Widow Seven Zero will be with them ...'

The three guys playing their parts moved and stood together.

'And then the Battery Commander and the convoy leader will be in position here overnight.' The BC and another guy I'd never met before sat down.

'At whatever time it is, minus L hour – and I don't know how long it'll take them to move – the convoy will then depart the gun position.'

The convoy guy moved round to the north-west.

'At the same time, Patrols Platoon and the mortars, with Widow Seven Zero, are going to move forwards to secure the LS.'

They moved forward on the sand map to the site of the intended LS.

The 3 Para Ops Officer said, 'Right, what's the next thing we're going to hear?'

The Patrols Platoon Commander put his hand up. 'LS secure.'

'Right, the LS is secure – that means we can go ahead with it. At that point, we're going to send out the Chinooks with B Company and the CO's JTAC. With them will be the first wave of Apaches.'

As four Chinook guys, four passengers, Pat and Chris walked to the LS, the BC said, 'At this point we'll be registering – we'll be firing into this area, to make sure our guns are ready.'

The Mortar Platoon Commander said, 'And at this point, I'm going to be firing too.'

The aircrew could see where the gun line was, where the mortar line was, how they were going to get in, how they were going to get out and the location of the gun-to-target line they needed to stay out of. The four Chinook pilots headed back to the Bastion Coke can where we stood.

The CO, 2i/c and Ops Officer of 3 Para threw in a constant stream of questions.

'What happens if that compound fires at you now?' the CO asked.

'I would call you and D Company, sir. D Company would put fire down and your JTAC would get those two Apaches onto it.'

The whole rehearsal was done at speed but relative to the timeframe so everyone knew where everyone else was, what they would be doing or saying at any point along the line. We walked out and replaced Pat and Chris and the rotations continued until everyone at the RoC drill was standing back at the Bastion Coke can.

The rehearsal ended, a host of questions answered.

Later, we talked through the brief again within our squadron. We ironed out how we would RIP at any given moment because even on the day we wouldn't know how slowly or quickly each phase of the Op would take.

There was still one nagging doubt in my mind.

I knew I had to voice it.

I had to address our operational effectiveness with the boss again. It had degraded to the point that we rarely hit our targets with a first burst. The main reason was the gun Dynamic Harmonisation (DH).

'We RIP'd with Dan the last time we tried to get into Musa Qa'leh,' I said. 'Dan had fired 250 rounds at the Taliban and we still don't know if they got a hit.'

Major Black tried to laugh it off. 'Maybe his shooting's not very good.'

I took a deep breath.

'His firing was good. In fact, it was brilliant. He would have hit first time if the gun had been on. Pat had exactly the same problem on Op Mutay. He couldn't even fire in zoom field of view because his rounds landed outside of what he could see.'

The boss hadn't known because he'd only fired forty cannon rounds and a Hellfire, but the current policy between crews was to test fire into the desert on the way to a scramble. If they didn't hit they would register in which direction the gun was off and aim off accordingly. It was ridiculously costly in time and munitions, dangerous to the point of a blue-on-blue, and a serious degradation in combat effectiveness.

'If the gun fails to hit first time, the Taliban get a clear warning and the crews end up chasing their tails, not knowing where to aim to get a kill. And a whole lot of Taliban are living to fight another day.'

He wasn't having it. He said he didn't have enough flying hours to let us DH the guns.

I tried to keep the red mist at bay.

'The Apache is an attack helicopter, sir. Its primary role is to fire weapons at the target. If the weapons aren't accurate we're not doing our job properly. If we fire at a target and it dies, we've succeeded. So we either waste time at the target or we use the time profitably by DHing the guns beforehand. The flying hours are the same, but the success rate is hugely better.'

'I said no, Mr Macy.'

I felt like banging my head against the wall again. Our sister squadron, 664, had just landed at Kandahar and was coming up to replace us soon after this operation. What would they think when they saw our gun tapes? As the SWO I felt deeply embarrassed that we hadn't completed an essential procedural task.

'I will be briefing the next squadron commander on what I think we've failed to do, sir.'

Major Black returned my glare. His jaw clenched then he turned on his heel and walked away.

OPERATION SNAKEBITE

SUNDAY, 6 AUGUST 2006
Camp Bastion

0213 hours local

The neon strip lights that hung above our cots burst into life. I shielded my eyes and scrutinised my right wrist.

'Time to get up, freaks,' Jon said.

'Wanker,' someone shouted.

I swung my legs over the side of the bed and peeled off my lightweight – but still clammy – sleeping bag liner. Jon lifted the tent's door flap and disappeared while Pat, Chris, Tony, Carl, Jake, Billy and I slowly came round. The scratching of arses, stretches and chorus of yawns would have done a bunch of gibbons proud.

I arrived in the Ops tent smack on 2.30 a.m. We'd been in earlier but Patrols Platoon had wanted more time to get through the minefield on the ridge, and to ensure the LS was clear before securing and marking it. Getting an hour's kip here and an hour's kip there was not conducive to flight safety, but we didn't have much choice when it was this busy.

Things were looking good. 3 Flight were told to be ready to take off at 0440 hours. L hour had slipped to 0500 and would most likely slip again, but they'd lift regardless. We completed a final brief at 0300 hours with a strong black coffee and walked to the aircraft half an hour later. I knew that today was going to be a long operation even if the bloody Taliban didn't turn up. And I was already knackered.

We'd be RIPing with Pat's flight, but stayed on the APU instead of taking an extra two and a half hours' rest. We had come a long way since Op Mutay. 3 Flight had taken the first Deliberate Ops callsigns, Wildman Five Two and Wildman Five Three, and needed to make their takeoff time. We'd have our aircraft running at the same time, so if either of theirs started with a fault, they could whack their kit into one of ours and leave us to sort out the shagged one with the technicians.

Jake would command 2 Flight from the front seat of Wildman Five Four with Jon flying; I'd command Wildman Five Five from the front with Billy flying. Simon was back at KAF, briefing the new squadron commander and his 2i/c.

3 Flight were in bays 3 and 4, Jon and Jake were in 5 and we had 6. The techs looked like zombies these days, but still had six aircraft lined up and ready to go. The boys were chirpy as ever as they stood around our four Apaches, but they were no oil paintings either. The whole squadron was feeling the strain. Even Billy was looking a bit rumpled.

Billy sparked up our aircraft. We tested the weapons, the sights, the sensors, defensive aids suite, video; checked that the data transfer cartridge had uploaded the mission correctly, that the comms came up in the right order and that the IDM – Improved Data Modem – had configured Pat's patrol with ours so we could communicate with each other digitally.

Our Apache woke up in a good mood but Jake was experiencing comms problems again. I checked in with Pat's patrol to make sure mine were working. They were. I kept the door open. Normally you'd close it to keep the cab air-conditioned, but there was a strong breeze from the east, making it an unusually cool morning on the flight line.

3 Flight lifted on time while Jake and Jon got their comms sorted. We sat on the APU. There was no way we would close down now. If something happened en route to the drop-off point or they had a problem we would need to get there asap.

We led the taxi out five minutes early, turning left to the top of the HALS. We lined up on the right; Jon and Jake forward left. We started to roll. Exactly two hours and thirty minutes after 3 Flight departed our wheels lifted off the metal runway. We took off south this time because of the wind.

'Saxon Ops. Wildman Five Four and Five Five … airborne …' I called. 'Zero Seven One Zero hours. Out.'

We took a left and climbed to 5,500 feet. Jon and Jake went up to 6,000. The visibility wasn't anything to shout about, but it'd do. It wasn't a particularly long flight to Musa Qa'leh, but we knew our kit was working so we could relax for a moment or two. On our IRT/HRF stint we'd been setting stuff up on the way, so things had been more fraught.

Flying north-east across the desert, we needed to establish the gun line. We knew our guns were south-west of the town. If they were operating, we didn't want to fly through them. We didn't want to restrict their fire or end up with a shell up our arse.

My MPD had the gun icon marked on the TSD – Tactical Situational Display – page, and a line from the guns to the point where the convoy track went through the Green Zone. That was roughly where the guns should be firing. I flipped the radar from air to air to ground targeting mode.

The radar immediately identified the guns so I flipped onto the TADS. Exactly where they said they'd be.

We now needed to locate 3 Flight. We didn't want to route north of the guns to find out they were south of the gun-to-target line.

That would mean backtracking west, turning south around the guns and back to the east to do a RIP.

'Wildman Five Two, this is Wildman Five Four – routing in, five minutes to run, send sitrep.'

'Wildman Five Two. The gun line is active. Guns are registering. The LS has changed to grid Forty-One-Sierra, Papa-Romeo, Six-Four-Six-Zero, Eight-One-Two-Nine and active.'

Jake read the grid back to confirm.

'Stand by,' Pat said. 'Come north of the gun line. We've got people fleeing north. Come to my position and maintain over-watch.' Pat and Tony were north of the gun-to-target line.

As we headed north-east past the guns Chris and Carl's Apache should have been operating at the same height and hopefully in the same area. The Longbow radar picked them up and confirmed their position from five miles away. We climbed to 6,500 feet. If they were in a battle we didn't want to be below them. Visibility was still hazy, but TADS was on the case.

There was no action yet or they would have given us a target. The boys were on the ground and the LS was active. The second wave had just landed and the new LS was a mile north-west of the choke point where the track entered the Green Zone. Our concerns were for Taliban moving into the area, and combat indicators of people moving out of it.

'Wildman Five Five, this is Wildman Five Four,' Jake called. 'Five Four will concentrate on the immediate area where the troops are. Can you check out those movements to the north and let me know as soon as you know the convoy's position, and that it's still safe?'

'Wildman Five Five, copied.' Jake always thought of the big picture and never got bogged down in detail that didn't concern him.

Jon kept tight in to the gun line. We moved steadily further north, away from them. Billy had the radar spinning to detect the convoy. I set up my acquisition source for the FCR ready for when he found them. They were supposed to be north-west, so we would have to pass them at some point.

'Gunner – Target – FCR – Tracked and wheeled vehicles – Stationary – Range five point nine klicks,' Billy reported. No sooner said than done.

I hit slave on the ORT and before Billy had finished reading out what the FCR had detected I was looking at a group of LAVs, Scimitars and trucks. They'd formed a big corral for all round defence, just like the wagons in the Wild West movies I used to watch on a Saturday with my granddad.

They were on the western side of a south-pointing spur between two huge adjacent wadis that joined to form a Y. This was a great place to hide and gave them access to the major wadi system leading down to 3 Para and the choke point between the urban area and the Green Zone three klicks south-east. I offset the laser to prevent any eye damage and lased their position.

Up flashed 41S PR 6332 8226.

I sent it to Jake over the IDM, giving him details of the convoy's set-up.

We had a good look around the main wadi leading north from Musa Qa'leh to make sure no one was heading west to intercept it. Several groups of women and children were heading north up the wadi, but no males. They were 2.5 klicks north of the choke point already. All the combat indicators I'd learned in Northern Ireland were telling me that something was going down and the locals knew it.

I spotted our first three males – two in dark robes, one in white – heading south. They seemed to be ignoring everyone rushing to escape on donkeys and on foot, clutching their bags and possessions. They didn't seem to be carrying weapons and I couldn't see any unusual bulges in their dishdashes.

Saxon called. The boss had intelligence that Taliban were to the north.

'Wildman Five Four, this is Saxon Ops. We've got an intelligence grid. Grid, Forty-One-Sierra, Papa-Romeo, Six-Three-Eight-Seven, Eight-Triple-Three. Read back.'

Jake read it back and I checked that what I'd punched into my keyboard was correct then hit Enter. I'd stored it as a red icon – so it came up on my MPD as enemy.

'Correct. Taliban are in that area. Zero Alpha would like you to look.' Zero Alpha was Major Black, back at base.

'Wildman Five Five, Wildman Five Four. That's to the north. It's your area. Can you investigate?'

'A-firm,' I said. 'Stand by.'

Jake was in the south over the LS. The grid was just over a klick and a half north-west of me but – alarmingly – just a fraction over a klick north-east of the convoy.

We didn't need to move and we weren't about to advertise to the Taliban that we knew where they were, so we stayed over the fleeing civilians. Billy was watching for anyone heading south and I slewed the camera to the intelligence grid with a push of a button. It was a small cut-out in the ridge on top of a wadi wall, but there was nothing there. It was a great vantage point to look south-west towards our convoy, but they were on the reverse slope of the spur and out of sight.

A hundred metres north-west, however, was a house and a compound; a little farmstead. Just north-west of that were four large tents, with cooking pots still over a fire pit. I couldn't tell if anyone was inside.

These tents were huge, not at all your traditional nomadic arrangement. Nomads kept all their shit in one sock. These things were black tarpaulin palaces, about five metres by eight, held up by poles and pegged down by lengthy guy ropes. The place seemed deserted. The fire was still smoking, but it looked like someone had just dropped the pan and run. I shifted the radar down to see if I could pick up any vehicles. There were none hiding under cover and the radar would know. All I could see in the entire area was the convoy.

We moved overhead. It looked well set up, but there was no perimeter fence. These guys were either genuine nomads, or the Taliban. Nomads were curious tribesmen that were always fascinated by our helicopters. I didn't see why they would have done a runner; they knew they had nothing to fear. If they had left the camp, they would be around the top with goats. There were no goats in the area, no indicators telling me this was friendly. But nor was there anything to suggest otherwise; no big vehicle tracks, nothing. We could have dropped to ten feet and flown an arc around them, peeping under their tarpaulin, but that wasn't our job. We were there to protect the convoy and the ground troops. If there were Taliban hiding here, their day would have to wait.

'Wildman Five Four, Wildman Five Five,' I reported back to Jake. 'Looked into that area. All I can see is a deserted camp 1,200 metres north-north-east of our convoy. I can't see if it's enemy or not. I'm going to search the convoy route.'

The first thing we did was over-fly the route our convoy would take, looking for any likely IEDs or mined areas, in case the Taliban, indicated by intelligence had left.

'Wildman Five Four, Wildman Five Five and Top Man. Both guns and mortars finished and the troops are shortly going to move off. Stand by.'

'Wildman Five Four, acknowledged.'

'Wildman Five Five, acknowledged.'

'Top Man, acknowledged.' I looked at my black brain for the sync-matrix. The British Harrier would soon be replaced by a US B1 bomber.

The boys were about to face their first real threat, about to stand up and move down a forward-facing slope into what could be an enemy position.

My pulse started to race. The pressure was up. If something was going to go bang, this was the time and place. I imagined the enemy looking up the long slope to their west, hidden behind little portholes they'd poked through walls. For them, it was about to become a target-rich environment. A swarm of Paratroopers was about to walk towards them in extended line.

If the Taliban had been told to fight, they were going to start hitting our boys early. I had visions of World War One squaddies being mercilessly mowed down by the most technologically advanced weapon of the day, the machine gun. If they hadn't been told to fight, then they would be legging it backwards. Either way, our job was to find them – and then to nail them. We couldn't have them reappearing from around another corner later that day.

We were over the Green Zone now and I was looking at the urban area north of the east–west track the convoy would take through the choke point. It was from here that the community lived and farmed the Green Zone.

There were three long tracks running north–south between compound walls fifteen feet high and, in places, four feet wide. The main tracks all paralleled the Green Zone; the right-hand one separated the Green Zone and the first row of compounds.

Each compound was a walled garden that backed onto the next without break. They all ran into each other as they sprawled northwards from the choke point. Seven compounds north there was a break: an east–west alleyway connecting the right-hand and centre tracks. The alleyways between them were just wide enough to take a small vehicle.

On the left of the centre track was another set of sprawling compounds. Each walled garden bordered the next, with the odd alleyway connecting to the final north–south track.

Each compound had been given a number on the satellite imagery. When the troops were moving through, they could tell their commanding officer which had been cleared. The guys were going to have to enter each and every one of them. Ideally, it would be completely methodical, one compound after the other. But CO 3 Para didn't have the time; he instructed them to get through there at warp speed. This was a close-quarter-battle area, he said, and they'd have to clear them as fast as they could.

Tootal had taken the brave and unusual decision to tell his men they didn't have to wear body armour. He'd suffered more injuries through heat exhaustion than he had from bullets and shrapnel. A lot of the lads decided to risk it, because it was roasting out there and they were going to be doing this for hours.

We divided up the compounds between us. I'd take everything from the choke point next to Compound 1 northwards to Compound 35, and Jake from 36 to 70. Billy and Jon would maintain a watchful eye on the advancing troops and on each other.

My blood pressure had risen; I could feel my temples pumping against my helmet. Something was about to go horribly wrong. I knew I could take out anyone that fired at them and smash their hideaways, but if they did open up I was only going to be killing the killers who'd just killed a fuck lot of Paratroopers.

I was tired and needed to stay focused.

I started searching the western side of the built-up area first, the side facing the slope, compound by compound. There was no one hiding behind any of the walls, just livestock.

'B Company are up, Ed,' Billy said. 'They're beginning to move east towards the compounds. They're not hanging around. Mind you, neither would I in the wide open.'

I flicked in and out of FLIR to look for heat sources. All I could see were cows, goats, chickens and more cows, goats and chickens. Most of the compounds contained between three and five terraced buildings, mostly against the northern wall, opposite the compound entrance, where the meagre sunlight could still warm them in winter. They usually had one or two in another corner for the livestock, and a low square shelter in the centre where the locals kept their chickens and the Taliban hid their weapons. This was quite an affluent area. They had solid roofs.

We normally expected to see civilians. The men would be in the Green Zone tending their crops, the women around the cooking pot and the children playing. There were no schools. The Taliban had destroyed them all.

There were no men today, and no women, children or cooking pots. The whole place looked deserted. It gave me the heebie-jeebies. Had they fled? Or were they in there, too afraid to come out?

You didn't have to be Stephen Hawking to figure it out. The residual heat from the fire pits and fire places should have been white hot on FLIR. They hadn't had a sudden attack of the colly-wobbles. They'd been tipped off nice and early; that was why the place was stone cold dead, and why there were relatively few civil-ians still fleeing north. They must even have known it was going to be a one day op, because they'd left all their livestock behind.

We'd seen men walking back towards the area. We hadn't seen any of fighting age leaving. I was feeling more uncomfortable by the minute.

Jake was covering the northern part of B Company's urban area. I worked my way south through the village until I got to the build-ings by the choke point.

I spotted thirty or so barrels stacked against the southern wall of Compound 1, where the track the convoy would take was at its narrowest.

I flicked on the radio. 'Widow Seven Zero, this is Wildman Five Five – I've got a potential IED at Compound Zero One.'

'Stand by.'

He'd be telling the CO.

'Widow Seven Zero, copied.'

'It's at the narrowest part of the choke point, on the northern side of the track. Copy so far?' I pictured Tootal sitting in the dirt, his finger tracing the relevant section of the map.

'Copied.'

'I can see about thirty barrels neatly stacked against the southern wall of this compound, right next to the track. It's the perfect IED spot. If you had to hit the convoy as it passed through the built up area, this would be the place to do it.'

'Stand by.'

Billy dropped our height to take a closer look.

'Widow Seven Zero, Wildman Five Five – I can see no command wires.'

'Wildman Five Five, this is Widow Seven Zero. I want you to destroy that target with high-sap.'

I could almost feel Billy's eyebrows disappearing beneath his hairline. 'High-sap?'

He was right. High Explosive Incendiary Semi-Armour Piercing rockets were not precision weapons. How could I hit a barrel with a rocket? They were free-flight, and since the launchers were haphazardly aligned to the Apache in the first place, they could go anywhere.

'I know we wouldn't use them against this target, Ed,' Billy said. 'But have you aligned the rockets on this cab?'

'I can't guarantee that the launchers haven't been swapped. They could go anywhere, buddy.'

I'd decided to use HEDP.

'Widow Seven Zero, this is Wildman Five Five – negative. I'll fire Hedpee as this is likely to initiate any explosives or fuel employed.'

'Widow Seven Zero, clear hot.'

'Wildman Five Four, Wildman Five Five – did you copy the last?'

'Wildman Five Four, A-firm, go ahead.'

'Where are they, Billy?' I didn't want to fire at Jon and Jake, and didn't want to take my eyes off the target to look for them either.

'They're clear, and so is B Company.'

We were still in an orbit and flying clockwise at seventy knots. Billy kept it low and slow.

I dropped to a ten-round burst setting, lined the crosshair up on the centre of the barrels, steadied, and lased the target with my right middle finger. I didn't use my index finger; some of its muscles were linked to the thumb which controlled the crosshair.

The MPD showed 1,699 metres – a mile away.

'Firing!' I called.

I pulled the left trigger and held it until the gun stopped firing. Ten rounds came off, and missed the target completely. They landed low and left – in the middle of the track.

'Fucking Gun DH!' I was absolutely threaders with the boss.

'Thank God we weren't firing close to troops.' Billy had been watching on his MPD. My crosshairs were bang over the target and there was no drift. Those rounds should have been spot on.

I aimed up and right the distance I'd missed by, and fired another ten-round burst. A huge cloud of dust enveloped the compound. When it settled there was a little smoke and plenty of hot spots in the barrels, but over half of them hadn't been touched.

'Widow Seven Zero, this is Wildman Five Five. Delta Hotel but no IED detonation.'

'Wildman Five Five – is it safe?'

They'd all been thrown around, but I couldn't guarantee that one of the barrels at the bottom of the pile didn't still contain an active initiation device.

'Negative. Not 100 per cent. A 500-lb bomb would be advisable. Dart Two Four is available.' According to my sync matrix Dart Two Four was a B1 from Diego Garcia and had been on task for fifteen minutes.

D Company, the CO and his JTAC were still up the slope. They had full view of the entire route, all the way down to B Company's position just short of the urban area.

Patrols Platoon were covering the high ground and guarding the wadi to the west, where the convoy would emerge.

It had just set off from the spur, and was making its way slowly down the most secure route they could find – the wide, flat, dry river bed. You could see by its colour that it had been flooded during the wet season, so any mines left from the previous defence of Musa Qa'leh would have been washed away, and any fresh ones would have been laid in the last twenty-four hours. The recce cars were working overtime.

B Company were now just above the compounds, ready to go.

It was a tense moment. A Taliban sniper team could have a field day here. B Company would be pinned down in the open, and we'd be the ones who'd have to flush them out. If they'd all fired together and their weapons were nice and dry, it would be like finding a handful of needles in a haystack.

'Bring them in.'

CO 3 Para wasn't messing around. He understood the threat all too well. Every single vehicle was going to have to go through the choke point. And he needed B Company out of the potential killing ground asap.

I called Dart Two Four. An attractive-sounding female American voice told me she couldn't drop without strato clearance. I had no idea what that meant, or if she was the pilot or offensive systems officer. Strategic clearance, maybe? Did she have to get permission from somebody out of theatre?

I called Widow Seven Zero and passed on the message.

Widow Seven Zero contacted Dart Two Four direct. He said he was the commander on the ground. This was extremely high risk, a possible IED; he had men in the open and it must be removed.

After a ten-minute wait, she confirmed that she had strato clearance to drop. The B1 Lancer had a synthetic aperture radar. She could only see a radar-mapped area of the ground, not the real thing – and Compound Zero One wouldn't mean anything to her. She mapped the target and was talked onto the southern wall of the compound. She was about to deliver a JDAM – Joint Direct Attack Munition – an inertial and GPS kit strapped to a dumb bomb to guide it with pinpoint accuracy.

'Ready three zero,' she called. Time of flight, thirty seconds.

There was an almighty boom and a pillar of black earth blasted 150 feet into the air. When the dust cleared, we could see that it had demolished the southern wall with pinpoint perfection, gouging a hole some ten feet wide and four feet deep in the ground. There wasn't a single barrel left.

'Dart Two Four, Wildman Five Five. That's a Delta Hotel. Nice hole.'

Widow Seven Zero told us the mortars were about to fire. We were instructed to move east to the wadi.

The Green Zone was only a couple of hundred metres thick, but the trees overlapped to form a canopy. I tried to see if there was anything beneath it that might pose a threat to the convoy. I had a sporadic view of the track running through it; there were plenty of potholes, but I couldn't see any fresh holes or unusual heat shapes.

The trees overhung the point where the buildings came to an end and the Green Zone began. It was the most hazardous area for the convoy because it could be viewed – at ground level – from a distance, and command detonated from cover with deadly accuracy. Once in the Green Zone, the Taliban bomb-makers would have to depend on a pressure pad trigger, which our engineers could find without the threat of a remote detonation.

When the mortars stopped Billy took us low over the western side of the compounds as the boys went firm, ready for the assault.

I noticed a roadblock just past the bomb crater, where the track disappeared into the trees.

'Widow, Wildman Five Five. I've seen what looks like a roadblock at the entrance to the Green Zone. Copy so far.'

'Widow Copied.'

I continued to describe what I saw. Just under the canopy, the right-hand side of the track was blocked by what looked like two forty-five gallon concrete barrels with a steel pole stretched between them spanning the right side of the track. Any vehicle passing to the left of them would then be forced to swing hard right by another set. It was a tight chicane and not one that you could ram aside at high speed. It was designed to slow traffic to a crawl. There were no ANP checkpoints here, which meant it was down to the Taliban.

Widow acknowledged and informed his search engineers.

As we kicked over to the east, I looked down and saw a man with a gun. On closer inspection I realised it wasn't a gun and he was very old. Dishdashes and full face beards made it hard to tell the age of some Afghans from this height, but his gait, stoop, pace and the way he held his shoulders earned him pensioner status in my book.

No more than 500 metres north-east of where the bomb had gone off, and north of the track that ran east–west through the Green Zone, he ducked inside a small, door-less dome constructed out of four poles overlaid with grasses. It wasn't a home, but a place to rest while working the fields, just large enough to lie down in with his feet poking out.

I told Widow Seven Zero he was no threat. I didn't want one of the lads to pop round a corner and get spooked by a harmless old man with a stick.

A few seconds later, the Widow said B Company was going to start clearing the compounds.

They moved from building to building with incredible speed. It was as much as we could do to stay one step ahead of them. I couldn't cover everything they were doing. They weren't grenading. They pairs fire-and-manoeuvred through each doorway. They were treating the place with respect while aggressively clearing compound after compound.

Before we knew it, 3 Flight was back out to do a RIP with us. That was how long it had taken to get in there, clear the IED, and get B Company in.

I was very surprised B Company had got down the slope without a contact. It was a golden opportunity. The Taliban knew that the built-up area had great killing fields. Perhaps the Now Zad experience had made them think twice. We were directly overhead and if they did open up, they would die wherever they fired from. If they made a break for it, they'd just die tired.

They'd wait until the Green Zone to attack. They would 'shwhack 3 Para on their terms, in their backyard.

We had to route back around the north to avoid the gun-to-target line after briefing Pat about the roadblock and the old-timer. As we flew past the three guns, I could see they were no more than twenty metres apart.

Billy and I bypassed Camp Bastion. We went straight onto the range just to the west of the camp and fired fifty rounds to DH my cannon.

We took a suck of gas and a 30 mil ammo upload then taxied back out onto the runway just fifteen minutes later. With the gun DH, the refuel and upload we only had nineteen minutes on the end of the HALS before we roared off again.

I flicked semi-automatic onto automatic on the HIDAS and Billy power-climbed into the haze.

The artillery were firing straight in. We went north of the guns and waited for an opportunity to call Pat.

I spoke to the patrol ahead. Pat said the troops had cleared the roadblock. It *was* a Taliban checkpoint. We were to clear them immediately due east, and watch the boys move through the Green Zone.

We'd left them not too far short of it. They'd taken so long to get past the Taliban checkpoint they'd hardly moved. The engineers had needed to go forward first to make sure it wasn't booby-trapped.

The old man's crops had been immaculate when we left. They were now trampled in snaking lines. It did look as if the Taliban had been waiting in ambush.

There were also 2,000-lb bomb craters by the road and in the fields. They'd been dropped as pre-emptive strikes.

The old-timer was still taking refuge in his hut. I saw his head poke out every now and again.

The boys began their clearance of the Green Zone. Two Paras ran forward through an open field and put a wooden frame against a solid wall and ran back again. Mouse-hole charges. After the explosion they ran back to the wall with half of their group; the other half had their weapons up, ready to fire. They went through the freshly blown hole in pairs, then down on their belt buckles. The whole process was repeated over and over again, field after field. They weren't prepared to go through doorways. One patrol even head butted their way through one of the flimsier walls.

We did another RIP when they were halfway through the Green Zone. That was how long this mission was taking.

The Taliban still hadn't kicked off. They weren't ones for shying away from a fight in the Green Zone, no matter how outnumbered they were. So they had to be biding their time. They knew about the convoy. They were deliberately avoiding any confrontation with 3 Para. They wanted the convoy: an easy target that couldn't fight back.

If it wasn't an IED or an ambush, what could they have planned? Whatever it was, I prayed that our boys would all still be alive and unscathed when we returned.

We parked up when we got back. We had thirty minutes or so to spare this time because we didn't need to go on the range. While Billy sorted out the aircraft, Jon and I borrowed the lads' 'Mimic' – it looked like a WMIK, but without any weapons or weapon mounts – and we drove like men possessed to the 3 Para cookhouse. It was closed. We should have guessed; every swinging dick was at Musa Qa'leh. We begged for some grub. They handed us a doggie bag of turkey mash sandwiches and wedges of cheesecake and we belted back.

Jon glanced over his shoulder and began to laugh. 'The fuzz are after us.' A wagonload of Royal Military Police (RMP) with flashing blue light and siren blaring were in hot pursuit because we were speeding. Still wearing our Apache helmets with visors down – helmets were mandatory in convertibles and this one didn't have a windscreen – I kept my foot to the floor. They weren't allowed inside the flight line, so had to stop at our barrier.

We were ravenous, but had no time to eat before we jumped in the aircraft, so we stuffed our faces as we sat waiting to taxi.

Taff plugged in and told me the RMPs were going to charge the driver of the Land Rover and his name was on the work ticket.

'Tell them it was me and there's a fucking war going on out there,' I said.

He smiled. 'Thank you, sir.'

I was chinstrapped. We'd been strapped into the Apache for nearly eleven hours and they hadn't even got into the DC yet. I immediately felt guilty. At least I was fighting from an air-conditioned seat, while 3 Para were out there on the ground.

The radio transmissions came through sporadically as Billy threw the engine power levers forward, ready to move out again.

The vehicles were crossing the wadi and Chris had found the Taliban.

I'd spoken too soon.

SNIPER TEAM

SUNDAY, 6 AUGUST 2006
Musa Qa'leh

We rolled out onto the runway, took off and climbed away from the sun. It was a welcome release. My eyes burnt through lack of sleep and staring into the TADS for days on end. I felt like I needed a regular supply of ice cubes down my trousers to keep me awake.

Must focus, I kept telling myself. Must focus ...

Pat and Chris were tracking Taliban so we didn't interrupt them. We skirted north of the guns. All three fired in unison as we passed. Dust billowed around them, carried by the radial shockwave.

I was trying to get my head around what the Taliban were up to. They'd learned a thing or two over the past three months. What was I missing? There were no IEDs so far today and no mines either. It wasn't as if they didn't know we were coming and hadn't had time to prepare. And they sure as hell weren't scared. Their primary aim was to send the British infidels home in body bags, and they weren't going to get many better chances than this.

Trying to stay one step ahead of them was what was focusing my mind, but my mind was as knackered as my increasingly emaciated body. They clearly weren't going to take on 3 Para, but how could they take out the convoy without getting close? Their mortars, RPGs and rockets weren't accurate enough.

'Wildman Five Five this is Wildman Five Four.' Jake broke through my tortured thoughts. He'd taken advantage of a lull in the radio traffic and spoken to Pat.

The convoy was in the DC and shortly to depart. B and D Companies were in position on the western side of the wadi, covering east. The Pathfinders and Danes were at the end of the Bazaar road, on the eastern side of the wadi, covering west. Pat and Tony were orbiting the track across the wadi as a deterrent. Chris and Carl were to the south, short of gas, looking for Taliban from an intelligence hit.

We were in the north, approaching the ridge, with the Patrols Platoon below us.

Jake told us to take over from Chris; he would stay close to the convoy route.

Bollocks.

The guns were firing. We were told we'd have to route back west, around the rear of them, and come back east to meet up with Chris and Carl.

Billy muttered, 'No way, José.'

He dropped the nose, and within a heartbeat we were thirty feet off the deck, banging southbound across the desert floor at max chat. The guns were firing but he knew that their trajectory would take the shells over our heads. It was a no-no to fly through the gun line, but needs must. We weren't going to waste any more gas flying three sides of a square.

Then Billy nosed us up vertically and all I could see was sky.

Chris told me to look out for a white car, which would be our anchor point, and sent me a grid via the IDM. I slaved the TADS. When I looked down, there was the white car by a small stream just off the main wadi. Three men were making a poor show of pretending to wash it.

Chris wasn't a slave to the digital environment; he was a head-out-of-the-cockpit kind of guy. Any directions he gave me now would always begin at this anchor point.

We were now three klicks south of the crossing point and too far away from the boys to either defend them or act as a deterrent. The last time we'd been on overwatch was after the IED killed three of our guys five days ago. We'd had an intelligence hit then too, only thirty klicks away to the north-east.

We'd tried to fob it off, but the head sheds at Lashkar Gar were highly excited; they believed it was a high value target, 'a sizable force that was preparing to set off and kill our troops'. We pointed out that its location meant it had no bearing on the troops we were protecting, but were ordered to go.

It was too far to send a lone Apache, so we both went, leaving our guys with no Intimate Support – only to be greeted by a couple of men in the open, waving their dishdashes to prove they didn't have any concealed weapons.

As we got back to the area we were supposed to patrol, Dan's flight had just arrived to RIP us. The Taliban were crawling all over the place. We were lucky we hadn't taken any further casualties.

This seemed like an action replay to me, and I resolved to get back to the convoy as soon as possible.

'Five hundred metres south-west of anchor is a group of about fifteen compounds,' Chris said.

I saw them out of the window and copied.

'There is a back-to-front, J-shaped tree line oriented west.' Okay, looking west I will see a J with the hook pointing north – ﮌ – got it.

'Visual with a J tree line,' I acknowledged. 'It has fields to the north and west, buildings to the south and east.'

'Correct. In and around the hook of the J I've got two pax, possibly Taliban.' Chris went on to say that they were hiding from him, possibly with a SAM or an RPG, and maybe personal weapons as well.

Carl couldn't hang around any longer; they headed back to refuel.

His final words confirmed my worries. 'I wouldn't hang around down here, if you know what I mean …'

I knew exactly what he meant. I called Widow Seven Zero. 'The area we're looking in isn't a direct threat to your convoy route.'

'Try to find them and ascertain if they've got weapons. If they have, you're clear hot.'

If I'd found them on my own I couldn't have fired because they were not a threat to the convoy. He must have had better intelligence to clear me hot. Either way, he couldn't see them so I was going to have to give him a full picture and then request his clearance again.

One man was trying to conceal himself under the trees at the very end of the hook of the J. He had something hanging over his shoulder. I didn't want to hang around so the best thing, I reckoned, was to provoke some form of response. If I fired close to but not at him, he'd run away empty-handed, or fire back at me or at least reveal a weapon.

I put down a warning burst about fifty metres away, in the field to his west.

Nothing.

We turned away to see if we could tempt him at least to move or draw a weapon. He got up and sauntered under the tree line.

As we turned back towards him, he went static again. Maybe he thought we couldn't see him because he was in shadow and wearing black. It looked like he was carrying some kind of flag. I tried to get an angle on him as we came round, but he stayed behind a tree trunk as we circled.

'Keep it up,' I said. 'He's going to move into the sunlight in a minute; maybe we'll be able to spot something.'

As he moved round to avoid us the sun glinted on something long and thin across his shoulder. It couldn't have been a weapon. Weapons don't glint. Gunmetal is dull, for good reason.

Billy said, 'Maybe it's a sword.'

We completed a full orbit and found another two men. One of them had what looked like another flag. Two flags? What was this, the opening ceremony of the Taliban Olympics?

We brought Widow up to speed. He was clearly taking these guys seriously. 'Do they have concealed weapons?'

'Stand by,' I said. 'I'll put down another ten-round warning burst.'

All three were now just across the track from the compounds.

This time I aimed the burst so close they all got a free pedicure. The third man whipped across to a doorway in the compound wall, but couldn't get through. This was a big combat indicator to me. This wasn't their turf; they had to be Taliban. Had they been locals he would have known the other side of the door was bricked up.

His two mates set off east along the track, towards the woods. I finally got a good view of them. The lead man had a swathe of cloth over his shoulder, and had something long underneath it. Chris was right. My money was on an RPG or a SAM. The one behind him had something similar under his arm, similarly concealed. It must have weighed a bit; he was using both hands to keep it under his armpit. It was long and chunky enough to have been a recoilless rifle.

But they were walking away from the fight and I couldn't positively identify weapons. Our ROE didn't support shooting them. There was another flash of reflected sunlight. It was an antenna. He had a radio.

'*Contact!*' Widow called.

Billy spun us on a sixpence.

The radios went manic. The convoy had come under fire in the wadi from Yellow 14.

I was absolutely fuming at myself. While we'd been mincing around, trying to coax these three into doing something stupid so we could either identify or discount them, the convoy had been hit three klicks away. We had only one Apache over it; *it* should have been our priority.

We raced north.

The convoy was still strewn across the wadi. I glanced at Yellow 14 on my spot map; it was 200 metres north of B Company, 700 metres west of the Norsemen in Musa Qa'leh and about 300 metres north-west of the centre of the convoy.

The airwaves were suddenly flooded with chatter. We found out why there wasn't a raging firefight going on. There had only been a single shot from Yellow 14.

The dense vegetation of the Green Zone thinned out as you moved further north, and gave way to an open expanse of irrigated farmland. Right in the middle of it was a small copse – otherwise known as Yellow 14.

The next thing we heard was that a soldier had been killed on one of the vehicles.

'Fuck,' Billy said.

Yellow 14 had a direct view across to the convoy, and would have made sense as a firing point – but for one thing.

I said, 'Can't be there, mate.'

'It's got to be,' Billy said. 'That's Yellow 14.'

'Look at the distance. It was a single shot, and that's too far for anything other than a sniper. There's no way a sniper would shoot from there.' It was too close to the Paras and there was no escape route. They'd be a sitting target. As soon as he pulled that trigger again, the artillery would come down and he'd become a magnet for every British soldier in Musa Qa'leh.

'Widow Seven Zero, Wildman Five Five – Yellow 14 cannot be the firing point. It must be somewhere else,' I said. 'Has anyone else got a better steer on where the shot came from?'

'B Company heard the shot from there, and he's been shot straight through the head.'

'Ohhh no,' Billy groaned.

I cursed the Taliban and blamed myself. The most vulnerable part of the convoy's journey was when they were crossing the wadi. I knew it, and I hadn't been there for them. How could I have been so fucking stupid? I should have insisted on getting back to the priority task of protection.

I felt sick to my stomach.

'It might have been a single shot, Billy. But there are at least two of them out there, buddy – possibly four – and they're *not* at Yellow 14.'

I'd learned about terrorist sniping in Northern Ireland. A head shot needed maximum concentration. He wouldn't have looked up from his sight for anything. So he will have had a spotter. The spotter must have been watching Jon's aircraft, to let the sniper know when it was safe to fire. If they felt 100 per cent safe there might just have been the two of them. It was my guess they'd have some muscle with them, too, in case of a follow-up. One or two heavies deployed as lookouts to ensure that they weren't being outflanked or compromised. RPG men most likely; men with weapons that could buy them time in the getaway.

'Wildman Five Five, Wildman Five Four – you take a look around here; we'll stay over the convoy.'

'Wildman Five Five, copied.'

The convoy had slowed to a halt. The dead soldier, we gathered, was the driver of one of the vehicles.

I looked out of the cockpit window and scoured the area for good fields of fire.

Jake and John dropped lower than they should have. They trundled round and round in the same piece of sky, deliberately setting themselves up to attract fire away from the convoy and ID the firing point.

The pressure was on. If it was a sniper, and he thought we didn't know where he was, he might be tempted to try it again. Chances were, though, that he'd be making his getaway. I pictured him looking through his sight, watching the body jerk then slump. He'd be up for it now, and we'd become the focus. What we did next determined what he'd do next.

'Billy, keep over this side of the wadi and don't turn tail on the north-western area of the Green Zone. We must make them think we can see them. It's our only way of preventing a shot until I can work out where they are.'

I'd learned fieldcraft during my time with 2 Para: how to patrol, how to manoeuvre, how to set ambushes. I was taught how to pick routes that gave cover from view and cover from fire.

As a Gazelle pilot, I'd given top-cover to the boys on the ground, and I knew what to look for to keep them safe. The IRA knew exactly how we patrolled. They'd had lads in the TA; they'd had lads defect and come across. They knew how to set an ambush so that no one escaped, and how to get away before the security forces turned up.

They'd be sure to hit us from the greatest distance and had perfect killing fields. And so did our new enemy. Yellow 14 had cover from view, but that was it. It was on its own. It was a shit position.

But where else was there?

They needed to have a good escape route, one that provided cover from above so they could get away from the hot firing point if incoming started, or we attempted to flush them out with recce-by-fire – firing into all the most likely places until we got a response.

They'd need to move back, and that meant somewhere north-west. Once they'd broken free they'd hide their weapons and turn into Afghan locals waving their dishdashes to prove they were just on their way to the mosque.

The IRA quartermaster would bag all the stuff and drive away, leaving the sniper team to separate and blend in with whoever else was around.

But there was one phase neither could avoid: they'd have to extract from the firing point first.

Where were they?

'What about those bushes?' Billy aimed at them with his monocle.

They followed an irrigation ditch. It was a good position, right on the eastern side of the Green Zone. But they only ran part of the way, which meant they'd end up in an irrigation ditch for fifty metres before getting back into cover.

Widow Seven Zero pressed us for an update.

'Wildman Five Five. Negative,' I said. 'Looking.'

'Widow Seven Zero, Wildman Five Four – give Wildman Five Five some space. It's like looking for a needle in a haystack.'

I gave Jake a silent thank you and kept searching.

It all looked the bloody same. Just west of the wadi were fields and irrigation ditches with tree lines and hedgerows but none was unbroken. There must be a continuous hedgerow somewhere, or a tree line, or a mixture of both … but I couldn't find anything and I was getting to the limits of a long-range sniper shot.

Just west of these fields was the edge of the Green Zone. Could he have scored a hit from this distance? Yes. But the fields were in full crop, and the crops were high, so he couldn't possibly have got a clear shot at the convoy.

'Where the fuck …?'

That's where they are.

'There ... Pilot ... Target ... HMD! Right! One o'clock! Tree line east–west, looks like an inverted Y.'

Billy's crosshair matched mine in my monocle.

'Seen,' he said.

Running south from a group of compounds was a thin but unbroken line of trees which forked after 200 metres. One row went south-west and buried itself in thick crops too high to see over. The other went east for about 300 metres before turning south-east and continuing to the very edge of the wadi. Trees didn't survive in Afghanistan unless there was plenty of water, so there had to be irrigation ditches right alongside them.

I lased and stored the junction of the Y in the Apache's computer in case we needed it.

'From the very bottom of that row, buddy.' I pointed with my right eye, knowing that Billy was following closely with his. 'At the very end of the south-eastern leg, you can see straight down the wadi, all the way down to the convoy.'

'It's a long way,' Billy said.

He had a point. It was between 500 and 700 metres. It was 600 metres to the centre of the wadi.

It was pretty much like the sniper position outside Crossmaglen. A long clear shot from a concealed wood. It had a good escape route with cover. And it led to an urban area where they could dump the weapons and melt away.

But what about the distance?

I needed to commit to a search or discount it on range, and quickly.

'Six hundred metres is about 660 yards.' I was thinking aloud. 'One minute of arc at 660 is up to a six and a half inch error. He can hit a head at that range. If the convoy stopped for a second or if he led the target by about a second, he could still hit a head.'

'There's nowhere else he can be,' Billy said. 'Look at the size of those crops ...'

'Wildman Five Four has a possible firing point north up the wadi. Investigating.' I needed to keep everyone off my back.

Billy kept the aircraft on an offensive heading, without pointing directly at the tree line. We wanted them to stay exactly where they were.

I searched very carefully under the trees, flicking the TADS from DTV to FLIR, FLIR white-hot to FLIR black-hot. Sometimes it stood out better when heat was displayed as black and cold as white. I was afraid I'd miss something. My eyes were stinging with tiredness, and from not blinking.

I started from the edge of the compounds and worked south. I didn't want them to escape while I was searching for the possible firing point. I had an awesome picture. It was working a treat.

The trees were well established along this route. The bottom of the tree canopy was between four and twelve feet proud of a foot-path, beside which ran an irrigation ditch. It looked fairly deep. They'd be glowing if they were silhouetted against it.

Nothing.

I rubbed my eyes.

I searched again and this time looked into the trees too, to see if they'd taken the koala route up into them.

Still nothing.

My back was killing me. I'd been strapped in one position for too long, hunched over a five-inch screen, looking for a shagging pixel to move.

'They're nearly across,' Jon called. 'You see anything yet?'

'Negative. If they're in there, we're going to have to sucker them out.'

It was a long way to extract and they must have felt safe so far north. They *had* to be there.

With Jon orbiting below us, we were heading west over the convoy.

'Billy, fly an orbit clockwise, making the centre point well south of them. As we come round onto east they'll think we're looking at something to the south of us. They may make a break for it.'

We flew the arc, everything peeled.

'Nothing yet.' Billy was using the thermal PNVS.

We were now facing north-east, in a slow right-banked orbit with the inverted Y to our north. I had a perfect view. As we passed through north I saw what looked like a footbridge about six to eight feet wide, about ten metres to the right of the Y, under the trees. I hadn't spotted it earlier.

I flicked from DTV to FLIR and back again, in and out on maximum zoom.

'I think I've cracked it, mate. There's nowhere else. Do you see that?'

The aircraft was banking away from the bridge, but the TADS was staring directly at it.

'Seen.' His crosshair matched the TADS crosshair.

We continued around the arc.

'Keep pointing the aircraft in this direction,' I said. 'Make it look as if we're flying away.'

'Good thinking.'

'I don't know what else to do,' I said.

I zoomed in on the bridge as we got further and further away.

We both stared at the MPD, not daring to blink.

'There,' Billy yelled over the intercom. 'We've found one. Stand by.'

A head appeared from under the bridge.

'Hold it,' I said to Billy. 'Hold it …'

I was right on the edge of the TADS hard stop; I didn't want him to turn the aircraft and lose them.

'I have it.'

Out came the shoulders. FLIR had him glowing against the ditch water.

The sun was at the best possible angle, so I flicked from FLIR to DTV. His black dishdash stood out beautifully against the far bank of the irrigation ditch. He slung his RPG over his shoulder and a sack of warheads on his back.

As he started to climb, out came Number Two.

I felt a surge of excitement.

'Steady, steady ...' I kept counting.

The second guy had a weapon too – an assault rifle of some description, but I couldn't make out a distinctive AK47 magazine. Right behind him, pushing him hard, was Number Three.

The fourth, in white, also had an RPG, but it was Number Three that got my pulse racing. As he stretched forward to scramble up the bank, he had a long, thin-barrelled weapon at his side.

'Sniper,' we said in unison.

'Bring it round to the right, but don't give the game away.'

'We've found the sniper team, stand by for data,' Billy updated Jon and Jake and sent them the Y junction grid.

If they'd been in fire positions, we could just have flipped the aircraft over and poured rounds down on them. But they weren't; they were trying to escape.

We didn't want to spook them. We had to lull them into thinking they'd got away with it. We were in a big lazy turn, when what we really wanted to do was flip the aircraft round and blow them away.

We lost sight of them as the TADS locked out, but they were moving cautiously. By the time we rolled out they would be at the junction of the tree line running north to the compounds.

As he turned the aircraft and we passed 180 degrees from the stored Y grid, the TADS swung from full left to full right. It was ready to lock on the second it came within 120 degrees.

I cursed the IPT. I'd been asking all tour for the Flechette restriction to be lifted. It was deemed an inhumane weapon by the legal boffins; they thought the place would end up looking like George A. Romero's version of the World Darts Championship. We knew the clearance was on its way, but if we used the best weapon the Apache had to nail them in this wood right now, we'd be breaking the law.

'Widow Seven Zero, Wildman Five Four, this is Wildman Five Five. We've located the sniper team. Widow, call when ready to copy.'

'Widow ready to copy.'

'Four armed men in a tree line egressing north from Grid Forty-One-Sierra, Six-Five-Nine-Two, Eight-Zero-Nine-Three. Setting up to attack.'

I took a deep breath and forced myself to stay alert.

The sun was right above us and baking through the glass. The cockpit was air-conditioned, but my flameproof clothing, escape jacket and helmet combo didn't allow the cool air to get through. I was baking.

My hands had barely come off this big PlayStation control for over twelve hours. My thumbs felt like they couldn't move another millimetre. My lumbar spine was on fire and my eyes were dry and stung like hell. My lids felt like they were lined with sandpaper every time I blinked.

Anxious to see every minute detail, I'd been getting closer and closer to the screen. I'd been looking north most of the day, using the sun to aid the TADS, which meant I needed to keep my visor up to see the MPDs – which meant the air-conditioning gasper poking out of the console kept hitting me smack in the face.

As front-seater, I'd sat still for so long my buttocks felt like they were pressing down on a couple of golf balls. I'd been lifting one cheek, then the other for ages now, but it didn't relieve the pain. To round things off, leaning over perpetually made my body armour dig deep into my bladder.

In the turn I checked the cannon was set to a twenty-round burst, then selected HEISAP rockets to two. As we approached the 120 degree TADS stop, I actioned the cannon and felt the comforting thud as it moved fully right to intercept the target.

Widow confirmed this was a known position; other lads had also been contacted from here. *Bloody hell, Widow.* It would have been useful to have known that earlier.

If the lads had been contacted from there it was obviously on the way in, not on the way back out.

The TADS image whipped past then froze. The bottom of the Y filled the screen. I just caught sight of the hem of a set of white robes as the last man disappeared under the trees, heading north.

I nearly whooped with excitement.

'The sniper team are all in the wood, heading north. Come in after us fast with rockets; we'll kick right out of your way. Don't wait for us to say clear, just fire as soon as you can. Then we'll swarm the target. We'll take the northern cut-off, you take the south.'

'Copied,' Jon said.

I zoomed to the top of the tree line, at the south-east corner of the first compound wall. Awesome. There was a fifteen-foot gap they'd need to cross to get to the wall. The wall itself ran fifty metres east and twenty-five metres north without a single hole or access point.

'We've got them buddy,' I called. 'They've nowhere to go.'

They'd just killed one of our lads. Now I was going to make sure they would never do it again.

My eyes were out on stalks, watching the TADS for the slightest movement.

We rolled out north and began running in. I estimated them to be nearly halfway along the irrigation ditch. They wouldn't be able to see us now.

Jake and Jon were running in behind us.

The plan was for me to fire cannon rounds towards the top of the tree line to stop them in their tracks, fire a pair of HEISAP rockets to check their alignment and finally to make the necessary correction and hit them hard with another flurry of rockets.

At that point we'd push right and fly up the eastern side of the trees, watching the gap at the top to make sure they didn't escape.

Jake and Jon would follow suit.

Both of us would then circle like a pair of avenging eagles: we were responsible for the northern escape point; they'd cover the southern fork.

I held the crosshair three-quarters of the way up the tree line, lasing constantly. I squeezed the weapons release trigger hard and called, 'Engaging' over the Mission Net.

The second the gun stopped firing I lowered the crosshair to the centre of the wood and actioned the rockets with a flick of a button.

'Come co-op, Billy.'

'Co-op,' he yelled back, letting me know that we were ready to fire rockets co-operatively.

The cannon rounds smashed into the trees with incredible accuracy. I knew they would; we'd DH'd it some hours earlier and got it spot on. The HEDP rounds would be sending shrapnel, fire, branches and splinters all over the place, right across the sniper team's path. There's no way they'd run into that lot.

'Match and shoot.' My crosshair was dead centre.

'Engaging,' Billy called over the radio to let Jake and Jon know it would be their turn in a moment.

A pair of rockets peeled off each side of our airframe and roared towards the target with their arses on fire.

Before they had even impacted I could see they were going too high and to the right.

'Fucking IPT ...' I set the quantity to eight HEISAPs. We needed a tool to align these launchers and they still wouldn't buy one.

They landed in the field just right of the gap between the trees and the corner of the wall. I adjusted low and left and called for another volley.

'Match and sh—'

There was a tremendous whoosh as eight rockets rippled off the wings.

'My gun.' I was ready to smash these Taliban to pieces at the same time Jon and Jake fired.

'Kicking right.' Billy let the others know they were up.

FUCK ...

I had a TADS FAIL and LOS INVALID message in my monocle as soon as the rockets fired. The weapons computer suddenly didn't know where the TADS was pointing or I was looking. It was a catastrophe. The computer wouldn't allow me to fire any weapons if it couldn't corroborate an accurate sight.

All eight rockets cracked straight into the canopy. Splintered branches, trunks and leaves burst out of the centre of the tree line. At least we'd got top marks for adjustment.

'My gun,' Billy called. He was as fast as they came in the Apache world and knew from this point onwards that I was just talking baggage. I had no offensive capability beyond firing the weapons in their restrictive head-on-only redundant mode. He could still fight using his monocle.

Jon and Jake were running in on the same approach path. I looked at the gap through the cockpit window to make sure the sniper team hadn't reached it and quickly ran my eyes southwards.

'Billy, left and low,' I called. He wouldn't see my crosshair now so I had to talk him on.

The trees ran north, bordered by tall crops on either side, and I glimpsed a stretch of track on the right. I could see two of the team almost directly below us.

'Halfway down the tree line ... this side ... two men ...'

'Seen.'

As the cannon growled into life the leading Taliban wanted to run, but couldn't manage much more than a hobble. His companion staggered to a halt and waved frantically to someone behind him, as if trying to hurry him on.

I spotted the third. He was bent double, moving slowly about ten metres behind his mates. He wasn't in good shape at all, and could barely put one foot in front of the other.

A huge explosion burst through the foliage above their heads.

Taliban Number Three disappeared in a cloud of dust and leaves. Jake and Jon's rockets had impacted spot on target, a fraction of a second before Billy's HEDP rounds sent a series of ghostly orange pulses along the track. He'd fired using his monocle and even though we never saw what they struck, the flashes told us his aim was spot on.

The dust wasn't settling. The ground was like talcum powder. There wasn't a breath of wind. The gap was still clear.

'Have I got them?' Billy said.

'No idea. But they haven't escaped north. I've got that covered.'

'Engaging.' He fired three further bursts into the billowing cloud.

We pulled into a tight orbit and dropped down low.

Jon was flying in the same direction, clockwise, and 180 degrees out. We swarmed the target, waiting for the first sign of life.

'Wildman Five Four, Wildman Five Five,' I called. 'Three Taliban were hit indirectly by your rockets and we think directly by our cannon. They've gone unsighted in the dust. Confirm the southern escape route was secure and the fourth man never leaked out that way.'

'Negative. We can confirm one Taliban dressed in white jumped into the haystack before our rocket hit it.'

What fucking haystack?

We didn't need to look hard. On the western side of the tree line, just north of the Y junction, was a pall of grey smoke. The haystack was burning ferociously.

Billy and I needed Flechette clearance, and soon. The HEISAP rockets were magic against buildings but rubbish in the open.

When the dust settled, there was nothing left but the smouldering remains of a haystack, a line of burning trees, a succession of craters, splintered branches and fragments of rock. The four Taliban had completely disappeared.

Jon and Jake reported a heat source in the crops to the west, but no movement, and it was debatable if it was big enough to be human.

The crop was about eight feet high and must have had a very damp base to reflect sunlight. If their legs and arms were in the water, or if they were lying hunched up, trying to look smaller, all we'd see was a glowing torso.

Billy and I looked at his PNVS image. We'd just lost a British soldier and the DC had been under months of relentless sniper fire. The only Afghan we had seen down here was the old-timer in the grass shelter by the crossing point. We were sure these scumbags had killed our boy and Widow had taken fire earlier from this very spot. We didn't want a single one of these guys to fight another day.

Billy opened up with another twenty-round burst.

Mud, water and shredded foliage blossomed along the line of fire and the heat source disintegrated.

We had a perfect view under the trees at this low altitude. We continued to search. But there was no one there.

'Wildman Five Four, Widow Seven Zero. That's the convoy in the Green Zone. Send sitrep.'

Jon called on the inter-aircraft radio, 'We'll get that.'

'Widow this is Wildman Five Four,' Jake said. 'The sniper team has been destroyed. We are short of gas but will hold on for as long as possible. We'll be overhead in two minutes.'

'Wildman Five Four. Wildman Five Two Flight will be with you in two minutes for RIP,' Pat called. 'Send update.'

We were just about to cover the convoy back up the slope. There wasn't much to say.

We broke off and tanked it back across the desert.

I felt relieved, but numb. Billy and I were now fighting on redundant systems, in more ways than one. I'd lost all line of sight, which meant I had no control of the TADS. If I needed to fire I'd have to fix the cannon forward and then point the aircraft directly at the target and dive at it.

There wasn't any dialogue between us. The next patrol was out, so they had primary use of that radio frequency. We could flip onto another frequency for a chat, but then we wouldn't hear what was going on at the pointy end. We still had to keep listening to what was happening behind us, in case we were needed to relay something back to base. We could have sent text messages to each other, but none of us was in the mood for doing anything unless we really had too. It was all too much effort.

3 Flight was out there now, watching the convoy pass through the Green Zone.

I was still trying to fix my aircraft. We might find ourselves straight back out if one of 3 Flight got hit. If I succeeded by the time we got to Bastion, we'd just need a suck of gas and ammunition.

I disconnected and reconnected my helmet, trying to bore sight it. Nothing. I switched over the systems processors. Nothing. I ran diagnostic checks on the equipment and attempted to reboot the systems. Nothing. I had no control over the line of sight. Nothing worked.

We listened to the fading sounds of the battle as we flew back across the desert.

I heard a beep and saw a text message.

Send FARMC

Jake wanted to know what we had left. We'd fired 120 rounds of 30 mm HEDP and ten HEISAP rockets. I typed my reply into the keyboard:

F 490 LBS – Fuel remaining

A 180 – Ammo. 30mm remaining

R 28 HEISAP – Rockets remaining

M 4 – Missiles. All of our Hellfires remain

C Full – Countermeasures. All of our chaff and flares remain

TECHNICIAN TO REPAIR TADS FAIL INVALID LOS

'Saxon, Saxon,' Jake called. 'Wildman Five Four and Wildman Five Five are RTB to you. With you in two zero minutes. Stand by for farm-c.'

Saxon Ops acknowledged.

'We require 140 rounds of thirty mike mike, eighteen high-sap, and can you get a Greenie to the radio to speak with my wingman? He has a Tango Alpha Delta Sierra fail and an invalid Lima Oscar Sierra.'

A moment or two later, an avionics technician's voice came through my earpiece. He sounded tentative. The techies didn't much like talking on the radio.

'Erm … Technician speaking … erm … over.'

He told me there was no way I could repair the fault in mid-flight and that it would have to wait until I got on the ground.

'I'll be ready when you get on the ground, sir. No problems, sir. Over and erm … out, sir.' He gratefully signed off.

Calls between Pat and Chris were still coming through loud and clear. The vehicles were making their way up the slope to freedom. D Company and B Company were peeling back through the Green Zone at warp speed.

We landed, taxied, and pulled across to the refuel point. The spring in the groundies' step had disappeared over the last few weeks. They connected the hose and started to refuel. The Greenie tech made his way to the door and pointed towards the arming bays. I signalled a '6' to him and he set off to meet us there. He walked like a zombie. I knew the last thing he needed was hours and hours of work repairing my chariot. I had no idea how they managed to fix these flying computers when they could hardly keep their eyes open.

Billy taxied along the hardened area in front of the hangar and pulled into bay 6. As we ground to a halt, I heard Pat on the radio.

'Saxon Ops, this is Wildman Five Two. That's the convoy safe, in the wadi to the west. All troops now making their way back towards the LS. Send in the CH-Forty-Sevens to collect.'

We wouldn't have to go out again.

I looked at the Up Front Display.

17:15:08 … 17:15:09 … 17:15:10 …

We'd been on the go for fifteen hours, and that didn't include getting up to discover the timing had slipped.

I'd jumped into this aircraft at 3.45 this morning. Actually, maybe 'jumped' was too big a word.

I dipped my head and gave my eyes a rub.

When the blurriness cleared I looked left out of the cockpit window towards my wingman.

Jon was slumped back, arms by his side, head resting on the back of the seat, his visored face pointing upwards.

Jake had his arms crossed over the ORT in front of him. They were all that prevented his head from touching his feet.

Their ALPC waited patiently for a thumbs-up so he could plug in.

I looked up and left at the mirror in the corner of the cockpit frame. Billy had flaked out, just like Jon. All I could see was his chin-strap.

It was over.

Automaton-like, I placed my right arm on the ORT and my left on top of it. I lowered my head until the browpad of my helmet was resting on my arms. Then I closed my eyes.

I heard the click of a comms lead being plugged into the wingtip. There was a long silence before a broad Welsh lilt filled my earpieces.

'You all right, sir?'

Billy was dead to the world, and I was too ball-bagged even to lift my head.

'No, mate,' I replied. 'I'm totally and utterly fucked.'

EPILOGUE

I only flew three more sorties after Operation Snakebite.

The Taliban took the death of their sniper very badly, and they didn't take it lying down. They hit Musa Qa'leh DC day after day with everything they had but without his elite marksmanship skills they failed to hit our boys again, and for us, every mission became a turkey shoot.

We were in predictably high spirits on our final return to Camp Bastion, knowing we were only one night away from being whisked back to the UK to catch some well-earned zeds. And this was my last tour; my twenty-two years were up. I'd miss the camaraderie of the squadron, and I'd miss the awesome Apache gunship, but the damage I'd sustained in that car accident was starting to take its toll, and I'd finally be able to give my family the time they so richly deserved.

Billy bet me that the RAF's big white freedom bird wouldn't turn up and we'd be stuck in the Desert of Death until the end of time. I typed Emily's coordinates into the computer; it told me she was 3,601 miles away. If Billy was right, at a walking speed of 4 mph it would only take us 900 hours to get there. I told him that if we kept going for ten hours a day we'd be home on 7 November.

We both burst out laughing. It was the date he was due to return to Afghanistan for his next tour. I said I'd raise a pint of Guinness to him at my local – but as it turned out, he had the last laugh.

Brigadier Ed Butler, Commander of 16 Air Assault Brigade, was now hailing the Apache as 'mission essential', and we certainly felt we'd done our bit to bring it centre stage. Whitehall was ecstatic. The visits programme was now crammed full with Members of Parliament, random dignitaries and anyone they could usher from the corridors of power in front of a fully tooled-up Apache gunship.

During 664 Squadron's tour immediately after ours, the mangled remains of an AA gun mount were discovered in the alleyway behind the building we Hellfired in Now Zad. I heard a rumour that the gunner had been Iranian-trained and brought in to deal with the 'mosquitoes'. Whether or not that's true, we'd come a long way since taking pot shots at the drone on Salisbury Plain.

But as we prepared to land at Brize Norton and I gazed out at the startlingly green Oxfordshire countryside, I couldn't help wondering what we'd really achieved. We'd been sent on a reconstruction mission to a patch of desert no bigger than 150 square miles and one government minister thought we might return without having fired a single shot. We ended up covering an area ten times that size, found ourselves constantly under siege and unable to patrol far from any of our bases without our ground troops being at significant risk, and fired off more ammunition than even Taff cared to think about.

We were also told that our mission had nothing to do with the Taliban or the narcotics trade. But during the three sweat-soaked months we spent with 3 Para in Helmand we were in contact with the Taliban every single day and found ourselves fighting for survival in villages that grew vast quantities of raw opium that ended up as heroin on the streets of the UK.

Sitting in the window of a coffee bar in broad daylight on my first trip to London after getting home, I was asked if I'd like to buy some.

It wasn't my only rude awakening.

The army was short of Apache Weapons Officers. In fact, they had none. They wanted me to go back for another tour. I guess it wasn't that surprising. For every soldier or marine accepted as a candidate for pilot selection, eighteen were shown the door. Over 2,000 applicants fell by the wayside just to get one of us through the course and onto operations.

We were lucky. Out of the fourteen on my grading, four went on to become pilots – an attrition rate of three and a half to one instead of the more normal five.

As we prepared ourselves to head out to Afghanistan once more, Scottie, my friend and instructor, decided to move Down Under with his family. He now teaches Attack Aviation to the Aussies. After years of abusing him about his outrageous watch collection, in a moment of madness I bought two of the twenty-five limited edition titanium Breitlings commissioned by the 656 Squadron aircrew to commemorate being the UK's first Apache attack pilots. They had a dark blue face with a rippling Union Flag at three o'clock and an Apache AH1 – complete with our trademark weapons fit – replacing the nine.

After more than two decades in the British Army I couldn't exactly put a Hellfire missile in my trophy cabinet, but at least I had a couple of suitably muscular timepieces to hand down to my young sons in case they ever need reminding that Dad wasn't always a boring old fart.

AFTERWORD

JULY 2009

As I sit writing this from the comfort of my home friends continue to keep me informed about what's happening in Afghanistan. Andy Wawn sends me regular emails even now, three years beyond that epic tour.

He and his fellow Apache pilots are firing more ammunition and flying more hours than we ever did. Repetition of tours is becoming more frequent, and the team is utterly ball-bagged.

A Major in the US Marines recently informed me that they are currently coming up against particularly heavy resistance in a place called Jugroom Fort. He thanked me for writing *Apache* and giving them a heads up.

GLOSSARY OF TERMS

1BIT: one standard 7.62 mm ball round for every one tracer round (1Ball1Tracer = 1BIT)

2i/c: second in command

30 mil: 30mm High Explosive Dual Purpose Apache cannon rounds

.50 cal: British Forces L1A1 Heavy Machine Gun – 12.7 mm (.50 inch) calibre tripod-mounted or vehicle-mounted automatic

A109: Agusta 109 helicopter used by the SAS

AA: Anti-Aircraft – known as 'Double A'. A large calibre gun used against low-flying aircraft

AAC: Army Air Corps – corps of the British Army that operates helicopters and fixed wing aircraft

ABFAC: Airborne Forward Air Controller

ACC: Army Catering Corps

ACTI: Air Combat Tactics Instructor

AK47: Soviet assault rifle – 7.62 mm automatic

ALPC: Arming and Loading Point Commander

Altitude: Height above sea level, rather than ground level

AMTAT: Air Manoeuvre Training and Advisory Team – senior instructors with expertise in multiple disciplines who were there to train, coach and test to ensure see that the Apache was worked up to its full fighting potential prior to being declared fully operational

ANA: Afghan National Army

ANP: Afghan National Police

ANSF: Afghan National Security Force

Apache: Apache AH Mk1 – the British Army Apache Attack Helicopter – built by AgustaWestland and fitted with the Longbow radar

APC: Armoured Personnel Carrier

APU: Auxiliary Power Unit – an engine used to power up the main engines or to provide power to an aircraft on the ground

AQ: Al-Qaeda

Armée de l'Air: French Air Force

ASE: Aircraft Survival Equipment

ATO: Ammunition Technical Officer

Attack helicopter: A helicopter that is designed around being a complete weapon system, rather than a weapon system designed to fit a helicopter

B1: B1 Lancer bomber – US Air Force high altitude long-range supersonic strategic bomber

Bag, the: A blacked-out cockpit used to teach Apache pilots how to fly at night with sole reference from the monocle

Battlegroup: A battalion-sized fighting force

BATS box: BATUS Asset Tracking System Box. A transponder that transmits to the exercise controllers the exact position of a vehicle during live firing training on BATUS

BATUS: British Army Training Unit Suffield – training unit at Canadian Air Force base, Suffield, Alberta

BC: Battery Commander

BDA: Battle Damage Assessment

Bergen: Army slang for a rucksack

Berm: A man-made ridge of earth, designed as an obstacle

Bird table: A table (often strewn with maps) that all of the main players gather around to discuss and brief the details of operations

Bitching Betty: The Apache's female cockpit voice warning system

Black brain: The black kneeboard Apache pilots fly with on their thigh that contains everything that can't be committed to memory and may be needed instantly in flight

Bob-up box: A piece of symbology displayed in the monocle that remains fixed in space. It allows the crew to know how far they are from a self-generated known point in space they were hovering over when it was created.

Bonedome: Helmet

Brick: A term used in Northern Ireland for a four man patrol

Broken Arrow: A base or fort that has been overrun by the enemy

BRU: Boresight Reticule Unit

C-17: RAF transport plane

CAG: Combined Air Ground

Calibre: The inside diameter of the barrel of a weapon

Carbine: Short-barrelled SA80 with an additional grip at the front – used by Apache pilots and tank crews – 5.56 mm automatic

CAS: Close Air Support

Casevac: Casualty Evacuation

CH47: Chinook – a large wide-bodied helicopter with two rotors on the top. Used by many countries for carrying troops – may also carry equipment inside or underslung below.

Chicken fuel: Just enough fuel to make it back direct and land with the minimum fuel allowance

Chicken plate: Triangular armoured plate to shield the vital organs within the chest cavity from bullets and shrapnel

Chippies: De Havilland Chipmunk T10 training aircraft

Choke point: A point where a natural narrowing occurs in a route – like a bottleneck.

CMDS: Counter Measures Dispensing System

CO: Commanding Officer – Lieutenant Colonel in charge of a regiment, battalion or the Joint Helicopter Force

Collective lever: The flying control to the left-hand side of the pilot's seat; held in the left hand; when raised the Apache climbs and when lowered it descends

ComAO: Combined Air Operation

Co-op: Co-operative rocket shoot – both of the Apache's crew working together to fire the rockets at the target

Cow: Taliban slang for the Chinook helicopter

Crabs: Slang term for the RAF

CRV7: Canadian Rocket Vehicle 7 – the Apache's rockets

CTAF Net: Common Tactical Air Frequency Net

CTR: Conversion To Role

CTT: Conversion To Type

Cyclic stick: The flying control between the pilot's legs, held by the right hand and used to speed up, slow down, dive and turn the Apache

Danger close: The proximity to a weapon's effect that is considered the last safe point when wearing body armour and combat helmet

Dasht-e-Margo: Desert of Death

DC: District Centre – the commercial/political/military centre of a particular area. Usually a building that once held power

Deliberate Operations: Preplanned operations like escort missions and deliberate strikes

Delta Hotel: Phonetic alphabet for DH – air speak for Direct Hit – call made when a weapon system hits its intended target accurately

Dfac: American Dining Facility

Dishdash: Loose kaftan-style outfit worn by many Afghan men

DoS: Days of Supply

DTV: Day television – black and white TV image generated from the day camera in the TADS

DVO: Direct View Optics

ECM: Electronic Counter Measures

ETA: Estimated Time of Arrival

ETD: Estimated Time of Departure

EWI: Electronic Warfare Instructor

Excon: Exercise Control

FAC: Forward Air Control/Controller

FARMC: Fuel, Ammunition, Rockets, Missiles, Countermeasures (farm-c)

Fast air: Offensive military jet aircraft

FCR: Fire Control Radar – the Apache's Longbow radar

Fenestron: A tail rotor that is housed in a Venturi

FIBUA: Fighting In a Built-Up Area

Flares: Hot flares fired to attract heat-seeking missiles, luring them away from the Apache

Flechette: Five-inch tungsten darts fired from a rocket travelling above Mach 3.3

Flick: Military slang. When something has been signed over to you and you are held accountable for it

FLIR: Forward Looking Infrared – Sights that generate a thermal picture – an image produced by an object's heat source above absolute zero

FOB: Forward Operating Base

Frag: Fragments of hot metal that break away from a shell when it explodes

FRV: Final Rendezvous point

GAFA: Great Afghan Fuck All – Dasht-e-Margo – the Desert of Death

Gazelle: British Army helicopter – generally employed for training, liaison and reconnaissance

GMPG: British Forces General Purpose Machine Gun – 7.62 mm bipod machine gun

GPS: Global Positioning System – satellite navigation equipment

Greenie tech: Nickname for an aviation technician. Aviation technicians are responsible for all electrical equipment on an aircraft

Green Zone: Lush habitation of irrigated fields, hedgerows, trees and small woods on either side of the Helmand River, bordered by arid deserts

Ground crew: People who work with aircraft when they are on the ground, but not technicians

Groundie: Military slang for ground crew

Ground school: Academic lessons on flying and all to do with flying: meteorology, law, engines, etc.

Gunship: An aircraft that has the capability of firing its cannon/s from the side instead of having to strafe head-on

Gun tape: The video tape put into an Apache that records what the selected sight sees

HALS: Hardened Aircraft Landing Strip: small runway

Harrier: British designed military jet aircraft capable of Vertical Short Takeoff and Landing (VTOL) – often called the 'Jump Jet'

HEDP: High Explosive Dual Purpose (Hedpee) – 30 mm cannon rounds

Height: The height above the ground expressed in feet

HEISAP: High Explosive Incendiary Semi-Armour Piercing (high-sap) – kinetic rocket fired by the Apache

Hellfire: AGM-114K SAL (Semi-Active Laser) Hellfire is a laser-guided Hellfire missile fitted to the Apache

Hesco Bastion: Square metal meshed cubes lined with hessian and filled with rubble and/or sand. Used as defensive ramparts to protect bases and platoon houses from fire

H Hour: The moment offensive action begins – first bullet, bomb or the moment troops walk towards their intended target to attack

HIDAS: Helicopter Integrated Defensive Aids System – protection from SAMs

HIG: Hezb-I Islami Gulbuddin – major group of the old Mujahideen with ties to Osama bin Laden

HLS: Helicopter Landing Site

HMD: Helmet Mounted Display

Hot: Air speak for clearance or acknowledgement that live bombs can be dropped

HQ: Headquarters – the nerve centre for planning and execution of operations

HRF: Helmand Reaction Force – two Apaches and a Chinook full of soldiers on standby at Bastion used to bolster any troops on the ground quickly

IAT: Image Auto-Track

IAT: International Air Tattoo. Now RIAT (Royal International Air Tattoo)

Icom: A make of radio scanner used by coalition and the Taliban to monitor each other's transmissions

ID: Identification

IDM: Improved Data Modem

IED: Improvised Explosive Device – home-made bombs or multiple mines strapped together

IEFAB: Improved Extended Forward Avionics Bay (eefab) The slabs that stick out either side of Longbow Apaches below the cockpits

IntO: Intelligence Officer

IOC: Initial Operating Capability

IPT: Integrated Project Team

IRA: Irish Republican Army – Northern Irish paramilitary group

IRT: Incident Response Team – Apaches, Chinooks, doctors, medics and Ammunition Technical Officer (ATO) responsible for the immediate recovery of personnel in danger or injured

ISAF: International Security Assistance Force – multinational military force in Afghanistan

ISTAR: Intelligence, Surveillance, Target Acquisition and Reconnaissance

JDAM: Joint Direct Attack Munition – inertial navigation and GPS guidance system bolted onto a 500 to 2000-lb bomb to make it an accurate all-weather weapon

JHC: Joint Helicopter Command – the UK-based command headquarters and operating authority for all British military helicopters in the UK and abroad

JHF: Joint Helicopter Force

JHF(A): Joint Helicopter Force Afghanistan – 'Main' at Kandahar and 'Forward' at Camp Bastion – the Afghanistan helicopter headquarters operating under authority of the Joint Helicopter Command (JHC)

JOC: Joint Operations Cell – the functioning control centre of operations in the Helmand province

JTAC: Joint Terminal Attack Controller (Jaytac) – soldier responsible to his commander for the deliverance of air ordnance from combat aircraft onto a target. The airspace controller for a battle, normal callsign is Widow

KAF: Kandahar Airfield

KIA: Killed In Action

Klick: military slang for kilometre

LAV: Light Armoured Vehicles. Canadian 8x8 wheeled Armoured Personnel Carrier

Leakers: Taliban that are attempting to escape (leak) from a target area

L-Hour: The moment the first helicopter lands on an LS during an operation

Lima Charlie: Phonetic alphabet for LC – air speak for Loud and Clear

Loadie: Loadmaster responsible for passengers and equipment in military troop-carrying helicopters or transport aircraft. Often mans one of the crew-served guns

LOAL: Lock-On After Launch (low-al) – missile is launched then it acquires a laser lock

LOBL: Lock-on Before Launch (lobel) – the missile locks onto the laser energy when it is still on the Apache

Longbow: The Longbow radar is the Apache's Fire Control Radar. It looks like a large Swiss cheese and sits on top of the main rotor system

LOS: Line of Sight

LS: Landing Site – any unprepared Helicopter Landing Site

LSJ: Life Support Jacket – survival waistcoat – escape jacket

LWRS: Laser Warning Receiving System

Lynx Mk7: British Army anti-tank helicopter armed with missiles on each side

ManPADS: Man Portable Aid Defence System – shoulder-launched heat-seeking missile

MAWS: Missile Approach Warning System

Max chat: As fast as possible

MC: Military Cross – awarded in recognition of exemplary gallantry during active operations against the enemy on land.

MIA: Missing In Action

Mission Net: An encrypted frequency used to coordinate the mission during operations

MoD: Ministry of Defence

Monocle: The pink see-through glass mirror over an Apache pilot's right eye that displays green symbology and images from the onboard computers and sights

Mosquito: Taliban slang for the Apache

MPD: Multi-Purpose Display – one of two five-inch screens on the console in each Apache cockpit

MPOG: Minimum pitch applied to the main rotor blades when on the ground

MPSM: Multi-Purpose Sub-Munition

Mujahideen: Afghan opposition groups – fought the Soviets during the Soviet invasion and each other in the Afghan Civil War – plural for the word mujahid meaning 'struggler'

Multiple: A Northern Ireland patrol consisting of two or more bricks

MWR: Moral, Welfare and Recreation. Large US facility in which to unwind with the freely provided games, refreshments, TVs, Cinema, computers, gaming stations, DVDs and the internet

NATO: North Atlantic Treaty Organisation

Negative: Air speak for 'no'

Negative Lima: No laser

Nimrod: A long-range maritime patrol aircraft modified for surveillance

NVG: Night Vision Goggles – night sights that magnify light by 40,000 times

OC: Officer Commanding – major in charge of a squadron or company group

OP: Observation Position

Ops: Operations – as in Ops tent, Ops room, Ops Officer or literally an operation

ORT: Optical Relay Tube – the large console in the front seat with PlayStation-type grips on either side

Pairs fire-and-manoeuvre: One static soldier aiming or shooting whilst his buddy manoeuvres to a position forward or backwards of him. They swap roles and do this continually manoeuvring with one foot on the ground at all times

Para: Nickname for a soldier from the Parachute Regiment or the Regiment itself

Pathfinder Platoon: a small unit designed and trained to fight behind enemy lines; 16 Air Assault Brigade's equivalent of the SAS

Pax: Official military term for people

P-check: Northern Ireland term for checking the details of a car from its number plate

PFL: Practice Forced Landing – practising landing without the use of any engines

PID: Positive Identity

Pinzgauer: Small 4x4 all-terrain utility truck

PNVS: Pilot's Night Vision System (Pinvis) – the thermal camera that sits above the TADS on the Apache's nose

Port: Left-hand side of an aircraft or vessel

PRT: Provincial Reconstruction Team

PMI: Power Margin Indicator

QHI: Qualified Helicopter Instructor – flying instructor

RA: Royal Artillery

RAD: Ram Air Decelerator

Radome: A dome that shrouds a radar head

RAF: Royal Air Force

Rearm: Reload the Apache with ammunition

Red Top: Gazelles painted anti-collision Day-Glo red, flown by range officers whose job is to ensure that troops, vehicles and aircraft are within safety limits

Replen: Military slang for replenishment

RF: Radio Frequency

RIP: Relief In Place – Apache flights handing over the battle between each other, maintaining support to the ground troops

RMP: Royal Military Police – British Military Police

RoC: Rehearsal of Concept

ROE: Rules Of Engagement – law set by a country's government laying down the rules governing how arms are brought to bear

ROZ: Restricted Operating Zone

RPG: Rocket Propelled Grenade – shoulder-launched rocket with a powerful grenade warhead on the front

RQHI: Regiment's Qualified Helicopter Instructor

RTA: Road Traffic Accident

RTB: Return To Base

RTM322: Rolls-Royce engines for the Apache

RTS: Release To Service – the document that details what can and can't be done with the Apache regarding flight, firing, etc.

RV: Rendezvous – designated meeting place

RWR: Radar Warning Receiver

SA80: British Forces rifle – 5.56 mm automatic

SAL: Semi-Active Laser

SAM: Surface-to-Air missile

SAS: Special Air Service – an independent British Special Forces unit of the British Army

SBS: Special Boat Service – an independent British Special Forces unit of the Royal Navy

Scratcher: Military slang for bed

SF: Special Forces – e.g. SAS and SBS

SFI: Senior Flying Instructor

Sitrep: Situational Report

Starboard: Right-hand side of an aircraft or vessel

Stinger: US-designed Surface-to-air ManPADs (Man Portable Air Defence System) Missile. Taliban slang for any shoulder-launched surface-to-air missile

SupFAC: Supervisory Forward Air Controller

SWO: Squadron Weapons Officer

Symbology: Flying and targeting information beamed onto the monocle

T-33: Lockheed T-33 Shooting Star. An old military jet built under licence by the Canadians and renamed the CT-133 Silver Star

TA: Territorial Army

TADS: Target Acquisition and Designation Sight – the 'bucket' on the nose of the Apache that houses the Apache's cameras

Taliban: Collective term used in this book for Taliban, Al-Qaeda and Hezb-I Islami Gulbuddin (HIG)

Tanky: A member of one of the tank Regiments – tank commander, driver or gun loader

TFAD: Task Force Availability Date

Theatre: Country or area in which troops are conducting operations

Thirty mike mike: Military slang for thirty millimetre or the Apache's cannon rounds

Thirty mil: Alternative name for thirty mike mike

TOC: Tactical Operations Cell

Topman: Callsign for the British Harrier

TOW: Tube-launched Optically tracked Wire-guided missile – fired from the British Army Lynx helicopter

Tracer: Bullets that burn with a red, orange or green glow from 110 metres to 1,100 metres so that they can be seen

TSD: Tactical Situational Display

UFD: Up Front Display – an LED instrument that displays critical information to the Apache crews

USAF: United States Air Force

Venturi: A tubed duct that changes pressure to speed air up

VP: Vulnerable Position

WAH-64D: British version of the Apache

WI: Weapons Instructor

Widow: Callsign for JTACs in Afghanistan

Wildman: British Apache callsign from May 2006 to October 2006

Wingman: The other aircraft in any pair of aircraft

WMIK: Weapons Mounted Installation Kit – an odd-looking Land Rover with bars all over it to which weapons can be attached

WO1: Warrant Officer Class One – a soldier who holds a Royal Warrant is known as Warrant Officer; Class One is the highest non-commissioned rank in the British Army

WO2: Warrant Officer Class Two

Zero-zero: A term used to describe a specific type of approach to land in a helicopter

ACKNOWLEDGEMENTS

I owe a great debt of gratitude to Captain Paul Mason, Army Air Corps, the Apache guru who (as he constantly reminds me) taught me all I knew. You were an inspiration to me Paul.

My sincere thanks to the Attack Helicopter Force Commander, Lieutenant Colonel David Turner AAC, and the Director of Army Aviation, Brigadier David Short CBE ADC, for their support throughout, and for letting me tell it the way it was.

A special thank you to Paula Edwards at the MoD for her habitually elegant tightrope act.

The dedication, time, enthusiasm and friendship of the HarperCollins team has been nothing short of monumental. John Bond and Arabella Pike, thank you for believing in me.

I couldn't have written this book without the guidance of Nick Cook and Martyn Forrester. You have helped nurture and shape my narrative in a way that I could never have achieved on my own. Thank you both so much.

Thanks to all my army buddies, friends and family for your continued support.

I owe my sanity to TFM's Gary Philipson for letting me in the Zoo at night to talk to the Love Slug!

I'd always assumed an agent was someone who took money off you for licking the odd stamp when he could find the time. I now realise it doesn't stop there. I can't thank Mark Lucas enough – for your tireless promotion, advice and, above all, priceless edits. You're my agent, literary scholar, adviser and above all friend.

Emily, you are my foundation. You support everything that I dream of and you always hold firm when times are rough. Without you I could never even begin to chase my dreams.

To my children, my little AAC: you are my world.

INDEX